Redefining the Sacred

BEITRÄGE ZUR
ARCHITEKTUR- UND KULTURGESCHICHTE
LEIBNIZ UNIVERSITÄT HANNOVER

Abteilung Bau-/Stadtbaugeschichte
Fakultät für Architektur und Landschaft

8

CONTEXTUALIZING THE SACRED

Previously published volumes in this series are listed at the back of the book.

VOLUME 1

Redefining the Sacred

Religious Architecture and Text in the Near East and Egypt 1000 BC – AD 300

Edited by

Elizabeth Frood
and Rubina Raja

BREPOLS

British Library Cataloguing in Publication Data

Redefining the sacred : religious architecture and text in the Near East and Egypt, 1000 BC - AD 300. -- (Contextualizing the sacred ; 1)
1. Sacred space--Middle East--History.
2. Sacred space--Egypt--History.
3. Religious architecture--Middle East--History.
4. Religious architecture--Egypt--History.
5. Architecture, Ancient--Middle East.
6. Architecture, Ancient--Egypt.
7. Architecture and society--Middle East--History.
8. Architecture and society--Egypt--History.
9. Middle East--Religious life and customs--History.
10. Egypt--Religious life and customs--History.
I. Series
II. Frood, Elizabeth editor. III. Raja, Rubina, 1975- editor.

726'.0932-dc23

ISBN-13: 9782503541044

D/2014/0095/48
ISBN: 978-2-503-54104-4
Printed in the EU on acid-free paper

Contents

Places, Communities, and Individuals

List of Illustrations

Colour Plates

Figures

Maps

Acknowledgements

We would like to thank the participants in the ESF Exploratory Workshop for their contributions, out of which this volume was developed: Christoph Bachhuber, Heather Baker, Martin Bommas, Emmanuelle Burfin, Jenny Cashman, Filip Coppens, Joachim Ganzert, Jack Green, Rudolf Haensch, Virginia Rimmer Herrmann, Carina van den Hoven, Jiří Janák, Ted Kaizer, Andreas Kropp, Kristina Lahn Dumke, Anne Lykke, Jesper Majbom Madsen, Erika Meyer-Dietrich, Frederick Naerebout, Beate Pongratz-Leisten, Frances Reynolds, Cynthia May Sheikholeslami, and Claude Traunecker. The workshop was held at the University of Oxford in March 2009, hosted by the Ioannou Centre for Classical and Byzantine Studies, St John's College, and St Cross College, and was generously funded by the European Science Foundation, the John Fell OUP Research Fund, and the Novo Nordisk Foundation. We are grateful to Aleksandra Warda and Alice Reid for their help throughout the workshop, and Bernie for his patience! We owe a huge debt of gratitude (and many cocktails) to Annette Højen Sørensen for all her hard work editing the volume and to Ditte Maria Damsgaard Hiort and Anne Ditte Kougstrup Høj for compiling the index. We would also like to thank the editorial team at Brepols for helping us to establish the series and for consulting with us and advising throughout its development. We look forward to the several books that are soon to follow this launch volume within an area of work that we consider of utmost importance.

Elizabeth Frood and Rubina Raja
Oxford and Aarhus, May 2013

Colour Plates

Plate 1. Hatschepsut metamorphosis: a conventional monochrome reconstruction of the Hatschepsut Temple (left) juxtaposed with a colour reconstruction sketch with vegetation (right). Sketch © J. Ganzert.

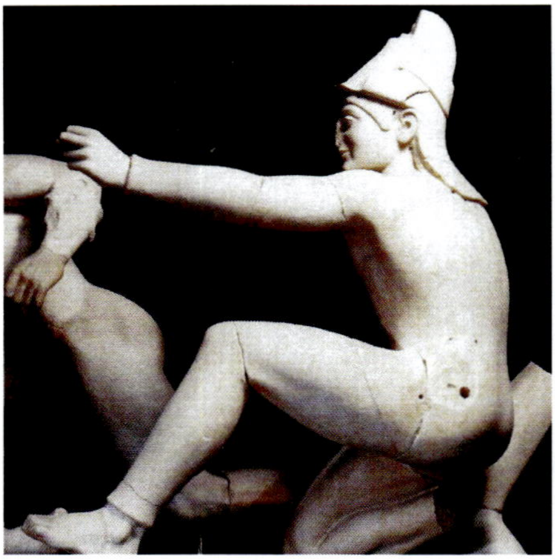

Plate 2. **Left**: Archer, west gable of the Temple of Aphaia in Aigina, Glyptothek Munich (condition in 2003). After Brinkmann, Hornbostel, and Wünsche, *Bunte Götter*, p. 97, fig. 146 (R. Kühling).
Right: Section of the west gable of the Temple of Aphaia in Aigina (coloured, 2005). After Brinkmann, Hornbostel, and Wünsche, *Bunte Götter*, p. 110, fig. 178 (V. Brinkmann).

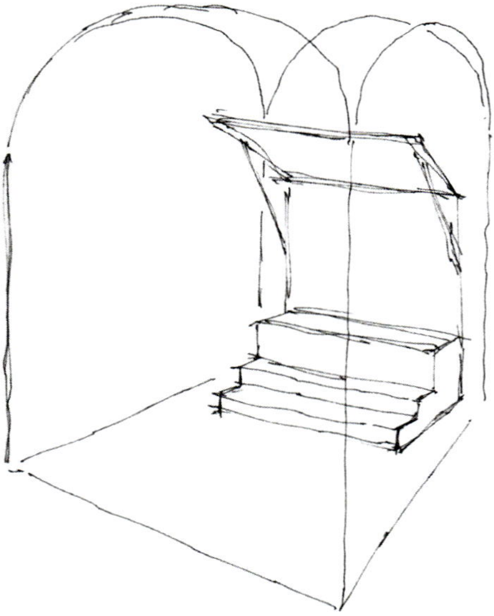

Plate 3. **Left**: Lüneburg Town Hall, lower court of justice, chair with opened baldachin.
Right: Lüneburg Town Hall, lower court of justice, chair with opened baldachin, schematic location sketch. © J. Ganzert.

Plate 4. Schloss Neuschwanstein, throne niche in the throne room.
After Desing, *Königsschloss Neuschwanstein*, p. 16, fig. 41.

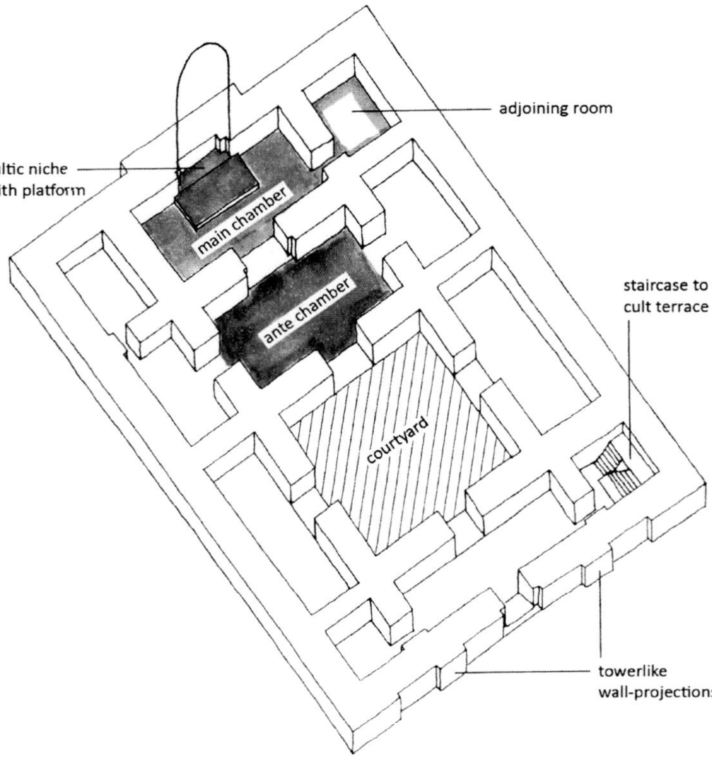

Plate 5. **Above**: Schematic synopsis of ancient Oriental temple layouts. © J. Ganzert.
Below: The Ninmah Temple in Babylon (reconstruction: R. Koldewey, 1911).
After Koldewey, *Die Tempel von Babylon und Borsippa*, fig. 1.

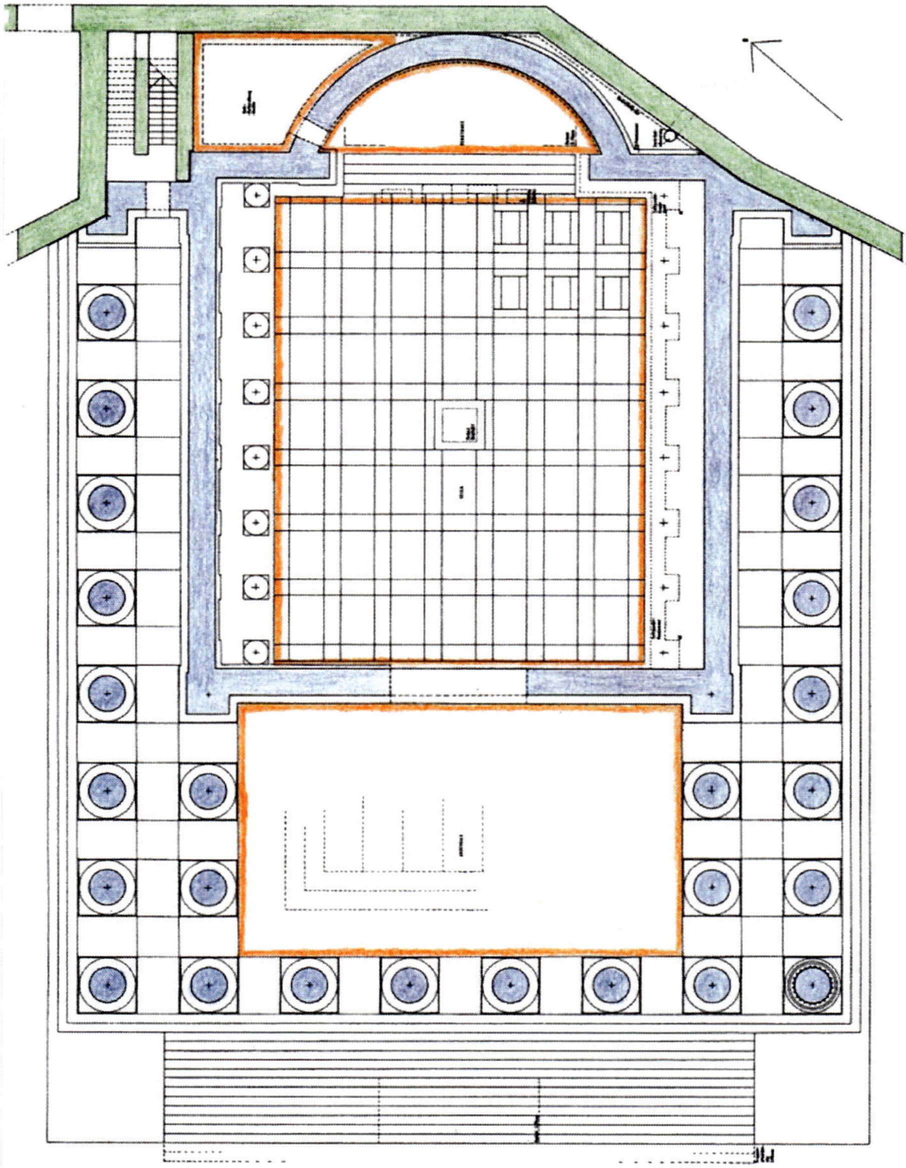

Plate 6. Rome, the Temple of Mars Ultor, layout (antecella, cella, penetrale with annex). © J. Ganzert.

Plate 7. **Top**: Rome, the Temple of Mars Ultor, computer-simulated corner view.
After Ganzert, *Im Allerheiligsten des Augustusforum*, p. 97, fig. 163.
Bottom: Rome, the Temple of Mars Ultor, cella, computer-simulated interior view with apse.
After Ganzert, *Im Allerheiligsten des Augustusforum*, p. 99, fig. 166.

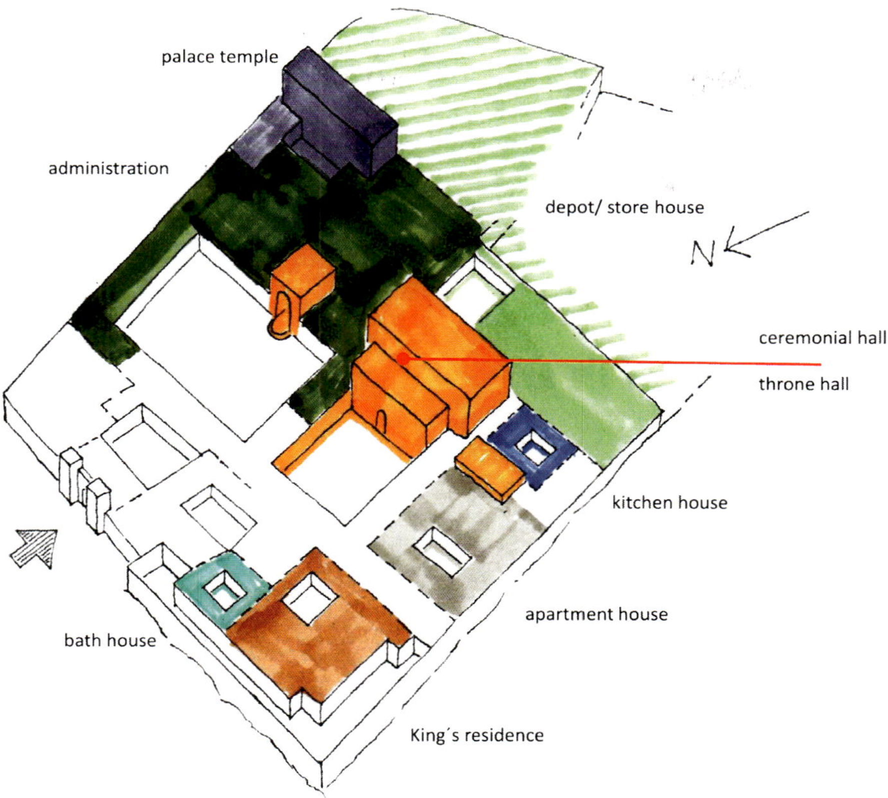

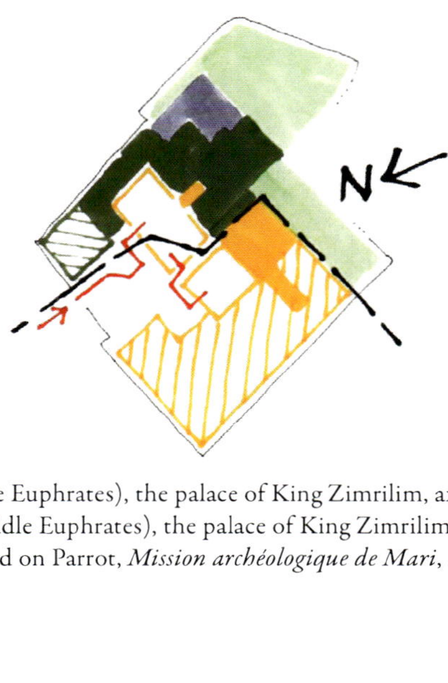

Plate 8. **Top**: Mari (Middle Euphrates), the palace of King Zimrilim, axonometric projection.
Bottom: Mari (Middle Euphrates), the palace of King Zimrilim, schematic plan
© J. Ganzert, based on Parrot, *Mission archéologique de Mari*, enclosed plan.

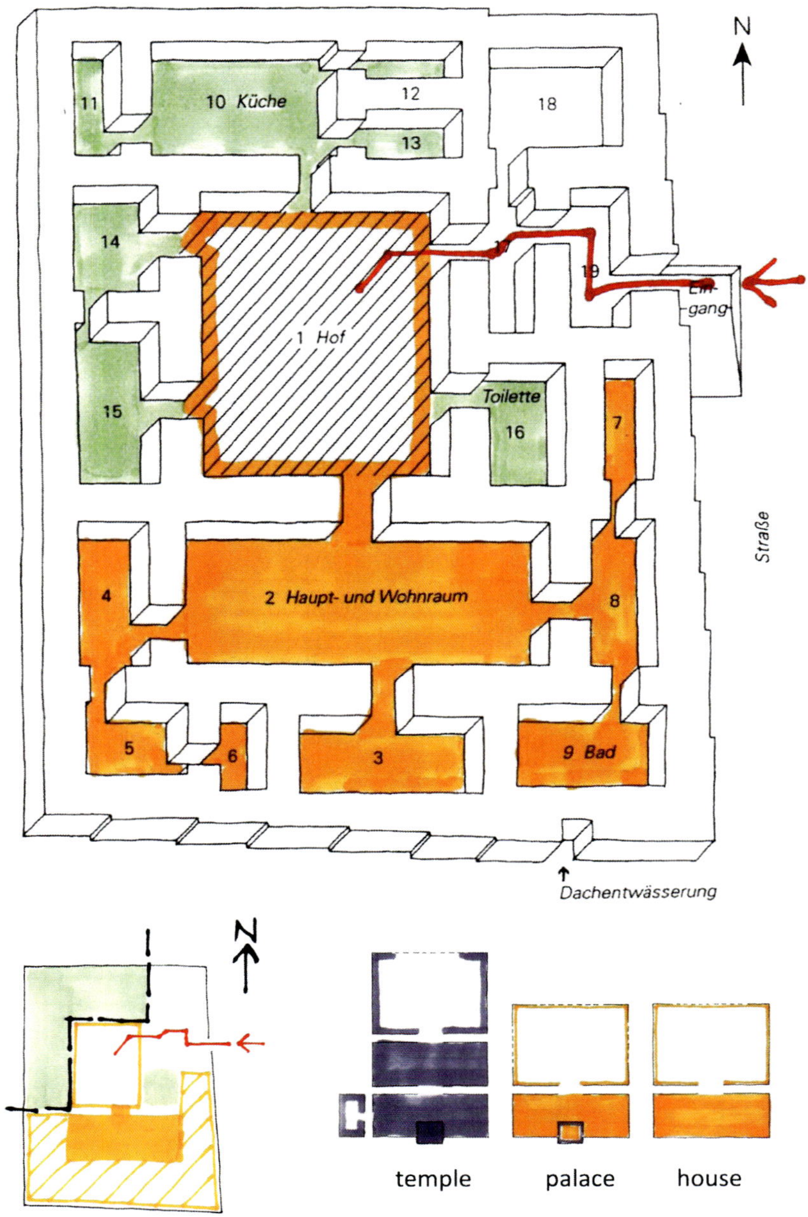

Plate 9. **Top**: Babylon, House I: plan. **Below left**: Schematic layout.
Below right: Conceptual schemata. Axonometric projection
© J. Ganzert, based on Reuther, *Die Innenstadt von Babylon*, p. 81, fig. 62.

Introduction: Material Culture and Religious Identity in the Ancient Near East and Egypt

Elizabeth Frood and Rubina Raja

This volume and the series it launches were initiated by a European Science Foundation exploratory workshop held in Oxford in 2009 entitled 'Redefining the Sacred: Religious Identity, Ritual Practice, and Sacred Architecture in the Near East and Egypt, 1000 BC – AD 300'. The workshop was generously supported by the European Science Foundation, the John Fell OUP Research Fund, and the Novo Nordisk Foundation.[1] The idea for the workshop has a longer history, developing out of our shared research interests in sacred architecture and religious identity in Egypt and the ancient Near East. We both received training in our respective fields (Egyptology and classical archaeology) at a time when the 'spatial turn' in the social sciences was impacting archaeology,[2] and the various directions this has taken in our subjects continues to shape our work in different but complementary ways. We saw the workshop as an opportunity to bring our mutually developed ideas and

[1] See the conference information at <http://www.orinst.ox.ac.uk/conferences/redefining_the_sacred/index.html> [accessed May 2013].

[2] See, for example, Blake, 'Space, Spatiality, and Archaeology', pp. 230–43, for a general summary, which includes key references.

Elizabeth Frood (elizabeth.frood@orinst.ox.ac.uk) Faculty of Oriental Studies and St Cross College, University of Oxford.

Rubina Raja (rubina.raja@cas.au.dk) Department of Culture and Society, Section for Classical Archaeology, Aarhus University.

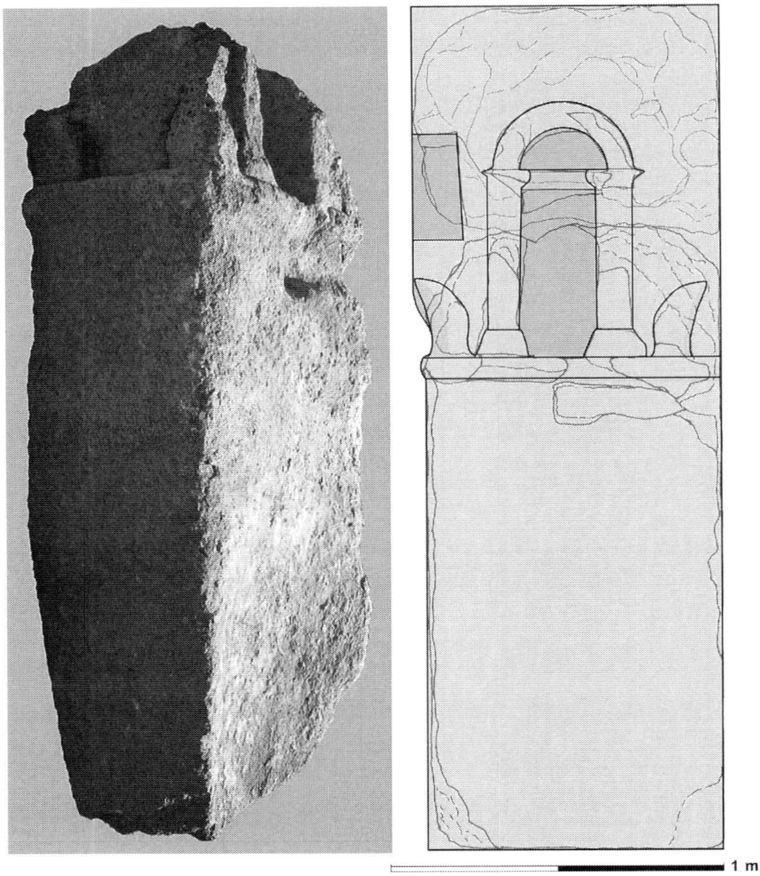

Figure 1.1. Late Hellenistic- to Roman-period monumental architectural limestone block from Jerash incorporating altar iconography, with a drawing of its reconstruction. Source: The Danish-German Northwest Quarter Project, Jerash. Drawing by Jens Christian Pinborg.

questions to a wider forum for discussion and debate. At the outset we aimed to lay a foundation for ongoing collaborations across disciplinary and regional boundaries; we hope that this volume goes some way towards establishing this foundation and intend that future volumes in the Contextualizing the Sacred series will take this work forward in new and different directions, ranging far beyond the issues we highlight here.

The series logo encapsulates some of the general perspectives we hope to explore through the series. It is an abstraction of a *c.* three-metre-high architectural element in the shape of an altar discovered in 2011 and excavated in 2012 during fieldwork at the ancient city of Jerash in Jordan, led by Rubina Raja and Achim Lichtenberger (Figure 1.1).[3] This element, which is late Hellenistic to Roman in date, poses a range of questions which relate to the series in general and to this volume in particular. The integration of an altar shape into a monumental architectural feature, which may have flanked a large entrance into a sanctuary and probably had a pendant standing opposite, allows us to consider the contextualization of the sacred in the ancient world as ever-changing, dynamic, and adaptable to new and specific situations. Its visual evocation of an altar may signal ritual practice or expectations of performance in some way. With such a statement we are also invoking a symbolic language, which was in many ways so generic that, although put into different media, the essence would have been understood by a wide group of recipients, communities of viewers, and/or participants. How such reinterpretations of something which so obviously stemmed from an 'older' tradition — namely the so-called horned altar motif of the Iron Age — were perceived by ancient actors and what these perceptions meant in relation to practice are central issues for this volume and series. In its secondary use, the element was built into an oil press, highlighting interpretive issues involved in the loss or transformation of its original meaning. What can modern scholars really know about how objects, architecture, and texts were used and perceived over time and space, extending beyond their 'original' contexts? This is, of course, assuming that ideas of 'origins' are appropriate and meaningful. With this introductory volume we hope to encourage critical assessments of approaches to material and textual culture with such broader issues in mind.

Whether something is 'in' or 'out' of context is crucial to how material culture is perceived and interpreted. This series, on the one hand, aims to give scholars across various subjects opportunities to contextualize and recontextualize material related to religious institutions and experience in antiquity through integrating, for example, archaeological, anthropological, and historical approaches. On the other hand, we also invite scholars to pose new questions of already well-contextualized material through diverse methodological and theoretical frameworks. An open and exploratory approach to these frameworks and methods of analysis and explanation will be one of the central aims and contributions of the series.

[3] Lichtenberger and Raja, 'Preliminary Report of the First Season of the Danish-German Jerash Northwest Quarter Project 2011'; Kalaitzoglou and others 'Report on the Geophysical Prospection of the Northwest Quarter of Gerasa/Jerash 2011'. The logo was designed by Jens-Christian Pinborg, architect for the Jerash project, and we are grateful to him for this.

Figure 1.2.
Roman-period horned limestone altar from Jerash. Source: Rubina Raja.

Let us briefly return to the Jerash element and the idea of it as a signpost for performance, as a focal point for attention in ritual practice, but also something that may have been, occasionally or frequently, restricted to specific users and audiences. An altar in its specific archaeological context invites us to interpret, for example, ritual practices and spatial layouts. For Roman-period sanctuaries in the ancient Near East there is considerable and various evidence for how altars were used. Altars for libations and for burning offerings were common features. For example, Figure 1.2 shows a Roman-period horned altar from Jerash with similar features to those found on the architectural element, demonstrating how this motif was used for functioning altars in this period. In the case of the Jerash architectural element, the level of abstraction used in its reinterpretation as an architectural feature evokes a generalized sense of space and practice, such as being a signifier of sacredness more than a usable feature. The Jerash element as the logo of this series foregrounds archaeological contexts of material culture, transformations of meaning across time (from religious space/feature to oil press) and space, and the potential levels of abstraction and generalization which can be involved in such transformations, here in the redefinition of an image and idea of an altar.

Redefining the Sacred

This collection of essays is not a conference proceedings in any straightforward sense, but rather presents some of the sources and concepts which were treated in the workshop in order to set the stage for the series and to put forward some initial material and approaches for wider discussion and critique. Some contributors participated in the original workshop while others kindly responded to later invitations as our design and aims for the volume crystallized and as we began to envisage it as the first of a new academic series. Thus the temporal and geographical scope of the papers here is representative of our aim for the series as a whole: crossing the Levant, Mesopotamia, Anatolia, and Egypt, from around 1000 BC through to *c.* AD 800. These are fluid boundaries; questions of definition, interaction, and change lie at the heart of this project, rather than any narrow material focus. For example, discussions in this volume touch on sites in Ibiza, Sicily, and Spain, and we hope that studies of material from Asia Minor as well as from further east (e.g. Iran) may be included in the series in future. The series also extends well into Late Antiquity thus covering periods of significant social and cultural change in the wider region, including early Christianity and the emergence of Islam. In contrast, Beate Pongratz-Leisten's essay here explores the configuration of space by king and elites for late third- and early second-millennium Mesopotamia, assessing early traces of a discourse that is fundamental to later periods. This *longue durée* perspective is enormously valuable for illuminating questions of continuity and change, central themes of this volume and the series. Overall, flexibility in selection of material allows for broad comparative approaches to be developed.

The essays explore questions related to the architectural development and multifunctional roles of temples and sanctuaries in the Near East and Egypt. By focusing on temples and their immediate environments, as well as the relationship between sacred sites and communities across regions, we begin with a seemingly traditional focus on architecture as a frame for people, action, and experience.[4]

[4] Cf. the complementary approach taken in Wescoat and Ousterhout, 'Afterword'.

This is a productive way to 'stage' and examine practice: despite vast differences of detail, we seem to share a common core understanding of the role of temples and sanctuaries in the creation, perpetuation, and display of elite world-views in the ancient world. The scope of these political dimensions is encapsulated initially by Joachim Ganzert's characterization of power relations between divine worlds and (elite) human spheres as 'healing sovereignty'. Exploration of the relationship between power and space has been a theme in humanities and social sciences for some time.[5] With Ganzert, we intend to look beyond space as sign of political hegemony and social power constructions to explore more detailed aspects of identity and the social production of space. His 'healing sovereignty' allows fine nuances to be approached, connected with human perceptions of the divine, personal relationships to gods, and the social significance of religion. All the contributions here point towards interactions of people and place in the articulation and transformation of personal and group identity and in the creative performance of sacredness. This focus on social space is in keeping with broader theoretical perspectives, highlighting the impact of individual or group choices, from the designers of Ptolemaic temples in Egypt (Coppens) to the implications of cultic reforms for communities in Hellenistic Uruk (Baker).

Questions relating to the definition and meaning of sacred space and what characterizes the sacred are also at the heart of Ganzert's paper and are a common thread through many of the other essays. The ancient Near East was the cradle of many transregional polytheist cults as well as Judaism, Christianity, and Islam. Over the last thirty years a particular paradigm has dominated the study of religious life in ancient societies in the Near East, asserting that ancient religions can only be understood within narrow regional and temporal frameworks.[6] We hope to help challenge this paradigm through creating a forum in which can be examined the elements these religions might have had in common, how they influenced each other, and the common pool of conceptions on which they drew, all of which should be grounded in the detailed examination of archaeological sources (including texts).[7] This said, we are not seeking to determine religious 'anthropological constants'; rather we intend to embed these religions, their practices and related experience, in their historical and

[5] E.g. the essays in Inomata and Coben, *Archaeology of Performance*.

[6] E.g. Millar, *The Roman Near East*; *contra* Sartre, *D'Alexandre à Zénobie*, in the tradition of Braudel, *La Méditerranée et le monde méditerranéen à l'époque de Philippe II*.

[7] Cotton and others, *From Hellenism to Islam*, represents an important attempt at tackling such issues, encompassing contexts outside the religious sphere.

material contexts — contextualizing the sacred. These religions did not develop in isolation but were shaped by transreligious communication and competition on several levels. This is in part what we refer to when we speak here of 'redefining the sacred' alongside contextualizing it: a profound (re)consideration of the transreligious elements, which are often overlooked since it is periods and data sets that have defined views and discussions. Redefinition can take place when scholars from different disciplines, subjects, and regions engage with material in closely related areas, exploring differences and similarities, questioning terminologies and definitions. We believe that there is considerable unexplored potential in such work.

Architectural language, especially through its translation into ground plans and architectural drawings, offers a productive starting point for thinking about definition and delineation, especially as it seems to offer clear distinctions between inner and outer, sacred and profane and graduations of transition, as articulated by Pongratz-Leisten elsewhere for Mesopotamian temples: 'the specific construction of the ground plan produced an intensified sacralization by means of numerous courtyards and gates — zones of passage that emphasized the transition between the temple and the outside world'.[8] Comparable patterns can be interpreted for temples in Egypt and elsewhere in the ancient Near East and seem to be a broadly cross-cultural fashioning or 'translation' of monumental sacred architecture. This highlights the meaning of the liminal and the transitional, and how those transitions, 'contact zones',[9] are governed and, in their own way, ritualized and sacralized. For instance, could the Jerash element delineate a transition, or does its meaning point in other directions? Such definitions and ideas of gradations and intensifications in contexts where everything was infused with the sacred may focus too much on boundaries,[10] and perhaps our approaches to sacredness are too much shaped by our own ideas of governance of space. As G. J. Wightman points out in his global survey of sacred space in the ancient world, simply being a locus of interaction (between divine and mundane) does little to characterize the interaction.[11] Interrogating the implications of social/spatial interactions through delineations and gradations of architecture are very productive, as many of the papers here suggest.

[8] Pongratz-Leisten, 'Sacred Places', p. 253.

[9] For which see Ashley and Plesch, 'The Cultural Processes of Appropriation', pp. 1–15.

[10] Cf. Wescoat and Ousterhout, 'Afterword', pp. 365–75.

[11] Wightman, *Sacred Spaces*, p. 904.

Volume Overview

Ganzert's position paper, which opens the volume, sets out approaches and perspectives ranging from ancient temples and houses to modern churches. The volume is then divided into two parts, moving from three essays that present global perspectives on the configuration of landscapes and religious territories in the first, to four that examine personal or community positions in the second. This structure was inspired in part by Ganzert's paper, which moves from an ultimate in macro, the Milky Way, to an ultimate in micro, a carbon atom in a human body, in order to illustrate the 'unfathomable infinite' in all dimensions and contexts. By replicating this organization we are not seeking to separate local from universal, but rather to create a coherent relationship between essays. Ganzert uses both perspectives to come to the same point about sacredness in terms of capacity and potential, and this is an approach that we find inspiring.[12] Within the two sections, the essays are partly ordered chronologically and partly topically. The intention has been to position papers with particularly closely related, or contrasting, frameworks next to one another. In all cases, we seek to facililtate 'conversations' of method and material.

Alongside differences in data, approaches to the analysis of space here are also variable, from essays that take sacred space as a 'given', as a formalized, structured concrete reality to be 'read' and examined from comparative perspectives (Morstadt and Coppens), to those that explore the contingency of sacred space and its performance by groups and individuals (Pongratz-Leisten, Herrmann, and Baker). This distinction could also be characterized in terms of the descriptive and the explanatory. Description is a powerful tool, as the implications of Bärbel Morstadt's essay for the diversity of Phonecian practice make clear. Surveys and detailed descriptions are fundamental to our project because they open up material to scholars from different subjects and because description embeds human action, practice, and behaviour in context. In complement, the explanatory modes explored in others of these essays focus around the dynamic interaction of architecture and people in the production and displacement of social relationships.

The introductory paper by Ganzert mobilizes the 'readability' of architecture, architectural 'footprints', in a way that has points of comparison with the well-developed idea of a 'temple grammar' integrating text and architecture in Graeco-Roman temples in Egypt.[13] This architectural language has the

[12] Cf. Kaizer, 'In Search of Oriental Cults', p. 27.

[13] E.g. Derchain, 'Un manuel de géographie liturgique à Edfou', pp. 31–65. An excellent,

potential to illuminate other contexts. Ganzert's 'macro to micro' vision offers insights into ways of working with what we might term 'high definition' perspectives, in which empirical evidence can answer broad questions if analysed in detail. The following chapters provide diverse examples of the application of such approaches.

The first part of the volume deals with regional perspectives. The three papers present case studies from three different time periods and regions, thus raising core questions that are echoed in the papers in the second part. For example, Pongratz-Leisten assesses the active social production of space in Southern Mesopotamia, newly configured through text. She advances close readings of nested metaphors in late third- and early second-millennium BC texts in order to examine how relations between urban elites and the king were 'inscribed' into landscapes, creating and legitimizing new configurations of divine/royal power.

A key point of discussion throughout the 2009 workshop was whether we are using appropriate terminology and the extent to which terminology matters. This problem is highlighted for a single culture and its translation by Morstadt's survey of Phoenician terms for sacred structures and areas. More broadly, many of the essays here confront issues of translation and interpretation across regions, periods, and the domains of scholarship that lay claim to these regions. Morstadt's paper also allows exploration of the extent to which diasporic communities forge relations to space in comparison with other groups in order to underscore their belonging and contextualization. Thus a survey of sacred sites contributes to discussions of diaspora, acts of displacement, and new place-making;[14] she describes a Phoenician temple built on an abandoned sacred site in Cyprus, then meeting its own end hundreds of years later with the integration of the island into the Ptolemaic Empire. One related question is, how did changes in power structures impact expressions of religious identity in religious architecture? Such issues are also addressed by Heather Baker and Achim Lichtenberger, and are crucial for understanding how sacredness and religious identities were used and shaped by elite decision-makers, and vice versa.

The presence and actions of human 'designers' and participants in the diverse sacred places discussed in the essays test notions of architecture as a 'readable' medium that is comparable to text. Mechanisms for community

accessible overview is Wilson, 'Temple Architecture and Decorative Systems', pp. 794–96. See, more generally, Wescoat and Ousterhout, 'Afterword', p. 373, for comments on the idea of 'reading' architecture.

14 Fisher, 'Elite Place-Making and Social Interaction', pp. 183–209.

agency are crucial to Filip Coppens's discussion of the role of Egyptian priests of the first millennium in designing temples; these were selected, shaped, and adapted to requirements and in response to ancient traditions and ideal models. The apparently conservative 'readability' of such complexes elides the complex decision-making processes behind them. Coppens shows that knowledge and translations of traditions offered groups wide-ranging and innovative possibilities for shaping expressions of contemporary religious identities. Architecture is also a stage within which the sacred is performed, requiring action and response, as set out by Ganzert and encapsulated by the structures Coppens treats. In this dynamic, performative, and adaptable understanding of sacred space, ephemeral spaces, practices (ceremony, ritual), and procession are vital. Approaching the performance of the sacred therefore suggests phenomenological frameworks, hinted at here in Morstadt's discussion of incense and water in Phoenician temples and Coppens's treatment of light.

The grounding of individual and group experience and practice within wider spatial and social topographies lies at the heart of Virginia Rimmer Herrmann's fine-grained analysis of the contexts of the stela of Kuttamuwa discovered in the lower town in Zincirli, southern Turkey, in 2008. Her discussion suggests how locales, practices, and beliefs that were previously thought exclusive to the royal mortuary cult may have extended through Syro-Hittite society in the ninth and eighth centuries to a newly (or more visibly) self-assertive aristocracy. Through her paper we get a sense of how a place and a monument might be embedded in the ordinary day-to-day of a group, while emulating, or connecting with, central temple practices. Her study also opens up possibilities for modelling non-elite experience. Sacredness perhaps suffused the elite world, as Ganzert evokes, but we know little beyond the world of the elites. This is due, in part, to the nature of the evidence and, in part, to aims of scholarship.[15] In order to access non-elites, different analytical frameworks as well as data sets are required.[16]

Heather Baker raises related questions in her examination of temple organization and cultic reform in the southern Babylonian city of Uruk during the

[15] A new ERC Advanced Grant Project begun in 2012 headed by Jörg Rüpke (Universität Erfurt) and Rubina Raja (Aarhus University) examines aspects of lived ancient religion, focusing on the experience of the individual and especially non-elite perspectives. Website: <http://www.uni-erfurt.de/max-weber-kolleg/projekte/kooperationsprojekte/lived-ancient-religion/> [accessed May 2013].

[16] Cf. Baines, 'Modelling the Integration of Elite and other Social Groups in Old Kingdom Egypt', pp. 117–44.

late Achaemenid period. Like Herrmann, she evaluates the intimate relationship of sacred places and institutions to urban communities, in this case via material pertaining to temple personnel at a time when structures and practices were undergoing radical reform. Times of crisis, departures from 'norms', are highly productive for crystallizing values, for allowing what is considered crucial to group, family, and individual identity to be thrown into vivid relief, alongside strategies developed by groups to secure position and to profit from transformation and uncertainty. That the reforms, for example, changed processional routes and street networks in the city has implications for theorizing potential impacts of comparable changes in regions where such detailed integration of textual and archaeological evidence is not yet possible.

Achim Lichtenberger's chapter demonstrates this. He questions the extent to which continuity and discontinuity of local and regional traditions in religious architecture and practice in the Decapolis in Northern Jordan can be traced through the material evidence and the written sources. Crucially he highlights the role of monuments in memory making and in forgetting,[17] as well as in new creations, redefinitions, and appropriations of memory. His survey may be compared with Baker's discussion of the closure of the Eanna temple in Uruk by Xerxes as 'conscious demotion and deliberate neglect'.

Finally, Volker Menze presents a case study of an individual from the early Christian period, the Syrian late antique poet Ephrem. Ephrem's self-awareness as a Christian of a Syrian origin in the later Roman Empire is central to the essay, and the assessment of his provincial perception of imperial power and the imperial office in relation to the Church is pivotal. Menze uses Ephrem's poetic writings — his instructional hymns — to examine expressions of religious identity and strategies of self-understanding (both Ephrem himself as an individual, but also as someone interpreting Christianity for a broader audience). Like Pongratz-Leisten's essay, the first of the case studies in this volume, Menze highlights the salience of literary sources for the interpretation of space. Here, the centrality of understanding the historiography surrounding literary evidence is also emphasized, an area of work still underdeveloped in many areas of archaeological analysis. Menze's essay serves as a natural conclusion to the volume not only because it is the last chronologically, but also because it concerns one individual's display of his own interpretation and contextualization of the sacred in relation to the surrounding world.

[17] Cf. Küchler and Forty, *The Art of Forgetting*.

Looking Ahead

Problems of approach and interpretation in relation to religious transformation in the ancient and classical Near East are highlighted by numerous scholars and treated in numerous volumes. With this new series, we hope to open up the exchange of ideas and approaches relating to sacred space and ritual practice across disciplines and areas of study which do not normally come into close contact. We consider such exchanges vital, not least because of geographical interconnection and ideas of continuity and change. We hope the series will contribute to a transdisciplinary discourse and interaction and enable new collaborations through the interpretive lenses of region (ancient and classical Near East) and theme (sacred space). Thus we welcome contributions to the series that will take these aims further. By beginning to assess this common foundation through different regions and times, we can enrich our perspectives, question approaches, share material, change frameworks, and provide a base from which to explore. In the end, this is an investigation of the superabundant potentials of sacred space in terms of interpretation and engagement with human actors. In this, our primary interest is social, as all the case studies in this volume reflect. Thus we hope to contextualize the sacred across disciplinary, temporal, and geographic borders within a region that continues to play a primary role in global politics and religious developments.

Works Cited

Secondary Studies

Ashley, K., and V. Plesch, 'The Cultural Processes of Appropriation', in *The Cultural Processes of Appropriation*, ed. by K. Ashley and V. Plesch, special issue, *Journal of Medieval and Early Modern Studies*, 32.1 (2002), pp. 1–15

Baines, J., 'Modelling the Integration of Elite and Other Social Groups in Old Kingdom Egypt', in *Élites et pouvoir en Égypte ancienne: actes du colloque Université Charles-de-Gaulle – Lille 3, 7 et 8 juillet 2006*, ed. by J. C. M. García, Cahiers de Recherches de l'Institut de Papyrologie et d'Égyptologie de Lille, 28 (Lille: Université Charles-de-Gaulle – Lille III, 2010), pp. 117–44

Blake, E., 'Space, Spatiality, and Archaeology', in *A Companion to Social Archaeology*, ed. by L. Meskell and R. W. Preucel (Oxford: Blackwell, 2004), pp. 230–54

Braudel, F., *La Méditerranée et le monde méditerranéen à l'époque de Philippe II* (Paris: Armand Colin, 1966)

Cotton, H. M., R. G. Hoyland, J. J. Price, and D. J. Wasserstein, eds, *From Hellenism to Islam: Cultural and Linguistic Change in the Roman Near East* (Cambridge: Cambridge University Press, 2009)

Derchain, Philippe, 'Un manuel de géographie liturgique à Edfou', *Chronique d'Égypte*, 37 (1962), 31–65

Fisher, K. D., 'Elite Place-Making and Social Interaction in the Late Cypriot Bronze Age', *Journal of Mediterranean Archaeology*, 22.2 (2009), 183–209

Inomata, T., and L. S. Coben, eds, *Archaeology of Performance: Theaters of Power, Community, Politics*, Archaeology in Society (Oxford: AltaMira, 2006)

Kaizer, T., 'In Search of Oriental Cults: Methodological Problems Concerning "the Particular" and "the General" in Near Eastern Religion in the Roman Period', *Historia*, 55.1 (2006), 26–47

Kalaitzoglou, G., and others, 'Report on the Geophysical Prospection of the Northwest Quarter of Gerasa/Jerash 2011', *Annual of the Department of Antiquities of Jordan* (forthcoming)

Küchler, S., and A. Forty, eds, *The Art of Forgetting* (Oxford: Berg, 1999)

Lichtenberger, A., and R. Raja, 'Preliminary Report of the First Season of the Danish-German Jerash Northwest Quarter Project 2011', *Annual of the Department of Antiquities of Jordan* (forthcoming)

Millar, F., *The Roman Near East: 31 BC – AD 337* (Cambridge, MA: Harvard University Press, 1993)

Pongratz-Leisten, B., 'Sacred Places', in *Religions of the Ancient World: A Guide*, ed. by S. I. Johnston (Cambridge, MA: The Belknap Press of Harvard University Press, 2004), pp. 253–55

Sartre, M., *D'Alexandre à Zénobie: Histoire du Levant antique. IVe siècle av. J.-C. – IIIe siècle ap. J.-C.* (Paris: Fayard, 2001)

Wescoat, B. D., and Robert G. Ousterhout, 'Afterword', in *Architecture of the Sacred: Space, Ritual, and Experience from Classical Greece to Byzantium*, ed. by B. D. Wescoat and R. G. Ousterhout (Cambridge: Cambridge University Press, 2012), pp. 365–75

Wightman, G. J., *Sacred Spaces: Religious Architecture in the Ancient World*, Ancient Near Eastern Studies Suppl., 22 (Leuven: Peeters, 2007)

Wilson, P., 'Temple Architecture and Decorative Systems', in *A Companion to Ancient Egypt*, Blackwell Companions to the Ancient World, 2 vols (Malden: Wiley-Blackwell, 2010), II, 781–803

Contextualizing the Sacred

Joachim Ganzert

Prelim 1

We are all familiar with these freeze-frames of a fictive journey from deep space to our planet by Ray and Charles Eames, on which each picture, magnified tenfold from its predecessor, brings us closer to the Earth and its living human beings until we delve into their atomic structure.[1] From their long series of images we present just ten — zoomed in very different magnifications and schematically sketched — as an illustration (Figure 2.1; the red square is not always ten times larger in the next picture but usually x times larger).

The series begins with an image that is actually ten million light years across and shows the Milky Way as a single point, one of twenty galaxies.

The second image has jumped one tenfold magnification and is 'only' a hundred thousand light years across. It depicts the Milky Way with its approximately one hundred billion stars, zoomed in on the Magellannic Clouds.

We now miss out fourteen magnification stages (the pictures are similar in that they zoom in on new masses of stars) that lead from the 'Orion' spiral arm on whose margin our sun lies, through the solar system, the orbits of Venus,

[1] *Powers of Ten*. A film dealing with the relative size of things in the universe and the effect of adding another zero. Made by the office of Charles and Ray Eames for IBM, 1977. The nine-minute film, which may also be watched at <http://www.youtube.com/watch?v=0fKBhvDjuy0>, is based on the book by Boeke, *Cosmic Views*. *Powers of Ten* has been continually revised, most recently in 1998.

Joachim Ganzert (j.ganzert@igt-arch.uni-hannover.de) Abteilung Bau-/Stadtbaugeschichte, Institut für Geschichte und Theorie der Architektur, Fakultät für Architektur und Landschaft, Leibniz Universität Hannover.

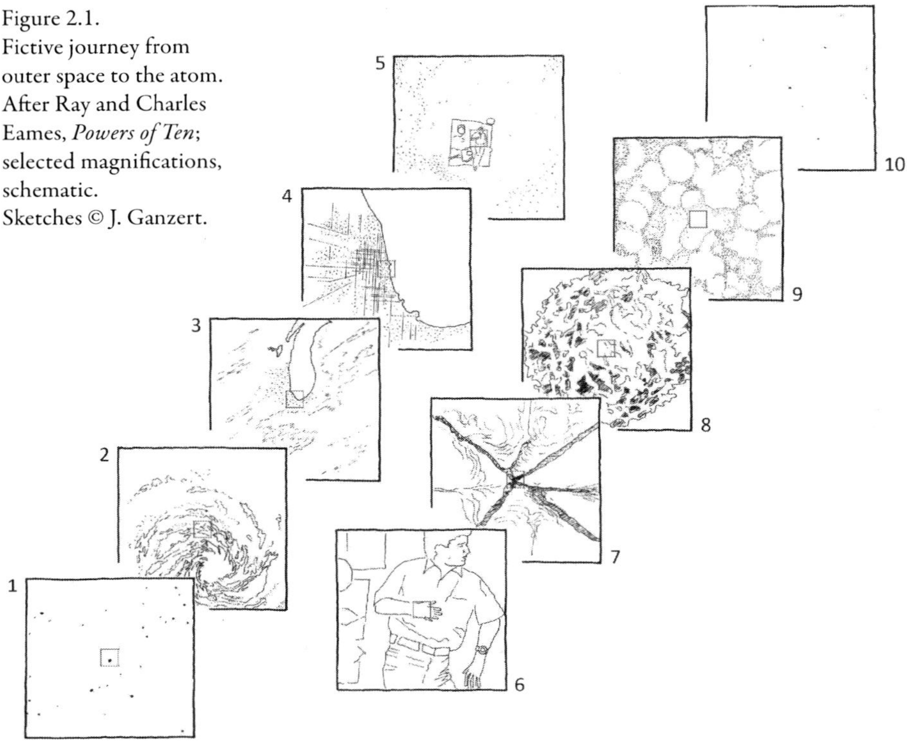

Figure 2.1.
Fictive journey from outer space to the atom. After Ray and Charles Eames, *Powers of Ten*; selected magnifications, schematic.
Sketches © J. Ganzert.

Earth, and Mars to the lunar orbit and the planet Earth. We approach it through the clouds and look down in the third image on a 1000-km wide section — what we could call the astronaut's eye view of Lake Michigan with Chicago on its south-west shore; in the fourth picture we see Chicago in a 100-km section.

Again we jump several magnifications and in the fifth (10 m wide) and sixth (1 m wide) images zoom in on a picnic site near the Chicago World Exposition Grounds and on a human being lying on a blanket. This is the everyday scale to which our senses are attuned.

In the seventh image we have again missed out two magnifications and see, in a 1-mm section, the pattern of wrinkles on the skin (the back of the resting person's hand) under the microscope — the gateway to the microcosmos.

With the eighth image we enter the realm of the cells and see a white blood cell in a section ten micrometres wide.

Omitting the next magnification stages, which lead us towards the hereditary molecules, we land in the ninth image in the molecular chains of DNA in the territory of molecular biology.

And with the tenth, 10-picometre wide, image we have passed through the magnification stages of the carbon atom wreathed in its cloud of electrons and approached the atomic nucleus, three steps away from the smallest particles of all.

Taking this journey through the dimensions may, perhaps, provoke two sorts of response:

Response 1: We only have to keep on zooming and sooner or later everything — or nearly everything — will be investigated and understood; the dimensions of the incomprehensible seem capable of being reduced to a minimum that may be discounted. That is to say: it would be possible to make the apparently 'unfathomable infinite' more or less comprehensible and thus susceptible to domination.

Response 2: No matter in which direction we zoom, there will always be new, endlessly vast areas with another, always different abundance of dots on an unknown background. We would be dealing with 'the relative size of things in the universe and the effect of adding another zero', as expressed in the subtitle to *Powers of Ten*. An 'unfathomable infinite' would gape, one that lay beyond the limits of our comprehension, understanding, and domination. It would suffuse us with astonishment and awe, and we associate it with what one could denote as 'sacred'.

Cautiously expressed, one could probably say that nowadays the spontaneous readiness to adopt the first response is generally greater than in the past. We consider ourselves lords of the macro- and the microcosm; other power relations are the stuff of history. It may even be asked whether the dimensions that we would nowadays regard as the 'unfathomable infinite' or, lying beyond our control, as 'sacred', are nothing less than inversely proportional to those of earlier times. Even to regard such an 'unfathomable infinite' as something that could exercise 'salvatory domination' or 'healing sovereignty' over us, to recognize and accept it as something 'completely, normally holy' and to deal with it as part of the anthropological basic constitution may again — because of negative experiences with such a stance, especially in the twentieth century — inversely proportional to earlier times, be met with the deepest scepticism.

It would follow from this that such a contemporary perception, in considering historical finds, would present us with a 'world turned upside down' image of past realities and that we would have to put on an inverting prism if we wished to avoid imposing inadequate or inappropriate modern positivist ideas on historical evidence. This, at least, would be a first step towards contextualizing the sacred.

Figure 2.2.
'The church is open' – sign in front of a Hannover church.
© J. Ganzert.

Prelim 2

At numerous churches today, not only in Hannover for instance, one finds an emphatic notice by the entrance that the church is 'open'; this derives from the situation that most churches are almost always closed — apparently useful, at most, for the two or three hours of the Sunday service or for concerts. At one church the notice was secured by a padlock (Figure 2.2); it seems that being open is also liable to be stolen. Whatever the case may be, the least that one can induce from this (and it is born out in reality) is that there is no natural need to frequent the church every day. Even if this example from the Protestant north of Germany may seem rather extreme and the Catholic south of Europe, Italy for instance, differs considerably, I still believe that in this connection we can — indeed, we will have to — work on the general basis of relatively inverse proportions to earlier times.

Prelim 3

A look — just to take one example — at the town of Lüneburg[2] near Hamburg in the closing years of the fifteenth century, that is, shortly before the Reformation, can help elucidate this. Back then this modest town had, for its

[2] Cf. Rümelin, *St. Nicolai in Lüneburg*, pp. 17–30.

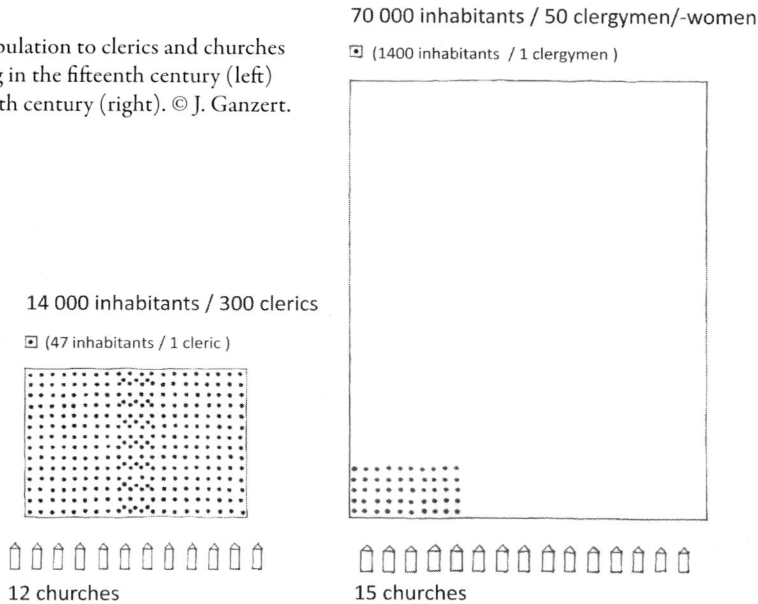

Figure 2.3.
Ratio of population to clerics and churches in Lüneburg in the fifteenth century (left) and twentieth century (right). © J. Ganzert.

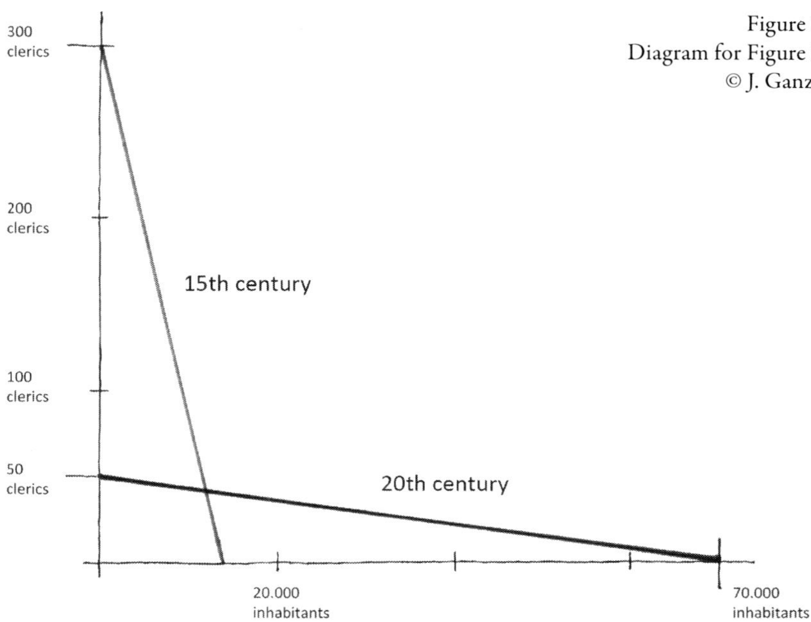

Figure 2.4.
Diagram for Figure 2.3.
© J. Ganzert.

Figure 2.5. Left: Frankfurt am Main, the Frauenfriedenskirche (architect H. Herkommer; early 20th century). After Wasmuth, *Wasmuths Lexikon der Baukunst*, II, 187. Right: Design for a 'four-wall church', the entrance (architect R. Schwarz; 1920s). After Raith, *Der Heroische Stil*, p. 61, fig. 46.

fourteen thousand inhabitants, twelve churches and three hundred clerics — a cleric for every fifty residents. To this may be added around thirty sodalities / spiritual brotherhoods (*fraternitates, societates*, etc.), and 376 benefices were attached to 113 altars in the Lüneburg churches. There was also a synagogue. I've attempted to portray these relations schematically here (Figure 2.3, left).

Today, Lüneburg has seventy thousand inhabitants (five times as many), but the number of churches is roughly the same as in the fifteenth century — of course, distributed across an urban area at least ten times greater — and there are, at the most, fifty clergymen and clergywomen (Figure 2.3, right). The proportions are, as we see, more than inverted (Figure 2.4).

An even higher concentration of sacred buildings of various sizes, by the way, could be found in medieval Damascus[3] where the city area (160 hectares)[4] was comparable with that of Lüneburg (around 150 hectares):[5] along with the Great Mosque (which already covers 1.2 per cent of the city's entire area), there are another 210 mosques and places of prayer, eleven churches (Armenian Catholic, Armenian Orthodox, Greek Catholic, Greek Orthodox, Syrian Catholic, Jesuit, and others), and four synagogues.[6]

[3] Sack, *Damaskus*, pp. 23–24.

[4] The old town (*intra muros*) without the suburbs is meant; cf. Sack, *Damaskus*, pl. 2.

[5] Rümelin, *St. Nicolai in Lüneburg*, map 1 between pp. 824/825.

[6] Sack, *Damaskus*, pl. 4.

Prelim 4

If we understand architectural evidence as 'footprints' of the functions, conceptions, cults, rituals etc., they may be read like inscriptions containing quite direct 'word meanings' that in normal linguistic usage no longer appear or are subject to taboos. Considering the question of what we nowadays associate with the terms 'sacred' and/or 'holy', then, looking at architectural evidence can be helpful.

We should, in my view, consider two apparently contradictory conceptions. One — let us call it the abstract conception — expressed itself in the first half of the twentieth century through an almost colossal church architecture (Figure 2.5) characterized by histrionic loftiness and over-proportioned voids; not inappropriately, this school of design was designated the 'Heroic Style'.[7]

> The auratic effect of buildings in the Heroic Style arises from their status as self-sufficient works of art, from the elevation of a building, whether it be church or memorial, to the status of monument. [...] the utterly ungraspable quality of the space [...] imbues in the visitor a feeling of his total nullity and insignificance — an experience that Rudolf Otto [...] considered one of the most powerful epiphanic forms of the Holy: the suspension of individuality that occurs in the transgression, even the complete overpowering of the personality seems to make an authentic experience of the Other, the Holy, possible.[8]

Perhaps one should also regard the almost menacing effect of these monumental manifestations as a response to Nietzsche's 'God is dead', inasmuch as one sought to 'suspend' or 'freeze' sacredness in a martial-evocative abstraction, to secure the 'Holy' in a heroic unconditionality, to compel it to appear with all this force and massivity.

Interestingly, this hermetic, cold style was also favoured by Fascism (Figure 2.6). Such an intimidating and also fascinating frigidity offered the preconditions for an overpowering 'saviour' ('Heiland' in German) whose specific acts could be sanctioned with a 'Heil Hitler',[9] however 'unfathomably tangible' this may actually have been. This literally forceful-authentic manifestation may explain the fascination that so few people were able to resist. In any case, such extremely remote abstraction excludes all the gradations of human mediating

[7] Raith, *Der Heroische Stil*.

[8] Raith, *Der Heroische Stil*, p. 60.

[9] Cf. von Hehl, 'Sakrales im Säkularen?', pp. 226–43, specifically p. 240.

Figure 2.6.
Nuremberg, Zeppelinfeld, the main stand with the Hall of Honour (architect A. Speer; 1930s). After Wasmuth, *Wasmuths Lexikon der Baukunst*, v, 413.

and polychromatic differentiation that could have allowed something colourful and vital to emerge out of this black-and-white.

This is also expressed in contemporary graphic reconstructions of historic architecture, such as of Egyptian, ancient Oriental, or Greek temples, that not only reflect this architectural style but also the idea of unapproachable, other-worldly 'holiness' typical of the times. Almost exclusively in hard black-and-white contrast, mostly bombastically overproportioned and with the details only schematically surmisable, these drawings present the 'power of fate' in all its implacability.

One recalls, for example, reconstructions of the 'Tower of Babel' by Robert Koldewey,[10] the 'City of Assur' by Walter Andrae[11] (Figure 2.7), and the 'Temple of Solomon' by Hugh Ferris[12] (Figure 2.8). By the way, back then sky-scraper design sketches were drawn in a similar manner to the last example. But it is not only in the graphic but also in the built reconstructions that one can see this style: the early twentieth-century reconstruction of the Hatshepsut Temple (Figure 2.9), to mention an Egyptian example, can here be compared with examples of 1930s and 1940s architecture. To stay with the Hatshepsut

[10] Schmid, 'Der Tempelturm – Befund und Rekonstruktion', p. 93, fig. 64.

[11] Andrae, *Das wiedererstandene Assur*, fig. 37.

[12] Neumann, 'Der Turmbau zu Babel und das Hochhaus', p. 93, fig. 51.

Figure 2.7 (left).
Above: Reconstruction of the Tower of Babylon (R. Koldewey; early twentieth century). After Ganzert, *Der Turmbau zu Babel*, p. 93, fig. 64. **Below**: Reconstruction of the city of Assur with the Assur Temple (W. Andrae; 1930s). After Andrae, *Das wiedererstandene Assur*, p. 54, fig. 37.

Figure 2.8 (right).
Design for the Temple of Solomon by F. Helmle, H. W. Corbett, and J. W. Kelchner; drawn by Hugh Ferris; 1925. After Ganzert, *Der Turmbau zu Babel*, p. 79, fig. 51.

Figure 2.9.
Egypt, Temple of Hatshepsut in Deir el-Bahri (reconstruction; early twentieth century). After Wasmuth, *Wasmuths Lexikon der Baukunst*, I, 68.

Figure 2.10. Hannover: the Melanchthon Church (post-war). © J. Ganzert.

Temple for the moment, here is another comparison (Plate 1): the usual black-and-white reconstruction on the left and a coloured, very provisional sketch on the right that shows the holy place with vegetation and a gaily clad procession. I've captioned the whole thing 'Hatshepsut Metamorphosis' to pose the question of whether there shouldn't be, analogous to the 'polychrome debate' (Gottfried Semper) of the nineteenth century, a similar 'biology debate' in which we would have to add a little vegetal-colourful nature to the stonily monotone reconstructions. And this comes to pass; in a more recent graphic reconstruction of the Mentuhotep Temple the draughtsman has, however modestly, given a little thought to the plantings.[13] And most recently, the colourfulness of earlier sacred architecture and sculpture has become the subject of sophisticated technical-scientific investigation; in place of the former pure white classical plaster casts, architecture and sculpture can to some extent be reconstructed very colourfully (Plate 2).

[13] Wildung, *Ägypten*, p. 78.

The other opinion of the 'sacred' — we can call it the concrete conception here as opposed to the abstract — generally expresses itself in the latter half of the twentieth century after the Second World War, in church architecture that was modernist, mostly coolly functional, not of particularly large dimensions, even, one could say, lower middle class and banal (Figure 2.10), in which the congregation could gather around the altar without a sense of intimidation and awe. (The Second Vatican Council made its own contribution to this from the Catholic side.) In contrast to the pre-war era, the attempt was made to create a concrete, almost familial proximity to the 'sacred', which has to be seen as antithetical to aforementioned distanced abstraction of what one conceived of as 'healing' and 'holy' before the Second World War (and then also during it). This seemed, somehow, desperately necessary if one wanted to, and had to, distance oneself from what, in the 1930s and 1940s, had been revered as god-like ('Heil').

That this second conception, in reacting against the first, is also of course dependent upon it makes it necessary to insert an inverting prism in front of them both if we are to penetrate to a more fundamental consideration of the 'sacred' that we encounter in such multifarious forms in historic finds.

Section I

Let us return to the city of Lüneburg (Figure 2.11). On the north-east corner of the town hall stands what is known as the 'Niedergericht' — the 'lower court of justice' — probably dating from the fifteenth century at the latest. Beneath a cross-vaulted alcove looking out on the market square, a bench is set whose back, opened up into the horizontal, forms a kind of baldachin on whose plafond the Holy Trinity is depicted (Plate 3). In the niche revealed by raising a flap on the back wall the Judgement of Solomon is depicted, captioned with a quotation from the Old Testament.[14] More pictures and inscriptions of biblical quotations on the walls refer to the administration of justice in God's name:[15] the judge, sitting under the baldachin, pronounced judgement as His repre-

[14] II Samuel 14. 17: 'SINT IVDICES SICVT ANGELVS DOMINI VT SINE AFFECTV HVMANO AVDIANT ET IVDICENT BONVM A MALO' (A judge should be disposed as an angel of the Lord and free of human motives; whatever matters he may hear, he should be able to distinguish between good and evil).

[15] See note 14: 'SICVT ANGELVS DOMINI' (as an angel of the Lord).

Figure 2.11.
Lüneburg Town Hall, eastern side, on the right the lower court of justice alcove. © J. Ganzert.

sentative. The vaulting above his chair allows the place and its function to be defined as an overarched vaulted place of justice.

That the town hall was principally to be seen as a place of just and legitimated rule is also made plain, for example, by the picture cycles and woodcarvings in the former council chamber. Along with depictions of 'Heavenly Jerusalem' or portraits of representatives of the Pagan, Jewish and Christian world, they also refer to Daniel's visions of the great empires of the Babylonians, Persians, Greeks, and Romans. This revised elucidation of the council's legitimation addresses the world historical dimension that identifies the Holy Roman Empire's German nation in the spirit of *translatio imperii* with the Roman Empire. In the depiction of 'The Visions of Daniel' of the four realms of the Earth, ancient lore conveyed through Christianity and humanism was extended and fused into a coherent programme that expressed a claim to embed the rule and judgement of Lüneburg's authorities in the great 'Universal Encyclopaedia' of the history of ideally respected rulers and justice — to provide legitimation.

I offer a further example, from the nineteenth century: Let us look at Schloss Neuschwanstein, of which the Bavarian King Ludwig II laid the foundation stone in 1869.[16] Probably the many copies that Walt Disney has placed all over the world are better known, but the original was recently proposed for a list of today's Wonders of the World. Be that as it may, its important features for our purposes are the throne room and its apsidal, arched, and semi-domed vaulted termination (Plate 4). As the castle remained 'romantically unfinished' — that is, was never really completed — the throne in the apse is missing.

Let us take a brief tour of the visual programme in the throne room:

- In the apsidal dome, Christ is shown sitting on a rainbow, flanked by Mary and John and adoring angels;
- to the left and right of the staircase, the twelve Apostles embody divine law;
- in the highest arch above the entrance wall, the Roman Emperor Augustus symbolizes the 'Lex Romana', with Zarathustra on his left and Solon on his right;
- on the opposite wall, Moses with the tablets of stone, symbolizes Old Testament law;
- on the wall facing the apse, the star of the Wise Men with the Three Kings is a symbol of the Christian moral law of the New Testament.
- The rest are other portrayals of justice and mercy.
- The mosaic floor shows the globe with its animals and plants.
- The dome above it symbolizes the heavens with the sun and stars.
- The chandelier is in the shape of a Byzantine crown — symbol of the king as mediator between heaven and earth.

Here too, then, in the throne room of Schloss Neuschwanstein — just like in Lüneburg Town Hall — a cultural-historical compendium for the idealized exercise of authority and just judgement is evoked to legitimize its claims which, as we shall see, obey an archetypal legitimation imperative.

Thus we connect to the ancient world, for this interpretive programme and both the judge's chair at the Lüneburg lower court of justice and the throne planned for the apse but missing in Neuschwanstein lead us among other places to ancient Oriental realms, which, for instance, were already apparent from the

[16] Cf. Desing, *Königsschloss Neuschwanstein*, pp. 16–21.

depictions of Moses and Zarathustra in Neuschwanstein and Old Testament quotations in the Lüneburg court.

I will take the city of Babylon as an example, whose name is derived from 'Bab-ilim', meaning 'the gate of God' — which may, incidentally, be pictured as an arched gate.[17]

The ancient Oriental — and that would to some extent also include the Old Testament — world view concerned itself very thoroughly with the relationship of heaven to earth, of the divine to the earthly sphere, the relationship of the godhead to mankind and the (god) king as mediator between heaven and earth — that is to say, with power relationships — and this manifested itself in temple and palace buildings.

This power relationship between the divine and earthly spheres may be characterized as a perception of hierarchy, namely in the etymological sense of 'hieráe-archáe', roughly translatable as 'healing sovereignty / authority'. To provide the divine sphere's own denizens and the 'healing sovereignty' that was understood to emerge from it with ingress to the earthly sphere, this was the purpose of this religion and its temple buildings, whereby the divine sphere and the godhead itself are seen as of such universal dimensions that the godhead was never tangible in its real presence — its being — but only as appearance.[18] This image of the godhead is celebrated in its envisionment as cult statue or, more often, performed as sacred theatre. And for these epiphanic religious performances, the architecture provides the necessary infrastructure.

The epiphany of the godhead is usually presented in a portal capped by an arch, constructed as a false portal, a niche with an arched vault connotated as the vault of heaven. In the sacral 'epiphanic play', human beings attempt to comprehend their relationship to the universal whole 'theatrically' or to realize it — in the actual sense of the word: to re-present, to make present. For this performance, a stage-like platform is needed, a room for the cult members to prepare, and further, a room to create distance from the sacral performance, capable of lending the events an appropriate significance and to augment their effect.

In this way a fundamental concept for sacred buildings was created (Plate 5), which may be summarized as 'antechamber, main chamber, cultic niche with platform and adjoining room'. This concept could be variously furbished and also have additional rooms, but these variables alter nothing in the fundamen-

[17] Klengel-Brandt, 'Babylon', col. 1042.

[18] Cf. Assmann, *Herrschaft und Heil*, p. 43.

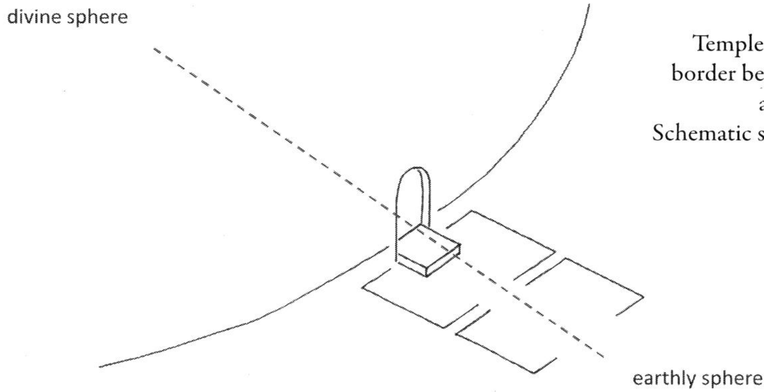

Figure 2.12. Temple cultic niche on the border between the heavenly and earthly spheres. Schematic sketch © J. Ganzert.

tal conceptional constancy; it is to be found in practically every temple — and not only in temples, as we will see.

Additionally enhanced significance can be imparted to this concept of a lower temple by adding a ziggurat, a temple tower with a high temple closer to the divine sphere. The ziggurat of Babylon is familiar to us as the Tower of Babel.[19] At the temple in Kar-Tukultininurta, temple and ziggurat have even melded into a unity.[20]

This tripartite spatial arrangement reflects in general the Semitic-ancient Oriental conception of two different spheres, their 'hier-archical' relationship and the corresponding (con)junctual or communicative possibilities in the sense of religion and ritual (Figure 2.12): on the one hand, beyond the temple, the sphere of the godhead, to be conceived as of otherworldly dimensions corresponding to its significance and dignity, in its 'healing' holiness; on the other hand the earthly sphere, on whose borders the temple facilitates the contingence of the two spheres and their appropriate communication. The temple is not, however, the actual dwelling place of the godhead but rather the setting for its appearance, its epiphany, as a representative cultic image, for the making-present, the real-ization of its 'healing sovereignty' and for its re-presentational 'envisioning': the temple is the setting for the realization of the 'hierarchical' relationship between the divine and the earthly spheres. 'Representation' or 'realization' — in this case 're-presentation' — are the key qualitative terms for communication between the two spheres and for the architecture that makes it possible; representative architecture is thus 'envisioning, realizational architecture'.

[19] Cf. Ganzert, *Der Turmbau zu Babel.*

[20] Andrae, *Das wiedererstandene Assur*, p. 136, fig. 117.

In the self-revelatory 'hierarchical', and thus also envisioned, relationship between the spheres that plainly manifested the relationship of 'healing sovereignty' of the godhead over humankind in a fundamentally valid way and as the archetypical definition of the power relationship, we may find not only a quasi-universally authoritative reason for the accepted validity and attractiveness of this conception, but also for its model and exemplary function. And to this extent such a conception — as we will shortly see — may be found in the context of royal palaces but also in residences and ordinary houses albeit in reduced forms.

This absolutely fundamental concept of the sacred building, presented here of course in very brief and compressed form,[21] was not only shaped and developed in innumerable variants but was also, above and beyond the image of the state or theologically derived formal variable, compatible with the ceremonial and the presentation of a 'healing sovereignty' and/or the epiphanic religious re-presentation of hierarchical power relationships for various cultures, and as a legitimation constant or imperative, a generally indispensable legacy to the future.

Various cultures means that the re-presenter — the proxy of the divinity — could be a 'God King', or in the later Hellenic era, for example, a godlike ruler or 'Heros', or in the subsequent Roman Empire the deified Emperor, or in the following Christian era Pope, Emperor, or King, and these conceptions were accordingly adopted, the tradition persisted and/or acculturated.

Greek religion also largely avoids the epiphanic religious concept dealt with here but is in the final analysis only understandable in relation to it. And to this extent we also encounter, in Greek sacred buildings, very many more and varyingly differentiated mixed concepts — for example, the Lower Italian-Sicilian temple — than a truly durable counter-design. The Eastern legacy of sacred building was too weighty and came from too long a tradition to be discarded.

[21] More extensive accounts from this author: Ganzert, 'Der Mars-Ultor-Tempel auf dem Augustusforum in Rom', pp. 36–59; Ganzert, *Der Mars-Ultor-Tempel auf dem Augustusforum in Rom*; Ganzert, *Im Allerheiligsten des Augustusforum*; Ganzert, 'Zum Verhältnis von "Erscheinung und Wirklichkeit"', pp. 275–96; Ganzert, '"Hier-archische" Herrschaftsverhältnisse und ihr Repräsentationsritual als Legitimationskonstante?', pp. 15–29; also, Ganzert, 'Spielraum "Neu-ORIENT-ierung" bzw. "Neuorientierung"', pp. 177–206.

An Excursion to the Sicilian Concordia Temple in Agrigento

The Concordia Temple in Agrigento, like many temples in Lower Italy and Sicily, not only has an adyton and, together with the pronaos and naos, epitomizes the antechamber–main room–cultic niche concept but, on either side of the naos entrance, also has flights of steps. As the only temple with this feature, however, at the Concordia Temple the window-like apertures in the naos walls right below the upper edge of the roof, and also the staircases and additionally the tympanoi, have been preserved, and this would permit further enquiry.[22] That the staircases served purely technical purposes, as has been proposed by researchers often enough,[23] seems to me a positivist fallacy. It seems equally impossible that the steps led to a cultic performance in the attic;[24] how would this be imaginable in such a low and, in Sicily, overheated attic space, leaving aside the fact that one could only have entered the attic from the staircase by stooping! The sole sensible possibility would appear, as in Egyptian[25] and Oriental temples too, to reconstruct a cult terrace (cf. the later Temple of Bel in Palmyra).[26] From the naos, the procession would have led via the staircase to the cult terrace (Figure 2.13) and back, and on this terrace, open to the vault of heaven, incense sacrifices were made and the associated epiphanic ceremonies performed — through the revelatory doorways in the pronaos-tympanon. This ritual, in which the priesthood above participated directly and the congregation indirectly from below, 'beholding', together with the ritual in the naos and adyton, constitutes a part of the cult that one must see together with that at the altar in front of the temple, like the two differing conceptions in the architectural form: namely, ambivalent and coalesced through acculturation. That this would have to be verified by investigation of the structure[27] is just as urgent a

[22] Mertens, *Der Tempel von Segesta und die dorische Tempelbaukunst des griechischen Westens in klassischer Zeit*, pl. 56,1.

[23] Krencker and Zschietzschmann, *Römische Tempel in Syrien*, p. 292.

[24] Mertens, *Der Tempel von Segesta und die dorische Tempelbaukunst des griechischen Westens in klassischer Zeit*, pp. 172, 173.

[25] In the Ptolemaic Horus Temple in Edfu reliefs have survived on the staircase walls showing processions of gods leading up the sun kiosk on the roof; cf. Stierlin, *Baukunst der Pharaonen*, p. 199.

[26] Seyrig, Amy, and Will, *Le Temple de Bel à Palmyre*, Album pl. 140.

[27] For initial considerations of the architectural evidence, see Ganzert, *Der Mars-Ultor-Tempel auf dem Augustusforum in Rom*, pp. 248–49 and fig. 57; Ganzert, *Im Allerheiligsten des Augustusforum*, p. 84 and figs 142–46.

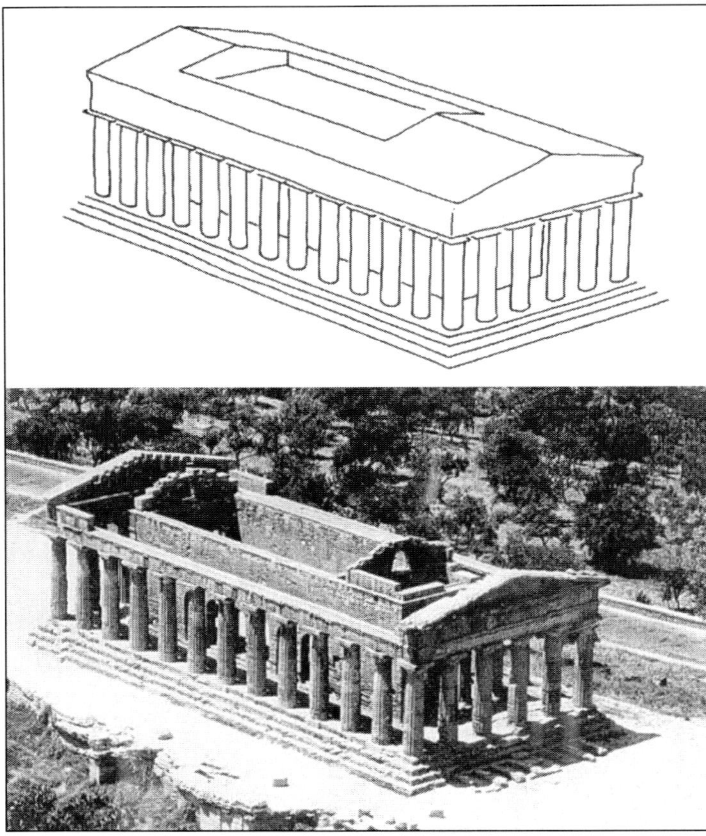

Figure 2.13. **Above**: Agrigento, the Concordia Temple with cultic terrace. Schematic sketch © J. Ganzert. **Below**: Agrigento, the Concordia Temple. After Mertens, *Der Tempel von Segesta und die dorische Tempelbaukunst des griechischen Westens in klassischer Zeit*, pl. 56,1.

research desideratum as the necessity to extend the term 'Near East and Egypt' to include the entire Mediterranean world. Carthaginian-Phoenician, but also Egyptian influence is nothing unusual in Sicily.[28]

The Sicilian examples show that the concepts addressed here are not concerned with a specification identical to just one 'uni-form' stereotype, but with a fundamental conception that could be variously shaped and mixed through acculturation with other traditions.

[28] On this, see Koldewey and Puchstein, *Die griechischen Tempel in Unteritalien und Sizilien*, pp. 193–95.

This fundamental conception was then subjected to further alteration in Roman times, inasmuch as the consistently rectangular cult niche of the ancient Orient and Near East was formed as a curved apse.[29]

With the adoption of Persian court ceremony in the Roman Empire[30] the reverential concept was received as a new concept of *maiestas*, of dignity, into Roman temples, imperial cultic shrines, the throne halls and auditoria of Roman imperial palaces just as fully as the multipurpose halls at the Roman Fora, the *basilicae*, which were not only 'regal' (basiliké) in their dimensions and dignity but also served the purpose of the 're-presentative' — envisioning and representative — dispensation of justice. Apses or exedrae were the places of tribunal.[31]

One of the first Roman temples with an apsidal, vaulted termination is the Augustan Temple of Mars Ultor on the Forum of Augustus in Rome (Plate 6).[32] Even so, it is not the apse alone — perhaps only a formal design variation — but the entire devotional (*maiestas*) conception of the temple interior, as 'antechamber, main room, cult niche termination with podium and adjoining room', and that stands out with its coloured marble from the mainly white marble exterior. The podium in the broad apse, which was structured across its full width by a prospect of steps ornamented in precious alabaster and from whose level a cult preparation room, a kind of sacristy, was connected, offered the cult setting that dominated the entire temple interior (Plate 7); on it the Roman standards brought home to the shrine from Oriental campaigns[33] and the associated theology of victory and peace were brought to 'epiphany'.[34] The

[29] Here the Diodoreion in Pergamon offers an interesting example; its cultic room had a rectangular cult niche which was converted to a semi-circular apse in the early Imperial era; Radt, *Pergamon*, p. 280, figs 138, 139.

[30] Alföldi, 'Die Ausgestaltung des monarchischen Zeremoniells am römischen Kaiserhof', pp. 1–118.

[31] Cf. Vitruvius, *De Architectura*, V, 1, 8.

[32] Ganzert, *Der Mars-Ultor-Tempel auf dem Augustusforum in Rom*; Ganzert, *Im Allerheiligsten des Augustusforum*.

[33] *Res gestae* Divi Augusti 29.

[34] Conversely cf. Beat Brenk, who sees statues set up in the apse, but unfortunately without taking account of the architectural fundamentals (Brenk, *The Apse, the Image and the Icon*, pp. 34–37). To deposit 'the typological question of "temples with apses" in the wastepaper basket', as Brenk believes to have done (Brenk, *The Apse, the Image and the Icon*, p. 37), one should firstly consider the architectural and static conditions: statues cannot float in mid-air; they need a solid foundation, and it is precisely this which is not possible in the case of the apse

temple, however, also served the Senate as a meeting place to deliberate on wars or triumphs;[35] from here provincial governors departed in a celebratory procession to take up their commands, and here the victorious generals brought the trophies of their triumphs, which they probably offered up on the apse steps. At the centre of the cella, a tripod on a podium symbolized the hearth.[36] But it can also be supposed that the Collegium of the Salii gathered here for banquets.[37]

In the same way that the temple interior was distinguished from the exterior in its colours, the apse and its arched semi-domed vaulting was invisible from the outside (Plate 7), where Greek-influenced vertical-horizontal structure architecture was dominant. The actual bearer of meaning, however, was the temple interior with its round-arched epiphanic framework in the holy of holies.

Therefore this conception is continued in Christian sacred buildings, and in this connection one of the key edifices is the Old Church of St Peter in Rome.[38] Before Constantine, the church as the Christian cultic space corresponded to no binding type of building, whereby the direct quotation from ancient models was plain. The merger of imperial and Christian representation mirrored the contemporary official ideas in the area of art and ceremony: the Christian cult and reverence for the Emperor belonged together. And the appropriate available concept was that which we have considered so far, now with the elements: gateway in style of the triumphal arch (?) – atrium – church nave – transept and apse. And it is interesting that in the apse, not only of Byzantine churches, to be precise in the apsis calotte, the image of the ruler of the world appears, shown as Pantocrator.

I will not at this juncture look at the equivalent consequences in connection with the triumphal arch,[39] but would interpret it as an epiphanic frame, the threshold between the two spheres: the godlike/triumphal and the earthly world.

in the Mars Ultor Temple! (Comprehensively demonstrated in Ganzert, *Der Mars-Ultor-Tempel auf dem Augustusforum in Rom*, p. 135 and p. 144.)

[35] C. Suetonius Tranquillus, *Divus Augustus*, 29.

[36] Ganzert, *Im Allerheiligsten des Augustusforum*, p. 99, fig. 166; p. 106, fig. 174.

[37] Herz, 'Zum Tempel des Mars Ultor', pp. 266–81; specifically pp. 276–77.

[38] Arbeiter, *Alt-St.Peter in Geschichte und Wissenschaft*.

[39] Ganzert, *Im Allerheiligsten des Augustusforum*, pp. 89–96 (pp. 94–96: Die '*arcus*'-Geschichte zwischen '*fornix*' und '*arche*'); Künzl, *Der römische Triumph*; Versnel, *Triumphus*.

Section II

Unlike a dualistic juxtaposition of heavenly and earthly realms and/or relations, it seems, above all in ancient examples, that we are concerned with the re-presentation of a power relationship that was extraordinarily finely gradated in its intensity, always tangible and all-pervading; gradated literally, too, in the sense of steps, stairs, rostra, podia, elevated areas, terraces, or platforms. A very important mediatory or 'representational' field on this scale between the heavenly and earthly spheres or, in other words, between temple and house, is the royal palace with its differentially gradated componential areas. And to this extent the temple concept elucidated above may be found in the context of royal palaces, for the proxy or representative of God on Earth was the 'god-king', who appeared to his human subjects in the throne room or audience chamber of his palace like the divinity in a sacred building — but in personam, enthroned on rostrum in a niche below a vault, from where he exercised his 'salvatory authority', pronounced judgement, and thus dispensed justice. Unlike the temple, the significance and realization were less intensively enhanced; even so, the niche as a false portal created the frame for the envisioning, representative ritual. Conception and ceremonial emphasize the sacred function of the royal office as God's representative, its proxy 'salvatory authority' and 'dispensation of justice' derived from it — the vaulted false portal thus becomes the gateway to judgement.

Let us consider a particularly strong example (because it is well preserved): the palace of King Zimrilim (1782–1759 BC) in Mari on the middle Euphrates from the early Babylonian era (Plate 8).[40]

The palace comprises several more-or-less independent areas. A substantial part of it served, to the north, as the wonderful entrance area of the palace as a whole and, to the south, as the economic centre, administration, trading station (Plate 8, dark green) and the depots and stores (Plate 8, light green) arranged around the palace-temple at the highest point of the palace grounds (Plate 8, violet) and extending to the south-east; the stores were thus in a way under the protection of the palace-temple.

A slightly lower-lying section to the east was the ceremonial area with Throne Hall and halls for festivities, conferences, and banqueting on one side (Plate 8, orange-yellow) and the kitchens (Plate 8, blue), offices of the civil service, royal apartments (Plate 8, reddish brown), and bathhouse (Plate 8, turquoise) on the other.

[40] Cf. Parrot, *Mission archéologique de Mari*, enclosed plan.

Access between these areas was via antechambers and courtyards and almost entirely along path and corridor axes (Plate 8, red, sharp-angled lines in the small schematic drawing) that turned many corners, making both direct access and direct views impossible. Narrow doors or corridors were followed by large rooms and courtyards, so that a constant series of surprising contrasts and cumulatively intense moments of entering opened up. The route to the representative areas may be described as a ceremonial mise en scène. It began at the palace entrance in the north, from whence one passed through the gatehouse, a courtyard, and the adjacent waiting room into the central palace courtyard. Audiences without a ceremonial act of state could be conducted in the audience chamber that opened onto the courtyard (Plate 8, marked orange-yellow within the dark green administration area, with semi-circular open staircase).

Through one of the many doors in the corners of the courtyard one could proceed from the north along the north-western access corridor, which turned three corners, to reach the second largest courtyard (Plate 8, outlined in orange-yellow), the one in front of the Throne Hall.

The ceremonial rooms were partly shaped by the strictest symmetry with vistas or sight lines that were chiefly oriented on the position of the royal throne; this was on the one hand the 'display', that is, the appearance or epiphany of the King, and on the other hand the 'beholding' or 'marvelling' of the participants in the royal audience.

The Throne Hall portal lay on the sight line directly opposite the courtyard entrance, through which one looked towards the royal throne on a podium at the midpoint of the broad rear wall. Apart from the portals on the central sight line, the courtyard walls were sectioned by doors set symmetrically in the corners. For participants of the royal audience entering the courtyard, the throne in the cool, shady area or in the semi-darkness of the Throne Hall must have been only gradually revealed, so that the appearance of the King may be imagined as a strikingly cumulative procedure.

The throne stood on a podium accessed by steps from either side beneath a baldachin; to the right, on the Throne Hall's long transverse axis, was another place for a throne with a charcoal brazier in front of it, probably for burning cultic incense. Apart from the central sight-line portal, the doors to the wide Throne Hall were also set symmetrically in the corners.

Beyond the Throne Hall, further heightened in importance, lay the large 'Ceremonial Hall', once again with entrances symmetrically positioned in the corners. On its long axis, the King's throne beneath a baldachin was to the right, and at the opposite end was a high stage reached by a flight of steps. The portal reveals of the stage were recessed, and to the right and left in front of them probably stood figures of gods on pedestals.[41] Charcoal braziers were also set up here in front of both the throne and the stage. As the stage clearly fulfilled a sacred function, the position of the King on the throne across from it was inverted: from that of apparition into that of one beholding the divine epiphany; beholding as an act of visualization. Whether this hall was also the venue for ceremonial banquets or whether these were held exclusively in what is called the 'Conference and Banqueting Hall' directly adjoining the kitchens must remain unresolved.

To summarize, it may be said that the layouts of both the entire palace and also the ceremonial areas were subordinated to a series of differentiated stages of sacred importance. As the palace-temple with the storehouses assumed the highest position in the palace area, so the Ceremonial Hall beyond the Throne Hall and the courtyard lying before the Throne Hall lay at a middle, that is, a mediating level. Seen from the town below — most palaces in the ancient Orient were situated on a raised platform — the palace area was ceremonially accessed.

A later example is offered by the palace of Nebuchadnezzar II (sixth century BC) in the southern castle of Babylon from the later Babylonian era.[42] The throne room is a transverse space, again on the south side of a courtyard, and the throne stood flanked by double reveals opposite the central portal in front of or in a niche. Located to the east of the throne room were two further courtyards, where the portal from the first (eastern) courtyard to the second (middle) courtyard apparently served as the place of judgement.[43] Like the other important gateways it was flanked by towers. Whether this first courtyard was actually allotted the title 'House of the adoration of the people',[44] as mentioned in a royal inscription, is not certain; such an expression emphasizes the significance of 'beholding' in sacred and semi-sacred contexts.

A similar arrangement has come down to us from ancient Egypt. In the palace of Rameses III in Medinet Habu,[45] for example, the King was not only enthroned on a podium in front of a niche but revealed himself to his subjects gathered in the courtyard before the palace through a higher window.[46]

[41] Cf. Heinrich, *Die Paläste im Alten Mesopotamien*, pp. 68–81.

[42] Koldewey, *Die Königsburgen von Babylon*, pl. 2.

[43] Conjecture of R. Koldewey and E. Heinrich, in Heinrich, *Die Paläste im Alten Mesopotamien*, p. 209.

[44] Langdon, *Die neubabylonischen Königsinschriften*, p. 137.

[45] Hölscher, *The Excavation of Medinet Habu*; Hölscher, *Die Wiedergewinnung von Medinet Habu im westlichen Theben*.

[46] Hölscher, *The Excavation of Medinet Habu*, p. 37, fig. 15.

An inscription on the window frame relates: 'The King appeared like the morning sun in his magnificent palace.'[47] The palace courtyard is also the first courtyard behind the entrance pylon to the temple and thus directly linked with the temple area.[48]

'Medinet Habu' means, incidentally, 'the city of Habu',[49] making it clear that the entire temple and palace area was comprehended as an urban unity. This raises the question of to what extent the way we use the term 'town' is applicable to ancient and probably also later urban archaeological findings. Similarly to the ancient Orient, the complex included both extensive administration and storage areas and greenspace and water features, all of which fulfilled various sacred functions.

Section III

As the final link in the chain of mediatory and/or visualization scale, let us take a brief look at a residential house, 'House I' in Babylon from the later Babylonian era (Plate 9).[50] It was entered indirectly via a double corner (Plate 9, red, sharply angled line) that prevented any direct view and through two lobbies, beside them a room that was probably for visitors or the doorkeeper. The heart of the house comprised the inner courtyard with the main living room on its shady side (Plate 9, orange-yellow), a broad transverse room entered through double doors. This adjoined seven smaller rooms, probably sleeping apartments and annexes including the bathroom. On the west and north sides of the courtyard were storerooms, servants' rooms, and workrooms (Plate 9, green) including a kitchen.

The residential house also, then, consisted of a southern formal and private area, a northern commercial area, and an entrance area to the north-east. The private area was for the family and women and was the most prestigious.

Comparing private house, palace, and temple (Plate 9, below right, schematic drawing) allows us to work out a few conceptional parallels that are even more explicit in the residence with its reduced configuration.

[47] Hölscher, *Die Wiedergewinnung von Medinet Habu im westlichen Theben*, p. 26.

[48] Hölscher, *Die Wiedergewinnung von Medinet Habu im westlichen Theben*, p. 17, fig. 1.

[49] Hölscher, *Die Wiedergewinnung von Medinet Habu im westlichen Theben*, p. 13.

[50] Cf. Ganzert, *Der Turmbau zu Babel*, p. 27, fig. 15; see also Reuther, *Die Innenstadt von Babylon*, p. 81, fig. 62.

First, access was not simple and direct but complex and indirect: looking in, or 'beholding', was also here manifestly connotated at least as semi-sacred (through its parallels with temple and/or palace access systems), only possible via appropriate diversions and pre-stages and, when directly, only across an appropriate distance and only to the correspondingly prestigious objectives. In the temple, this is further accentuated by means of other antechambers. Access and beholding, then, as acts of visualization.

Second, the main room is typified by its location, only accessible by crossing the courtyard, in the shaded, cooler area to the south, by the central double gates on its north side, by its transverse shape, broader than it is deep, and by the large number of adjacent rooms or groups of rooms.[51] In the palace and the temple, the location of the throne or cultic image was further accentuated by its position in front of or within a niche in the long wall.

Finally, the prestigious, formal area with such characteristics can be recognized as the area of the family and the women, and indicates, also for this area, an at least semi-sacred status. When one also considers that the holy of holies in the temple was also called 'thalamos', that is, sleeping apartment, and the 'holy wedding' (*ierós gamós*) was a sacred ritual, then the sacred position of the family and women's areas in the house is plain. The apportionment, especially of Assyrian palaces, into 'babanu' (gatehouse, entrance lobby) and 'bitanu' (house, residence)[52] generally emphasizes this enhancement of significance; this tradition is continued, incidentally, in Islamic apartments and residences with their division into 'haramlik' and/or 'selamlik', alternatively 'Diwan-i-Am' and/or 'Diwan-i-Khas'.

Conclusion

In striking contrast to the modern-secular view, the sacred in earlier connections was represented neither by a lifeless, larger-than-life abstraction nor by a banal-concrete anthropomorphism, but rather quite clearly in a practice of visualization incorporating the whole of life and the whole world view that could be expressed to variously differentiated degrees on an extended scale of possibilities: from the residential house through the palace to the temple — yes, and

[51] These characteristics — variously shaped — apply to the other excavated houses in Babylon; cf. Reuther, *Die Innenstadt von Babylon*, pl. 17.

[52] Cf. Heinrich, *Die Tempel und Heiligtümer im Alten Mesopotamien*, p. 249; and Heinrich, *Die Paläste im Alten Mesopotamien*, p. 81.

even to the high temple on the ziggurat and the roofs of the houses. The extent to which we, in observing historic truths, will have to assume an inverted prism may also be plain from the inversion in meaning of two terms.

In German, the term 'Repräsentation' is mainly used in the sense of, or substituted for, 'Selbstdarstellung'. 'Selbstdarstellung', literally self-presentation or ostentation, is, however, the opposite of the meaning of 'Repräsentation' in which English comes closer: re-presentation. And much the same applies to the term 'hierarchy', which is almost exclusively used in the sense of a higher-to-lower ranking and mostly associated pejoratively with evil, despotic (often Oriental) power relationships. The etymologically appropriate meaning of 'hieráe-archáe' as 'healing sovereignty' — and this meaning would be the opposite of 'Unheil', meaning evil or harm — is seldom reflected upon[53] and almost always tabooed.

To this extent it is probably also difficult to talk of 'sacred and/or representative rooms or spaces' — in contrast to profane spaces? For what was not sacred space, what was not comprehended in the sense of 'healing visualisztion' or as 'salvific world view'![54] House, palace, and temple were quite obviously suffused on a daily, everyday basis with a living cultic practice — in the broadest sense of the word — that incorporated almost everything in life, as Ernst Heinrich illustrated,[55] with which the most various people were occupied, from the priests through the artists who created the cultic images and their adornments, the musicians, actors, craftsmen of every kind through to the servants and workers in the fields.[56] For the daily cultic acts, touching on 'worship', beholding, and sacrifice, that is, for the sanctification and offering of sacrifices, one can assume a large number of participants. The sacrificial offerings, often enough foodstuffs, had to be produced, stored, administered, and distributed, food offerings had to be prepared, the several cultic images clothed and cared for. For the sacrificers, admission to the temple and to the holy of holies, often fitted with numerous divine images, cannot have been refused. The sacrifice foodstuffs included meat, so we must consider stalls for livestock. And stalls were above all needed for the white processional horses. Such processions and temple feasts, which could last several days in the area of the temple but also in the city and across the land, required enormous logistical effort and numerous

[53] Assmann, *Herrschaft und Heil*.

[54] This offers no support for an idealistic-euphemistic assessment of the evidence!

[55] Heinrich, *Die Tempel und Heiligtümer im Alten Mesopotamien*, pp. 243–46.

[56] Heinrich, *Die Tempel und Heiligtümer im Alten Mesopotamien*, p. 244.

personnel for their preparation and conduct. Feasts were celebrated for all the major gods, some of them over several days and sometimes also several times a year.[57] For processions in which gods, either alone or accompanied by others, went to visit their co-divinities in the city or participated in festivities for other gods, a least half the population must have been involved. Even the temple and palace roofs were the destinations of processions and incense sacrifices. Some cities had several feasting houses, and the description of Babylon speaks of fifty-three shrines to the major gods alone; additionally one assumes that there was an altar or cultic place on every corner. The cultic life kept the city constantly and literally 'on its toes', as apparently some gods were on the move almost every day.

The palaces were not stony, barren places but should be imagined as enriched with luxuriant vegetation in gardens and parks. Plants that the King had brought back from his campaigns were planted around the royal residence: willow, oak, laurel, and lilac, but also pear trees, quince, medlar, figs, grape vines, or the date palm — and for the care of such plants we must also envisage the necessary gardeners and servants. For construction of the palaces the timber of various trees was imported: box, mulberry, cedar, cypress, pistachio, tamarisk, poplar, and many more.[58] All the gods were invited to the feast to mark completion of the building work, but also all who had worked on its construction: from civil servants to indentured labourers from the furthest corners of the empire, everyone was there and was sumptuously feasted. Thousands of guests are mentioned.

The way ancient Oriental cultures are addressed here is also valid for later cultures; such a temple as Mars Ultor also served, as we have seen, to fulfil multifarious functions and was crammed — one could almost speak of a 'fair' — with colourful, sacred-theatrical ceremonial life,[59] but a life which did not divide the sacred from the profane.

Simple as it may seem to look through an inverting prism and set an upside-down two-dimensional picture the right way up, it is correspondingly difficult to imagine, and to convey, the all-encompassing multidimensionality and differentiated degrees of what we call the sacred in earlier ages, or to appreciate it without inappropriate prejudices. The architectural evidence would indicate an

[57] Heinrich, *Die Tempel und Heiligtümer im Alten Mesopotamien*, p. 245.

[58] Heinrich, *Die Tempel und Heiligtümer im Alten Mesopotamien*, p. 245.

[59] On this, see Ganzert, '"Hier-archische" Herrschaftsverhältnisse und ihr Repräsentationsritual als Legitimationskonstante?', p. 21.

all-pervasiveness in everyday life, in consciousness, indeed, in the whole world view of the sacred, and conversely the pervasion of the sacred with the 'worldly'. Indeed, for the greater part of human history no division between these two areas seems to have existed,[60] for the indivisibility of the spheres seems, in their mutually legitimizing references, to have been inherent, and to have demanded realization; and realization means the opposite of separation, even excludes the possibility of separation because earthly authority and justice could only be legitimized with reference to the salvatory-divine sphere. The legitimation fulfilled through envisioning created a holistic sacrality that apparently encompassed everything from the temple through the palace to the house. Does that not also signify 'contextualizing the sacred'? Subsumation within the sacred, or sacred inclusion, were probably such self-evident preconditions for one's entire life that the overly one-dimensional and heroic-monumental 'assertions of holiness' of the modern era (see 'Prelim 4' above) were superfluous. Indeed, our overview of the architectural evidence for various eras could reveal that the epiphanic conception with regard to legitimation not only played a crucial role in ancient contexts, but also that through the centuries legitimation has been constantly renewed through reference to this conception and its acculturation; that we are concerned with an archetypical legitimation imperative.

This, however, raises the question of what role legitimation actually plays today, and who would be prepared to respond at all to the solicited legitimation imperative — and why not? Thereby the issue of '(salvatory) power relationships' and the legitimation of authority and justice would be addressed as of central importance. This, however, would present itself as one of the most difficult and complex issues for us to deal with today, as much seems suspect to us — particularly after the experiences of the twentieth century — from the terminology alone and in part encumbered with sweepingly defamatory and revulsive reflex reactions; to a large extent our entire self-conception with regard to this issue seems to been turned upside down. This demonstrates, though, how important it is not to proceed from today's conditions and mental dependencies, or to judge historical evidence too quickly using contemporary criteria, if we wish to concern ourselves with the long-overdue attempt to contextualize the sacred.

[60] It would nevertheless be worth examining to what extent today's so-called 'division of State and Church' reflects reality or rhetoric.

Works Cited

Secondary Studies

Alföldi, A., 'Die Ausgestaltung des monarchischen Zeremoniells am römischen Kaiserhof', *Mitteilungen des Deutschen Archäologischen Instituts, Römische Abteilung*, 49 (1934), 1–118

Andrae, W., *Das wiedererstandene Assur* (Leipzig: Hinrich, 1938)

Arbeiter, A., *Alt-St.Peter in Geschichte und Wissenschaft* (Berlin: Gebr. Mann, 1988)

Assmann, J., *Herrschaft und Heil: Politische Theologie in Altägypten, Israel und Europa* (Darmstadt: Wissenschaftliche Buchgesellschaft, 2000)

Boeke, K., *Cosmic Views: The Universe in 40 Jumps* (New York: John Day, 1957), available at <http://www.vendian.org/mncharity/cosmicview/> and <http://ned.ipac.caltech.edu/level5/Boeke/frames.html> [accessed 15 June 2011]

Brenk, B., *The Apse, the Image and the Icon: An Historical Perspective of the Apse as a Space for Images* (Wiesbaden: Reichert, 2010)

Brinkmann, V., W. Hornbostel, and R. Wünsche, eds, *Bunte Götter: Die Farbigkeit antiker Skulptur, Ausstellung Museum für Kunst und Gewerbe Hamburg* (München: Mediahaus Biering, 2007)

Desing, J., *Königsschloss Neuschwanstein: Schlossbeschreibung, Baugeschichte, Sagen* (Lechbruck: Kienberger, 1998)

Ganzert, J., '"Hierarchische" Herrschaftsverhältnisse und ihr Repräsentationsritual als Legitimationskonstante? Zur architektonischen Kult-Infrastruktur', in *Zwischen Kult und Gesellschaft: Kosmopolitische Zentren des antiken Mittelmeerraumes als Aktionsraum von Kultvereinen und Religionsgemeinschaften, Akten Symposion Archäologisches Institut Universität Hamburg 2005*, ed. by I. Nielsen, Hephaistos Themenband, 24 (Augsburg: Camelion, 2006), pp. 15–29

——, *Im Allerheiligsten des Augustusforum: Fokus 'oikoumenischer Akkulturation'* (Mainz: Philipp von Zabern, 2000)

——, *Der Mars-Ultor-Tempel auf dem Augustusforum in Rom*, Sonderschriften Deutsches Archäologisches Institut Rom, 11 (Mainz: Philipp von Zabern, 1996)

——, 'Der Mars-Ultor-Tempel auf dem Augustusforum in Rom: Ein Bericht über die laufenden Bauforschungsarbeiten und Beitrag zur Sakralbau-Entwicklung', *Antike Welt*, 3 (1988), 36–59

——, 'Spielraum "Neu-ORIENT-ierung" bzw. "Neuorientierung"', in *Orient – Orientalistik – Orientalismus: Geschichte und Aktualität einer Debatte*, ed. by B. Schnepel, G. Brands, and H. Schönig, Postcolonial Studies, 5 (Bielefeld: Transcript, 2011), pp. 177–206

——, ed., *Der Turmbau zu Babel: Maßstab oder Anmaßung?* (Biberach: Biberacher, 1997)

——, 'Zum Verhältnis von "Erscheinung und Wirklichkeit": Annäherungen an entsprechende Befundhinweise aus der Augusteischen Architektur', in *Propaganda – Selbstdarstellung – Repräsentation im römischen Kaiserreich des 1.Jhs.n.Chr.*, ed. by G. Weber and M. Zimmermann, Historia Einzelschrift, 164 (Stuttgart: Steiner, 2003), pp. 275–96

Hehl, U. von, 'Sakrales im Säkularen? Elemente politischer Religion im Nationalsozialismus', in *Die Sakralität von Herrschaft: Herrschaftslegitimierung im Wechsel der Zeiten und Räume*, ed. by F.-R. Erkens (Berlin: Akademie, 2002), pp. 225–43

Heinrich, E., *Die Paläste im Alten Mesopotamien*, Denkmäler antiker Architektur, 15 (Berlin: De Gruyter, 1984)

——, *Die Tempel und Heiligtümer im Alten Mesopotamien: Typologie, Morphologie und Geschichte*, Denkmäler antiker Architektur, 14 (Berlin: De Gruyter, 1982)

Herz, P., 'Zum Tempel des Mars Ultor', in *Der Mars-Ultor-Tempel auf dem Augustusforum in Rom*, ed. by J. Ganzert, Sonderschriften Deutsches Archäologisches Institut Rom, 11 (Mainz: Philipp von Zabern, 1996), pp. 266–81

Hölscher, U., *The Excavation of Medinet Habu*, vol. III: *The Mortuary Temple of Ramses III, Part I*, Oriental Institute Publications, 54 (Chicago: University of Chicago Press, 1941)

——, *Die Wiedergewinnung von Medinet Habu im westlichen Theben* (Tübingen: Wasmuth, 1958)

Klengel-Brandt, E., 'Babylon', in *Die Religion in Geschichte und Gegenwart*, vol. I, ed. by H. D. Betz, 7 vols (Tübingen: Mohr Siebeck, 1998), col. 1042

Koldewey, R., *Die Königsburgen von Babylon*, vol. I: *Die Südburg*, Deutschen Orient-Gesellschaft, 54 (Leipzig: Hinrichs, 1931)

——, *Die Tempel von Babylon und Borsippa*, Deutschen Orient-Gesellschaft, 15 (Leipzig: Hinrich, 1911)

Koldewey, R., and O. Puchstein, *Die griechischen Tempel in Unteritalien und Sizilien* (Berlin: Asher, 1899)

Krencker, D., and W. Zschietzschmann, *Römische Tempel in Syrien* (Berlin: De Gruyter, 1938)

Künzl, E., *Der römische Triumph* (München: Beck, 1988)

Langdon, S., *Die neubabylonischen Königsinschriften* (Leipzig: Hinrich, 1912)

Mertens, D., *Der Tempel von Segesta und die dorische Tempelbaukunst des griechischen Westens in klassischer Zeit* (Mainz: Philipp von Zabern, 1984)

Neumann, D., 'Der Turmbau zu Babel und das Hochhaus im 20. Jahrhundert', in *Der Turmbau zu Babel: Maßstab oder Anmaßung?*, ed. by J. Ganzert (Biberach: Biberacher, 1997), pp. 70–89

Parrot, A., *Mission archéologique de Mari*, vol. II: *Le Palais, Tome I: Architecture*, Bibliothèque archeologique et historique, 68, 5 vols (Paris: Paul Geuthner, 1958)

Radt, W., *Pergamon* (Ostfildern: Dumont 1988)

Raith, F.-B., *Der Heroische Stil: Studien zur Architektur am Ende der Weimarer Republik* (Berlin: Bauwesen, 1997)

Reuther, O., *Die Innenstadt von Babylon (Merkes)*, Ausgrabungen der Deutschen Orient-Gesellschaft in Babylon, 3; WVDeutschen Orient-Gesellschaft, 47 (Osnabrück: Otto Zeller, 1968; repr. of the 1926 edn)

Rümelin, H., *St. Nicolai in Lüneburg: Bauen in einer norddeutschen Hansestadt 1405–1840*, Veröffentlichungen der Historischen Kommission für Niedersachsen und Bremen 248; Beiträge zur Architektur- und Kulturgeschichte, Leibniz Universität Hannover, Abtlg. Bau- Stadtbaugeschichte, Fakultät für Architektur und Landschaft, 2 (Hannover: Hahn, 2009)

Sack, D., *Damaskus: Entwicklung und Struktur einer orientalisch-islamischen Stadt*, DamForsch, 1, Deutsches Archäologisches Institut, Station Damaskus (Mainz: Philipp von Zabern, 1989)
Schmid, H., 'Der Tempelturm — Befund und Rekonstruktion', in *Der Turmbau zu Babel: Maßstab oder Anmaßung?*, ed. by J. Ganzert (Biberach: Biberacher, 1997) pp. 90–101
Seyrig, H., R. Amy, and E. Will, *Le Temple de Bel à Palmyre*, Bibliothèque archeologique et historique, 83 (Paris: Paul Geuthner, 1968)
Stierlin, H., *Baukunst der Pharaonen* (Paris: Finest S.A./Editions Pierre Terrail, 1992)
Versnel, H. S., *Triumphus* (Leiden: Brill, 1970)
Wasmuth, G., ed., *Wasmuths Lexikon der Baukunst*, 5 vols (Berlin: Wasmuth, 1929–32, 1937)
Wildung, D., *Ägypten: Von der prähistorischen Zeit bis zu den Römern*, ed. by H. Stierlin (Köln: Taschen, 2004)

Regional Perspectives

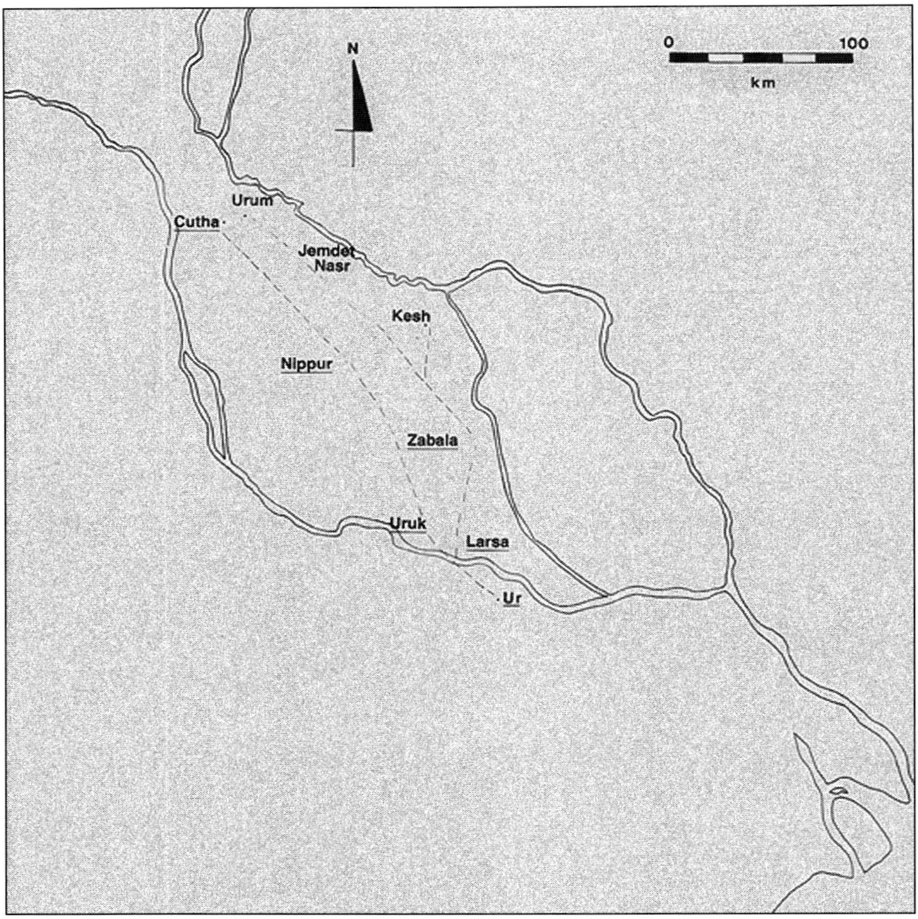

Map 1. The early cities of Sumer.

Sacred Topography of the Empire: Inscribing Social Order into the Cosmic Order

Beate Pongratz-Leisten

Logographic writings of city names such as ud-AB (sanctuary of (the sun god) Utu/Shamash) for the city of Larsa, AB-ùri (sanctuary of (the moon god) Nanna) for Ur, and mùš-AB (sanctuary of (the goddess) Ishtar) for Zabalam bespeak the notion of a close link between the temple of a god or goddess and the community settled around their temple already during the Archaic period (3200–2900 BCE).[1] From the city seals of the same

* I would like to thank Elizabeth Frood and Rubina Raja for having brought me to Oxford to attend their stimulating conference. I would also like to thank them for generously agreeing with my request to contribute a paper differing substantially in content from my original talk, as I plan to include this former material into a forthcoming book I am writing on the Assyrians.

[1] Englund and Nissen, *Die lexikalischen Listen der archaischen Texte aus Uruk*; Michalowski, 'On the Early Toponomy of Sumer', pp. 119–33; Szarzynska, 'Offerings for the Goddess Inanna in Archaic Uruk', p. 24 with n. 13. Sallaberger, 'The City and the Palace at Archaic Ur', p. 33, assumes a more general sense of AB as 'place' because in the UD.GAL.NUN orthography AB/UNUG corresponds to *ki* 'place'. His argument that because the office of the sanga, generally considered an administrator of the temple, is associated also with the é-gal in Lagash, AB should be interpreted as a profane institution is not persuasive as the administrative complex of the queen in Lagash is dedicated to the goddess Bau, and so our modern distinction between sacred and profane does not apply for the ancient conditions. Wang assumes that the early writing for Nippur is EN.KID in the Archaic City Seal designating a toponym /nibru/ and only later was read as /ellil/: Wang, *The Metamorphosis of Enlil in Early Mesopotamia*, pp. 41–59, 218–19.

Beate Pongratz-Leisten (bpl2@nyu.edu) Institute for the Study of the Ancient World, New York University.

period,[2] which contain multiple such names in various constellations, we know of a number of such urban communities, which emerged in the alluvial plain of Southern Mesopotamia at the time (Map 1). Among these the city of Uruk stands out due to its impressive monumental urban landscape and text finds, which inform us about the nature of this large-scale, populous, politically centralized, and socially stratified polity.[3] Inanna's sanctuary in Uruk probably was the recipient of regular deliveries from these cities mentioned in the sealings found on jars and tablets, which identified the receipt of food deliveries destined for Inanna of Uruk.[4] While within the city walls archaeological evidence attests to a diligent layout of various monumental buildings around Inanna's temple precinct, Uruk's spatial dimension is enhanced through its economic relationship with other cities, which creates a cultic hierarchy with Inanna's temple representing the cultic centre among these various cities.

The regular deliveries from various cities to a cultic centre represent an important strategy of how to bind various parts of a region to a centre; what is more, the translation of such an economic measure into the iconography and writing of the city seal demonstrates a major cognitive step in transferring the conceptualization and ordering of space and its mapping into a different medium, the text. Combining the various names on the seal is a further conceptual step of expressing the spatial relationships and cultural cohesion between the major centres of Sumer, which came to be called the 'land' (*kalam*) in Sumerian in contrast to the 'foreign land' (*kur*). It further reflects the interdependence of these cities who engaged in intercity activities such as canal building, for instance.[5] Unfortunately, we are far from fully understanding the city seals of which various sealings have survived from various cities on tablets as well as jars combining different sets of names. While in this early period economy seems to have been the driving motor behind mapping the coherence of a particular space, in later periods this strategy was primarily used by the kings to convey a sense of communal coherence.

[2] Matthews, *Cities, Seals and Writing*, pp. 40–47 and figs 12–125; Steinkeller, 'Archaic City Seals and the Question of Early Babylonian Unity', pp. 253–54; Wang, *The Metamorphosis of Enlil in Early Mesopotamia*, pp. 219–22.

[3] Stein, 'Understanding Ancient State Societies in the Old World', p. 353.

[4] Steinkeller, 'Archaic City Seals and the Question of Early Babylonian Unity', pp. 255–56; Sallaberger, 'The City and the Palace at Archaic Ur', p. 33, is critical of that interpretation because sealings of those seals have been also found on doors in Archaic Ur.

[5] Wang, *The Metamorphosis of Enlil in Early Mesopotamia*, p. 221.

The particular manner of writing the name of a city with reference to its patron deity survives in various cases throughout the history of Mesopotamia and, together with the city seals, indicates that these communities had a strong sense of communal identity bound up with their patron gods. Personal identity, by contrast, was primarily anchored in the family with its adherence to a particular family god, and only secondarily with the patron deity and pantheon of the city. The family and the temple as the seat of the patron deity, consequently, were key elements in fostering the strength of the local elites.

The social structure of the early Mesopotamian cities was determined by a mixture of tribal and urban elements, the latter playing out in the diversification of labour, social stratification, and the concentration of wealth in the hands of a few. Indeed the interesting historical phenomenon Marc van de Mieroop has observed for Mesopotamia is that, 'with the progressive territorial expansion of the political units' into empires, 'the cities and their representatives gained increased political independence'.[6] This political independence was grounded in an economic independence. From the Old Babylonian period (1800–1595 BCE) onwards, the economy rested on three sectors: the palace, the temples, and the private citizenry. While the temple personnel were originally in charge of all supervision, with private citizens being engaged as sharecroppers or as contracted herdsmen to take care of the day-to-day work, van de Mieroop observes an increasing fragmentation of temple offices during the Old Babylonian period. Kept within the family, the temple offices became inherited property to be divided among the sons at the death of the office holder. It thus became impossible for the temple attendants to maintain the supervision of all the economic affairs, and private entrepreneurs were instead contracted for this work. At the time that the temple changed its daily administration by privatizing many of its functions, the palace drew administrative duties away from the temple and began to use its own offices to take care of its business.[7] A similar impact of private entrepreneurship is evidenced in the Neo-Babylonian period (626–539 BCE), when individuals and families belonging to the old, hereditary urban elite often owned prebends and held offices in the local temples.[8]

[6] This 'is the reverse of the currently predominant view that Mesopotamian history evolved from a "primitive democracy" to a totalitarian state headed by an all-powerful king': van de Mieroop, *The Ancient Mesopotamian City*, p. 133.

[7] Van de Mieroop, *Society and Enterprise in Old Babylonian Ur*.

[8] Bongenaar, *Interdependency of Institutions and Private Entrepreneurs*, p. 2; Beaulieu, 'A Finger in Every Pie', pp. 43–72.

This private entrepreneurship may account for the power of the urban citizenry throughout Mesopotamian history.

With the growth of the territorial states into empires, this power is apparent in the institution of exemption from royal taxation, corvée, and military duties, called *kidinnu*, a privilege that the king had to grant to the ancient cult centres in Babylonia such as Babylon, Borsippa, Nippur, Sippar, and Uruk,[9] and later, during the Sargonid period (721–627 BCE), to Assur and Harran as well in order to guarantee their loyalty to the crown.[10]

In addition to this delicate balance between monarchical power and the elites of the cities, maintaining internal stability and cohesion in the face of external threats and internal growing heterogeneity in ethnic, political, and administrative elements turned more and more difficult over the millennia of Mesopotamian history. The rapid and often brutal expansion of the borders added in hostility and hatred, and the fact that the organization of power was based primarily on kinship ties and ties with the wealthiest families of the elites increased the danger for 'internal power struggle and disruption of dynastic succession'.[11]

Regional, territorial, or even imperial unification under the control of one centre, consequently, always posed a particular challenge to the individual rulers. Hence, an entire league of professional experts worked at creating a world view that allocated each individual his or her place in society and bound its various members in a system of mutual obligations. Their cosmogonies, consequently, not only defined the physical space, but also legitimatized the existing social organization and its hierarchy.[12] The Sumerian cosmogonies, in particular, as the 'religion of "there"',[13] that is, the public sphere, are much informed by the elements of urbanism emphasizing technological achievements, as is the case in the Sumerian debate literature. Further, the organizing and categorizing of individual and communal experiences by demarcating boundaries of time, space, group, and status[14] is obvious in a variety of cosmogonies concerned with the creation of the cities, kingship, and humankind. The list of the ME in

[9] Further terms describing the privileges of the elites are *andurāru*, *zakûtu*, and *šubarrû*. See Postgate, *Taxation and Conscription in the Assyrian Empire*, pp. 238–43.

[10] Chamaza, 'Sargon II's Ascent to the Throne', pp. 21–33.

[11] Parpola, 'Neo-Assyrian Concepts of Kingship', p. 35.

[12] Gladigow, 'Welche Welt paßt zu welchen Religionen?', p. 18.

[13] Smith, 'Here, There, and Anywhere', esp. pp. 27–29.

[14] Douglas, *Purity and Danger*.

the Sumerian myth *Inanna and Enki*[15] reveals that institutions, technological achievements, and professions, as well as positive and negative aspects of human behaviour, are considered essential elements of the cosmic order. Originally associated with the creator god Enki/Ea, patron deity of the most ancient cultic centre in Sumer, Sumerian literary tradition as represented in the myth *Inanna and Enki* then passed the supervision of the ME to the goddess Inanna of the city of Uruk.[16] Inanna in turn acted as intermediary between the divine council and the king in Babylonia, and later between Assur and the king in Assyria. Although with the second millennium BCE the notion of the ME is superseded by the concept of the fate decreed by the chief god, it continues to underpin the concept of the cosmic order until the end of Mesopotamian history.

In the early cosmogonies, therefore, the creation of the city or its symbol, the temple as the abode of the gods on earth, often precedes any other element of the creation process, and the creation of humankind and kingship remains always secondary to the idea of the city. Mythic reasoning thus presents kingship as the institution necessary to carry on the work once started by the gods on the basis of its managerial and organizational capacities. It is exactly for that reason that the kings in their inscriptions always emphasize their meeting of divine expectations in their canal building, resulting in an abundance of grain and consequent prosperity not only for the people but also for the cultic offerings. This is also why they celebrated successful building undertakings commissioned by the gods, such as the construction and restoration of temples, walls, and flood-control systems. Maintaining the entire system that guaranteed the provisioning of the cult and thus satisfied the needs of the gods served to maintain the harmonic balance of the human–divine relationship — with the king on the institutional level, and on the individual level with the balanced relationship between the person, his or her protective genius, family god, city god, and the other members of the pantheon including ultimately the chief god.

The city, consequently, is also the epitome of social order as illustrated by the Sumerian *Hymn to Enlil in the Ekur*, his temple in Nippur. This hymn lists all the social taboos that were forbidden in the city:

> It [Nippur] cuts short the life of those who speak too mightily. It permits no evil word to be spoken in judgment (?). ......, deception, inimical speech, hostility, impropriety, ill-treatment, wickedness, wrongdoing, looking askance (?), violence,

[15] The Electronic Text Corpus of Sumerian Literature, 1.3.1.

[16] This has been demonstrated by Jean-Jacques Glassner by means of contextual reading with other texts, primarily myths and hymns: Glassner, 'Inanna et les ME', pp. 55–86.

> slandering, arrogance, licentious speech (?), egotism and boasting are abominations not tolerated within in the city.[17]

Ultimately it was the duty of the ruler to guarantee that such abominations would not happen within the city by means of enacting the law.[18] Hence, the royal inscriptions can be read as justifications cast into stylized narratives about the successful fulfilment of accomplishments expected to be carried out by the ideal king. Consequently, the responsibilities of the royal institution consisted of guaranteeing the continuity of the civilization and cosmic order as laid out in the physical setting of the city states in the alluvial plain and as represented in the social order of their communities established by the gods in the mythical past.

Faced with the strong ideological rhetoric of the ancient kings and oblivious of the programmatic message of myth as laid out above, modern historiography of the political history of the ancient Near East has tended to overlook the fact that the monarchical systems of the city states, territorial states, and empire states at least to some extent depended on the loyalty and cooperation of the political and religious elites to sustain the stability and longevity of their government.[19] Indeed, in their official self-representation the kings of ancient Mesopotamia generally neglected the contributions of their officials, and, consequently, their official inscriptions have been often dismissed as pure propaganda. However, the more abbreviated and formulaic these inscriptions are the more we are required to scrutinize their messages in this regard,[20] and my preliminary remarks delineating the interface between social order and cosmic order are meant to sensitize the reader towards the rhetoric used by ancient rulers in their inscriptions in which they publicize their control over a particular territory. As they are primarily concerned with the question of whether they have met the challenge of balancing the two, the kings generally tend to refer to the cities as abodes of the temples rather than as communities of people, a phenomenon that can only be explained within the framework of the ancient world view as described above. The exclusion of the political and scholarly elites and their impact on the operation of power in the royal inscriptions is dictated by the world view that ranks the maintenance of the cosmic order

[17] The Electronic Text Corpus of Sumerian Literature, 4.05.1:18–25.

[18] Glassner, 'Droit et divination'.

[19] See, however, Tadmor, 'Monarchy and the Elite in Assyria and Babylonia', pp. 203–22, and Pongratz-Leisten, 'All the King's Men'.

[20] This point has been made in Liverani, 'Critique of Variants and the Titulary of Sennacherib', pp. 225–57.

highest among the royal duties and therefore in all media — text, ritual, and image — prioritizes the king's close cooperation with the gods rather than with earthly communities.[21]

Some texts, however, are a little more explicit with regard to the multilayered system of social order directly interfacing with cosmic order, as for instance the prologue of Gudea's Building Hymn[22] or the prologue of Hammurabi's (1792–1750 BCE) Law Code,[23] which demonstrate that divine command in ancient Mesopotamia was considered to be channelled from the head of the pantheon through the patron deity of the city or regional state or capital of the territorial state — Ningirsu of Girsu in the first case, and Marduk of Babylon in the second case — down to the ruler, who in turn presided over a pyramidical structure of command terminating in a horizontal network including the political elites of the various urban centres. The notion of the divine will was thus not an abstract concept, but was rather Enlil's decision — without which 'no city would be built, no settlement would be founded, no cow-pen would be built, no sheepfold would be established, no king would be elevated, no lord would be given birth, no high priest or priestess would perform extispicy'[24] — materialized directly in the physical and social landscape of the ancient communities and their political and religious elites.

The larger the territory that had to be controlled the more the king and his scholars had to invent cultural strategies that created and secured a consensus between the political centre and the urban elites of the other cities, so that ultimately social order could guarantee the cosmic order.

In this article, I will focus primarily on texts from the late third and first half of the second millennium in order to demonstrate how the king and his

[21] The king's address to Assur, the gods of the Assur temple and the pantheon of Assur, the city (URU/*ālu*) and its people (*nišišu*), as well as the palace as the political institution in Sargon's report on his eighth campaign to the god Assur is unusual and has to be read with these questions in mind; see Thureau-Dangin, *Une relation de la huitième campagne de Sargon*, pl. 1, ll. 1–4. Things seem to have worked further differently in the periphery as demonstrated by the Statue of Tell Fekherye dedicated by Adad-id'i, the governor of Guzan 'for the well-being of his house, offspring, and people' (l.15: 'šulum bītīšu zērīšu u nišīšu') and 'that his utterance please gods and men' (l. 25: 'qibīt pîšu eli ilī u nišī ṭubbi'), see Greenfield and Shaffer, 'Notes on the Akkadian-Aramaic Bilingual Statue from Tell Fekherye', pp. 109–16.

[22] Edzard, *Gudea and his Dynasty*, E3/1.1.7.CylA+B.

[23] Roth, *Law Collections from Mesopotamia and Asia Minor*, pp. 71–142; for the inclusion of the cuneiform and interpretation of the grammar of this text, see Richardson, *A Comprehensive Grammar to Hammurabi's Stele*.

[24] The Electronic Text Corpus of Sumerian Literature, 4.05.1:110ff.

scholars designed the ideological discourse revolving around the interaction between temple, community, and ruler in order to convey an image of spatial coherence. In addition to imagery, architecture, and ritual, text was used as a potent means of projecting the idea of the king performing his political tasks in compliance with the institutional duties that accompanied the divinely decreed office. I would like to demonstrate that close reading provides hints as to royal recognition of the importance of creating a consensus among the elites, and my inquiry will focus particularly on the strategy of producing the idea of a relational space, in which political elites of the periphery bond with the political centre under divine surveillance. Relational space in which they lived, conceived, and perceived realms represent interconnected domains of human life and thus require the active participations of the producers as well as all the other subjects was a major theme pursued by Henri Lefebvre, and in his vein also by Edward W. Soja and Adam T. Smith.[25] My own approach to the sacredness of political space rests on the ancient cultural strategy of inscribing the relationship between the urban elites and the body of the divinely authorized king into the landscape, textually and archaeologically.[26]

Such rhetoric arose for the first time in Mesopotamian history in the twenty-third century BCE when King Lugalzagesi of the city state of Umma succeeded in bringing the city states of the south under his control and boasted of his political achievement in the titulary of his inscription:

> Lugalzagesi, king of Uruk, king of the Land, priest of An, lumah of Nisaba, son of Bubu governor of Umma, lumah of Nisaba, looked on favorably by An king of all lands (lugal.kur.kur.ra), chief governor of Enlil, granted wisdom by Enki, chosen by Utu, high vizier of Sin, general of Utu, provider for Inanna, son born of Nisaba and suckled on the milk of Ninhursag, man of Mes-sanga-unuga, brought up by Ningirim the lady of Uruk, and high steward of the gods.[27]

Lugalzagesi interestingly describes his control of the cities by means of pointing out particular offices he performs for their patron deities, thus virtually establishing a relationship by means of central roles guaranteeing the functioning of the cult far beyond the administration of the temple itself. Rather than following a geographical organization, these deities are further arranged in such a way that they follow to at least some degree the theological ranking as represented

[25] Lefevbre, *The Production of Space*; Soja, *ThirdSpace*; Smith, *The Political Landscape*.

[26] For a detailed overview on the definition of the urban landscape and city, see Pezzoli-Olgiati, *Immagini urbane*.

[27] Frayne, *Presargonic Period*, E1.12.7.

in the early god lists with the sky god An of Uruk heading the list of deities who all represent major cultic and political centres in Sumer:

An (Uruk)
Nisaba (Ereš)
Enlil (Nippur)
Enki (Eridu)
Utu (Larsa)
Sin (Ur)
Inanna (Uruk)

Lugalzagesi further includes the key metaphor of kinship alliances with the divine world, a device originally invented by Eannatum of Lagash, with his claim of being born by Nisaba, suckled by Ninhursaga, and brought up by the incantation deity Ningirim of Uruk while inserting again a title emphasizing his administrative function with the epithet 'man of Mes-sanga-unuga', a deity who bore the title chief governor of Inanna (ensi$_2$.gal ^{d}inanna).[28]

Having established his proper relationship with the divine world through the performance of roles that guarantee the functioning of the cult and by claiming of divine parentage, thus anchoring himself legitimately as *body politic* within the cosmic order, Lugalzagesi only then proceeded to explicitly delineate his interaction with these cities on the human level. In column ii of this same inscription there occurs a short passage in which Lugalzagesi makes it look as if the cities pertaining to the former Kiengi League — Uuk, Ur, Larsa, Umma, Zabala, and KI.AN — including the governors of the foreign countries, did indeed *decree* his sovereignty for him, that is, they deliberately chose him to be their overlord:

bára-bára-ki-en-gi énsi-kur-kur-ra ki-Unuki-ge me-nam-nun-šè mu-na-tar-e-ne

[The shrines of Kiengi, the governors of all countries, and the region of Uruk decreed the role of ruler for him.][29]

Interestingly, when it came to the league of the Sumerian city states, he chose again to represent them as the major cultic centres rather than as political entities ruled by former city rulers. The rulers of the foreign lands by contrast are referred to directly, probably because they maintained some kind of vassal sta-

[28] Krebernik, 'Mes-sanga-unuga', pp. 94–95.

[29] Frayne, *Ur III Period*, 1 E1.14.20.1 ii 21–25. My translation deviates from Frayne and rather follows Postgate, *Early Mesopotamia*, p. 35.

Figure 3.1.
Eannatum Stele Front. After Bahrani, *Rituals of War*, p. 148; drawing Elizabeth Simpson.

tus. Not surprisingly, the city of Uruk concludes the list, as its patron deity Inanna is directly associated with the institution of kingship.[30]

The second time such rhetoric is visible in the historical record is during the Akkad Dynasty, which ruled southern Mesopotamia in the twenty-fourth and twenty-third centuries BCE. In the twenty-fourth century BCE the rise of the dynasty of the kings of Akkad put an end to the former loose confederation of the Sumerian city states in Southern Mesopotamia. An unprecedented process of enforced unification and political centralization followed, binding the former city states to the centre by means of a centralized tax system. The creator of the dynasty, Sargon of Akkad (2334–2279 BCE), founded his new capital in Akkad in the strategic location of modern Baghdad whence he could control the entire south as well as extend more easily his presence towards the north. Far-flung forays into Elam in the East and into the areas of the Upper Tigris and the Upper Euphrates aimed at securing and monopolizing trade routes. In the wake of these military achievements, the traditional royal title 'king of Kish' (*lugal kiš*) came to mean 'king of the world', 'using the similarity of the name of the city of Kish and the Akkadian term for "the entire inhabited world", *kishshatum*'.[31]

The centralized hegemonic rule of the Akkadian kings met fierce resistance, and the kings had to suppress various rebellions of the former Sumerian city states. Conscious of the challenges posed by imperial politics the Akkadian rulers created a new image of kingship, which centred on the figure of the king in the public arts and public display ceremonies.[32] Having crushed one of major rebellions, which included the entire south, King Naram-Sin (2254–2218 BCE) sought for a new way to symbolically express his exalted status, which elevated him among the rest of the political elites. Several strategies can be observed: He emulated the depiction of the warrior god Ningirsu in Eannatum's *Stele of the Vultures*[33] (Figure 3.1) by representing himself as superhuman in size and capable of commanding life and death (Figure 3.2). The unique artistic choice

[30] Westenholz, 'King by Love of Inanna', pp. 75–89.

[31] Van de Mieroop, *A History of the Ancient Near East ca. 3000–323 BCE*, p. 64.

[32] Westenholz, 'The King, the Emperor, and the Empire', p. 99.

[33] Steible and Behrens, *Die altsumerischen Bau- und Weihinschriften*, pp. 120–45; Cooper, *Reconstructing History from Ancient Inscriptions*, pp. 45–47; Winter, 'After the Battle Is Over', pp. 11–32; Winter, 'Eannatum and the "King of Kiš"?', pp. 205–12; Heuzey, *Decouvertes en Chaldée par Ernest de Sarzec*, pls. xxxviii–xlii (copies and drawings showing the position of the text in relation to the relief); Alster, 'Images and Text on the Stele of the Vultures', pp. 1–10. On a different interpretation, see Selz, 'The Divine Prototypes', p. 22, who interprets also the obverse as the ruler in the role of the divine triumphator.

Figure 3.2. Naram-Sin Stele (Reconstruction Drawing, Nigro). After Winter, 'How Tall was Naram-Sîn's Victory Stele?', p. 144.

made in this monument of war, however, is that, in contrast to Eannatum's stele, it 'presents events not linearly or sequentially but hierarchically. Naram-Sin, the mighty king of Akkad, is the telos of the temporal narrative. The king is therefore the culmination of the event'.[34] His body is deployed emerging as a silhouette against the sky, walking on the mountaintop, and crossing into territory hitherto unchartered by the kings of Mesopotamia. The inclusion of such imagery, depicting the king mastering unknown territory, is a new element in the iconography. Although the stele commemorates the historical event of Naram-Sin's campaign against the Lullubu in the eastern mountains, his visual representation transforms him into an icon of victory mastering and controlling the universe. The gesture of the warrior god Ningirsu, whose hold on the enemies in his net on Eannatum's *Stele of the Vultures* indexes the glorious outcome of the battle, is now replaced by that of the King, shown in the heroic action of trampling the defeated enemy. Unlike the *Stele of the Vultures*, victory here is portrayed as a human achievement performed by the ideal king. Naram-Sin has fully emulated the role of the divine warrior deity Ningirsu/Ninurta who by the end of the Early

[34] Bahrani, *Rituals of War*, p. 109.

Dynastic Period at the latest had become established as son of Enlil, chief god of the Sumerian pantheon, and as patron deity of Nippur.[35]

The ideal royal image is a combination of a variety of elements that all contribute to the sacralization of kingship: the perfect body, the king's superhuman size, and his demonstration of victorious action not in the alluvial plain but in the wilderness of the mountains.

In Naram-Sin's stele, in addition, all these tropes defining the image of the ideal king are combined with the horned crown, which signals the new divine status of the King. This visual icon is further complemented by the writing of the King's name with the divine determinative in the inscription. Naram-Sin's stele thus serves as a visual expression of the new conception of kingship,[36] standing at the historical juncture of the change from a period of independent city states to a unified empire with a centralized kingship. While kingship had, until the Akkad period, been conceived of in 'limited terms and within the local structure of the city-state', it 'now came to be defined as *sovereign* power'.[37] The accompanying text, reporting on the historical event of crushing the insurgence of the Lullubi mountain tribes, can also be read on a mythic level as narrating the royal victory over chaos.[38]

What is of particular interest for our investigation in the creation of a sacred topography of the empire is the manner in which Naram-Sin projected the vision of a unified territory under divine control in the text inscribed on the so-called Bassetki statue, named for a village close to Mosul, where the statue was found.

> Naram-Sin, the Mighty,
> king of Akkade:
>
> *Summary of the great revolt* (ll. 5–19)
> When the Four Quarters (of the world)
> All together revolted against him,
> He won nine battles in only one year

[35] The Barton Cylinder provides evidence for this: Alster and Westenholz, 'The Barton Cylinder', pp. 15–46; see also the discussion by Wang, *The Metamorphosis of Enlil in Early Mesopotamia*, p. 192.

[36] Why some scholars want to read the DINGIR category marker as a logogram for *ilum* 'god' and thus introduce a distinction in the act of divinizing between the deified king and other deified entities such as statues, steles, cultic paraphernalia, etc. remains opaque to me; see the recent discussion by Král, 'Naram-Sin's Deification', pp. 75–86.

[37] Bahrani, *Rituals of War*, p. 102.

[38] Westenholz, 'The King, the Emperor, and the Empire', p. 102.

Through the love Ishtar showed to him
And he captured the kings
Who had risen against him.

Request for deification (ll. 20–56)
Because he preserved
The base of his city
in these times of crisis,
(the citizens of) his city
asked
from Ishtar in Eanna, (in Uruk).
from Enlil in Nippur
from Dagan in Tuttul,
from Ninhursag in Kesh,
from Ea in Eridu,
from Sin in Ur,
from Shamash in Sippar,
(and) from Nergal in Kutha
that he be the god of their city
and they built a temple for him
in the midst of Akkade.[39]

Having violently suppressed the rebellion of the cities, Naram-Sin asks nothing less than that those established political and cultic centres acknowledge his elevation to divine status and accept him as the 'god of Akkad'.[40] Instead of engaging himself in conversation with the elites of these cities, however, he claimed that the elites of his own city addressed the respective patron deities of these cities, insinuating a consensus achieved between himself and his own community and a consensus achieved with the patron deities of these cities, evoked as representatives of the respective political and religious elites. Again, as in Lugalzagesi's inscription, no mention is made of an interaction between the elites of the respective cities and Naram-Sin himself. Rather, in the ideological discourse, it is the patron deities who are turned into active players in creating the vision of a unified territory under divine control. Military and political success are presented as a result of the relationship established between the

[39] Translation: Kienast, 'Inscriptions of Narām-Sîn', p. 244.

[40] The title 'god of Akkad' is attested in several inscriptions of seal impressions, a seal, a plaque, and a hemispherical bowl dedicated by either his servants or family members. Frayne, *Sargonic and Gutian Periods*, E2.1.4.2003, E2.1.4.2013, E.2.1.4.2014, E2.1.4.2020, E2.1.4.2023 (seal impressions); E.2.1.4.53 (seal cylinder); E2.1.4.2018 (plaque); E2.1.4.2007 (bowl).

gods and the king, thus tying Naram-Sin's action as an individual ruler into the general world view of the institution of kingship originating with the gods.

It is noteworthy that Naram-Sin's list of the cities is headed by Inanna of Uruk, and only then followed by the Sumero-Babylonian chief god Enlil of Nippur in the south and Dagan of Tuttul in the far north delineating at least to some extent the sphere of Akkadian control[41] to be concluded by the major cities of Babylonia: Kesh, Eridu, Ur, Sippar, and Kutha. Such a choice of hierarchy could be explained by the fact that the office of kingship is closely related with Inanna, as she is the one who empowers the king by means of her love, acting as intermediary between Enlil and the king. Though Inanna, according to her self-praise, has many hypostases associated with a variety of cities in Mesopotamia, among them Uruk, Zabalam, Nippur, Ur, Girsu, Adab, Kish, Kisiga, Akshak, Umma, and Akkad, it is Inanna of Uruk who is associated with the royal office. With the exception of Inanna of Uruk who was closely linked with the institution of kingship, the sequence of the cities is notable insofar as Enlil and Dagan can both be classified as divine leader figures, the former in Southern Babylonia and the latter in Syria. The sequence of the cities that follow in Naram-Sin's list are not listed in geographical order. Rather it seems that the text producers had the hierarchical order of the Akkadian pantheon in mind with Ninhursaga of Kesh interestingly preceding Ea of Eridu, to be followed by Sin of Ur, Shamash of Sippar, and Nergal of Kutha.

While Naram-Sin's victory stele was originally set up in a temple and thus of limited access, another strategy of visualizing the king's image as the invincible emperor also introduced by Naram-Sin was setting up such steles at the borders of the empire to mark his military expansion. Such a stele, commemorating Naram-Sin's military victory over the settlements in the Tigris basin, has been found at the northern frontier of the Akkadian empire at Pir Hüseyn, about 25 km north-east of Diyarbakır.[42] In contrast to his victory stele, which shows the triumphant king trampling on his enemy, Naram-Sin is the only person represented on this stele. In addition to the similarity in hair and beard styles, his depiction differs from the victory stele with regard to the beehive-shaped hat with crossed lines, which has been related to headdresses from Ebla

[41] The choice of Dagan of Tuttul is interesting insofar as Dagan served as a third party in the conclusion of interregional treaties during the Early Dynastic Period (2900–2350 BCE); see Eidem, Finkel, and Bonechi, 'The Third-Millenium Inscriptions', p. 100.

[42] Westenholz, 'The King, the Emperor, and the Empire', fig. 2 after Börker-Klähn, *Altvorderasiatische Bildstelen und vergleichbare Reliefs*, no. 25.

in Syria.[43] This particular style, which links the stele to the Syro-Anatolian tradition, further shows in the arrangement of text and image, as the text seems to flow right out of the mouth of the king, a pictorial element familiar from much later steles found at Zincirli in Northern Syria. Naram-Sin's strategy of marking either the boundaries of the empire or indicating the King's forays into hitherto unexplored and unknown territory by means of steles would be revived by the later Assyrian kings.

Naram-Sin's newly introduced practice of dedicating shrines to the living king intended to enforce a community building that centres as much on the king as protective genius of the city as on the patron deity continued throughout the Ur III period (*c.* 2100–2000 BCE) becoming an important means of creating a relational space that bonded the controlled territory with the political centre. From economic texts recording the deliveries for these shrines we can reconstruct four sanctuaries in the cities of Umma, KI.AN, Gu'abba, and Girsu dedicated to King Shulgi, two in Umma and Girsu dedicated to King Amar-Sîn, and no less than five in Umma, Ur, Adab, Girsu, and Eshnunna dedicated to King Shu-Sîn. Shu-Sîn in particular stands out for not continuing the ambitious building activities, dedicated to constructing temples of various cultic centers of the empire, of his predecessors. Instead, numerous temples to Shu-Sîn himself were built by governors in several cities of the Ur III empire,[44] demonstrating their loyalty with the ruler. Shu-Sîn might have copied the model provided by Naram-Sîn, since it was only after having conquered the people of Simanum and resettling the inhabitants in a newly built town on the border of Nippur that he declared himself as their city god.[45] A door socket informs us of the builder of Shu-Sîn's shrine, in this case Ituria, the governor of Eshnunna:

> [For the deified] Shu-Sîn,
> Whose name had been called
> by Anu,
> beloved one of Enlil,
> the king whom Enlil
> had chosen in his pure heart
> for shepherdship of the land
> and the four banks,

[43] Westenholz, 'The King, the Emperor, and the Empire', p. 106, with reference to Matthiae, 'Appunti di iconografia eblaita, II', p. 41.

[44] Reichel, 'The King Is Dead, Long Live the King', pp. 133–55, with reference to Sallaberger, 'Ur III-Zeit', pp. 121–414, esp. pp. 170–71.

[45] Frayne, *Ur III Period*, E3/2.1.4.1 iv 44–46: 'the god of their town was Shu-Sîn'.

mighty king
king of Ur,
king of the banks,
his [i.e. Ituria's] god:
Ituria,
governor
of Eshnunna,
his [i.e. Shu-Sîn's] servant,
[has built] his [i.e. Shu-Sîn's] temple
for him.[46]

Note that in this inscription emphasis is laid on Shu-Sîn's control of the land by means of his shepherdship (*nam-sipa-kalam-ma*), thus providing for the social order first, before continuing with his control of the four river banks, that is, the cities along the Euprates and Tigris rivers. Note also that the governor calls King Shu-Sîn his god. Soon after Shu-Sîn died Ituria's son Shu-iliya followed his father in the office as governor of Eshnunna, adopting the title 'king' (lugal) instead of 'governor' ($ensi_2$) and also claiming divine status.[47] Shu-Sîn's shrine at the capital is also attested in the inscriptions directly related with the building. Incised on six door sockets from Ur the inscription records the construction of a temple dedicated to the deified Shu-Sîn by the governor Lugal-magure:

1–5 For (the deified) Shu-Sîn, beloved of the god Enlil, the king whom the god Enlil lovingly chose in his (own) heart,
6–9 mighty king, king of Ur, king of the four quarters, his god,
10–14 Lugal-magure, lieutenant of the watch, governor of Ur, his servant,
15–16 built his temple for him.[48]

Only one archaeological example of the royal sanctuaries survives, the one adjacent to the governor's palace in Eshnunna dedicated to Shu-Sîn, the fourth king of the Ur III period. A major point made already by Günter Martiny is that the orientation of the shrine deviates from the orientation of the palace. That is not only to be explained by the fact that it was built about forty years later than the palace itself. The main reason for the anomaly, rather, is to be sought in the aligning of the shrine with the location of the capital of the

[46] My translation follows Frayne, *Ur III Period*, E3/2.1.4.12 with the exception of the translation for 'an-ub-da-límmu-ba' which I prefer to translate as the 'four banks' (of the Tigris and Euphrates rivers) rather than the 'four regions of the world'.

[47] Reichel, 'The King Is Dead, Long Live the King, p. 136.

[48] Frayne, *Ur III Period*, E3/2.1.4.15.

Ur III kings. As pointed out by Martiny, the axis running through the Shu-Sîn Temple points towards the city of Ur, located some 300 km to the south-east of Eshnunna.[49] These close ties between Ur and Eshnunna at the periphery of the empire were reinforced by a cult performed by members of the royal family for the local goddesses Bēlat-teraban and Bēlat-šuhnir.[50] These goddesses otherwise played no role in the cult of Ur.

With the king appropriating the role of the patron deity as carrier of identity and protective genius of the city, the Akkad and Ur III periods thus present us with a major shift in the strategies used to create a communal sense, now putting the king at centre stage. By contrast, the building hymn of Gudea, the ruler of the city state of Lagash, whose reign overlapped at least partially with that of King Ur-Namma, founder of the Ur III dynasty, introduces a different message, and one wonders whether this is due only to the genre, with the building hymn focusing on the king's restoration of Ningirsu's temple, or whether it is due to the fact that Gudea never controlled an extended territory, and thus was simply unable to make any imperial claims. It is worth noting that, unlike the iconographic repertoire chosen by the rulers of the Early Dynastic Period and Akkad and the royal self-laudatory hymns of the Ur III period, Gudea never depicts himself as the victorious warrior. Instead he obtains everything — labour and raw materials — needed for the building of the temple through persuasion and request.[51] Indeed, even the gesture that reflects coercion, namely the conscription of the various tribes to carry out the construction, in this literary utopian vision is supported by divine consent. The clans are conscripted with the help of divine standards that belong to the patron deities of the main three cities of Gudea's territory, Ningirsu with his main temple in Girsu,[52] Nanshe with her main sanctuary in the city of NINA,[53] and Inanna with her temple Ibgal located in Lagash.[54]

[49] Reichel, 'The King Is Dead, Long Live the King, p. 137, with reference to Martiny, 'The Orientation of the Gimilsin Temple and the Palace Chapel', pp. 92–96.

[50] As pointed out by Reichel, 'The King Is Dead, Long Live the King, p. 138, Shulgi-Simtum, the wife of King Shulgi, performs offerings for these two goddesses in Drehem, and the title 'Sanga-Priest of Bēlat-teraban and Bēlat-uhnir' was held by Bābāti, brother of Amar-Suen's wife Abī-smtī, who around 2035 at least temporarily resided at Eshnunna.

[51] Pongratz-Leisten, 'Gudea and his Model of an Urban Utopia', pp. 45–59.

[52] Selz, *Untersuchungen zur Götterwelt des altsumerischen Stadtstaates von Lagaš*, p. 250.

[53] Selz, *Untersuchungen zur Götterwelt des altsumerischen Stadtstaates von Lagaš*, p. 185.

[54] Selz, *Untersuchungen zur Götterwelt des altsumerischen Stadtstaates von Lagaš*, p. 154.

Gudea A xiv 7–28

In those days the ruler made a conscription in his country, in his realm [...] in Ningirsu's Gu-edenna he made a conscription. He made a conscription in his built up cities, his rural settlements, in Nanshe's Gu-gishbarra. There was a conscription for him among Ningirsu's clans (im-ru-a) (having the emblem) 'Rampant fierce bull that has no one to oppose it' (and) 'White cedar passing along(?) for its master', and he let go their magnificent standard 'King who makes the mountain tremble' in front of them. There was a conscription for her on Nanshe's clans 'both river banks and shores rising from the water, the huge river, abounding in water, whose abundance spreads everywhere', and he let go the 'White Swan'(?) Nanshe's emblem, in front of it. There was a conscription for her on Inanna's clans, 'Snare stretched out for the beasts of the steppe', and 'Choice steeds, famous team, team beloved by Utu', and he let go the rosette, Inanna's standard in front of it. In order to build Ningirsu's House.[55]

The relationship of these cities was reinforced through cultic performance not only during the ritual preceding the restoration process of Ningirsu's temple in Girsu but also during other festivities (Figure 3.3), which included the journey of the gods and the king.

The idea of the channelling of the divine command from the Sumero-Babylonian chief god Enlil through the city god down to the ruler, who then created his horizontal web of relationships with the various urban communities, is carried on into the Old Babylonian period (1800–1595 BCE). Concomitantly, one can observe the strategy of the cosmicization of power in equating the king with the sun,[56] which made the state unlimited in duration and right to rule. Hammurabi's (1792–1750 BCE) description of his appointment to the throne in the prologue of his Law Code best illustrates this development:

at that time, the gods Anu and Enlil, for the enhancement of the well-being of the people, named me by my name: Hammurabi, the pious prince, who venerates the gods, to make justice prevail in the land, to abolish the wicked and the evil, to prevent the strong from oppressing the weak, to rise like the sun-god Shamash over all humankind, to illuminate the land.[57]

Hammurabi created this stele probably after the thirty-eighth year of his rule, which is why the 'text projects a sense of achievement: the king had completed

[55] Edzard, *Gudea and his Dynasty*, p. 78.

[56] Gladigow, 'Welche Welt paßt zu welchen Religionen?', p. 14.

[57] Codex Hammurabi, col. i, ll. 27–49, quoted after Roth, 'The Laws of Hammurabi', p. 336.

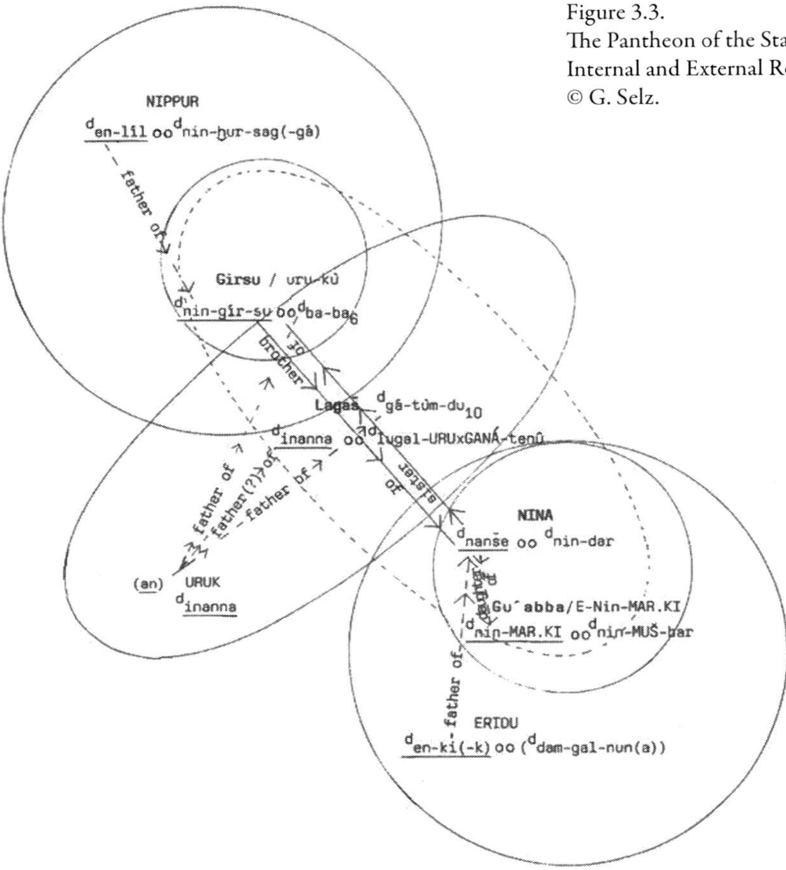

Figure 3.3.
The Pantheon of the State of Lagash: Internal and External Relationships.
© G. Selz.

a string of conquests and in celebration he set up this special record',[58] which, in the prologue, lists all the conquered cities that make up a territory nearly as large as the earlier empire of the Ur III dynasty.

While in the text the chief gods Anu and Enlil authorize Hammurabi's rulership of Babylonia, and the goddess Mami of Kesh bestows on him the regalia of kingship, in the iconography the role of Mami is taken on by the sun god Shamash. Hammurabi, in turn, adopts the role of the sun god as judge watching over law and justice in his land. As with Gudea, Hammurabi makes no reference to his earlier military subjugation of the cities now under his rule, instead portraying himself as the caretaker of their cults. The sequence of the list of

[58] Van de Mieroop, *King Hammurabi of Babylon*, p. 110.

the cities does not follow geographical rules (Map 2). Instead, if one includes the first section describing An and Enlil choosing Marduk, the son of Ea, for the patron deity of Babylon, the text reflects the hierarchy of the supraregional pantheon of Babylonia of the time.

> Anu (Uruk)
> Enlil (Nippur)
> Ea (Eridu)
> Marduk (city god of Babylon, capital of Hammurabi's Babylonia)
> Sin (of Ur)
> Shamash and Aya (of Sippar and Larsa)
> Anu and Ishtar (of Uruk)
> Zababa and Ishtar (of Kish)
> Erra (of Kutha)
> Tutu (of Borsippa), Urash (of Dilbat), Mami (of Kesh)
> Ishtar goddesses (of Zabalam, Akkad, Niniveh, Babylon)
> Adad (of Karkar), Ea and Damkina (of Malgium)
> Dagan (of Mari and Tuttul)
> Tishpak and Ninazu (of Babylon)[59]

All of the above deities are mentioned in terms of their function as patron deities representing the local communities associated with the cities in Hammurabi's political domain. Hammurabi's capital of Babylon must have hosted a large number of deities, and yet these deities also acted as carriers of identity for particular cities under Hammurabi's rule. This situation is reflected in the local manifestations of a deity such as Ishtar, who is found in association with various cities. Likewise, Amurru, who was probably projected by the Sumerians onto the foreign population of the Amorites as their carrier of identity already during the Ur III period,[60] and thus is the *heros eponymos* of Hammurabi's own tribe, is associated not with Babylon but with the city of Larsa. In his official inscriptions, Hammurabi takes great care to present himself as representative of both constituencies of the local communities. While he often employs the royal title 'king of Babylon', he also portrays himself as 'father' or 'king of the Amorite land', emphasizing his tribal affiliations.[61]

[59] See Groneberg, *Die Götter des Zweistromlandes*, p. 245.

[60] Beaulieu, 'The God Amurru as Emblem of Ethnic and Cultural Identity', pp. 31–46.

[61] Van de Mieroop, *King Hammurabi of Babylon*, p. 3.

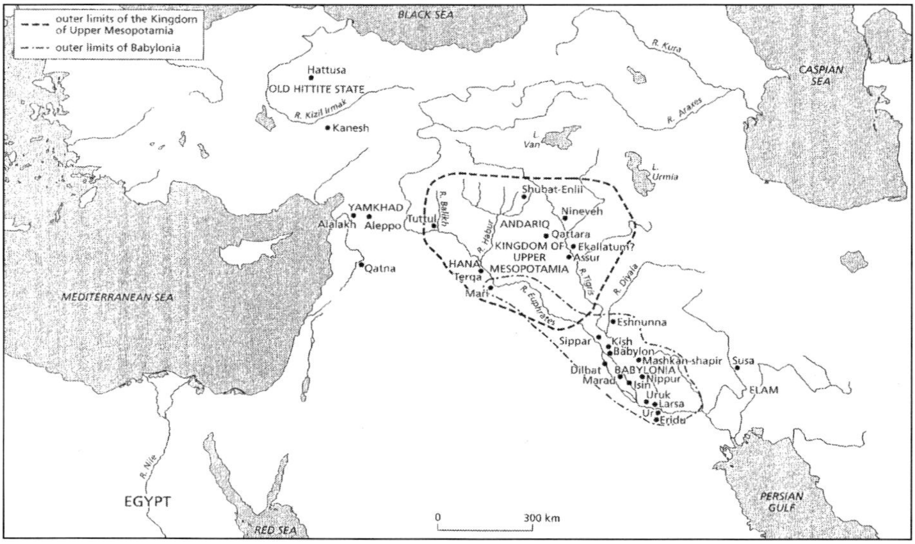

Map 2. The territorial states of Hammurabi in the South and Shamshi-Adad I in the North. After van de Mieroop, *A History of the Ancient Near East ca. 3000–323 BCE*, Map 6.1.

All the textual examples listed above demonstrate how cosmology and religion combine to become an authoritative system that legitimates existing political and social hierarchies and royal control over space. The latter ultimately serves the integration of the known world into the cosmic order as envisioned by the gods. Much later, when faced with the challenge of fostering an 'enduring perception of geopolitical relationships',[62] the Assyrians will develop an entire system of strategies to amplify the royal body as the focal point of social identity and make the various populations take on the normative pressures of a monarchical regime with imperial claims.

[62] Smith, *The Political Landscape*, p. 135.

Works Cited

Secondary Studies

Alster, B., 'Images and Text on the Stele of the Vultures', *Archiv für Orientforschung*, 50 (2003/04), 1–10

Alster, B., and A. Westenholz, 'The Barton Cylinder', *Acta Sumerologica Japanensis*, 16 (1994), 15–46

Bahrani, Z., *Rituals of War: The Body and Violence in Mesopotamia* (New York: Zone, 2008)

Bauer, J., R. K. Englund, and M. Krebernik, *Mesopotamien: Späturuk-Zeit und Frühdynastische Zeit*, Orbis Biblicus et Orientalis, 160.1 (Freiburg: Academic Press Fribourg, 1998)

Beaulieu, P.-A., 'A Finger in Every Pie: The Institutional Connections of a Family of Entrepreneurs in Neo-Babylonian Larsa', in *Interdependency of Institutions and Private Entrepreneurs: Proceedings of the Second Mittheilungen aus den Orientalischen Sammlungen, Königliche Museen zu Berlin Symposium, Leiden 1998*, ed. by A. C. V. M. Bongenaar (Leiden: Nederlands Historisch-Archaeologisch Instituut Te Istanbul, 2000), pp. 43–72

——, 'The God Amurru as Emblem of Ethnic and Cultural Identity', in *Ethnicity in Ancient Mesopotamia: Papers Read at the 48th Rencontre Assyriologique Internationale Leiden, 1–4 July, 2002*, ed. by W. H. van Soldt (Leiden: Nederlands Instituut voor het Nabije Oosten, 2005), pp. 31–46

Bongenaar, A. C. V. M., ed., *Interdependency of Institutions and Private Entrepreneurs: Proceedings of the Second Mittheilungen aus den Orientalischen Sammlungen, Königliche Museen zu Berlin Symposium, Leiden 1998* (Leiden: Nederlands Historisch-Archaeologisch Instituut Te Istanbul, 2000)

Börker-Klähn, J., *Altvorderasiatische Bildstelen und vergleichbare Reliefs* (Mainz: von Zabern, 1982)

Chamaza, G. M. Vera, 'Sargon II's Ascent to the Throne: The Political Situation', *State Archives of Assyria Bulletin*, 6 (1992), 21–33

Cooper, J. S., *Reconstructing History from Ancient Inscriptions: The Lagash-Umma Border Conflict*, Sources from the Ancient Near East, 2.1 (Malibu: Undena Publications, 1983)

Douglas, M., *Purity and Danger* (London: Routledge & K. Paul, 1966)

Edzard, D. O., *Gudea and his Dynasty*, The Royal Inscriptions of Mesopotamia: Early Periods, 3.1 (Toronto: University Press of Toronto, 1997)

Eidem, J., I. Finkel, and M. Bonechi, 'The Third-Millenium Inscriptions', in *Excavations at Tell Brak*, vol. II: *Nagar in the Third millennium* BC, ed. by D. Oates, J. Oates, and H. McDonald (Oxford: British School of Archaeology in Iraq, 2001), pp. 99–120

The Electronic Text Corpus of Sumerian Literature <http://etcsl.orinst.ox.ac.uk/>

Englund, R. K., and H. J. Nissen, *Die lexikalischen Listen der archaischen Texte aus Uruk* (Berlin: Gebr. Mann, 1993)

Feinman, G. M., and T. D. Price, eds, *Archaeology at the Millennium: A Sourcebook* (New York: Kluwer Academic/Plenum, 2001)

Frayne, D. R., *Presargonic Period (2700–2350 BC)*, The Royal Inscriptions of Mesopotamia: Early Periods, 1 (Toronto: University of Toronto Press, 2008)

——, *Sargonic and Gutian Periods (2234–2113 BC)*, The Royal Inscriptions of Mesopotamia: Early Periods, 2 (Toronto: University Press of Toronto, 1993)

——, *Ur III Period*, The Royal Inscriptions of Mesopotamia: Early Periods, 3.2 (Toronto: University Press of Toronto, 1997)

Gladigow, B., 'Welche Welt paßt zu welchen Religionen? Zur Konkurrenz von "religiösen Weltbildern" und "säkularen Religionen"', in *Religion im Wandel der Kosmologien*, ed. by D. Zeller (Frankfurt: Lang, 1999), pp. 13–31

Glassner, J.-J., 'Droit et divination: deux manières de rendre la justice. À propos de dīnum, uṣurtum et awatum', *Journal of Cuneiform Studies* 64, (2012), 39–56

——, 'Inanna et les ME', in *Nippur at the Centennial: Papers Read at the 35e Rencontre Assyriologique Internationale, Philadelphia, 1988*, ed. by M. de Jong Ellis, Occasional Publications of the Samuel Noah Kramer Fund, 14 (Philadelphia: Samuel Noah Kramer Fund, 1992), pp. 55–86

Greenfield, J. C., and A. Shaffer, 'Notes on the Akkadian-Aramaic Bilingual Statue from Tell Fekherye', *Iraq*, 45 (1983), 109–16

Groneberg, B., *Die Götter des Zweistromlandes* (Düsseldorf: Artemis & Winkler, 2004)

Heuzey, L., *Decouvertes en Chaldée par Ernest de Sarzec*, 2 vols (Paris: Leroux, 1884–1912)

Kienast, B., 'Inscriptions of Narām-Sîn', in *Context of Scripture*, vol. II: *Monumental Inscriptions of the Biblical World*, ed. by W. W. Hallo and K. Lawson Younger, Jr (Leiden: Brill, 2000), p. 244

Král, P., 'Naram-Sin's Deification', in *Shepherds of the Blackheaded People: The Royal Office vis-à-vis Godhead in Ancient Mesopotamia*, ed. by K. Šašková, L. Pecha, and P. Charvát (Plzeň: Západočeská universita v Plzni, 2010), pp. 75–86

Krebernik, M., 'Mes-sanga-unuga', *Reallexikon der Assyriologie und Vorderasiatischen Archäologie*, vol. VIII, ed. by M. P. Streck (Berlin: De Gruyter, 1993), pp. 94–95

Lefevbre, H., *The Production of Space* (Oxford: Blackwell, 1991)

Liverani, M. 'Critique of Variants and the Titulary of Sennacherib', in *Assyrian Royal Inscriptions: New Horizons in Literary, Ideological, and Historical Analysis. Papers of a Symposimum Held in Cetona (Siena) June 26–28, 1980*, ed. by F. M. Fales (Roma: Istituto per l'Oriente, 1981), pp. 225–57

Martiny, G., 'The Orientation of the Gimilsin Temple and the Palace Chapel', in *The Gimilsin Temple and the Palace of the Rulers at Tell Asmar*, ed. by H. Frankfort, S. Lloyd, and T. Jacobsen, Oriental Institute Publications, 43 (Chicago: University of Chicago Press, 1940), pp. 92–96

Matthews, J. R., *Cities, Seals and Writing: Archaic Seal Impressions from Jemdet Nasr and Ur*, Materialien zu den Frühen Schriftzeugnissen des Vorderen Orients (Berlin: Gebr. Mann, 1993)

Matthiae, P., 'Appunti di iconografia eblaita, II', *Studi Eblaiti*, 2.2–3 (1980), 41–47

Michalowski, P., 'On the Early Toponomy of Sumer: A Contribution to the Study of Early Mesopotamian Writing', in *Kinattūtu ša dārâti, Raphael Kutscher Memorial Volume*, ed. by A. F. Rainey (Tel Aviv: Tel Aviv University Institute of Archaeology, 1993) pp. 119–33
Mieroop, M. van de, *The Ancient Mesopotamian City* (Oxford: Oxford University Press, 1997)
——, *A History of the Ancient Near East ca. 3000–323 BCE* (Oxford: Blackwell, 2007)
——, *King Hammurabi of Babylon* (Oxford: Blackwell, 2005)
——, *Society and Enterprise in Old Babylonian Ur* (Berlin: Reimer, 1992)
Parpola, S., 'Neo-Assyrian Concepts of Kingship and their Heritage in Mediterranean Antiquity', in *Concepts of Kingship in Antiquity*, ed. by G. B. Lanfranchi and R. Rollinger (Padova: S.A.R.G.O.N. Editrice e Libreria, 2010), pp. 35–44
Pezzoli-Olgiati, D., *Immagini urbane: Interpretatzioni religiose della città antica* (Freiburg: Universitätsverlag; Göttingen: Vandenhoeck & Ruprecht, 2002)
Pongratz-Leisten, B., 'All the King's Men: Authority, Kingship, and the Rise of the Elites in Assyria', in *Experiencing Power, Generating Authority: Cosmos, Politics, and the Ideology of Kingship in Ancient Egypt and Mesopotamia*, ed. by Jane A. Hill, Phillip Jones, and Antonio J. Morales (Philadelphia: University of Pennsylvania Museum of Archaeology and Anthropology, 2013), pp. 285–309
——, 'Gudea and his Model of an Urban Utopia', *Baghdader Mitteilungen*, 37 (2006), 45–59
Postgate, J. N., *Early Mesopotamia: Society and Economy at the Dawn of History* (London: Routledge, 1994)
——, *Taxation and Conscription in the Assyrian Empire* (Roma: Istituto Biblico, 1974)
Reichel, C., 'The King Is Dead, Long Live the King: The Last Days of the Šu-Sîn Cult at Ešnunna and its Aftermath', in *Religion and Power: Divine Kingship in the Ancient World and Beyond*, ed. by N. Brisch, Oriental Institute Seminars, 4 (Chicago: The Oriental Institute of the University of Chicago, 2008), pp. 133–55
Richardson, M. E. J., *A Comprehensive Grammar to Hammurabi's Stele* (Piscataway: Gorgias, 2007)
Roth, M. T., *Law Collections from Mesopotamia and Asia Minor*, Society of Biblical Literature Writings from the Ancient World Series (Atlanta: Scholars Press, 1997)
——, 'The Laws of Hammurabi', in *Context of Scripture*, vol. II: *Monumental Inscriptions from the Biblical World*, ed. by W. W. Hallo and K. Lawson Younger, Jr (Leiden: Brill, 2000), pp. 335–60
Sallaberger, W., 'The City and the Palace at Archaic Ur', in *Shepherds of the Black-Headed People: The Royal Office vis-à-vis Godhead in Ancient Mesopotamia*, ed. by K. Šašková, L. Pecha, and P. Charvát (Plzeň: Západočeská universita v Plzni, 2010), pp. 31–36
——, 'Ur III-Zeit', in *Mesopotamien: Akkade Zeit und Ur III-Zeit*, ed. by W. Sallaberger and A. Westenholz, Orbis Biblicus et Orientalis, 160.3 (Freiburg: Universitätsverlag; Göttingen: Vandenhoeck & Ruprecht, 1999), pp. 121–414
Selz, G., 'The Divine Prototypes', in *Religion and Power: Divine Kingship in the Ancient World and Beyond*, ed. by N. Brisch, Oriental Institute Seminars, 4 (Chicago: The Oriental Institute of the University of Chicago, 2008), pp. 13–31

——, *Untersuchungen zur Götterwelt des altsumerischen Stadtstaates von Lagaš*, Occasional Publications of the Samuel Noah Kramer Fund, 13 (Philadelphia: Samuel Noah Kramer Fund, 1995)

Smith, A. T., *The Political Landscape: Constellations of Authority in Early Complex Polities* (Berkeley: University of California Press, 2003)

Smith, J. Z., 'Here, There, and Anywhere', in *Prayer, Magic, and the Stars in the Ancient and Late Antique World*, ed. by S. Noegel, J. Walker, and B. Wheeler (University Park: Pennsylvania State University Press, 2003), pp. 21–36

Soja, E. W., *ThirdSpace: Journeys to Los Angeles and Other Real-and-Imagined Places* (Cambridge, MA: Blackwell, 1996)

Steible, H., and H. Behrens, *Die altsumerischen Bau- und Weihinschriften*, vol. I: *Inschriften aus 'Lagaš'* (Wiesbaden: Franz Steiner, 1982)

Stein, G., 'Understanding Ancient State Societies in the Old World', in *Archaeology at the Millennium: A Sourcebook*, ed. by G. M. Feinman and T. D. Price (New York: Kluwer Academic/Plenum Publishers, 2001), pp. 353–79

Steinkeller, P., 'Archaic City Seals and the Question of Early Babylonian Unity', in *Riches Hidden in Secret Places: ANE Studies in Memory of Thorkild Jacobsen*, ed. by T. Abusch (Winona Lake: Eisenbrauns, 2002), pp. 249–57

Szarzynska, K., 'Offerings for the Goddess Inanna in Archaic Uruk', *Revue d'assyriologie et d'archéologie orientale*, 87 (1993), 7–28

Tadmor, H., 'Monarchy and the Elite in Assyria and Babylonia: The Question of Royal Accountability', in *The Origins and Diversity of Axial Age Civilizations*, ed. by S. N. Eisenstadt (Albany: State University of New York Press, 1986), pp. 203–22

Thureau-Dangin, F., *Une relation de la huitième campagne de Sargon*, Textes cunéiformes du Louvre, 3 (Paris: Geuthner, 1912)

Wang, X., *The Metamorphosis of Enlil in Early Mesopotamia* (Münster: Ugarit, 2011)

Westenholz, J. G., 'King by Love of Inanna: An Image of Female Empowerment', *NIN: Journal of Gender Studies in Antiquity*, 1 (2000), 75–89

——, 'The King, the Emperor, and the Empire: Continuity and Discontinuity of Royal Representation in Text and Image', in *The Heirs of Assyria: Melammu Symposia I*, ed. by S. Aro and R. M. Whiting (Helsinki: University of Helsinki, The Neo-Assyrian Text Corpus Project, 2000), pp. 99–125

Winter, I. J., 'After the Battle is Over: The Stele of the Vultures and the Beginning of Historical Narrative in the Art of the Ancient Near East', in *Pictorial Narrative in Antiquity and the Middle Ages*, ed. by H. L. Kessler and M. Shreve Simpson, Studies in the History of Art, 16 (Washington, DC: University Press of New England, 1985), pp. 11–32

——, 'Eannatum and the "King of Kiš"? Another Look at the Stele of the Vulture and "Cartouches" in Early Sumerian Art', *Zeitschrift für Assyriologie und Vorderasiatische Archäologie*, 76 (1986), 205–12

——, 'How Tall Was Naram-Sîn's Victory Stele?', in *On Art in the Ancient Near East*, ed. by I. J. Winter, 2 vols (Leiden: Brill, 2010), II, 133–50

Phoenician Sacred Places in the Mediterranean

Bärbel Morstadt

Problem Outline

Some Phoenician temples were most prominent and famous throughout Antiquity. The Phoenician temples in Tyre (Lebanon) and Cádiz (Spain) were especially mentioned by classical Greek and Roman authors who either described certain ritual and architectural aspects or reported important events of history. Some details: These two temples were dedicated to the god Heracles, who can only be interpreted as the Phoenician god Melqart.[1] Tyre, Phoenician Ṣur, was the most powerful and important city during the Phoenician expansion in the Mediterranean during the first half of the first millennium BC. Herodotus, the Greek historian of the fifth century BC reports that, according to the priests, the city and the temple of Melqart were founded 2300 years earlier — that is, 2800 BC. He also briefly describes the temple as being richly equipped with many offerings and two pillars, one of refined gold and the other of emerald.[2] The emerald pillar of the temple is also reported by Pliny the Elder, the first-century Roman natural philosopher.[3] In this temple, the resurrection of the god Melqart ('egersis') was celebrated every year in February/March.[4] Offerings were sent to this festival even by the inhabitants of Carthage

[1] Bonnet, *Melqart*, pp. 399–415.

[2] Herodotus II 43–44.

[3] Pliny the Elder, *Naturalis historia*, 37,74.

[4] Flavius Josephus, *Antiquitates Judaicae*, VIII 5,3; Flavius Josephus, *Contra Apionem*, I 117–19.

Bärbel Morstadt (baerbel.morstadt@ruhr-uni-bochum.de) Ruhr-Universität Bochum Institut für Archäologische Wissenschaften.

(Tunisia), thus testifying to the bond between the mother-city Tyre and their colony Carthage.[5] The fame and political importance of this temple were so outstanding that Alexander the Great intended to sacrifice there to the Tyrian god during his campaign in 332 BC. But when the Tyrian priests refused his request and barred him from entering the city, Alexander decided to conquer and subdue the city by force.[6] After having captured the city, he granted inviolability to the inhabitants of Tyre and the visitors from Carthage who had sought asylum in the temple.[7] He then organized games and a torch run there.[8]

The Tyrian temple of Melqart had its counterpart in the Phoenician temple in Gadir, modern Cádiz in southern Spain, on the modern island Sancti Petri / ancient Kotinoussa.[9] It was built in Phoenician style[10] and the performed religious rites were of Phoenician type.[11] The *sacra* (holy objects) from Tyre were also deposited there,[12] and here too a festival took place.[13] In the temple an enduring offering fire was burning on one of several altars[14] and statues of Alexander and Themistocles had been erected somewhere in the temple area.[15] No cult image, however, existed in the temple,[16] but the bronze doors were decorated with engravings, picturing the deeds of Heracles,[17] and two pillars gave information by engraved inscriptions about the total costs of this temple.[18] We are informed of politically important offerings in the temple at Gadir as well, for example, in 219 BC by the Punic military commander Hannibal. He made

[5] Quintus Curtius Rufus IV 2,10; Diodorus Siculus 17,41,8; 20,14.

[6] Quintus Curtius Rufus IV 2–18; Diodorus Siculus 17,40,2–17,46,6; Arrian, *Anabasis*, II 15,6–24,6.

[7] Arrian, *Anabasis*, II 24,5; Rigsby, *Asylia*, pp. 481–85.

[8] Arrian, *Anabasis*, II 24,6.

[9] Strabon III 5,5.

[10] Arrian, *Anabasis*, II 16,4.

[11] Appian, *Hispanica*, I 2; Arrian, *Anabasis*, II 16,4.

[12] Justinus XLIV 5,2.

[13] Pausanias X 6,4.

[14] C. Silius Italicus, *Punica*, III 30–31.

[15] Flavius Philostratus, *Vita Apollonii*, 5,4; C. Suetonius Tranquillus, *Julius Caesar*, 7; Diodorus Siculus 37,52.

[16] Arrian, *Anabasis*, II 16,4; Flavius Philostratus, *Vita Apollonii*, 5,5; C. Silius Italicus, *Punica*, III 30–31.

[17] C. Silius Italicus, *Punica*, III 32–44.

[18] Strabon III 5,5; Flavius Philostratus, *Vita Apollonii*, 5,5.

this offering after his victory in Saguntum and before his march from Iberia over the Pyrenees and the Alps into northern Italy, known as the Second Punic War. In doing so, he deliberately imitated the offering made by Alexander in Tyre.[19] Another event took place in 145 BC by the Roman consul Fabius Maximus Aemilianus on the eve of the campaign against the Lusitanians.[20]

Unfortunately, almost nothing remains archaeologically of these prominent temples, and not even their exact location is known today. Only the representation of a building on a bas-relief in the palace of the Assyrian King Sargon II in Khorsabad from the end of the eighth century BC, which probably pictures the flight of King Lulî / Elulaios of Tyre mentioned both by an Assyrian inscription[21] and the Roman historian Josephus Flavius,[22] could be interpreted as the front of the temple of Melqart in Tyre with its two pillars.[23] As for the location of the temple in Tyre, some scholars are convinced that it once stood in the place where the twelfth-century great cathedral was erected by the crusaders, using the foundations and some building materials from a Late Antique basilica. This basilica is supposed to have been built upon the old Phoenician temple.[24] This assumption, however, is very doubtful and cannot be proved by any further archaeological investigation since the area has already been studied and fully excavated.[25] The temple in Gadir, on the contrary, certainly can be located in a now underwater zone, and only several bronze male figurines of the eighth–seventh century BC in the attitude of the so-called Smiting god, possibly Melqart representations, have been recovered from the sea.[26]

The spatial arrangements, buildings, architectural elements, cultic installations, etc. of those temples and their surroundings could only be deduced by a critical analysis of the written sources and comparisons with other known

[19] C. Silius Italicus, *Punica*, III 12–13; Koch, 'Von Tarschisch bis nach Indien', pp. 567–78.

[20] Appian, *Hispanica*, 65.

[21] Frahm, *Einleitung in die Sanherib-Inschriften*, pp. 47–61 T. 4.

[22] Flavius Josephus, *Antiquitates Judaicae*, IX 14,2.

[23] Barnett, 'Ezekiel and Tyre', pp. 6–13; Aubet, *The Phoenicians and the West*, pp. 38–39; Keel, Knauf, and Staubli, *Salomons Tempel*.

[24] Bonnet, *Melqart*, pp. 90–94.

[25] A brief overview is given by Kamlah, 'Die Tempel und Heiligtümer Phöniziens', pp. 83–85, referring to Pringle, 'The Crusader Cathedral of Tyre', pp. 165–88 against Busink, *Der Tempel von Jerusalem*, pp. 458–59.

[26] Bonnet, *Melqart*, pp. 228–29; Romero, Fernández, and Rodríguez, 'Nuevos vestigios del santuario gadirita de Melqart en Sancti Petri', pp. 873–78.

Phoenician temples. The essential features which once were needed for the practice of specific cultic rites, the variable architectural additions and developments, and the potential individual forms of a Phoenician temple should therefore be generally clarified in order to regain an approximate image of these famous Melqart temples and other cult places. The aforementioned hint given by the second-century Roman historian Arrian[27] about the temple in Gadir surely points towards a well-known type of Phoenician temple, at least among his contemporaries.

Despite the many excavated and well-documented areas in the Phoenician settlements in the Mediterranean,[28] a detailed and comprehensive comparative analysis of Phoenician temples and rituals has not yet been done and a specific Phoenician style of temple is not yet identified. As a comparison and role model for the temple of Melqart in Gadir and others, the biblical temple of Jerusalem — which is not preserved — is very often considered: 'El Herakleion gaditano debía de parecerse al templo más antiguo de Kition, en Chipre, fechado en torno al año 800 a.C. [...] V. Karageorghis [...], en efecto, lo compara con el santuario de Jerusalén'.[29] It is reported in the Old Testament[30] that King Hiram I of Tyre sent cedar and cypress timber from the Lebanon Mounts as well as his craftsmen to King Salomo of Jersualem to have built the temple and made the furnishings such as two pillars of gold, the ten stands, the ten basins on the stands, the one sea, and the twelve oxen underneath the sea. But does this narration — of uncertain date and context — really serve as a reference point for describing the Phoenician temples? Regarding the methodology, the argumentation has to be turned upside down as has been correctly done by Theodor A. Busink in his reconstruction of the temple in Jerusalem, discussing it as the derivative of Phoenician temples.[31] A complete implementation of Phoenician sacred architecture and furnishing in Jerusalem has to be disclaimed since the cultic rites in Jerusalem possibly required different features in the architecture of the temple, organization of the sacred space, and furnishings than the Phoenician cultic rites in Tyre. The Phoenician rites, however, seem to have been of a certain, well-known type, if we take for granted again the above-mentioned report of the second-century Roman historians Appian

[27] Arrian, *Anabasis*, II 16.4.

[28] For example in Helas and Marzoli, *Phönizisches und punisches Städtewesen*.

[29] Blázquez, *Imagen y mito*, pp. 18–19, referring to Karageorghis, *Kition*, p. 95.

[30] 1 Kings 5. 15–32.

[31] Busink, *Der Tempel von Jerusalem*, pp. 566–89: 'Ableitung des Salominischen Tempels'.

and Arrian about the rites performed in the temple in Gadir.[32] We are likewise not well informed about the Phoenician rites, but some general aspects of worship and offerings can be deduced from finds as well as iconographic and epigraphic sources, for example, the incense-offerings.[33]

Furthermore, it has to be considered in this analysis that there never existed a sort of Phoenician Empire or united nation; rather the region consisted of rival city states with independent kingships. The term 'Phoenician' was used by the contemporary Greeks[34] for the inhabitants of the Levantine city states such as Sidon, Tyre, Byblos, etc. and therefore found its way through classical literature into modern scientific research. We certainly can refer to them as Phoenicians in terms of language and writing, political system and rivalry, religion and cult practice, and material culture. The precise geography, chronology, and identity of the 'Phoenicians' on the other hand are debatable. The Phoenician period is usually set from around 1200 (beginning of the Iron Age in the Levant) until 300 BC (Alexander the Great), not taking into account the continuation of certain cultural aspects from the Bronze Age and their persistence into the Hellenistic period. The Latin term 'Punic' has the same etymology as 'Phoenican' and is used for the period and area of the hegemony by the most famous Phoenician colony, Carthage, from the seventh/sixth century BC until its complete destruction in 146 BC by the Roman army. Due to the geographically and chronologically individual developments of the Phoenician culture, a comparison between Early Iron Age Tyre and Late Carthage therefore has to be undertaken very carefully.[35]

The Phoenician expansion from the Levantine city states into the western Mediterranean of course took place under divine protection. In the newly founded settlements far from the Phoenician homeland the colonists implemented their religion, cult and cult places, and rites. This can clearly be deduced by the examples of the Melqart temples in Tyre and Cádiz. According to Justin, the Late Roman historian, the Phoenician colonists even brought the 'sacra' from Tyre to Gadir and deposited them in the temple in Gadir.[36]

[32] Appian, *Hispanica*, I 2; Arrian, *Anabasis*, II 16,4.

[33] Morstadt, *Thymiateria – Zeugnisse des Orientalisierungsprozesses.*

[34] E.g. Homer, *Illiad*, 23,740–47.

[35] In the following the term 'Phoenician' is used, including the Carthaginian Empire, in order to simplify matters.

[36] Justinus XLIV 5,2.

The character, significance, and function of the various deities, however, could have changed according to the above-mentioned conditions in time and geography, as for example the well-attested Carthaginian deities, the goddess Tanit and the god Baal Hammon; both were once of rather moderate importance in the eastern Mediterranean.[37] The contact between the Phoenicians in the Mediterranean and the indigenous people (e.g. the Nuragic civilization in Sardinia, the people from Tartessos and the Iberians in southern Spain, and the Numidians in North Africa), as well as with other colonists (e.g. the Greeks in Sicily), once more led to individual developments in Phoenician culture and religion.

The analysis of Phoenician religion, cult, and rites therefore must be undertaken very carefully and in a detailed manner, which obviously requires a long-term and systematic investigation. Only a general overview and a case study can be given in the following pages in the hope of stimulating further comparative research projects.

The General Picture

Countless Phoenician sacred places once existed in the Mediterranean, and several of them have been identified and excavated. As mentioned above, a comprehensive and comparative analysis of Phoenician sacred places has not yet been done, but many compilations provide a general picture which will be reproduced in the following.[38]

Various Phoenician terms for sacred places and buildings are known from written sources, mainly 'bt' (house / palace / sanctuary) and 'mqdš' (sanctuary), but also 'qdš' and 'šr qdš' (sacred place), 'tw' (chapel), and 'ḥmn' (baldachin).[39] It could be assumed that 'bt' rather refers to the place and its architectural arrangements where the deity takes up its residence, while 'mqdš' may refer to the holy of holies in a sacred place. One could image the house of the deity as built and furnished like a royal palace, with several buildings, rooms, chapels, and courtyards, divided into private and public areas, and with different func-

[37] Lipiński, 'Baal Hamon', pp. 57–58; Lipiński, 'Tanit', pp. 438–39.

[38] Yon and Cecchini, 'Sanctuaries', pp. 387–89; Krings, *La Civilisation Phénicienne et Punique*, pp. 381–83; Lipiński, *Dieux et déesses de l'univers phénicien et punique*, pp. 417–38; Bonnet and Niehr, *Religionen in der Umwelt des Alten Testaments II*, pp. 134–40.

[39] Bonnet and Niehr, *Religionen in der Umwelt des Alten Testaments II*, p. 133, referring to Hoftijzer and Jongeling, *Dictionary of the North-West Semitic Inscriptions*.

tions for priests and the cultic community. At least in the Melqart temples in Tyre and Gadir, as mentioned above, there must have been enough space for processions and feasting,[40] for asylum seekers,[41] for several altars,[42] for a depository for the 'sacra',[43] for the installation of statues,[44] for simple store rooms, etc.

It is difficult to understand the precise meaning of these Semitic terms and to find an appropriate translation into our language. The term 'temple' shall therefore be used in the following according to the original meaning of the Latin word 'templum' as a sacred space for ritual purposes, which is not necessarily connected with a certain type of building. Within a temple a 'chapel' could have been erected, that is, a small building which served as a canopy and was not to be entered, and which probably contained the cult image or other cult objects ('sacra'). This 'chapel' could refer either to the term 'mqdš', 'tw', or 'ḥmn'. An unspecific place without any architectural arrangements shall be denominated 'sanctuary'.

Cave sanctuaries and other natural sites are always briefly cited, especially the Afqa grotto in Lebanon, the grotto Es Cuieram in Ibiza, and the Grotta Regina in Sicily. The Afqa grotto is a huge cavern in the mountain located in the upper valley of the Nahr Ibrahim river, 40 km north-east of Beirut, and is the water source of this river. This place is connected with the legend of Adonis and Aphrodite as narrated by the second-century rhetorician Lucian of Samosata.[45] In Roman times a temple of Aphrodite was built nearby.[46] The grotto of Es Cuieram lies in the north-eastern part of Ibiza in an area difficult to access. Around four hundred votive objects were found in the cave, almost exclusively terracotta figurines of a female goddess with a kalathos, dated from the fourth until the second century BC. A Neopunic inscription of the second century BC records a dedication to the goddess Tanit.[47] The Grotta Regina lies

[40] Flavius Josephus, *Antiquitates Judaicae*, VIII 5,3; Flavius Josephus, *Contra Apionem*, I 117–19; Arrian, *Anabasis*, II 24,6: games and torch run.

[41] Arrian, *Anabasis*, II 24,5.

[42] C. Silius Italicus, *Punica*, III 30–31.

[43] Justinus XLIV 5,2.

[44] Flavius Philostratus, *Vita Apollonii*, 5,4; C. Suetonius Tranquillus, *Julius Caesar*, 7; Diodorus Siculus 37,52.

[45] Lucian, *De Dea Syria*, 9.

[46] Jidejian and Bonnet, 'Afqa', p. 7.

[47] Aubet, 'La cueva d'Es Cuyram (Ibiza)', pp. 1–66; Aubet, *El santuario de Es Cuieram*; San Nicolás Pedraz, 'Nota sobre la tipología del santuario de Es Cuieram (Ibiza)', pp. 239–41; Ramón, 'Es Cuieram', pp. 225–53.

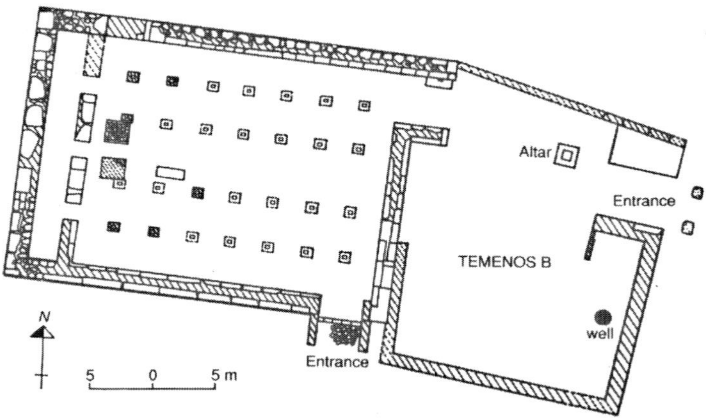

Figure 4.1. The temple of Astarte in Kition-Kathari in the mid-ninth century BC. After Reyes, *Archaic Cyprus*, p. 19.

at the north-eastern slope of the Monte Gallo, north of Palermo. The archaeological material goes back into prehistoric times, but Punic inscriptions and figurines of the fifth and fourth century BC, a Tanit symbol, and dedications to the god Shadrapha were discovered too.[48] Unfortunately, apart from their bare existence as cult places, no specific Phoenician features can be observed for the cave sanctuaries and other natural places — no specific architecture, votives, deities, etc. — and they are not connected with each other in any possible way. The cave sanctuaries and other natural sites therefore have to be considered as a general cultural phenomenon rather than a specific Phoenician phenomenon.

The Phoenician cult places are always somehow built up. They can even be built upon older structures such as the Astarte temples in Kition in Cyprus (Figure 4.1), and Tas-Silg in Malta. The Phoenician Astarte temple in Kition-Kathari was constructed around 850 BC, representing the earliest Phoenician presence in Cyprus. Among the archaeological finds are Phoenician terracotta figurines, amulets, jewellery, scarabs, pottery, and incense burners. The Phoenician temple was built on an ancient but abandoned temple area. Four building phases can be distinguished until its end in 312 BC when the integration of Cyprus into the Ptolemaic Empire was accompanied by a complete reorganization of the traditional religious and political structures. Throughout its lifespan of about five hundred years the temple consisted of two parts, an architectural building and an open courtyard. In the courtyard were an altar and two pillars that marked the entrance to the temple. One inscription points towards Astarte as the owner of the sacred place, but a dedication to Baal is also preserved.[49]

[48] Bisi, *Grotta Regina*.

[49] Karageorghis, *Fouilles de Kition*; Yon, 'Identifier les espaces urbains à Kition (Chypre)',

Figure 4.2.
A stele from the Tophet in Nora representing a three-pillar shrine. After Badisches Landesmuseum Karlsruhe, *Hannibal ad portas*, p. 320.

In Tas-Silg in the Bay of Marsaxlokk, the area of a Late Neolithic temple (*c.* 3000–2500 BC) was frequented by the Phoenicians and used as a sacred place from the end of the eighth century BC onwards. Its use can be confirmed by the archaeological finds. In the sixth century BC the Phoenicians remodelled this area by closing the concave façade of the Neolithic apse with a rectangular front building and by placing an altar. Two votive deposits were placed in the courtyard at the end of the fifth and the first half of the fourth century BC. These deposits held ephemeral material, a bronze ring, and an iron object. Another structure in the courtyard can be interpreted as a water basin connected with a cistern, and this basin was probably used for libation rituals. In the south-western area of this temple, the negatives of formerly erected stelae were detected. A rectangular forecourt in front of the building was plastered,

pp. 101–14. An attempt to establish a new chronology and fill the gap of around 100 BC between the two temples has been undertaken by Smith, *Art and Society in Cyprus*.

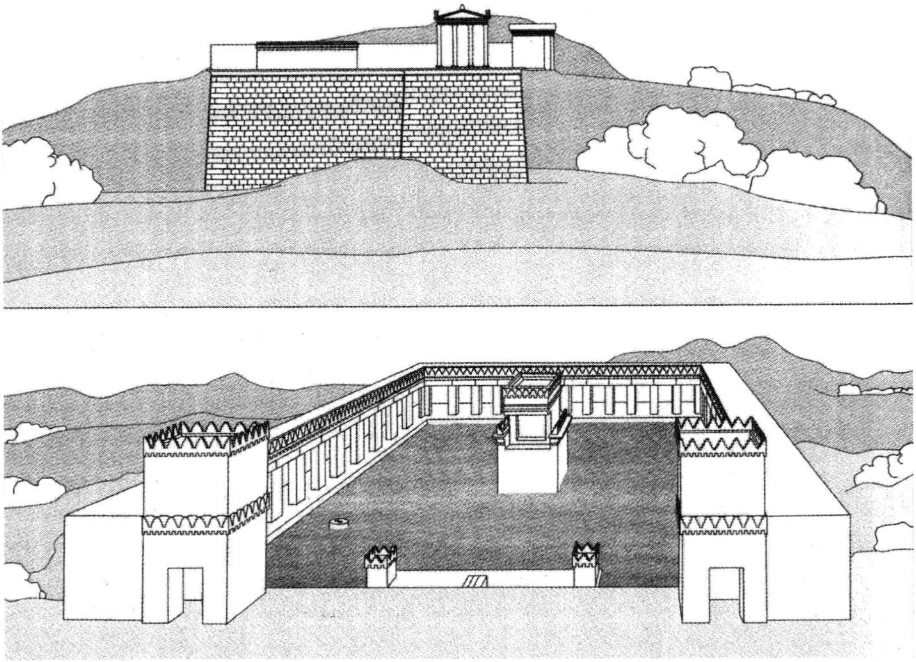

Figure 4.3. The reconstruction of the temple in Bostan esh-Sheikh near Sidon (above), and Amrit (below). After Kamlah, 'Die Tempel und Heiligtümer Phöniziens', p. 94.

and a small wall defined the area. To the altar was added a three-pillar shrine[50] which can be interpreted as one of the most important cultic objects in the Phoenician world. One of the most impressive examples is the three-pillar shrine in Kommos, Crete,[51] and numerous three-pillar shrines are presented on the so-called Tophet stele (Figure 4.2).[52]

Kommos was an important seaport already in the Bronze Age and had trade contacts with Egypt, Cyprus, and the Levant. After the destruction of Kommos around 1250 BC (LM III B), it was frequented as a small sacred place from 1050/20 BC on. A temple was built during this time and was in use until the end of the ninth century BC (temple A). Two building phases can be distinguished:

[50] Rossignani, 'Il santuario di Astarte a Malta', pp. 115–30.

[51] Pappalardo, 'Il tripillar shrine di Kommos', pp. 263–74; Shaw, 'Phoenicians in Southern Crete', pp. 165–83; Shaw, 'The Phoenician Shrine ca. 800 B.C. at Kommos in Crete', pp. 1107–19; Shaw, 'Der phönizische Schrein in Kommos auf Kreta', pp. 93–104.

[52] Bisi, *Le Stele puniche*.

the first from 1050/20 until 875 and a second from 875 until 800 BC. In both phases the building consisted of a rectangular chamber with an open access on the eastern side. In the second phase, abundant Phoenician material (pottery as well as glass and faïence beads) and layers of burned sacrifices were found. After its destruction a new temple building was erected (temple B) and was used as a sacred place by the Phoenicians until 600 BC. Since traces of Phoenician presence in the surrounding area are lacking, the precise interpretation of this cult place is highly debated. The temple, the finds, and the three-pillar shrine, however, are typically Phoenician, and even the installation in or on older structures was already observed for the Astarte temples in Kition and Malta. In Kommos no inscription gives information about the worshipped deity. In the temple in Malta a dedication inscription to Astarte was found. In the Late Hellenistic period the Maltese area was enlarged, several buildings were added, and a new altar was erected, all in the same alignment, and an inscription mentions Hera-Juno. Close to this Hera temple must have been a Heracles-Melqart temple as the second-century Roman mathematician and geographer Claudius Ptolemy reports.[53] The location of this temple is unknown today.

The Phoenician sacred places were sometimes located outside the settlement (*extra muros*) and occupied large areas such as the sanctuary in Bostan esh-Sheikh in the vicinity of Sidon, Lebanon (Figure 4.3a), or they were built in the residential quarter of a settlement (*intra muros*) as in Kerkouane, Tunisia (Figure 4.4). The temple in Bostan esh-Sheikh was built in the mid-sixth century BC as a truncated pyramid and remodelled several times. At the end of the sixth or the beginning of the fifth century BC a huge podium was erected in a second phase and was consolidated later on. A propylon gave access to the platform, on which a large building in Graeco-Persian style with two pillars in front and an architrave in the form of an Egyptian cornice once stood. During the fourth century BC this area was monumentalized by the erection of a building in pure Greek-Doric style and the installation of the so-called tribune of Eshmun, the basin and throne of Astarte, and the 'Batimênt des Enfants'. This temple was dedicated to Eshmun, but much evidence also points towards the veneration of Astarte. Many finds were recovered in this area and among them were Phoenician inscriptions and life-size Cypriote sculptures.[54]

[53] Claudius Ptolemaeus, *Geographia*, IV 3,13.

[54] Stucky and Mathys, 'Le Sanctuaire sidonien d'Echmoun', pp. 123–48; Stucky, 'Das Heiligtum des Eschmun bei Sidon in vorhellenistischer Zeit', pp. 66–86; Stucky, *Das Eschmun-Heiligtum von Sidon*; Xella and López, 'L'Inscription phénicienne de Bodashtart', pp. 119–29; Oggiano and Xella, 'Sidone e il suo territorio in età persiana', pp. 69–81.

Figure 4.4.
The ground plan of the temple in Kerkouane. After Fantar, 'La Chapelle carrée de Kerkouane', p. 195.

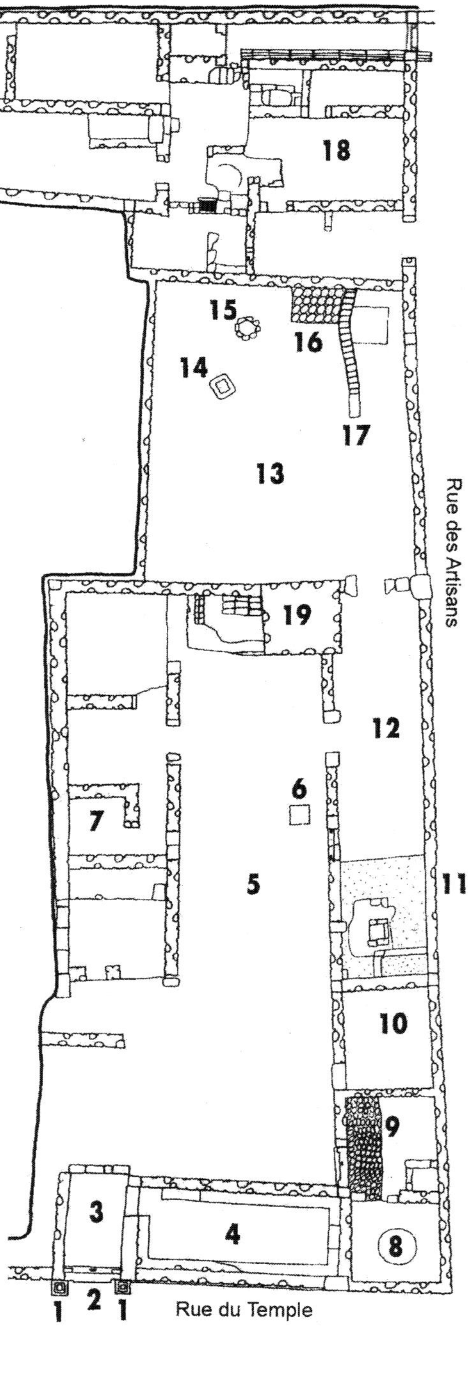

The two temples *intra muros* in Kerkouane on the peninsula Cap Bon are located right in the centre of the city. Kerkouane was founded in the sixth century BC, as is attested by its necropoleis and grave goods. The city was devastated at the end of the fourth century BC, probably during the campaign of Agathocles of Syracus in 310 BC, and finally destroyed and abandoned during the First Punic War, probably in the course of the campaign of the Roman consul Marcus Atilius Regulus in 256 BC. Right in the centre of the residential zone is an elongated, rectangular area. A front gate with two pilasters (nos. 1–3) gave access to a courtyard (no. 5), lined by small chambers for different purposes (nos. 4, 7–12), an altar in the courtyard (no. 6), and two podia in the background (no. 19). These podia could have been the foundations of chapels. At the right side of the podia is an entrance to a second courtyard (nos. 13–17). This large area is at first sight barely distinguishable from the surrounding houses, but the ground plan, the building arrangements, the terracotta finds, and especially the two podia clearly indicate the function of this area as a temple. Close by,

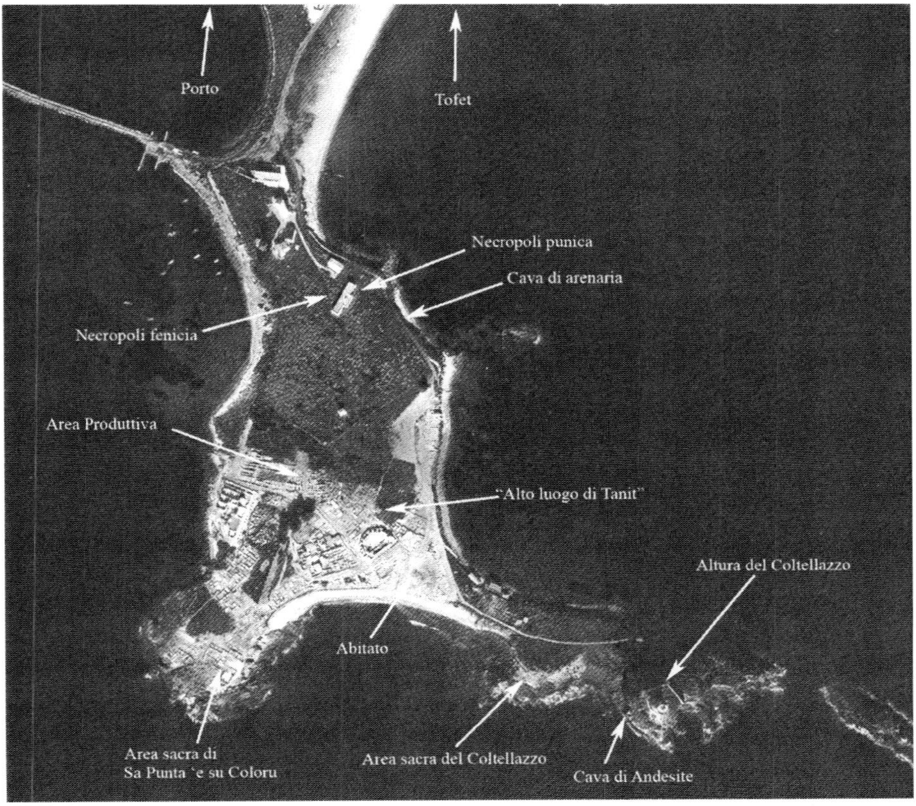

Figure 4.5. The city of Nora as an example of the strategic definition of urban space. After Oggiano, 'La "città" di Nora', p. 424 fig. 3b.

just across the street, a second sacred place is in the course of excavation. Here too, the entrance is decorated by two pilasters and opens into a courtyard which is dominated by the foundation of a small chapel and an altar. No inscriptions or finds record the owners of these two sacred places.[55]

The Phoenician temples (*extra muros* and *intra muros*) were usually strategically — and not arbitrarily — positioned in the city and its surroundings, as has been pointed out in a recent study of the Sardinian temples by Corinne Bonnet and Giuseppe Garbati.[56] The location of the temples, necropoleis, and

[55] Fantar, *Kerkouane*.

[56] Bonnet and Garbati, 'Spazi sacri fuori e dentro la città', pp. 343–67.

the Tophet contributes to the definition of the urban space, in addition to the geographical landscape with its coastlines, promontories, and hinterland. In Nora, to provide an additional example (Figure 4.5), the temples are located on the two promontories of the peninsula (the so-called Coltellazzo and Sa Punta 'e su Coloru), on a small hilltop overlooking the settlement ('high place of Tanit'),[57] and — as recent excavations seem to indicate — in the centre, beneath the later Roman temple of the forum.[58] Nora is supposed to be the oldest Phoenician settlement in Sardinia, and an inscription on a stele points towards the end of the ninth / first half of the eighth century BC. From the sixth century onwards it was under the supremacy of Carthage, and from 238 BC a part of the Roman Empire. The extensive excavations have brought to light the Phoenician remains under the Roman town, among them several temples, a necropolis, and a Tophet. Extensive building activities took place during the hegemony of Carthage.

The temple on the Coltellazzo was built at the end of the sixth century as a podium terrace, probably referring to much older oriental temple types. The 'high place of Tanit' is currently under excavation in order to better understand its poorly preserved structure. At Sa Punta 'e su Coloru once stood a small chapel which can be determined by its extant foundations and the preserved architrave, decorated with a winged sun. The chapel was probably erected in the fifth century BC. In Roman times a temple of Aesculapius was built close to the foundations of the older Phoenician chapel at Sa Punta 'e su Coloru. Since the Greek god Aesculapius was the interpretation of the Phoenician god Eshmun, it could be assumed that the chapel was once dedicated to the Phoenician god Eshmun. These chapels are widely attested, and they find their most famous comparison in the Phoenician temple in Amrit, where a large temple was built in the second half of the seventh or the beginning of the sixth century BC. A large water basin measuring 46.70 m in length, 38.50 m in width, and 3–3.50 m in depth was carved into the rock, and in the centre of the temple the chapel was positioned on a high podium (Figure 4.3b).[59]

Due to inscriptions the Phoenician temples can mostly be connected with one or two Phoenician deities who were worshipped in this specific sacred place. The Phoenician religion and various Phoenician and Punic deities are,

[57] Oggiano and Bonetto, 'Reise nach Westen', pp. 29–35; Oggiano, 'La "città" di Nora', pp. 419–34.

[58] Bonetto and Falezza, 'Scenari di romanizzazione a Nora', pp. 81–100.

[59] Dunand and Saliby, *Le Temple d'Amrith dans la pérée d'Aradus*; Lembke, *Die Skulpturen aus dem Quellheiligtum von Amrit*.

contrary to Phoenician temples, quite well studied on the basis of mainly written and iconographic sources:[60] Astarte, Melqart, Baal-Hammon, and Baal-Shamem to name just a few.[61] It is possible to characterize them while clarifying their origins, developments, persistence, and reception. A great part of the relevant sources concerning the Phoenicians in general and Phoenician religion in particular, however, are not written in Semitic but composed by classical Greek and Roman authors, using the Greek and Roman names of deities instead of the original Phoenician names. In most cases it is possible to reconstruct the meaning behind them,[62] but in some cases it is not sufficient to accept a simple translation of names. This approach rather seems to be oversimplifying and unsatisfying when precise contexts have to be analysed.

A good example for this on-going attempt to 'translate' the deities is the contract between the Punic military commander Hannibal and King Philip V of Macedon during the Second Punic War in 215 BC as reported by the Greek historian Polybius.[63] In order to guarantee the binding force of the contract, an evocation of several deities (under their Greek names) is added to the contract: Zeus, Hera, Apollo, the genii of Carthage, Heracles and Iolaos, Ares, Triton, Poseidon, the deities who are fighting on the side of Carthage, sun, moon, earth, rivers, lakes, and waters, every deity of Carthage. Numerous scholars have tried to translate the names and to identify the original Phoenician deities, coming to different results.[64] It is probably more effective to interpret the individual characters of these deities in their specific cultural area.[65] A detailed study of the written sources and their connection to archaeologically known temples or the religious topography of a Phoenician settlement could certainly further our understanding of the complex religious, political, and sociological systems in the Phoenician world. Unfortunately, this has not yet been done.

[60] Bonnet and others, *Religio Phoenicia*; Ribichini and Xella, *La religione e fenicia e punica in Italia*; Lipiński, *Dieux et déesses de l'univers phénicien et punique*; Costa and Fernández, *De Oriente a Occidente*; Xella, *Religione e religioni in Siria-Palestina*; del Olmo Lete, *Mythologie et religion des Sémites occidentaux*; Bonnet and Niehr, *Religionen in der Umwelt des Alten Testaments II*.

[61] See, respectively, Bonnet, *Astarté*; Bonnet, *Melqart*; Xella, *Baal Hammon*; and Niehr, *Ba'alšamem*.

[62] A listing is given in Huss, *Geschichte der Karthager*, pp. 521–25.

[63] Polybius VII 9.

[64] Charles-Picard, *Hannibal*; Barré, *The God-List in the Treaty between Hannibal and Philip V of Macedonia*; Huss, 'Hannibal und die Religion', pp. 223–38.

[65] Lee, 'Die Götter im Vertrag zwischen Hannibal und Philipp V'.

A Case Study: The Cult Topography of Carthage

In the following a case study of the available written sources and the archaeological material of a Phoenician city shall be given in order to compare this evidence and to assess the cult topography of a Phoenician city. This shall be done with the most famous and important Phoenician city in the western Mediterranean: Carthage. Carthage was founded at the end of the ninth century BC by Phoenician colonists from Tyre, as the founding myth reports. Nothing points towards the existence of a previous, indigenous settlement at this site; the city seems to have been founded on virgin soil. Carthage became the most dominant Phoenician city in the western Mediterranean from the seventh/sixth century BC onwards, exercising political control over North Africa, the Iberian Peninsula, Sardinia, and Sicily. Carthage was acting on the international scene, cooperating with and opposing the Etruscans, Greece and Greeks in Sicily, and Rome, absorbing and dispensing cultural elements. Quarrels over supremacy in the western Mediterranean led to various wars, and ultimately the city was destroyed by the Roman army and completely abandoned during the Third Punic War in 146 BC.[66] The city was, however, refounded around one hundred years later by the Romans as Colonia Iulia Concordia Carthago, and it regained its former grandeur from the second century on.

The Written Sources

We are informed by epigraphic sources of the fourth–second century BC about a temple of Melqart, 'bt Mlqrt',[67] and the cultic personnel of a Melqart temple in Carthage.[68] One inscription also mentions offerings for Tanit and Baal as well as Melqart,[69] and more than a thousand personal names from Carthage bear 'Melqart' as a name component.[70] The god Melqart literally is the king of the city. He is the most important deity of Tyre, the mother-city of Carthage. He can be characterized as a hero, protector of the collective, guarantor of its well-being, and

[66] Huss, *Geschichte der Karthager*, pp. 216–457; Badisches Landesmuseum Karlsruhe, *Hannibal ad portas*.

[67] *Corpus Inscriptionum Semiticarum*, I, 4894, 5575.

[68] *Corpus Inscriptionum Semiticarum*, I, 264.

[69] *Corpus Inscriptionum Semiticarum*, I, 5510.

[70] Bonnet, *Melqart*, pp. 165–86; Cadotte, *La Romanisation des dieux*, pp. 283–88.

expression of its identity.[71] The veneration of Sid-Melqart[72] and Milk-Ashtart[73] in Carthage are also attested by inscriptions[74] but are difficult to interpret. We have to assume that the deities of Sid-Melqart and Milk-Ashtart originated in a syncretism of the gods Melqart and Sid as well as Melqart and Ashtart on the basis of some specific similarities in their characters. They were therefore probably worshipped with analogous cultic rites and in the same cult places.[75]

The goddess Astarte is also known from several inscriptions of the fourth–second century BC mentioning her sole worship in a temple,[76] as well as her worship together with Tanit in a temple in Bordj Djedid, just outside the city of Carthage, in the fourth–third century BC.[77] A priest of Eshmun-Astarte is mentioned too.[78] The earliest evidence for Astarte is a small gold medallion, which was deposited as a funeral gift in the so-called tomb of Yadamilk and can therefore be dated in the eighth/seventh century BC.[79] Astarte is also worshipped in her specific form as Astarte of Eryx (Sicily).[80] Astarte was worshipped as the source of life, she elected and legitimized the king, and she also served as his companion.[81]

The worship of the goddess Tanit is testified by several thousand inscriptions on votive stelae from the Tophet at Carthage. She can be interpreted as one of the most important deities in the Carthaginian Empire.[82] She was seen as the protector of the genealogy, parenthood, and descendants.[83] According to Macrobius, a Late Roman grammarian and Neoplatonist philosopher, the Roman army even made an evocation in order to lure her out of the city during

[71] Bonnet and Niehr, *Religionen in der Umwelt des Alten Testaments II*, pp. 67–70.

[72] *Corpus Inscriptionum Semiticarum*, I, 256.

[73] *Corpus Inscriptionum Semiticarum*, I, 250, 2785, 4839, 4850, 5657.

[74] Cadotte, *La Romanisation des dieux*, pp. 283–88.

[75] Xella, '"Divinités doubles" dans dans le monde phénico-punique', pp. 167–75.

[76] *Corpus Inscriptionum Semiticarum*, I, 263, 255, 3779, 4842, 4843.

[77] *Corpus Inscriptionum Semiticarum*, I, 3914.

[78] *Corpus Inscriptionum Semiticarum*, I, 245.

[79] Donner and Röllig, *Kanaanäische und aramäische Inschriften*, no. 73.

[80] *Corpus Inscriptionum Semiticarum*, I, 3776, 4910; Bonnet, *Astarté*, pp. 97–105; Cadotte, *La Romanisation des dieux*, pp. 206–15.

[81] Bonnet and Niehr, *Religionen in der Umwelt des Alten Testaments II*, pp. 78–83.

[82] Benichou-Safar, *Le Tophet de Salammbô à Carthage*.

[83] Bonnet and Niehr, *Religionen in der Umwelt des Alten Testaments II*, pp. 83–85.

the Punic-Roman wars[84] — if Tanit is correctly identified as the Carthaginian Juno.[85] The temple of the Carthaginian Juno is also mentioned by Plinius the Elder and Vergil.[86]

The counterpart of the goddess Tanit was the god Baal Hammon, whose evocation is also attested on several thousand Tophet stelae, repetitiously using variations of the formula 'To Tanit, face of Baal, and Baal Hammon, dedicated by NN, son of NN, because they have heard his voice and blessed him'. Baal Hammon was the god of the dynasty, the ancestors, and religious traditions, and therefore the protector of the family and the whole community.[87] The Tophet stelae provide further names such as Baal Mgnm,[88] 'bdšgr,[89] and 'bdšd,[90] but we should not automatically assume that these deities also had their own cult places in Carthage.

To the god Eshmun, god of benevolence and health,[91] one of the richest and most renowned temples was dedicated on the citadel of Carthage,[92] if we accept the interpretation of Eshmun as Aesculapius.[93] The Carthaginian senate held its secret meetings there during the Punic wars,[94] and the Carthaginians sought asylum there during the capture of the city by the Roman army in 146 BC.[95] Several personal names from Carthage bear 'Eshmun' as a name component.[96] The temple of Eshmun on the citadel must be distinguished from another temple of Eshmun, if we accept his interpretation not only as Aesculapius but also as Apollo:[97] according to Appian and Valerius Maximus a temple of Apollo

[84] Macrobius, *Saturnalia*, III 9.

[85] Cadotte, *La Romanisation des dieux*, p. 73.

[86] Pliny the Elder, *Naturalis historia*, VI 36; Publius Vergilius Maro, *Aeneis*, I 441–444.

[87] Bonnet and Niehr, *Religionen in der Umwelt des Alten Testaments II*, pp. 66–67.

[88] *Corpus Inscriptionum Semiticarum*, I, 3778.

[89] *Corpus Inscriptionum Semiticarum*, I, 2669, 2988, 3993, 4514.

[90] *Corpus Inscriptionum Semiticarum*, I, 352, 696, 4555, 4556, 5098; Lipiński, *Dieux et déesses de l'univers phénicien et punique*, pp. 351–56.

[91] Bonnet and Niehr, *Religionen in der Umwelt des Alten Testaments II*, pp. 70–72.

[92] Strabon XVII 3,14; Appian, *Punica*, 130.

[93] Cadotte, *La Romanisation des dieux*, pp. 165–200.

[94] Livius XLI 22,2; XLII 24,3.

[95] Joannes Zonaras IX 30; Paulus Orosius IV 23,4.

[96] *Corpus Inscriptionum Semiticarum*, I, 1, 252; I, 3, 4834, 4835, 4836, 4827; Lipiński, *Dieux et déesses de l'univers phénicien et punique*, p. 166.

[97] Cadotte, *La Romanisation des dieux*, pp. 165–200.

stood in proximity to the harbour.[98] After the capture of the city by the Roman army, the golden statue of the god was removed from his temple in Carthage to the Circus Maximus in Rome.[99]

The cult of Baal Saphon, the protector of seafaring,[100] is testified by an epigraph which was found in Marseille in 1845.[101] The inscription regulates the offerings to the god Baal Saphon. Since the stone of this epigraph originates from a Carthaginian quarry, it was probably once erected in his temple in Carthage.[102] The god Shadrapha had at least one altar in the third century BC.[103]

Deities of Phoenician origin were not the only deities worshipped in Carthage: Diodorus Siculus, probably quoting Timaios of Tauromenium, reports the official implementation of the Greek goddesses Demeter and Kore at the end of the fourth century BC from Sicily.[104] The Carthaginians erected statues of them and worshipped them by using Greek priests and Greek rites.[105] This cult is confirmed by an inscription on an epitaph from the necropolis Ard el-Kheraib, dated to the fourth century BC, which mentions the priestess of the Kore.[106] As Edward Lipiński has pointed out, a Favissa with female terracotta figurines seems to be connected with this cult.[107] Perhaps in the same period, the cult of the Egyptian goddess Isis was introduced into Carthage, since an inscription of the third century BC mentions her cult and priests.[108]

This list does not claim to be a complete compilation of every cult and cult place in Carthage, but only a small collection of some of the best known

[98] Appian, *Punica*, 127; Valerius Maximus I 1,18.

[99] Plutarch, *Flaminius*, 1; Lipiński, *Itineraria Phoenicia*, pp. 484–92.

[100] Bonnet, 'Typhon et Baal Saphon', pp. 101–43; Bonnet, 'Baal Saphon', pp. 60–61.

[101] *Corpus Inscriptionum Semiticarum*, I, 165.

[102] Badisches Landesmuseum Karlsruhe, *Hannibal ad portas*, p. 320.

[103] *Corpus Inscriptionum Semiticarum*, I, 3921; Xella and Lipiński, 'Shadrapha', pp. 407–08; Cadotte, *La Romanisation des dieux*, pp. 253–81.

[104] Diodorus Siculus XIV 77, 4–5.

[105] Xella, 'Sull'introduzione del culto di Demetra e Kore a Cartagine', pp. 215–28; Lipiński, *Dieux et déesses de l'univers phénicien et punique*, pp. 374–78; Bonnet, 'Identité et altérité religieuses', pp. 365–79; Melliti, 'Religion, politique et hellénisme à Carthage', pp. 91–98.

[106] *Corpus Inscriptionum Semiticarum*, I, 5987.

[107] Lipiński, *Dieux et déesses de l'univers phénicien et punique*, pp. 372–76: Delattre, 'Une cachette de figurines de Déméter et de brûle-parfums votifs à Carthage', pp. 354–65; Delattre, *Une favissa à Carthage*.

[108] Beschaouch, 'Sur la localisation du temple d'Isis', pp. 323–30; Bonnet, 'Le Culte d'Isis à Carthage', pp. 43–56.

sources in order to gain a general picture. It can be concluded that most of the prominent and traditional Phoenician deities were present — Melqart, Astarte, Eshmun, Tanit, Baal Hammon, Baal Saphon — and additional smaller cults. Thus every social aspect of Carthaginian society was connected with a protector. Eventually they were complemented by foreign deities, who were worshipped according to their own rites. It seems that some of them were worshipped in the same place. Furthermore, no hierarchy among the cults can be observed — or at least Melqart did not maintain the religious and political primacy in Carthage as he did in Tyre.

The Archaeological Evidence

Carthage experienced many destructions and building activities in its history from the end of the ninth century BC until its final destruction in 146 BC. Under the UNESCO project 'Pour sauver Carthage' from 1972 to 1992, the historical topography of this city became more visible,[109] but there remain many blind spots. For example, the citadel (Byrsa) was completely remodelled in Roman times and the Punic arrangements removed.[110] Therefore nothing remains of the famous aforementioned temple of Eshmun on the citadel. We can only speculate that it had once been an impressive monumental building, occupying the best position in the city. It is unlikely that it was the only monumental structure on the citadel, and/or the biggest, since nothing indicates that Eshmun was the pre-eminent god in Carthage.

Only two areas with possible cultic activity have thus far been revealed by excavation, alongside the so-called Tophet. One was identified during the German excavations under the direction of Hans Georg Niemeyer, University of Hamburg, below the cross-section of the Roman Decumanus Maximus and the cardo X (Figure 4.6). The context was undisturbed and dates continuously from the mid-eighth century BC until the destruction in 146 BC, indicating eight rebuilding phases of a residential area. In phases V and VI (*c.* 480–400 and 400–350), a sanctuary was incorporated into this residential area during its restructuring. It comprises two rooms with different ground levels and a waterproof pavement. The pavement of the lower room is decorated with two symbols: the so-called Tanit symbol and another one, probably connected with Baal Hammon. A nearby small depression in the pavement with traces of sinter

[109] Ennabli, *Pour sauver Carthage*; Ennabli, 'Carthage', pp. 51–59.

[110] Lancel, 'La Colline de Byrsa', pp. 156–93 Lancel, *La Colline de Byrsa à l'époque romaine*.

Figure 4.6. The so-called sanctuary of Tanit in Carthage. After Niemeyer, Docter, and Schmidt, 'Die Hamburger Grabung unter dem Decumanus Maximus von Karthago', p. 174, fig. 4.

points towards ritual pouring (libation). Apart from that, no specific architectural features can be detected from this so-called sanctuary of Tanit.[111]

Not far away, in the excavation area below cardo XIII, an excavation directed by Friedrich Rakob of the German Archaeological Institute discovered another structure that was interpreted as a sanctuary. It consists of a huge wall, enclosing a courtyard, and a Favissa, containing architectural elements such as an Egyptian gorge, an Aeolic and Doric capital, fragments of pilasters, as well several thousand scarab-seals. Some scholars thought it possible to interpret these remains as the aforementioned Apollo temple.[112] The seals at least point towards the existence of a state archive, which could indeed have

[111] Niemeyer, 'Un nuevo santuario de la diosa Tanit en Cartago', pp. 635–42; Niemeyer and others, *Karthago*, I, 217–33; Niemeyer, Docter, and Schmidt, 'Die Hamburger Grabung unter dem Decumanus Maximus von Karthago', pp. 171–78.

[112] Appian, *Punica*, 127; Valerius Maximus I 1,18; Rakob, 'Ein punisches Heiligtum in Karthago und sein römischer Nachfolgebau', pp. 33–80; Rakob, 'Neue Ausgrabungen in Karthago', pp. 158–74.

been located in a temple.[113] A similar case is known from Selinunt, where a Punic archive was placed in a former Greek temple.[114] A current project at the German Archaeological Institute aims to evaluate and verify these data in the Carthaginian site.[115]

Just outside the city centre of Carthage, the so-called Tophet is situated. This term has been misleadingly understood from the Old Testament (beginning of the twentieth century BC) to designate certain areas in the Phoenician western Mediterranean as the locations of the child sacrifices reported by classical authors. Modern research inclines towards the interpretation of a Tophet not as a place of child sacrifice but as a cemetery for children. Whatever the correct interpretation might be,[116] a 'Tophet' certainly can be identified as a sacred place. The Tophet of Carthage comprises several phases of cremation burials from the first until the last days of the city (eighth–second century BC), including votive stelae, pottery, terracotta figurines, as well as some buildings: the so-called Chapelle Cintas and the Chapelle Carton.[117] Unfortunately these remains have now disappeared and have to be reconstructed through the notes of Pierre Cintas or Louis Carton. The Chapelle Cintas consisted of several walls and a pavement; it contained common grave furniture and is datable to the mid/end eighth century on the basis of the pottery (Figure 4.7).[118] The Chapelle Carton was a small building, decorated by architectural elements such as Ionic capitals, pilasters, kymation, and cornices. Various votive objects such as incense burners and pottery were found in a niche. The building technique and the finds point towards a date in the third or second century BC.[119] It can be assumed that these chapels once served as places to invoke the gods, make offerings, and deposit votive objects. In the Tophet in Mozia, Sicily, equally small buildings can be found.[120] In its first phase in the eighth–sixth

[113] Berges, 'Die Tonsiegel aus dem karthagischen Tempelarchiv', pp. 10–214.

[114] Helas, 'Die punischen Häuser in Selinunt', pp. 168–70.

[115] 'Karthago (Tunesien) – Rue Ibn Chabâat'.

[116] Benichou-Safar, *Le Tophet de Salammbô à Carthage*: Xella, 'Sacrifici di bambini nel mondo Fenicio e Punico', pp. 59–100.

[117] Ribichini, 'Il sacello nel "tofet"', pp. 425–39.

[118] Picard, 'Installations cultuelles retrouvées au tophet de Salammbo', pp. 189–99; Briese, 'Die Chapelle Cintas', pp. 419–52; Chelbi, 'La Chapelle Cintas', pp. 242–43.

[119] Carton, *Sanctuaire punique découvert à Carthage*; Ferchiou, 'Deux témoignages de l'architecture religieuse et funéraire de la Carthage hellénistique', pp. 15–45.

[120] Nigro, 'Il Tempio del Kothon', pp. 241–70.

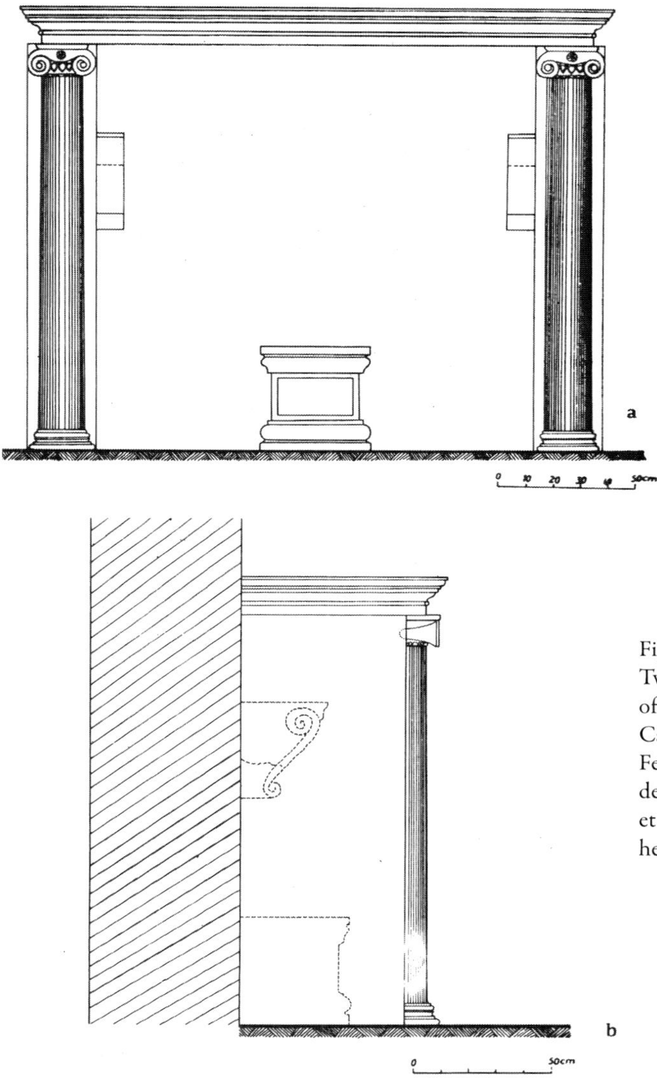

Figure 4.7.
Two possible reconstructions of the so-called Chapelle Carton in Carthage. After: Ferchiou, 'Deux témoignages de l'architecture religieuse et funéraire de la Carthage hellénistique', p. 38 fig. 3.

century BC, there was only one small chapel in Mozia, while in the mid-sixth century BC two other small buildings were added, one with a so-called throne of Astarte on a platform. A Doric capital found nearby can probably be connected with these buildings, and terracotta votives were also discovered in the area. These small chapels are widely known from Phoenician temples, such as the aforementioned example in Amrit, but no other examples are yet known from a Tophet. It would be productive to compare these remains in detail and to look for more evidence from other Tophets. These chapels seem to be some of the most important specific cultic elements of Phoenician sacred places.

Conclusions

A general overview and a short case study have been given in order to highlight the potential for further comparative analysis of Phoenician religious topography, bringing together written sources and archaeological evidence. The case study of Carthage has shown the abundant variety of the Carthaginian cults. The worshipped deities are part of a comprehensive system: every god and goddess thus contributing, according to their specific function, to the well-being of the city. No hierarchy among the deities can be discerned. Instead there is a pattern of specific functions. Their cults were spread all over the city, and we might expect at least one significant temple on the top of the citadel. In this temple the god Eshmun and probably also Astarte were worshipped. We can imagine this temple as a huge platform or open terrace with several buildings, among these a small chapel. This creates space for different purposes, such as the meeting of the Carthaginian senate. Literary sources indicate other temples in the centre of the city and its periphery. These, however, served different cults and rites, and thus, because of their architectural plans, they might be difficult to distinguish from the surrounding residential houses. Both would fit very well with the archaeological evidence from the two German excavations in Carthage. A temple of Melqart and Astarte, as well as the cult places of Sid-Melqart and Milk-Ashtart, would be appropriate and expected in the city centre. But even if those structures that came to light during the German Archaeological Institute excavation below the cardo XIII are correctly identified as a temple, the attribution to one or other deity will never be proven without an inscription. The cults of Demeter and Kore located 'extra-muros' according to the find-spot of an inscription and a Favissa containing terracotta figurines equally fit very well into this strategic distribution of sacred places. Finally we could speculate that there was a temple in the north-east part of the city too, in order to complete the picture of the strategic distribution. We still have to find and/or identify quite a number of temples in Carthage (Figure 4.8). The same phenomenon of a complex cult topography and the embedding of these cults in the urban structures is to be expected for Tyre and Cádiz: many important and many smaller cults as well as some foreign cults, situated in different types of buildings, and strategically placed within the city. Since no

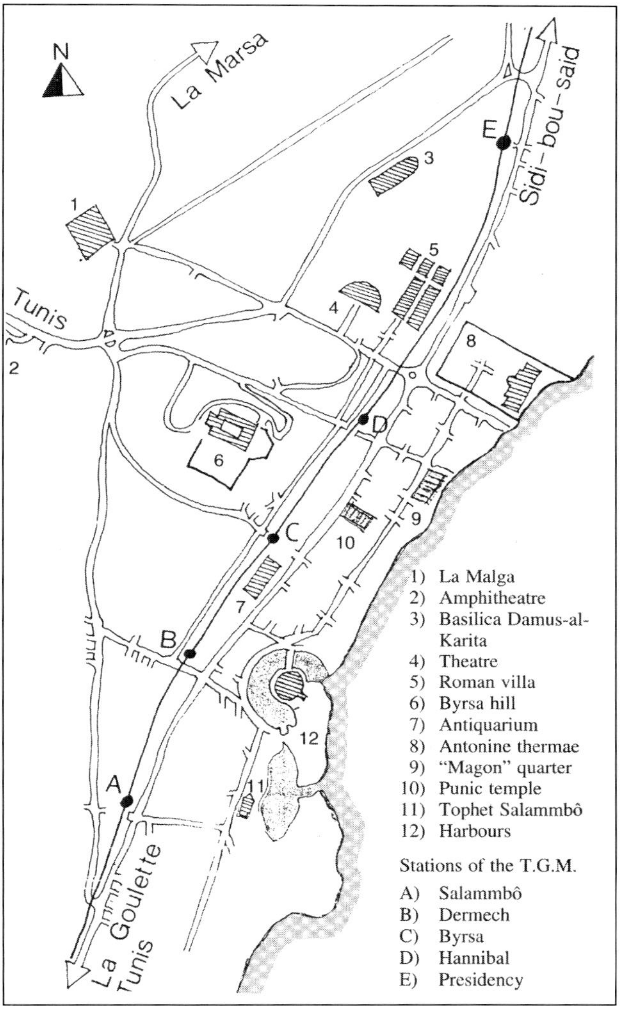

Map 3.
The ground plan of Carthage with its known ancient monuments. After Lipiński, *Itineraria Phoenicia*, p. 482.

monumental building and no specific architectural elements were obligatory, the temples are barely distinguishable from the surrounding residential houses. The temple of Melqart in Tyre could therefore have stood where the remains of the Crusader cathedral are now to be seen, but it has left no recognizable trace.

Works Cited

Primary Source

Corpus Inscriptionum Semiticarum ab Academia inscriptionum et litterarum humaniorum conditum atque digestum, vol. 1 (Paris: Académie des inscriptions et belles-lettres, 1881)

Secondary Studies

Aubet, M. E., 'La cueva d'Es Cuyram (Ibiza)', *Pyrenae*, 4 (1968), 1–66

——, *The Phoenicians and the West: Politics, Colonies, and Trade*, 2nd edn (Cambridge: Cambridge University Press, 2001)

——, *El santuario de Es Cuieram*, Trabajos del Museo arqueológico de Ibiza, 8 (Ibiza: Publicaciones de la Direccion General de Bellas Artes, Archivos y Bibliotecas, 1982)

Badisches Landesmuseum Karlsruhe, ed., *Hannibal ad portas: Macht und Reichtum Karthagos. Sonderausstellung Karlsruhe 2004–2005* (Stuttgart: Theiss, 2004)

Barnett, R. D., 'Ezekiel and Tyre', in *Eretz-Israel*, Archaeological, Historical and Geographical Studies, 9 (1969), pp. 6–13

Barré, M. L., *The God-List in the Treaty between Hannibal and Philip V of Macedonia: A Study in Light of the Ancient Near Eastern Treaty Tradition* (Baltimore: Johns Hopkins University Press, 1983)

Benichou-Safar, H., *Le Tophet de Salammbô à Carthage: essai de reconstitution* (Roma: École Française de Rome, 2004)

Berges, D., 'Die Tonsiegel aus dem karthagischen Tempelarchiv', in *Karthago II: Die deutschen Ausgrabungen in Karthago*, ed. by F. Rakob (Mainz: Philipp von Zabern, 1997), pp. 10–214

Beschaouch, A., 'Sur la localisation du temple d'Isis: topographie de Carthage romaine', *Comptes-rendus des séances de l'Académie des Inscriptions et Belles-Lettres*, 1991, 323–30

Bisi, A. M., *Grotta Regina*, Studi semitici, 33, 2 vols (Roma: Consiglio nazionale delle ricerche, 1969–79)

——, *Le stele puniche*, Studi semitici, 27 (Roma: Istituto di studi del Vicino Oriente, 1967)

Blázquez, J. M., *Imagen y mito: studios sobre religions mediterráneas e ibéricas* (Madrid: Ediciones Cristiandad, S. L., 1977)

Bonetto, J., and G. Falezza, 'Scenari di romanizzazione a Nora: un deposito di fondazione e un deposito votivo per la constituzione della Provincia Sardinia et Corsica, Sardinia', *Corsica et Baleares antiquae*, 7 (2009), 81–100

Bonnet, C., *Astarté: dossier documentaire et perspectives historiques* (Roma: Consiglio nazionale delle ricerche, 1996)

——, 'Baal Saphon', in *Dictionnaire de la civilisation Phénicienne et Punique*, ed. by E. Lipiński (Turnhout: Brepols, 1992), pp. 60–61

——, 'Le Culte d'Isis à Carthage: À propos de l'inscription funéraire punique CIS I, 6000bis', in *Ana Šadî Labnāni lū allik: Beiträge zu altorientalischen und mittel-*

meerischen Kulturen. Festschrift für Wolfgang Röllig, ed. by B. Pongratz-Leisten, H. Kühne, and P. Xella, Alter Orient und Altes Testament, 247 (Münster: Ugarit, 1997), pp. 43–56

——, 'Identité et altérité religieuses: À propos de l'hellénisation de Carthage', *Pallas*, 70 (2006), 365–79

——, *Melqart: cultes et mythes de Heraklés tyrien en Méditerranée*, Studia Phoenicia, 8 (Leuven: Peeters, 1988)

——, 'Typhon et Baal Saphon', in *Phoenicia and the East Mediterranean in the First Millennium B.C.*, ed. by E. Lipiński, Studia Phoenicia, 5 (Leuven: Peeters, 1987), pp. 101–43

Bonnet, C., and G. Garbati, 'Spazi sacri fuori e dentro la città: Strategie di occupazione e forme devozionali nella Sardegna fenicia e punica', in *Phönizisches und punisches Städtewesen: Akten der internationalen Tagung in Rom vom 21. bis 23. Februar 2007*, ed. by S. Helas and D. Marzoli, Iberia Archaeologica, 13 (Mainz: von Zabern, 2009), pp. 343–67

Bonnet, C., and H. Niehr, *Religionen in der Umwelt des Alten Testaments II. Phönizier, Punier, Aramäer* (Stuttgart: W. Kohlhammer, 2010)

Bonnet, C., and others, eds, *Religio Phoenicia*, Studia Phoenicia, 4 (Leuven: Peeters, 1986)

Briese, C., 'Die Chapelle Cintas – das Gründungsdepot Karthagos oder eine Bestattung der Gründergeneration', in *Archäologische Studien in Kontaktzonen der antiken Welt*, ed. by R. Rolle and K. Schmidt (Göttingen: Vandenoeck und Ruprecht, 1998), pp. 419–52

Busink, T. A., *Der Tempel von Jerusalem: Von Salomo bis Herodes – eine archäologisch-historische Studie unter Berücksichtigung des westsemitischen Tempelbaus* (Leiden: Brill, 1970)

Cadotte, A., *La Romanisation des dieux: l'interpretatio romana en Afrique du Nord sous le Haut-Empire* (Leiden: Brill, 2007)

Carton, L., *Sanctuaire punique découvert à Carthage* (Paris: Librairie Orientaliste Paul Geuthner, 1929)

Charles-Picard, G., *Hannibal* (Paris: Hachette, 1967)

Chelbi, F., 'La Chapelle Cintas', in *La Méditerranée des Phéniciens de Tyr à Carthage: Exhibition, Institut du monde arabe, Paris 2007–2008*, ed. by É. Fontan and H. Le Meaux (Paris: Institut du monde arabe, 2007), pp. 242–43

Costa, B., and J. H. Fernández, eds, *De Oriente a Occidente: los dioses fenicios en las colonias occidentals. 12. Jornadas de Arqueología Fenicio-Púnica* (Eivissa: Museu Arqueològic d'Eivissa i Fromentera, 1999)

Delattre, A. L., 'Une cachette de figurines de Déméter et de brûle-parfums votifs à Carthage', *Comptes-rendus des séances de l'Académie des Inscriptions et Belles-Lettres*, 1923, 354–65

——, *Une favissa à Carthage* (Tunis: Barlier, 1923)

Donner, H., and W. Röllig, *Kanaanäische und aramäische Inschriften* (Wiesbaden: Otto Harrassowitz, 1962–64)

Dunand, M., and N. Saliby, *Le Temple d'Amrith dans la pérée d'Aradus* (Paris: Librairie Orientaliste Paul Geuthner, 1985)

Ennabli, A., 'Carthage. La campagne internationale: aspects puniques', in *Carthago*, ed. by E. Lipiński, Studia Phoenicia, 6 (Leuven: Peeters, 1987), pp. 51–59
——, *Pour sauver Carthage: Exploration et conservation de la cite punique, romaine, byzantine* (Paris: UNESCO/INAA, 1992)
Fantar, M. H., 'La Chapelle carrée de Kerkouane: Nouveau témoignage de l'architecture religieuse punique', in *Phönizisches und punisches Städtewesen: Akten der internationalen Tagung in Rom vom 21. bis 23. Februar 2007*, ed. by S. Helas and D. Marzoli, Iberia Archaeologica, 13 (Mainz: von Zabern, 2009), pp. 191–201
——, *Kerkouane: cite puniqe du Cap Bon (Tunisie)*, 3 vols (Tunis: Maison tunisienne de l'édition 1984–86)
Ferchiou, N., 'Deux témoignages de l'architecture religieuse et funéraire de la Carthage hellénistique', *Rivista di Studi Fenici*, 15 (1987), 15–45
Frahm, E., *Einleitung in die Sanherib-Inschriften*, Archiv für Orientforschung Beiheft, 26 (Wien: Institut für Orientalistik der Universität Wien, 1997)
Helas, S., 'Die punischen Häuser in Selinunt: Wohnen zwischen punischer Tradition und griechischem Einfluß' (doctoral dissertation, Universität zu Köln, 1999) <http://kups.ub.uni-koeln.de/1481/> [accessed 6 August 2013]
Helas, S., and D. Marzoli, eds, *Phönizisches und punisches Städtewesen: Akten der internationalen Tagung in Rom vom 21. bis 23. Februar 2007*, Iberia Archaeologica, 13 (Mainz: Philipp von Zabern, 2009)
Hoftijzer, J., and K. Jongeling, *Dictionary of the North-West Semitic Inscriptions*, Handbuch der Orientalistik, Erste Abteilung, Der Nähe und Mittlere Osten, 21 (Leiden: Brill, 1995)
Huss, W., *Geschichte der Karthager*, Handbuch Der Altertumswissenschaften III, 8 (München: Beck, 1985)
——, 'Hannibal und die Religion', in *Religio Phoenicia*, ed. by C. Bonnet and others, Studia Phoenicia, 4 (Leuven: Peeters, 1986), pp. 223–38
Jidejian, N., and C. Bonnet, 'Afqa', in *Dictionnaire de la civilisation Phénicienne et Punique*, ed. by E. Lipiński (Turnhout: Brepols, 1992)
Kamlah, J., 'Die Tempel und Heiligtümer Phöniziens: Kultstätten im Kontext der eisenzeitlichen Stadtkultur in der Levante', in *Phönizisches und punisches Städtewesen: Akten der internationalen Tagung in Rom vom 21. bis 23. Februar 2007*, ed. by S. Helas and D. Marzoli, Iberia Archaeologica, 13 (Mainz: Philipp von Zabern, 2009), pp. 83–85
Karageorghis, V., *Fouilles de Kition*, 6 vols (Nicosia: Zavallis, 1974–2005)
——, *Kition: Mycenaean and Phoenician Discoveries in Cyprus* (London: Thames and Hudson, 1976)
'Karthago (Tunesien) – Rue Ibn Chabâat' <http://www.dainst.org/de/project/karthago?ft=all>
Keel, O., E. A. Knauf, and Th. Staubli, *Salomons Tempel* (Fribourg: Academic Press Fribourg, 2004)
Koch, M., 'Von Tarschisch bis nach Indien: Die Integration der Iberischen Halbinsel in das Weltherrschaftsschema des Alten Orients und seiner Erben', *Serta Palaeohispanica in honorem Javier de Hoz, Palaeohispanica*, 10 (2010), 567–78
Krings, V., ed., *La Civilisation Phénicienne et Punique: manuel de recherche*, Handbuch der Orientalistik I, 20 (Leiden: Brill, 1995)

Lancel, S., *La Colline de Byrsa à l'époque romaine* (Paris: Recherches sur les Civilisations, 1983)

——, 'La Colline de Byrsa et l'occupation punique, 7e siècle – 146 av. J. C. Bilan de sept années de fouilles', *Comptes-rendus des séances de l'Académie des Inscriptions et Belles-Lettres*, 1981, 156–93

Lee, J.-Y., 'Die Götter im Vertrag zwischen Hannibal und Philipp V', in *Interpretationes: phönizische, griechische und römische Gottheiten im historischen Wandel*, ed. by L.-M. Günther and B. Morstadt (forthcoming)

Lembke, K., *Die Skulpturen aus dem Quellheiligtum von Amrit: Studie zur Akkulturation in Phönizien* (Mainz: Philipp von Zabern, 2004)

Lipiński, E., 'Baal Hamon', in *Dictionnaire de la civilisation Phénicienne et Punique*, ed. by E. Lipiński (Turnhout: Brepols, 1992), pp. 57–58

——, *Dieux et déesses de l'univers phénicien et punique*, Studia Phoenicia, 14 (Leuven: Peeters, 1995)

——, *Itineraria Phoenicia*, Studia Phoenicia, 18 (Leuven: Peeters, 2004)

——, 'Tanit', in *Dictionnaire de la civilisation Phénicienne et Punique*, ed. by E. Lipiński (Turnhout: Brepols, 1992), pp. 438–39

Melliti, K., 'Religion, politique et hellénisme à Carthage: approaches historiques', *Semitica et Classica: International Journal of Oriental and Mediterranean Studies*, 3 (2010), 91–98

Morstadt, B., *Thymiateria – Zeugnisse des Orientalisierungsprozesses*, Alter Orient und Altes Testament, 354 (Münster: Ugarit, 2009)

Niehr, H., *Ba'alšamem: Studien zu Herkunft, Geschichte und Rezeptionsgeschichte eines phönizischen Gottes*, Studia Phoenicia, 17 (Leuven: Peeters, 2003)

Niemeyer, H. G., 'Un nuevo santuario de la diosa Tanit en Cartago', in *Actas del IV congreso internacional de estudios fenicios y púnicos: Cádiz, 2 al 6 de Octubre de 1995*, ed. by M. E. Aubet and M. Barthélemy, 4 vols (Cádiz: Universidad de Cádiz, 2000), II, 635–42

Niemeyer, H. G., R. F. Docter, and K. Schmidt, 'Die Hamburger Grabung unter dem Decumanus Maximus von Karthago', in *Phönizisches und punisches Städtewesen: Akten der internationalen Tagung in Rom vom 21. bis 23. Februar 2007*, ed. by S. Helas and D. Marzoli, Iberia Archaeologica, 13 (Mainz: von Zabern, 2009), pp. 171–78

Niemeyer, H. G., and others, *Karthago: Die Ergebnisse der Hamburger Grabung unter dem Decumanus Maximus*, 2 vols (Mainz: von Zabern, 2007)

Nigro, L., 'Il Tempio del Kothon e il ruolo delle aree sacre nello sviluppo urbano di Mozia dall'VIII al IV sec. a.C.', in *Phönizisches und punisches Städtewesen: Akten der internationalen Tagung in Rom vom 21. bis 23. Februar 2007*, ed. by S. Helas and D. Marzoli, Iberia Archaeologica, 13 (Mainz: von Zabern, 2009), pp. 241–70

Oggiano, I., 'La "città" di Nora: Spazio urbano e territorio', in *Phönizisches und punisches Städtewesen: Akten der internationalen Tagung in Rom vom 21. bis 23. Februar 2007*, ed. by S. Helas and D. Marzoli, Iberia Archaeologica, 13 (Mainz: Philipp von Zabern, 2009), pp. 419–34

Oggiano, I., and J. Bonetto, 'Reise nach Westen: Die Koloniestadt Nora auf Sardinien ist eindrucksvolle Zeugin des phönizischen Kulturtransfers', *Antike Welt*, 35 (2004), 29–35

Oggiano, I., and P. Xella, 'Sidone e il suo territorio in età persiana: Epigrafia e archeologia', in *Phönizisches und punisches Städtewesen: Akten der internationalen Tagung in Rom vom 21. bis 23. Februar 2007*, ed. by S. Helas and D. Marzoli, Iberia Archaeologica, 13 (Mainz: von Zabern, 2009), pp. 69–81

Olmo Lete, G. del, ed., *Mythologie et religion des Sémites occidentaux*, 2 vols (Leuven: Peeters, 2008)

Pappalardo, E., 'Il tripillar shrine di Kommos', *Creta antica*, 3 (2002), 263–74

Picard, C., 'Installations cultuelles retrouvées au tophet de Salammbo', *Rivista degli studi orientali*, 42 (1967), 189–99

Pringle, D., 'The Crusader Cathedral of Tyre', *Levant*, 33 (2001), 165–88

Rakob, F., 'Neue Ausgrabungen in Karthago', *Antike Welt*, 23 (1992), 158–74

——, 'Ein punisches Heiligtum in Karthago und sein römischer Nachfolgebau', *Mitteilungen des Deutschen Archäologischen Instituts, Römische Abteilung*, 98 (1991), 33–80

Ramón, J., 'Es Cuieram', *Noticiario arqueológico hispánico: Arqueología*, 20 (1985), 225–53

Reyes, A. T., *Archaic Cyprus: A Study of the Textual and Archaeological Evidence* (Oxford: Oxford University Press, 1994)

Ribichini, S., 'Il sacello nel "tofet"', in *Da Pyrgi a Mozia: Studi sull'archaeologia del Mediterraneo in memoria di Antonia Ciasca*, ed. by M. G. A. Guzzo, M. Liverani, and P. Matthiae, Vicino Oriente Quaderno, 3.2 (Roma: Università degli studi di Roma 'La sapienza', 2002), pp. 425–39

Ribichini, S., and P. Xella, *La religione e fenicia e punica in Italia* (Roma: Libreria dello Stato, Istituto poligrafico e Zecca dello Stato, 1994)

Rigsby, K. J., *Asylia: Territorial Inviolability in the Hellenistic World* (Berkeley: University of California Press, 1996)

Rossignani, M. P., 'Il santuario di Astarte a Malta e le successive trasformazioni del suo volto monumentale', in *Phönizisches und punisches Städtewesen: Akten der internationalen Tagung in Rom vom 21. bis 23. Februar 2007*, ed. by S. Helas and D. Marzoli, Iberia Archaeologica, 13 (Mainz: von Zabern, 2009), pp. 115–30

Romero, S. A. M., A. I. M. Fernández, and J. J. D. Rodríguez, 'Nuevos vestigios del santuario gadirita de Melqart en Sancti Petri (San Fernando, Cádiz)', in *El Periodo Orientalizante: Actas del III Simposio Internacional de Arqueología de Mérida: Protohistoria del Mediterráneo Occidental*, ed. by S. C. Pérez and J. J. Ávila, 2 vols (Mérida: Conseja Superior de Investigaciones Científicas, 2005), II, 873–78

San Nicolás Pedraz, M. P., 'Nota sobre la tipología del santuario de Es Cuieram (Ibiza)', *Archivo español de arqueología*, 56 (1983), 239–41

Shaw, J. W., 'The Phoenician Shrine ca. 800 B.C. at Kommos in Crete', in *Actas del IV congreso internacional de estudios fenicios y púnicos: Cádiz, 2 al 6 de Octubre de 1995*, ed. by M. E. Aubet and M. Barthélemy, 4 vols (Cádiz: Universidad de Cádiz, 2000), III, 1107–19

——, 'Phoenicians in Southern Crete', *American Journal of Archaeology*, 93 (1989), 165–83

——, 'Der phönizische Schrein in Kommos auf Kreta', in *Archäologische Studien in Kontaktzonen der antiken Welt*, ed. by R. Rolle and K. Schmidt (Göttingen: Vandenoeck und Ruprecht, 1998), pp. 93–104

Smith, J. S., *Art and Society in Cyprus from the Bronze Age into the Iron Age* (Cambridge: Cambridge University Press, 2009)

Stucky, R. A., *Das Eschmun-Heiligtum von Sidon: Architektur und Inschriften*, Antike Kunst: Beiheft, 19 (Basel: Vereinigung der Freunde Antiker Kunst, 2005)

——, 'Das Heiligtum des Eschmun bei Sidon in vorhellenistischer Zeit', *Zeitschrift des Deutschen Palästina-Vereins*, 118 (2002), 66–86

Stucky, R. A., and H.-P. Mathys, 'Le Sanctuaire sidonien d'Echmoun', *Bulletin d'archéologie et d'architecture libanaises*, 4 (2000), 123–48

Xella, P., *Baal Hammon: Recherches sur l'identité et l'histoire d'un dieu phénico-punique* (Roma: Consiglio nazionale delle ricerche, 1991)

——, '"Divinités doubles" dans le monde phénico-punique', *Semitica*, 39 (1990), 167–75

——, *Religione e religioni in Siria-Palestina dall'Antico Bronzo all'epoca romana* (Roma: Carocci, 2007)

——, 'Sacrifici di bambini nel mondo Fenicio e Punico nelle testimonianze in lingua Greca e Latina', *Studi Epigrafici e Linguistici sul Vicino Oriente Antico*, 26 (2009), 59–100

——, 'Sull'introduzione del culto di Demetra e Kore a Cartagine', *Studi e Materiali di Storia delle Religioni*, 40 (1969), 215–28

Xella, P., and E. Lipiński, 'Shadrapha', in *Dictionnaire de la civilisation Phénicienne et Punique*, ed. by E. Lipiński (Turnhout: Brepols, 1992), pp. 407–08

Xella, P., and J.-Á. Zamora López, 'L'Inscription phénicienne de Bodashtart in situ à Bustan Bustān ēš-Šēẖ (Sidon) et son apport à l'histoire du sanctuaire', *Zeitschrift des Deutschen Palästina-Vereins*, 121 (2005), 119–29

Yon, M., 'Identifier les espaces urbains à Kition (Chypre)', in *Phönizisches und punisches Städtewesen: Akten der internationalen Tagung in Rom vom 21. bis 23. Februar 2007*, ed. by S. Helas and D. Marzoli, Iberia Archaeologica, 13 (Mainz: Philipp von Zabern, 2009), pp. 101–14

Yon, M., and S. M. Cecchini, 'Sanctuaries', in *Dictionnaire de la civilisation Phénicienne et Punique*, ed. by E. Lipiński (Turnhout: Brepols, 1992), pp. 387–89

Designing the Sacred in Early Ptolemaic Times: A Continuum of Concepts

Filip Coppens

The Egyptian Temple in the Thirtieth Dynasty and the Ptolemaic Period

The end of the Pharaonic period, which came to a close with the native Thirtieth Dynasty in the course of the fourth century BC, witnessed the organization of some of the most extensive construction and restoration projects on temple domains all over Egypt. Under the auspices of the pharaohs Nectanebo I (Nakhtnebef), Teos (Djedhor), and Nectanebo II (Nakhthorheb), numerous existing temples were restored to their former glory and further embellished and expanded (such as with kiosks, gateways, and porticos).[1] At the same time several new sanctuaries were constructed at the site of ruined or dismantled temples, often occupying a much larger area than their predecessors.[2] These enlarged sacred spaces soon came to be filled with a series of smaller sacred monuments such as *mammisis* or birth temples, freestanding chapels, cult terraces, sacred lakes, and other constructions that often served as stages during processions. The entire sacred area was concomitantly separated from its immediate surroundings by the erection of a monumental mud brick enclosure wall

[1] For example, the extension of the Thoth temple in Hermopolis Parva, additions to the Ptah temple at Memphis, or the entrance kiosk to the Amun temple in Hibis (Kharga oasis), to name but a few.

[2] This is for instance the case at Elephantine (Khnum temple) and Tell el-Balamun (Amun temple), to name just two sites at opposite ends of ancient Egypt.

Filip Coppens (filip.coppens@ff.cuni.cz) Czech Institute of Egyptology, Faculty of Philosophy and Arts, Charles University, Prague.

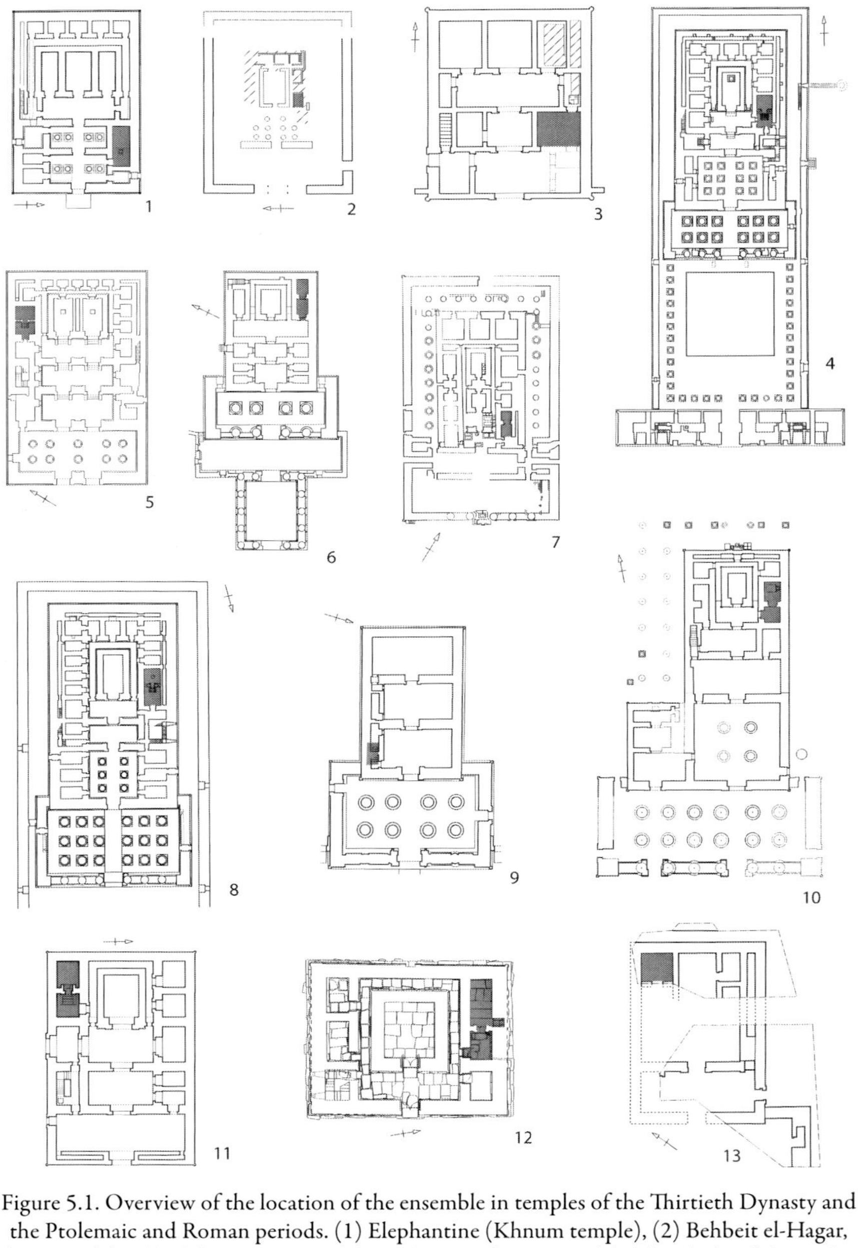

Figure 5.1. Overview of the location of the ensemble in temples of the Thirtieth Dynasty and the Ptolemaic and Roman periods. (1) Elephantine (Khnum temple), (2) Behbeit el-Hagar, (3) Philae, (4) Edfu, (5) Kom Ombo, (6) Elephantine (Satet temple), (7) Athribis, (8) Dendara, (9) Kalabsha, (10) Shanhur, (11) el-Qal'a, (12) Deir Shalwit, and (13) Komir. The grey-shaded area indicates the location of the complex in each individual temple. Drawing L. Vařeková.

— one of the most important and lasting contributions within the vast range of construction activities organized by the Thirtieth Dynasty rulers on the temple precincts.[3] This large-scale national building programme did not come to an end with the demise of the last native dynasty; it continued well into the Ptolemaic times (332–30 BC). The newly established Greek-Macedonian royal house, with the help and support of some of the Egyptian priesthoods, purposefully styled itself as the rightful heir of the indigenous dynasties. Part of their strategy for achieving this was their continuous support of major building and restoration activities on temple domains throughout the country — similar to the Thirtieth Dynasty pharaohs before them.[4]

At first glance the temple precincts of the Thirtieth Dynasty and Ptolemaic Egypt all seem to share a very basic set of architectural features or components in their general outlook and in the organization of the interior spaces of the temple and subsidiary sacred buildings — of course in keeping with the specific cultic function each space and the temple as a whole had to fulfil. This resulted in many of the temples of this period looking similar to one another *in general* (see for instance Figure 5.1). The specific manner in which the priestly designers of these monuments applied the basic architectural elements and concepts in the outlook or organized the exact sequence and location of chapels and halls in the interior from one temple to another resulted in each sanctuary also having its own particular flavour or style (again Figure 5.1). It is not too farfetched to claim that the temples of this era were designed on the basis of generally shared architectural concepts and features (with religious connotations), but at the same time the monuments received their own individual character owing to the specific manner in which these architectural concepts and components were applied in practice.

The basic layout of these temples appears to have been established over a relatively short period of time in the course of the Thirtieth Dynasty and the beginning of the Ptolemaic era in Egypt.[5] In essence, the typical temple of this period

[3] For instance the enclosure walls surrounding the temple domains in Karnak and Luxor or the sacred precinct of Coptos.

[4] On this topic consult for instance Hölbl, *A History of the Ptolemaic Empire*, pp. 77–123, or Fassone, 'The Last Indigenous Dynasties and the Ptolemaic Period', pp. 109–15.

[5] For a general introduction to the typical layout and the development of the temple in ancient Egypt from the end of the second millennium BC to the beginning of the first millennium AD (or from the Ramesside period to the Ptolemaic and Roman eras), consult for instance the overview in Assmann, *Ägypten, Theologie und Frömmigkeit einer frühen Hochkultur*, pp. 39–50; Finnestad, 'Temples of the Ptolemaic and Roman Period', pp. 185–237; Arnold,

Figure 5.2. The kiosk on the roof of the temple of Hathor in Dendara. © F. Coppens.

consists of a series of recurring spaces arranged in a linear scheme along an axis that leads from the heart of the temple to the exterior (once again Figure 5.1). The very core of the temple is usually formed by a freestanding sanctuary which often combines the role of the bark sanctuary and the home (in a monolith naos) for the statue of the main deity. The sanctuary is customarily surrounded by an ambulatory which leads to a series of chapels dedicated to the other gods residing in the temple.[6] Depending on the size of the monument and its state of completion, the sanctuary is preceded by one or more transversal halls.[7] These halls provide access to a series of side rooms and chapels and one or, in the case of some of the larger temples, two staircases to the roof of the temple. The roof of the temple survived to this day in only a few cases, but evidence exists that chapels dedicated to the resurrection of the god Osiris, associated with both

Temples of the Last Pharaohs; Niederberger, *Elephantine XX*, pp. 113–28; Spencer, *Naos of Nekhthorheb from Bubastis*, pp. 47–52; Wightman, *Sacred Spaces*, esp. pp. 123–43; and Zivie-Coche, 'Late Period Temples'.

[6] In a number of temples the ambulatory is not present. The sanctuary is then located against the rear wall of the temple, and the chapels dedicated to the other gods residing in the temple are usually positioned on either side of the sanctuary. See for example the temples of Isis at Philae (Figure 5.1/3), Satet at Elephantine (Figure 5.1/6), and Hathor in Deir el-Medina.

[7] These halls are sometimes referred to as the 'hall of appearance', the 'hall of offering', and the 'hall of the ennead' — the latter being located in front of the sanctuary. See for instance the online version of Gaber, 'The Central Hall in the Egyptian Temples of the Ptolemaic Period', with numerous references.

Figure 5.3. The pronaos of the temple of Horus in Edfu. © F. Coppens.

the netherworld and renewal, and a kiosk (Figure 5.2) appeared regularly on or near the roof.[8] The foundations and side walls of the temple often concealed entrances to hidden rooms and corridors (crypts).[9] In a number of temples, a pronaos with its typical screen walls (Figure 5.3), a large courtyard, and a massive entrance pylon were erected in front of the core of the monument.[10]

Like most other Egyptian temples, the monuments of this era have a tendency to an increased height of the floor level and decreased height of the ceiling as one nears the sanctuary, while the amount of daylight entering the temple becomes more and more limited towards its very core. The particular architectural layout of the temple clearly reflected the concept of a journey from darkness to light: the statues of the gods left the sanctuary immersed in darkness, and on their way out passed through ever-broader and brighter halls, to finally appear through the gate of the pylon like the morning sun on the horizon. These processions, reminiscent of the journey of the Sun, evoked notions of (re)birth, renewal, and revitalization. Another architectural feature typical of the temples of this period is the increased number of walls surrounding the temple proper.[11] This further separated the most sacred of spaces inside

[8] For instance the temples of Isis at Philae, Horus in Edfu, and Hathor in Dendara.

[9] Traunecker, 'Cryptes connues et inconnues des temples tardifs', pp. 21–46.

[10] Temples like Edfu, Kom Ombo, and Dendara (Figure 5.1/4, 5, 8) incorporate almost all of these elements, while other temples, like Deir Shalwit (Figure 5.1/12), were only equipped with the first transversal hall in front of the sanctuary.

[11] The best example of this practice is the temple of Horus in Edfu (Figure 5.1/4).

the already enclosed temple precinct from the outside world. These extensions especially suited the many processions taking place inside the temple: the increasing number of enclosure walls formed a series of large corridors that were used during the numerous festive processions which could thus take place in the open air but were still hidden from view.[12]

The ancient Egyptian priests designing the temples of the Late Period and the Ptolemaic and Roman eras did not create the typical layout of these sacred spaces *ab ovo*. The priestly designers had at their disposal a wide repertoire of traditions and concepts — whether in text, image, or architecture — from which specific elements could be selected and combined into distinctive combinations that would best suit the function a specific sacred space, whether the whole temple or a specific part of it, had to fulfil. These ancient concepts were not slavishly copied, but continuously analysed and (re)interpreted, resulting in the use of old traditions in an innovative manner and the introduction of (apparently) new elements against a backdrop of existing traditions. These new architectural elements did not appear out of thin air; as with any developments in architecture, new building elements are already anticipated in some form or other in earlier times.[13] It is the specific selection and combination of various elements that eventually results in apparent innovative alterations. A number of the constructions considered characteristic of temple precincts from the Thirtieth Dynasty and the Ptolemaic era, such as the cult terrace in front of the entrance pylon, the birth temple or *mammisi*, or the pronaos with its typical screen walls (see again Figure 5.3), all have their origin in eras preceding the Thirtieth Dynasty.[14]

The typical layout of the main temple — the focal point of any temple precinct — can also be traced back to earlier times. The basic form of the Late Period/early Ptolemaic temple type originated already during the Late New Kingdom. It finds its precursors in temples of the Ramesside period, such as the temple of Khonsu on the precinct of Amun at Karnak or the temple of Ramses III at Medinet Habu, but as already seen through the eyes of Kushite and

[12] Stadler, 'Procession', and Coppens, 'Temple Festivals', with many references to older studies.

[13] Certain architectural elements typical of Gothic churches, such as the ambulatory of the apse or the pointed arches, already appeared as separate elements in Romanesque architecture. It was merely the combination of these individual architectural elements within a single building that eventually gave rise to the Gothic style. See Arnold, *Temples of the Last Pharaohs*, p. 353, n. 2, and Pevsner, *An Outline of European Architecture*, pp. 50–71.

[14] Arnold, *Temples of the Last Pharaohs*, pp. 277–308, or Wightman, *Sacred Spaces*, pp. 126–31. On the *mammisi*, see also Kockelmann, 'Birth House (Mammisi)'.

Saite designers. It is in other words a Late Period interpretation of Ramesside architectural concepts.[15] It is difficult to establish how much of this development took place during the time of the Third Intermediate Period and the Late Period given that only a small number of temples remain from the first half of the first millennium BC.

The importance given to age-old traditions and concepts specifically in the priestly milieus of ancient Egypt should come as no surprise. The continuous presence of foreign rulers on the throne of the land throughout most of the first millennium BC might have been an important reason why so much attention appears to have been paid to indigenous traditions in text, image, sculpture, and architecture. But a priestly milieu — whether in ancient societies, medieval, or modern — is in essence always traditional or conservative. One should in this instance not be misled by the use of the terms 'tradition' and 'conservative', which in modern times have often received a pejorative connotation. The concept that a newly created sacred space in ancient Egypt was constructed in a traditional manner was not without importance. Keeping in touch with the age-old traditions infused these monuments with a notion of timelessness and provided them with a certain ancestral authority: something that had been proven to work for centuries, if not millennia, was not to be altered or abandoned on a mere whim. The use of traditional elements, dating back through the centuries, provided these temples with a notion of spatial and temporal unity, which was fundamental to the maintenance of social and cosmic order — the key function of any temple in ancient Egypt. The temple in this manner acquired a seemingly timeless architectural form. This does not imply that no new elements would be introduced into the layout and decoration of these sacred spaces. It is obvious, even to the casual observer, that the typical temple plan of the Ramesside period underwent numerous modifications throughout the first millennium BC before the basic layout of Thirtieth Dynasty and early Ptolemaic temples came into existence. The priests designing new temples were always balancing between maintaining the traditional and developing contemporary forms in architecture and decoration as they analysed and interpreted the work of their predecessors. The introduction of new elements was for the most part a gradual process taking place within a framework of traditions and rules. The pace of this process was not steady, but continuously changed over time. Major political events, such as the occupation or liberation of the coun-

[15] This is illustrated by, among many other authors, Arnold, *Temples of the Last Pharaohs*, pp. 25–28 and 305–09; Niederberger, *Elephantine XX*, pp. 113–15 and 118–21, and Wightman, *Sacred Spaces*, pp. 131–32.

try, usually provided the necessary input for a speedier inclusion of new ideas and concepts or led to a renaissance of older traditions.[16]

The ancient Egyptians themselves noted on more than one occasion that the temples of the Late Period and Ptolemaic and Roman times were built according to ancient models and rules. In temple inscriptions reference is sometimes made to the mythological origin or history of the temple. A mythological, imaginary prototype of the temple, erected in ancient times on a low mound in the river — the so-called primeval hill — is recalled and in detail described in order to justify the existence and specific layout of the new building. The newly created sacred space is represented as a direct descendant of this mythical monument.[17] Sets of inscriptions and scenes on the walls of the Ptolemaic temple of Edfu and the Roman pronaos of Dendara also suggest that the newly created sacred monument was organized and constructed following instructions of Imhotep, the famous architect of Djoser's step pyramid built in Saqqara in the Old Kingdom.[18] Although the historical accuracy of these statements is questionable at best, it is the idea behind these claims that is of particular importance. It is not the accuracy of the content that is important, rather than the mere fact that these statements were made and engraved for eternity on the temple walls. It indicates the importance the Egyptian designers attached to building within an existing framework of rules and traditions. The new temple thus became endorsed with ancestral authority.

The continuation of traditional concepts is not limited to temple architecture and layout; it is also attested in the text and images that were applied to the temple walls. This decorative programme, similar to the specific layout of the temple and its individual rooms, very much defined the sacred space and the ritual actions that took place within it. The priests who designed the decorative programme for the individual temple rooms appear to have had at their disposal an extremely rich repertoire of ancient traditions and texts that could be consulted in the temple libraries. The numerous inscriptions and reliefs engraved on the temple walls at this period in history represent the entire spectrum of ancient Egyptian religion, knowledge, and thought. The Ptolemaic temple walls contain ritual and foundation scenes and texts, hymns, proces-

[16] One can think for instance of the archaic tendencies in architecture and sculpture coming to the fore during Saitic times (Twenty-Sixth Dynasty), following the Nubian presence in Egypt (Twenty-Fifth Dynasty). On this topic, see for instance Tiradritti, *Pharaonic Renaissance*.

[17] Reymond, *The Mythical Origin of the Egyptian Temple*.

[18] Chassinat, *Le Temple d'Edfou*, VI, 10, and Cauville, *Le Temple de Dendara*, XIII, 58–59.

Figure 5.4.
The complex of *wabet* and court in the temple of Horus in Edfu. Photo: M. Frouz – Archive of the Czech Institute of Egyptology, Charles University in Prague.

sions, cosmogonies and cosmologies, religious calendars, astronomical depictions and texts, medical treatises, rules for priests, topographical lists of cultic sites, canals, trees, and mounds, recipes for the production of ointments, unguents, and other products, detailed descriptions of the different rooms within the temple (including their measurements, names, location, and function), and so much more.[19] Far from engraving mere copies onto the temple walls, the priests competently and purposefully used older material as a starting point for further developments and gave new life and purpose to numerous traditions through their innovative reworking, reinterpretation, and re-edition of the ancient material.

The priestly designers of the typical layout and decorative programme of the temples of the Thirtieth Dynasty and the Ptolemaic and Roman eras appear to have been very well aware of their position in the history of temple development in ancient Egypt. They were not only steeped in millennia-old traditions, nor did

[19] See the overview in Leitz, *Quellentexte zur ägyptischen Religion*.

they produce a mere copy of older monuments or texts. Instead they combined architectural, textual, and visual elements from various contexts in an innovative manner and added new ideas and concepts to create something that was not new but rather the next step in a process that had been going on for generations.

In the following sections of this paper I intend to take a closer look at how a specific sacred space appears to have been designed in this era. Since the characteristic layout of these temples was established over a relatively short period of time in the course of the Thirtieth Dynasty and the beginning of Ptolemaic Egypt, I will focus on a specific complex or ensemble of two rooms that appears — as if out of nowhere[20] — specifically in this particular period. The complex consists of an open court or light-well chamber and an elevated chapel (Figure 5.4). In Egyptological literature it is often identified as the *wabet* (*wᶜb.t*) or the complex of *wabet* and court,[21] although the ensemble is also regularly mentioned in inscriptions as the 'seat of the first feast' (*s.t ḥb tpy*).[22] I would like to start by defining this architectural complex in detail.[23] The analysis of the various ensembles has clearly revealed that each complex — despite local variations in its layout (often related to the size of the temple) and in the decorative scheme applied to its walls (due to intrusions of the local theology) — contains a number of recurring characteristic components that make it possible to define the essential elements of the ensemble.

In the final part of this paper I intend to identify and illustrate some of the processes at work when this sacred space was designed in the course of the Thirtieth Dynasty and the early Ptolemaic period. I will attempt to show that the typical layout and decoration that characterizes this complex is one of the coincidental results of developments that took place in the first millennium BC.[24] The complex has its roots in much older traditions and concepts that were gradually brought together and eventually resulted in the creation of this particular sacred space with its specific function in the temple. I do not wish to

[20] See for instance Zivie-Coche, 'Late Period Temples', pp. 9 and 10.

[21] Traunecker, 'Les Ouabet des temples d'el–Qal'a et de Chenhour', pp. 241–82, and Coppens, *The Wabet*.

[22] On the various terms in use for the complex, consult Coppens, 'A Variety of Designations', pp. 13–26, and Coppens, *The Wabet*, pp. 55–72.

[23] A much more detailed overview can be found in Coppens, *The Wabet*.

[24] I intend to sketch the broad lines in this development without going into too much detail on specific variations and exceptions. This format evidently implies the use of some generalizations, but a lot of specific aspects of this complex have already been analysed in depth in numerous previous articles, to which reference will be made at the appropriate place.

claim that this development was preordained; the complex of *wabet* and court was certainly not the only possible (let alone correct) outcome of a development in thought, decoration, and architecture. A different interpretation of religious, architectural, and decorative concepts employed at any time throughout the first millennium BC could have very easily resulted in a complex that might have looked very different, or it might not even have come into existence at all. It was the specific interpretation, selection, variation, and combination of various elements, sources, and concepts that eventually and coincidentally resulted in the apparent innovative appearance of this particular complex in the temple in the course of the Thirtieth Dynasty.

Defining the Wabet

The *wabet*, as with any other room in any other temple, was in essence a manufactured spatial framework designed for a specific interaction between this world and the divine. Its particular layout and the texts and images applied to its walls were carefully chosen as the entire space was consciously designed to serve very specific ceremonial needs. In order to comprehend the typical layout and decorative programme of this complex, one first has to understand the role this space was supposed to fulfil in the temple.

Numerous Egyptian inscriptions and reliefs provide a basic understanding of the main function of this complex: it was first and foremost an area in the temple to which statues of the main deities were brought (in procession) to be prepared for their renewal. The preparation involved a series of clothing rites (undressing, purifying, anointing, dressing with coloured linen, providing with protective regalia in the guise of necklaces and pectorals, and censing) and the offering of a wide variety of food and other products.[25] Once prepared, the act of regeneration or renewal was achieved by exposing the statues of the gods to the rays of the sun.[26] This ritual could take place in the open court of the com-

[25] For an overview, consult Coppens, 'Linen, Unguents and Pectorals', pp. 42–49; Coppens, *The Wabet*, pp. 195–206.

[26] Traunecker, 'Les Ouabet des temples d'el-Qal'a et de Chenhour', pp. 247, 251, 258–60, and 264–66, and Coppens, *The Wabet*, pp. 147–50. For instance Rochemonteix and Chassinat, *Le Temple d'Edfou*, I, 412, 14–15: 'Horus Behdety went round (to) the columned chapel (= the wabet) during his first feast, Hathor, the mistress of Dendara, was with him, while their enneads were with them, the day of the feast of the opening of the year for their union with the sun disc.' Similar inscriptions are included in Philae Bénédite 16, 9–10; Rochemonteix and Chassinat, *Le Temple d'Edfou*, I, 413, 12–16; 414, 2–7; Chassinat, *Le Temple d'Edfou*, VII, 16, 1–5; Chassinat,

Figure 5.5.
The court of the ensemble in the temple of Hathor in Dendara.
© F. Coppens.

plex (Figure 5.5), in a kiosk on the roof of the temple (Figure 5.2), or in the open space in front of the temple. The rite is known as the 'union with the sun disc' (*ẖnm-itn*),[27] but many inscriptions also refer to the statue being reunited

Le Temple de Dendara, IV, 149, 17–150, 1; 150, 5–7; 151, 11–13; 185, 14–186, 2; 186, 5–7; 233, 7–234, 1; 234, 6–10, and Pantalacci and Traunecker, *Le Temple d'el-Qal'a*, II, 166, and no. 195; and 167, and no. 215.

[27] For more information on this rite, consult Sauneron, *Les Fêtes religieuses d'Esna*, pp. 122–32; Daumas, 'Sur trois représentations de Nout à Dendara', pp. 373–400; and Coppens, *The Wabet*, pp. 12–13, 83–84, 141–44, and 195–98.

with the *ba* of the god.[28] The exact time frame of the rituals performed in the complex differed from one temple to another, but in general it seems to have revolved mainly around the final days of the last month of the year (Mesore), the five epagomenal days preceding the New Year, New Year's Day, and the first days of the first month of the New Year (Thoth). The period of the New Year was undoubtedly the best suited time for any act of renewal and rejuvenation as it coincided with the annual arrival of the Nile inundation which brought new life to the (agricultural) land of Egypt.

The importance of these renewal rituals went far beyond the scope of the individual statues or even the individual temple. In order to grasp their importance, one has to take into consideration the manner in which the ancient Egyptians viewed and understood their surroundings. The ancient dwellers at the Nile, like any other classical civilization, were keen observers of the world in which they lived. The livelihood of the individual, as well as of the state, was for a large part dependent on the knowledge of their natural surroundings and, especially, the ability to put this knowledge into practical use. Just as the ancient Egyptians tried to understand, shape, and control their natural surroundings, like the annual inundation, these various natural phenomena also greatly influenced the outlook and organization of the ancient Egyptian state and society. This happened on a practical level, for instance in the manner the country was administered and organized in relation to the annual floods, but also on a religious level. The ancient Egyptians' understanding and perception of their natural surroundings had an enormous impact on their religious thoughts and concepts, the myths created to provide insight into the order of the world and of the universe, and the organization and function of various religious activities and practices. By observing the skies during the day and night, the ancient Egyptians noticed that some heavenly bodies seemingly hardly moved (like the circumpolar stars), while others followed specific patterns. Most importantly, they noticed the cyclical nature of these movements. In the daily rising and setting of the sun, the monthly phases of the moon, the always similar movements of numerous stars and constellations, but also the yearly coming and going of seasons, or the ever-recurring annual inundation of the Nile, the Egyptians observed the cycli-

[28] For instance Rochemonteix and Chassinat, *Le Temple d'Edfou*, I, 417; Chassinat, *Le Temple d'Edfou*, VII, 16, 1–5, and Chassinat, *Le Temple de Dendara*, IV, 232, 5–233, 3. For the concept of the 'ba' of the god in ancient Egypt, i.e. the manifestation of its divine power and greatness, and the god's ability to assume or unite with a variety of physical forms, consult for instance Žabkar, *A Study of the Ba Concept*; Bell, 'Ancient Egyptian Personhood', pp. 39–40; and Janák, 'A Question of Size'.

cal aspect of many natural phenomena. This understanding influenced not only how the ancient Egyptians understood the world they lived in, but also their concept of time. Unlike the modern western world, which generally considers time to be linear, the Egyptians worked with a cyclical concept of time (*nḥḥ*) next to the linear one (*ḏt*). The cyclical concept was based on the constant recurring of the same patterns. Many ancient Egyptian rituals, festivals, and ceremonies (whether funeral, royal, or temple) appear to have been designed on the basis of these observations. Beside their cyclical nature, the many rituals and festivals, such as the daily temple sanctuary ritual or the annual celebrations of the New Year, concomitantly had the very crucial task of safeguarding and ensuring the continuation of the cyclical nature of the natural phenomena that inspired them — for instance making sure the sun would rise again in the morning or that the life-giving inundation would arrive again year after year. These rituals and festivities were in other words crucial to maintaining the cosmic order.

The time of the New Year did not revolve only around the renewal of the statues of the main deities residing in the temple. The related rituals were also very closely associated with the renewal and confirmation of kingship.[29] The presence in the *wabet* of several references to kingship and its confirmation is not really surprising given that the time of the New Year, when the renewal of the statues of the deities took place through their exposure to the sun, was in ancient Egypt also considered one of the ideal occasions for the ruler to be confirmed in his power as the legitimate heir to the throne.[30] In the decorative scheme the ruler is still depicted performing the necessary rites for which he is granted the kingship over the two lands, but it is the kingship of the gods — such as Horus in Edfu and Hathor and Isis in Dendara — and its confirmation and renewal that has taken the pride of place over the earthly kingship. Indirectly, through the confirmation of the divine kingship, the legitimacy of the Ptolemaic pharaoh and the confirmation of his rule are of course also evoked, but he is no longer the central figure of the festival. A small number of inscriptions and reliefs provide indirect references to the fact that the complex functioned not only at the time of the New Year in relation to the renewal and confirmation of kingship. These inscriptions indicate that the complex functioned during festivals organized to perform and celebrate the renewal and confirmation of the divine kingship on various occasions throughout the year.[31]

[29] See for instance Coppens and Vymazalová, 'Long Live the King!', pp. 73–102.

[30] Barta, 'Königskrönung', p. 532; Louant, 'Harsomtus the Child', pp. 225–49, and Hölbl, *A History of the Ptolemaic Empire*, pp. 88 and 108.

[31] See the overview in Coppens and Vymazalová, 'Long Live the King!', pp. 77–87.

To summarize, the complex of *wabet* and court appears to have functioned first and foremost as the place where the statues of the main deities of the temple were prepared for their renewal in the period surrounding the New Year and the arrival of the inundation. A series of preparatory rituals related to the renewal and confirmation of kingship — in the first place the divine kingship and through association the 'earthly' kingship — also took place in this ensemble at the time of the New Year and on several other occasions throughout the year.

Having familiarized ourselves with the function this sacred space was supposed to fulfil in the temple, the question can be asked, How was it designed to best serve these specific and ceremonial needs? The sacred space of the complex is characterized or defined by a large number of different aspects, such as its occurrence in time and space, its specific location within the temple, the typical architectural layout, the decorative programme applied to the walls, and the designations the ancient Egyptians used when referring to it. All these elements combined define the *wabet* and created the stage on which a set of rites related to renewal activities took place.

Time

The complex has so far been identified in nine and suggested for at least four other temples (see the table on the following page).[32] The nine ensembles illustrate the complex's occurrence in the temple over a period of almost half a millennium, approximately from the middle of the fourth century BC until the end of the first century or perhaps even the first half of the second century AD. Of the ten ensembles that have currently been identified with certainty, only one dates to the Thirtieth Dynasty, five to the Ptolemaic period, and four to the first century of Roman presence in Egypt.

The inscriptions refer for instance to various confirmations of the kingship of Horus in Edfu throughout the year, or the celebration and confirmation of the investiture or enthronment of the two main goddesses of the temple of Dendara: Hathor (on Thoth 1 and 20, and Paophi 5) and Isis (on the night of the fourth to the fifth epagomenal day).

[32] The identification of the ensemble in the temples of Isis and Osiris in Behbeit el-Hagar, Satet at Elephantine, and Anuket and Nephthys in Komir is not certain yet due to the absence of conclusive information: Traunecker, 'Les Ouabet des temples d'el-Qal'a et de Chenhour', pp. 267–69; Niederberger, *Elephantine XX*, pp. 120–28 and 137; and Coppens, *The Wabet*, pp. 20–22, 31–35, and 45–46.

Overview of the occurrence of the complex of *wabet* and court in time and space.

Temple	Architecture	Decorative Scheme
Elephantine (Khnum)	Nectanebo II	no remains
Behbeit el–Hagar	*Nectanebo II*	*Ptolemaios II*
Philae	Ptolemaios II	Ptolemaios II
Edfu	Ptolemaios III	Ptolemaios IV
Kom Ombo	Ptolemaios VI	Ptolemaios VI (fragmentary)
Elephantine (Satet)	*Ptolemaios VI*	*no remains*
Athribis (Wannina)	Ptolemaios XII	Ptolemaios XII (fragmentary)
Dendara	Ptolemaios XII	Cleopatra VII
Kalabsha	Augustus	undecorated
Shanhur	Augustus	Caligula
el-Qal'a	Augustus	Claudius
Deir Shalwit	first century AD	undecorated
Komir	*Antoninus Pius*	*no remains*

Space

Viewing the temples that contained an ensemble on the map of Egypt, one notes that, with the exception of Behbeit el-Hagar, all of these temples are located in Upper Egypt (Map 4). The location suggests that this ensemble might have been a typical component of the Ptolemaic and Roman temples of southern Egypt. But one has to keep in mind that the absence of complexes of *wabet* and court in temples to the north of Wannina might be due to the poor state of preservation and insufficient publication of the temples in the north rather than any purposeful geographical planning done by the ancient Egyptian priests. The constant need for building material for the ever-expanding cities of the Delta and Middle Egypt has led to at least partial if not total destruction of many temples in this part of the country, and their state of preservation often does not allow a detailed reconstruction of the exact layout of these monuments.[33] On the other hand, numerous temples from Ptolemaic and Roman times are known in the Fayum and the western oases. Not a single one of the better preserved temples in this area contains such an ensemble,[34] which does suggest that the complex could have been a typical architectural compo-

[33] For instance Hölbl, *Altägypten im Römischen Reich*, pp. 47–52 on the state of the Roman temple remains in the Delta and Middle Egypt.

[34] See for instance Willeitner, *Die ägyptischen Oasen*, and Hölbl, *Altägypten im Römischen Reich.*

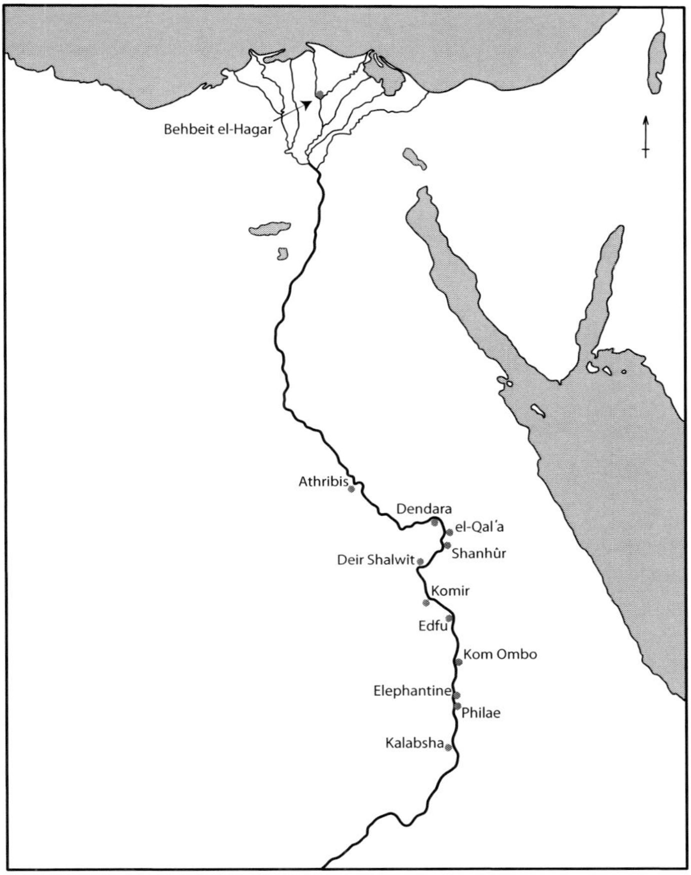

Map 4. The location of the temples containing a complex of *wabet* and court. Drawing L. Vařeková.

nent only in Upper Egyptian temples. Only further research and excavation of the monuments from this period in the Delta and Middle Egypt might eventually shed more light on this issue.

Location

The location of the ensemble in the temple appears to have been dictated by a simple rule under the Thirtieth Dynasty and in Ptolemaic times.[35] In a temple located on the west bank of the Nile (Edfu and Dendara) or on an island in

[35] Traunecker, 'Les Ouabet des temples d'el-Qal'a et de Chenhour', pp. 267–69; Niederberger, *Elephantine XX*, pp. 137, table 2; and Coppens, *The Wabet*, pp. 48–50.

Figure 5.6.
The complex in the temple of Hathor in Dendara.
© F. Coppens.

the Nile (Elephantine and Philae), the complex is always located to the right of the sanctuary, when looking from the outside in. In a temple erected on the east bank of the Nile (Kom Ombo), the complex is located to the left of the sanctuary (see Figure 5.1/4 and 8; 1, 6, and 3; 5). It seems that this rule was no longer followed so strictly in Roman times. The rule still applies for the temples of el-Qal'a and Deir Shalwit, but is no longer at work in Kalabsha (on the west bank, but complex on the left side), and Shanhur (on the east bank, but ensemble on the right side). The orientation of the complex in general follows the orientation of the temple. Only Philae (perpendicular to the temple axis) and Kalabsha (reversal of the orientation) are different.

The exact location of the complex in the temple moved over time from the vicinity of the hypostyle hall to the very core of the temple near the 'hall of the ennead' and the sanctuary (see Figure 5.1). In the temple of Khnum at

Elephantine (Thirtieth Dynasty), the ensemble was accessible through the first hypostyle hall which most likely functioned as the 'hall of appearance'. In the second oldest example — the open court at Philae from the reign of Ptolemaios II Philadelphos — the complex is already located closer to the very heart of the temple and features alongside the 'hall of offering'. It is connected with both the 'hall of appearance' and the 'hall of the ennead' by means of intermediary rooms. In the temple of Edfu, at the time of Ptolemaios III Euergetes I, the ensemble appears to have reached its characteristic and final location in the temple: accessible through the 'hall of the ennead' and (almost) at the height of the sanctuary — in other words in the most sacred part of the temple. In the temple of Edfu the ensemble is directly accessible through the 'hall of the ennead' in front of the sanctuary. In several monumental temples like Dendara and Kom Ombo, an intermediary room connected this transversal hall in front of the sanctuary with the complex. The same room often also connects the ensemble with a turning staircase to the roof of the temple. In the smaller temples the complex is accessed either immediately from the first transversal hall (Shanhur) or from the ambulatory (Deir Shalwit and el-Qal'a), while in Kalabsha the complex is located almost on the roof of the temple. The main entrance into the complex is positioned either in a lateral wall of the open court (Elephantine, Philae, Edfu, Shanhur, el-Qal'a, and Deir Shalwit) or looks directly towards the facade of the *wabet* (Kom Ombo, Dendara, and Kalabsha).

Layout

The ever-growing darkness each visitor encounters when proceeding from the temple entrance to the central sanctuary is in a number of temples chased away by the appearance of a few rays of sunlight in a small court or light-well chamber (Figures 5.4, 5.5, and 5.6). This court is part of an architectural ensemble with a very distinct layout: a court, open to the light of day, and a slightly elevated platform with a chapel, accessible from the court through a flight of steps. From the very beginning of its existence, at the end of the Thirtieth Dynasty, the ensemble consisted of these two very specific parts, which made the complex unique in more aspects than one. Any other chapel in the temple, whether accessible from the ambulatory or the transversal halls, consisted of a single room or at best a combination of two chambers, connected by a doorway.[36] The

[36] For instance the complexes of the 'Mansion of the Sistrum' and of the 'Throne of Ra' in the temple of Hathor in Dendara come to mind. On these complexes, see especially Preys, *Les Complexes de la Demeure du Sistre et du Trône de Rê*.

presence of a light-well chamber and an elevated chapel must have made (and still makes) the ensemble stand out in any temple of which it was a part.

The dimensions of the two distinct parts of the complex do not seem to have been governed by specific rules.[37] The difference in size between the Ptolemaic and Roman ensembles appears to be due to the diminished size of the entire temple in Roman times.[38] The ancient Egyptian description of the complex in the temples of Dendara and Edfu indicates that 8 square el/cubits[39] constitute the ideal dimensions for each part of the ensemble.[40] The complexes in the smaller Roman temples suggest a size of the open court of *c.* 4 square cubits and a slightly elongated chapel: *c.* 4 cubits wide and 5 to 8 cubits deep.

The two parts of the complex were always clearly separated from one another by a difference in the height of the floor level. The floor of the light-well chamber was in all temples located more or less at the same level as the floor in the other parts of the temple. The chapel was, however, always positioned on top of a platform, and the difference in floor level between the two spaces could be bridged by means of a small staircase.[41] It is surprisingly the only sacred space in temples of this era that has been positioned on a higher level than any other room in the temple, including the sanctuary that housed the statue of the main deity. This very characteristic feature has already been observed by many scholars that have studied this complex, but little attention has been paid to the reasons behind it. I will attempt to suggest a plausible reason for the specific outlook of the elevated chapel in the final section of this paper, when looking at possible precursors in the layout and decorative programme of this complex.

In the Thirtieth Dynasty and during the early Ptolemaic period, the separation between the two spaces — the open court and platform — appears to have been suggested only by a difference in the height of the floor level. During the reign of Ptolemaios III Euergetes I, the *wabet* in the temple of Horus at Edfu acquired the typical facade for the first time. In the wider ensembles, like

[37] See the overview in Coppens, *The Wabet*, p. 52, table III.

[38] Arnold, *Temples of the Last Pharaohs*, p. 226.

[39] One el or cubit being 52.30 to 52.50 cm: Arnold, *The Encyclopedia of Ancient Egyptian Architecture*, p. 61, and Arnold, *Building in Egypt*, pp. 10 and 251–52.

[40] Chassinat, *Le Temple d'Edfou*, VII, 16, 1–2; Cauville, 'Les Inscriptions dédicatoires du temple d'Hathor à Dendara', pp. 101–02, and Cauville and Devauchelle, 'Les Mesures réelles du temple d'Edfou', p. 24.

[41] The difference between the floor levels of the two spaces differs from temple to temple, but it is generally higher in the Ptolemaic monuments. It ranges from a few dozen centimetres to over a metre: Coppens, *The Wabet*, p. 52, table III.

in Edfu and Dendara (Figures 5.4 and 5.6), the facade of the *wabet* consists of three clearly defined components on either side of the small staircase in the middle: a screen wall, attached to the lateral walls of the complex, a column that carries the architrave above the doorway, and a broken door lintel that holds the wooden doors used to separate the complex from the court. In Roman times, when the size of the newly constructed sanctuaries could no longer rival the monumental temples of the previous Ptolemaic period and the ensemble diminished in size, the screen wall was often reduced to a very small wall (Kalabsha, el-Qal'a, and Deir Shalwit) or a mere carving into the pilaster that carried the columns (Shanhur).

The facade of the *wabet* with the broken door lintels, columns, and screen walls is a very typical architectural feature of the temples of this era.[42] The same type of facade was for instance also used for the colonnades surrounding the birth temples or for kiosks (Figure 5.2). The likeness to a kiosk is not without importance. Kiosks on the temple precincts often served as transitional spaces or resting stages during festive processions, a function also served by the complex as an important processional stage during renewal festivities. In combination with the light-well chamber, it also brings to mind the large open court and the pronaos preceding the most sacred area of the temple (Figure 5.3). The combination gives the impression that the complex is a temple within a temple.[43] The elevated platform upon which the chapel is placed might perhaps be a reference to the aforementioned primeval hill on which the first, mythical temple came into existence.

The combination of the open court with the facade of the chapel also creates an interesting (ritual) effect of light and shadow. The ensemble combines the openness and lightness of the court with the seclusion and darkness of the chapel lying beyond. The facade with columns and screen walls served to close off the space in the manner of a wall, but concomitantly rendered this boundary visually permeable, suggesting that the visual aspect (light/dark and hidden/open) must have been an important aspect of the ensemble's layout and the rituals performed within. The presence of rays of sunlight in the open court, falling on the facade and into the elevated chapel, strongly reminds us of the final stage of the rites performed in the complex: the renewal through the 'union with the sun disc' as the rays of the sun god fall upon the statues.

[42] Arnold, *Temples of the Last Pharaohs*, pp. 277–88, 303–04, and Arnold, *The Encyclopedia of Ancient Egyptian Architecture*, pp. 130, 180, and 211.

[43] See already Traunecker, 'Les Ouabet des temples d'el-Qal'a et de Chenhour', pp. 276–77.

Access to a crypt, located in the foundations of the temple, is another important recurring feature in the complex. In the case of the Thirtieth Dynasty examples it is at present not yet certain whether access to a crypt was located within the complex or in its immediate vicinity. In Ptolemaic times, in the oldest ensemble at Philae, access to the crypts of the temple is in an intermediary room that connects the complex with the 'hall of the ennead' and the sanctuary. From the time the ensemble was constructed in the temple of Edfu onwards, access to the crypt is usually located in the court (Edfu and Dendara) or in the immediate vicinity of the complex (Kom Ombo). In almost all Roman examples the *wabet* itself contains the entrance to the crypt (Shanhur, Kalabsha, Deir Shalwit), while in el-Qal'a the entrance is located under the staircase that connects both areas of the ensemble. The crypt could consist of a long corridor with a series of rooms (Dendara and Edfu) or a single small room/space (all Roman examples).

Claude Traunecker's study of crypts in first-millennium BC temples indicates that these hidden chambers could be used as a setting for ritual activities or to store different types of cultic material that would only be used at specific times.[44] The grand festivities surrounding important festivals undoubtedly required a much larger amount of cultic equipment than what was commonly used during the daily activities in the temple. The crypts also housed a large number of statues. Inscriptions from the temple of Dendara for instance refer to over a hundred statues housed in the underground crypts,[45] while the excavation of the crypt underneath the *wabet* in the temple of Shanhur brought to light several fragments of the statuary that was once stored there.[46] For most of the year, these statues were hidden from sight and were only brought out of the

[44] Traunecker, 'Krypta', pp. 823–30; Traunecker, 'Dimensions réelles et dimensions imaginaires des dieux de l'Egypte'; and Traunecker, 'Cryptes connues et inconnues des temples tardifs'.

[45] Traunecker, 'Dimensions réelles et dimensions imaginaires des dieux de l'Egypte', p. 60; Cauville, 'Les Statues cultuelles de Dendera d'après les inscriptions pariétales', p. 73–117; and Waitkus, *Die Texte in den unteren Krypten des Hathortempels von Dendara*, pp. 239–42. Similar but smaller and less preserved inventories can be found for instance in the Late Period temple of Mut in Karnak (reign of Taharqa) and the Ptolemaic and Roman temples of Opet in Karnak, Tod, and Armant, or on Demotic papyri, such as Papyri Berlin 23591 (in Zauzich, *Aegyptische Handschriften II*) and Papyri Berlin 6848 (in Spiegelberg, *Demotische Papyrus aus den Königlichen Museen zu Berlin*).

[46] The fragments included an Osirid figure, the top part of a statue of two cobras, and part of the head and torso of a goddess; see Traunecker and Willems, 'Chenhour: Rapport des travaux de 1996 et 1997', p. 127, plate 25B–C, and Coppens and Willems, 'Chenhour et la region Coptite', pp. 117–18, figs 51–52.

crypts when they had a role to play during a particular feast or festival, such as the festivities surrounding the New Year. In the temple of Hathor in Dendara, for instance, the inscriptions by the entrances to the crypts usually list in detail the specific statues that will be taken out at the time of specific festivities. The inscriptions on the doorjambs of room A in the west crypt no. 1, accessible from the light-well chamber,[47] for instance indicate that the statues from rooms A and F will be used during the festivities of the investiture or enthronment of Hathor (Paophi 5) and Isis (fourth epagomenal day).[48]

Wolfgang Waitkus's detailed study of the scenes and inscriptions from the three underground crypts in the temple of Hathor in Dendara, including the aforementioned west crypt no. 1, revealed that these underground chambers could symbolize the netherworld.[49] The prolonged presence of the statues in the crypts to the ancient Egyptian mind appears to have had consequences for the vitality of the statues.[50] The statuary came to be seen as deprived of its essence — the presence of the deity in the statue — and was regarded as lifeless.[51] In order for these statues to function once again, a number of cultic activities needed to be performed to reanimate and rejuvenate them and reunite them with their *ba* — the central purpose of the rite of the 'union with the sun disc' that took place in the complex. The presence of an access to an underground crypt in every single known complex of *wabet* and court indicates that the entrance to a crypt formed an essential part of this ensemble. Whether all these crypts served exactly the same purpose as the underground crypts in the temple of Dendara is impossible to establish due to the lack of inscriptions and reliefs in most of them. One can only assume that all these crypts housed the cultic material (including the (lifeless) statues of the deities) necessary for the optimal fulfilment of the ritual activities performed in the ensemble.

[47] Cauville, *Dendara V–VI*, pp. 65–67.

[48] Waitkus, *Die Texte in den unteren Krypten des Hathortempels von Dendara*, pp. 250–51 and 257; Cauville, *Dendara V–VI*, pp. 28–30; Coppens, *The Wabet*, pp. 176–77 ; and Coppens and Vymazalová, 'Long Live the King!', pp. 83–86.

[49] Waitkus, 'Zum funktionalen Zusammenhang von Krypta, Wabet und Goldhaus', p. 287; Waitkus, *Die Texte in den unteren Krypten des Hathortempels von Dendara*, p. 265; and Traunecker, 'Cryptes connues et inconnues des temples tardifs', pp. 25 and 42.

[50] Waitkus, 'Zum funktionalen Zusammenhang von Krypta, Wabet und Goldhaus', p. 287, and Waitkus, *Die Texte in den unteren Krypten des Hathortempels von Dendara*, pp. 265–66.

[51] For the Late Period concept of each god having a *ba* in heaven, an image on Earth, and a corpse in the netherworld, see Assmann, *Ägypten, Theologie und Frömmigkeit einer frühen Hochkultur*, p. 54.

The presence of a crypt in each complex is also interesting from another point of view. Three spheres or realms are in this manner linked within a single space: the underworld or subterranean realm (the crypt), the Earth (the complex looking like a temple), and the heavens (with the solar deity shining in the sky above the light-well chamber). The complex is connected with the heavens through the open court and also by means of a staircase that is always located nearby and leads to the kiosk on the roof of the temple (Figure 5.2) as one of the sites where the 'union with the sun disc' took place.[52]

Decorative Programme

In only five complexes have text and image been preserved to such a degree that a detailed study of the decorative programme can be carried out.[53] The decorative scheme in these five ensembles fortunately covers almost the entire period during which the complex occurred in Egyptian temples, including examples from early Ptolemaic times in Philae and Edfu, a late Ptolemaic example in Dendara, and two early Roman ensembles in Shanhur and el-Qal'a. The decorative scheme was clearly designed with the complex's function in mind. In text and relief, the focus is first and foremost on notions of rejuvenation and renewal attained through the rite of the 'union with the sun disc' or the exposure of the 'lifeless' statues of the gods to the rays of the sun. A secondary concept deals with the renewal and confirmation of kingship.[54]

The analysis of these decorative programmes has revealed that it is possible to distinguish two general themes: the safeguarding of the natural course of events, and the preparation of the deities for their rejuvenation. The idea that the statues of the gods are in need of a ritual act of revitalization implies that these statues are in a position of weakness and open to attacks from chaotic forces which are strongest precisely during the epagomenal days preceding the New Year.[55] A variety of scenes and inscriptions in the light-well chamber hence relate to the perpetual and undisturbed journey of the solar bark, the destruction of the enemies of the solar god, and the appeasement of the raging

[52] On the connection, see especially Waitkus, 'Zum funktionalen Zusammenhang von Krypta, Wabet und Goldhaus'.

[53] Traunecker, 'Les Ouabet des temples d'el-Qal'a et de Chenhour', pp. 242–67, and Coppens, *The Wabet*, pp. 73–194 (decorative programme of individual complexes) and 195–208 (general themes of the decorative programme).

[54] See the overview in Coppens and Vymazalová, 'Long Live the King!', pp. 77–87.

[55] Raven, 'Charms for Protection during the Epagomenal Days', pp. 275–85.

Figure 5.7.
The light-well chamber with altar in the Roman temple of Shanhur.
© F. Coppens.

goddess, whose destructive powers reached their climax during the five epagomenal days preceding the New Year. In the elevated chamber a series of amulets and protective spells are presented to the statues as another means of protection against these forces of chaos and destruction.

The second theme is usually found on the walls of the elevated chapel. An extensive number of scenes and inscriptions focus on a series of ritual acts to be performed prior to the actual rejuvenation of the statues of the gods: the festive procession of the statues in their shrines to the elevated chapel; the opening of the shrines and the revealing of the face of the deities; their subsequent purification with water, incense, and natron; clothing with linen; anointment with various unguents; and finally the presentation of protective amulets in the shape of necklaces and pectorals. Next to these activities in the elevated chapel, large offerings of food and beverages appear to have been presented in the open court, judging by the always present scenes of the 'large offering' (*ᶜ3b.t ᶜ3.t*) on its walls. In light of this it is worth mentioning that during excavations in the open court of the temple of Shanhur a part of a column was discovered against the south wall of the light-well chamber (Figure 5.7). The surface of the column had been smoothed and features a depression and discharge for libations, indicating that it had been reused at one point as an altar. The archaeological context in which this altar was discovered suggests that it predates the Coptic reoccupation of this monument,[56] but it is not entirely clear whether the altar/column was originally a part of the temple inventory. The excavation revealed that the base of the column had not been placed upon the original paving of the floor in the open court, which had at some unknown point in time been removed, but upon the temple foundations. Tempting though it may be, the question whether at one point in time this altar functioned as the setting for the 'large offering' in the light-well chamber must remain unanswered.

A final theme in the decorative scheme, which consists mainly of inscriptions, is most often found in text columns on the broken door-lintels and columns that separate the open court from the elevated chapel. These inscriptions regularly refer to the sun shining down on the statues of the gods and the joy it brings to the land — the actual result of a perfect execution of the rites in the ensemble.

Designations

The Egyptian priests who designed the inscriptions and reliefs for the walls of the ensembles used a large variety of designations to refer to the complex.[57] These various designations appear to illustrate quite different aspects of the ensemble, such as its architectural appearance and the nature and period of the ritual activities performed in it. Although the space is best known today as the *wabet*, the most frequently used term — from early Ptolemaic times well into the first century of Roman rule — appears to have been 'seat of the first feast' (s.t ḥb tpy). The association of this term with the ensemble is at times still problematic since it was shared with the kiosk on the roof of the temples of Edfu and Dendara. The designation clearly indicates that the complex and the kiosk played an important role during the 'first feast' (*ḥb tpy*) which took place during the last days of the old year and the first days of the New Year.[58] The transition from the old to the New Year represented to the ancient Egyptian

[56] Traunecker and Willems, 'Chenhour: Rapport des travaux de 1996 et 1997', pp. 123–27 and pls 23B, 24, and 25A.

[57] Coppens, 'A Variety of Designations', and Coppens, *The Wabet*, pp. 55–72.

[58] On the meaning of the term 'first feast', consult Chassinat, 'Quelques parfums et onguents en usage dans les temples de l'Egypte ancienne', pp. 123–28.

mind a period of renewal and rejuvenation, and this idea appears to have been a source of inspiration for a series of designations associated with the ensemble. A large number of terms refer to the concepts of death and burial and the subsequent resurrection and renewal of life. Although in general the term *wabet* (*wꜥb.t*) designates a workshop where all sorts of goods were prepared, it also has a mortuary connotation. It can be a place of embalming, where the body of the deceased was prepared, and even refer to the tomb itself. The term ḥ3yt ('chapel') also appears to point to this aspect of the complex as a mortuary workshop and tomb. The transitional region between this world and the next could well be represented by the use of the term *3ḫ.t* ('horizon') as one of the names for the ensemble, while the single occurrence of the designation *bw rnp* ('place of regeneration') would suggest the final stage in this process, from death to new life. The transitional period at the time of the New Year was also well known to be an unstable and life-threatening time, and this might well have inspired the use of the term *ḫw.t* or 'protective chapel' for the ensemble in Dendara. A series of other terms, like *w3ḏy.t* ('columned edifice') and *sbḫ.t* ('screen-walled portico'), refer to the architectural appearance of the ensemble and more specifically to the facade with columns and screen walls which separated the open court from the *wabet*. The designation *ꜥb3 ḏf3w* or '(court of) the food–altar' clearly suggests which type of activities took place in the open court. The latter is confirmed by the many depictions of the *ꜥ3b.t ꜥ3.t* or 'large offering' on the walls of the open court in most ensembles.

The characteristic layout and decorative scheme of the ensemble define the complex as a transitional space of great importance within the temple. It was used during some of the most crucial ritual festivals performed over the course of the year: the rejuvenation of the statues of the gods and the confirmation and celebration of the divine kingship. In summation, the ensemble was a simple or basic model of the whole universe and a stage for the annual transformation and regeneration rituals which ultimately involved the entire land and the cosmic order. The (statues of the) deities took centre stage in these activities, but the ruler remained an important participator through his performance of the rituals and his unique position as the intermediary between the earthly and the divine spheres.

Designing the Wabet

The very specific layout and the carefully designed decorative scheme applied to the walls of the ensemble certainly did not emerge entirely by accident. It was a well-thought-out construct designed to serve very specific ceremonial needs and based on extensive knowledge of various older ritual practices and monuments. The ancient Egyptian priest-designers did not leave behind any manuals that would provide exact information on the numerous sources that were used in this process. It is, however, possible to retrace some of these sources, for instance by focusing on particular characteristic aspects in the layout of the complex and comparing them with older monuments or by identifying already existing texts that were used in an edited form in the inscriptions and scenes on the walls.

The ritual activities performed in the elevated chapel — for example, the aforementioned clothing ritual — consist of a very basic sequence of acts that is known from a large variety of rituals from almost all periods of ancient Egyptian history. The basic structure revolves around approaching the statue of the deity, handling the statue, an offering ritual, and closing rites of purification and fumigation. The rites performed during the first two major stages of the ritual (i.e. approaching and handling the statue) can be further divided into six general acts: (1) approaching and opening the shrines which contained the statues of the deities, and revealing the face of the deity; (2) adoration of the god and prostration in front of the statue; (3) preparation of the statue for its adornment by removing the ointment and linen applied the day before and by purification with water, natron, and incense; (4) clothing the statue with four coloured cloths and anointing it with unguent and green and black eye paints; (5) attaching regalia, necklaces, and pectorals to the statue; and (6) final purification and fumigation of the statue. The basic steps of these ritual dressing activities appear to have existed in an almost unchanged form from the very beginning until the youngest periods of Egyptian history.[59] It is certainly not my intention to suggest a direct link between the clothing rituals performed on statues in, for instance, the Old Kingdom pyramid complexes and similar rites in Ptolemaic and Roman temples, but one cannot help noticing that a large number of rituals from different religious spheres share similar threads of structure. This has been shown in recent studies when comparing the structure of the Old Kingdom offering list, the offering ritual of the Pyramid Texts, the New Kingdom ritual of the 'Opening of the Mouth', and the temple sanctuary ritual.[60] The general structure of the rituals performed within the *wabet* clearly

[59] See for instance Vymazalová and Coppens, 'Statues and Rituals for Khentkaus II', or Coppens and Vymazalová, 'Linen for the God'.

[60] The as yet unpublished lecture of H. M. Hays, 'Composition and Syntax in Ancient Egyptian Rituals' presented at the seminar 'Egyptology and Anthropology' in March 2008 at Leiden University. I would like to thank Dr Hays for providing me with a printout of this paper. See also Hays, 'The Ritual Scenes in the Chapels of Amun', pp. 1–14.

formed part of a much older tradition and hence enhanced the authority (and effectiveness) of these ritual acts.

The typical and recurring decorative scheme the priests designed for the walls of the ensembles also shows traces of various re-edited older texts and decorations in combination with new material.[61] In order to best express the function of the ensemble in the decoration, its editors chose a (visual) language that was already well known. They found inspiration in a series of rites that also expressed the themes which played a central role in the function of the complex — the transfer from death, or at least a lifeless or deathlike state, to new life. The editors found this in the rites that in their mind had been performed successfully for many centuries and in various contexts: in temple rites (e.g. especially the temple sanctuary ritual),[62] in royal rituals (e.g. the confirmation of the pharaoh's power at the time of the New Year),[63] and mortuary rites (e.g. particularly the embalming process and the subsequent ritual of the 'opening of the mouth').[64] The influence of older rituals is, as one would expect, much more

[61] The scope and space of this volume does not allow an in-depth overview of all the sources involved, but studies on the subject have already been published. A detailed overview with many references can be found Coppens, *The Wabet*, pp. 119–21, 142–45, 157–60, and 206–08.

[62] The temple sanctuary ritual is a modern term for the performance of a (thrice) daily clothing and offering rite in the sanctuary. Depictions of the temple sanctuary ritual can be found for instance in the six chapels of the gods in the Nineteenth Dynasty temple of Seti I in Abydos or in the main sanctuary in the Ptolemaic temples of Edfu and Dendara. The description of the ritual is also known from a series of Twenty-Second Dynasty papyri, kept in Berlin (Papyri Berlin 3014, Papyri Berlin 3053, and Papyri Berlin 3055 in Möller, *Hieratische Papyrus aus den königlichen Museen zu Berlin 1*, also known as the ritual of Amun I, Amun II, and Mut). For more information consult Moret, *Le Rituel du culte divin journalier en Egypte d'après les papyrus de Berlin*; Alliot, *Le Culte d'Horus à Edfou au temps des Ptolémées*, pp. 1–195, and David, *A Guide to Religious Ritual at Abydos*, pp. 58–82. The presence of (re-edited) inscriptions from the temple sanctuary ritual on the wall in the complex of Philae was first observed by Traunecker, 'Les Ouabet des temples d'el-Qal'a et de Chenhour', p. 243, and is discussed in detail in Coppens, 'Creative Writing in Ptolemy II's Time', pp. 34–42. See also Coppens, *The Wabet*, pp. 92–107 (Philae), 157–58 (Edfu), and 202–07.

[63] The decorative scheme of the elevated chapel in the temple of Edfu is reminiscent of the preparatory clothing rituals performed during the confirmation of royal power according to the Late Period papyrus Brooklyn 47.218.50. The papyrus contains a set of directions for ritual acts to be performed during the commemoration of the enthronment of Horus and the confirmation of the pharaoh's power at the time of the New Year: Goyon, *Confirmation du pouvoir royal au Nouvel An*. See also the overview in Coppens and Vymazalová, 'Long Live the King!'.

[64] The embalming entails a series of similar activities and has the same aim as the rites performed on the statues of the gods in the *wabet*: the purification, anointment, and provision

detectable in the decorative programme that dates from the early period in the development of the ensemble and its decoration (i.e. in the temples of Philae and Edfu). In later examples, the editors kept the main decorative themes which derived from older rites and rituals, but their distribution and the inclusion of other themes in the decoration indicates a further development.

The precursors in text and image of the decorative scheme of the *wabet* can often, but certainly not always, be traced to older material that has been reinterpreted and edited in combination with new ideas and concepts. Retracing the typical layout of the complex of the light-well chamber and the chapel on the elevated platform to its plausible prototypes is a more problematic issue due to a lack of well-preserved temples from the period between the end of the New Kingdom and the early Thirtieth Dynasty. The presence of an open court, often accompanied by a platform or altar and a covered chapel, appears to have been a recurring architectural element in the layout of several temples of the New Kingdom and the Twenty-Fifth Dynasty.[65] The solar court of many New Kingdom temples,[66] the Twenty-Fifth Dynasty 'Edifice of Taharqa' near the sacred lake on the temple precinct of Amun in Karnak,[67] and the so-called dais room in a number of Amun temples in Nubia from the Twenty-Fifth Dynasty and Merotic times[68] appear to be closest in both layout and function to the later complexes of *wabet* and court in temples of the Thirtieth Dynasty and the Ptolemaic and Roman periods.

with linen (mummification) and protective amulets placed between the linen bandages is carried out in order for the body to be able to be revived and reunited with its *ba*. These ritual activities are for a large part repeated during the ritual of the 'opening of the mouth' whose aim was to return the senses to the deceased; see for instance Otto, *Das ägyptische Mundöffnungsritual*; Smith, *The Liturgy of Opening the Mouth for Breathing*; or Assmann, *Tod und Jenseits im alten Ägypten*, pp. 408–25. On the influence and use of various mortuary rituals and texts in the complex, see for instance Coppens, 'The *Wabet*', pp. 309–18, and Coppens, 'Funerary Practices in Ptolemaic and Roman Temples'.

65 For an in-depth overview of all possible precursors, see Coppens, *The Wabet*, pp. 209–22. See also Badawy 'The Approach to the Egyptian Temple', p. 90; Traunecker, 'Les Ouabet des temples d'el-Qal'a et de Chenhour', pp. 272–75, and Niederberger, *Elephantine XX*, pp. 114–18, 120–21, and 125–26.

66 Stadelmann, '*šwt-Rcw* als Kultstätte des Sonnengottes im Neuen Reich', pp. 159–78; Spencer, *The Egyptian Temple*, pp. 119–25; and Arnold, *The Encyclopedia of Ancient Egyptian Architecture*, p. 234.

67 Parker, Leclant, and Goyon, *The Edifice of Taharqa*, and Cooney, 'The Edifice of Taharqa by the Sacred Lake', pp. 15–47.

68 Rocheleau, *Amun Temples in Nubia*, esp. pp. 77–78.

The *šwt-Rc (Ḥr–3ḫty)* or solar court of several New Kingdom temples is generally considered to be the most likely architectural and functional precursor to the complex.[69] The solar court is archaeologically attested almost exclusively in the Theban region, and in particular on its west bank.[70] The typical monument usually consists of two distinctive parts: a court open to the light of day, and an elevated, roofed chapel that was accessible by a staircase and often located on or near the roof of the temple. The most typical feature of the open court was the presence of a large freestanding altar in its very centre. The central role the solar cult played in these chambers is evidenced not only by the fact that the court was open to the light of day. The still preserved inscriptions and reliefs on the walls of these ensembles all contain references to the diurnal and nocturnal journey of the sun and evoke the concept of its daily rebirth.

The location of the solar court in the temple is very similar to the location of the *wabet* and light-well chamber in later temples. The solar court is for instance always incorporated in the northern part of the temple, meaning to the right of the sanctuary in temples on the west bank and to the left in temples on the east bank. The distribution of the ensemble in Thirtieth Dynasty and Ptolemaic temples is the same: In a temple located on the west bank of the Nile (Edfu and Dendara) or on an island in the Nile (Elephantine and Philae), the complex is always located to the right of the sanctuary. In a temple erected on the east bank of the Nile (Kom Ombo), the ensemble is located to the left of the sanctuary. The location of the solar court in the immediate vicinity of

[69] Numerous scholars have suggested a connection between the New Kingdom solar court and the *wabet*. Consult for instance Werbrouck, *Le Temple d'Hatshepsout à Deir el Bahari*, p. 109; Daumas, 'L'Interprétation des temples égyptiens anciens', p. 266; Arnold, *Temples of the Last Pharaohs*, p. 277; Arnold, *The Encyclopedia of Ancient Egyptian Architecture*, pp. 234 and 255; Niederberger, *Elephantine XX*, pp. 114 and 120; Cooney, 'The Edifice of Taharqa by the Sacred Lake', p. 44, and Karkowski, *Deir el-Bahari VI*, p. 84.

[70] For instance the open court in the northern part of the upper terrace of the temple of Hatshepsut at Deir el-Bahari, the open court in the north-east corner of the Akh-Menu of Thutmosis III in Karnak, the open court to the north of the hypostyle hall in the temple of Seti I on the Theban west bank, the barely preserved court in the northern part of the Ramesseum, the north chapel or 'Pylon-/Kioskheiligtum' of Ra-Harakhte to the north of the temple of Ramses II in Abu Simbel, the open court in the north-west corner of the temple of Merenptah on the Theban west bank, and the open court no. 18 and rooms nos 17 and 19 in the temple of Ramses III in Medinet Habu (Figure 5.8). See the very detailed overview in Karkowski, *Deir el-Bahari VI*, pp. 85–118, for more information. On the relation between the New Kingdom solar courts and the Fifth Dynasty sun temples, see now Janák, Vymazalová, and Coppens, 'The Fifth Dynasty "Sun Temples"'.

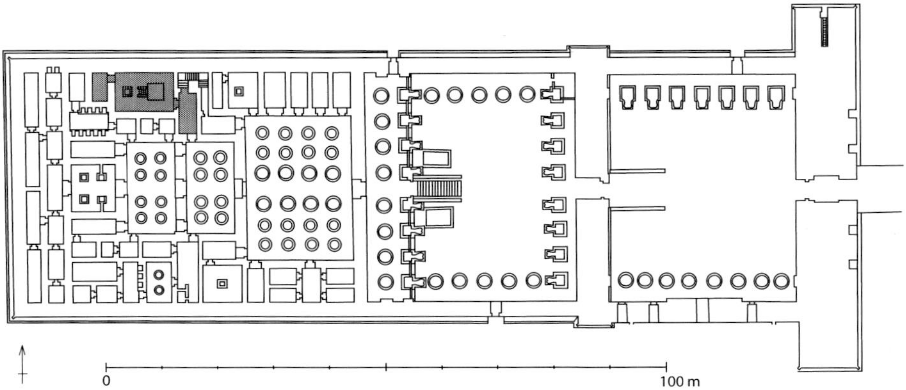

Figure 5.8. The solar court in the temple of Ramses III at Medinet Habu. Drawing L. Vařeková.

the temple sanctuary is also similar to the situation in the younger ensembles. The solar court in the temple of Ramses III in Medinet Habu provides in this perspective the most clear-cut example (Figure 5.8). The temple of Medinet Habu, together with the temple of Khonsu on the domain of Amun in Karnak, is generally considered to be the prototype or precursor to the typical layout of many temples from the Thirtieth Dynasty and Ptolemaic and Roman times.[71] It might have also fulfilled this role in the specific case of the complex of *wabet* and court. The solar court in the temple of Medinet Habu consists of an open court and a small covered chapel. The reliefs on the walls of the preceding room depict the introduction of the pharaoh into the temple and his purification. The room also provides access to the staircase to the roof of the temple. The general layout of these three rooms is very similar to the location of the ensembles and the nearby staircase in the temples of Edfu, Kom Ombo and Dendara (see Figure 5.1).

In the decorative programme of the solar court and its associated rooms, such as for instance in the solar court located on the upper terrace of Hatshepsut's temple in Deir el-Bahari or in the temple of Ramses III in Medinet Habu, two concepts are very much intertwined: the renewal of the creator/sun-god, and the renewal and confirmation of kingship.[72] Interestingly enough, the

[71] See the first section of this paper.

[72] See for instance Barguet, *Le Temple d'Amon-Re à Karnak*, pp. 291–96; Murnane, *United with Eternity*, p. 52; Daumas, 'L'Interprétation des temples égyptiens anciens', pp. 264–65; and Karkowski, *Deir el-Bahari VI*, pp. 59, 70, 72, 77, and 98–99. A series of rooms dedicated to

dominant role played by the king in the early examples (e.g. Deir el-Bahari, Eighteenth Dynasty) shifted towards a domination of the kingship of the gods in later complexes (e.g. Medinet Habu, Twentieth Dynasty).[73] This reflects the situation found later in the *wabet*, where the divine kingship also takes centre stage over the earthly kingship. The decorative scheme of the solar courts focuses primarily on the daily journey and renewal of the sun, but according to text and image, the pharaoh appears to have played a crucial role in helping to ensure this renewal happens. The return of the sun and the renewal of creation also implied the continuation and confirmation of the kingship of the pharaoh. At the same time the text and images in the covered chapel also introduce a funerary theme, particularly the concept of rebirth following a death-like state, by focusing on the diurnal phase of the solar cycle and the solar god's transformation in the middle of the night.[74]

It is not the concept of death but the victory over death and especially the renewal, rejuvenation, or reanimation of the deceased and their entry into a new life that is the central theme of the funerary notions that became incorporated in the temple and solar liturgy at this time. A continuation of these concepts can be found in a Twenty-Fifth Dynasty monument near the sacred lake in the Amun temple precinct of Karnak: the so-called Edifice of Taharqa.[75] The monument is only partially preserved, and its reconstruction, particularly with regard to the superstructure, is for the most part a mere hypothesis, but a large part of the inscriptions and reliefs that decorated the walls of the six underground rooms has been preserved.[76] The decoration of the subterranean chambers focuses on the rebirth and transformation of the god Amun. The

the renewal, continuation, and confirmation of the kingship of Hatshepsut and Thutmosis I are located exactly opposite the solar complex on the uppermost terrace of Hatshepsut's temple in Deir el-Bahari. This part of the temple, the so-called royal cult complex, contains numerous references and associations to the *sed*-festival and royal confirmation rituals. See Bialostocka, 'Hatshepsut's Regeneration in the Royal Cult Complex of her Temple at Deir el-Bahari', pp. 13–24.

[73] Karkowski, *Deir el-Bahari VI*, pp. 103–05.

[74] Karkowski, *Deir el-Bahari VI*, pp. 75 and 117–18.

[75] See note 67 above. Cooney, 'The Edifice of Taharqa by the Sacred Lake', pp. 39–45, was the first to link the 'Edifice of Taharqa' with the complex of *wabet* and court.

[76] For a detailed description of the decorative programme, see Parker, Leclant, and Goyon, *The Edifice of Taharqa*, pp. 10–79, and Cooney, 'The Edifice of Taharqa by the Sacred Lake', pp. 19–33. See also Karkowski, *Deir el-Bahari VI*, pp. 115–18, on the relation between the solar courts and the 'Edifice of Taharqa'.

scenes on the walls depict concepts of renewal and rebirth, such as the continual cycle of the sun setting and rising, the death of the solar deity and the rites to be performed to bring about his resurrection. The final result was the rebirth of Amun in the form of the solar deity Ra. According to the decorative programme, the pharaoh's participation was an important component for the rites to be successful and the sacred act of creation to be renewed.[77] The rebirth of the deity not only implied a restoration of the natural order, but also a confirmation and renewal of the kingship over Egypt.[78]

The decorative scheme of the edifice of Taharqa is of immense importance because it bears witness to a general development that took place in the course of the first millennium BC. The cult of the divine rebirth, which features in such detail on the walls of this monument, combines elements from a solar context with aspects from the cycle of Osiris. The syncretization of the solar deity Amun-Ra with Osiris has its roots in the New Kingdom, but it is especially in the Third Intermediate Period and the Late Period that Amun starts taking on many of the roles and concepts associated with Osiris.[79] The abundant presence of solar themes and funerary concepts, especially those related to death and the renewal of life, in the decorative scheme of the ensemble in the Thirtieth Dynasty and Ptolemaic and Roman times could be seen as a continuation of this syncretization. Taharqa's monument near the sacred lake in Karnak appears to be just an earlier version of this general development in the course of the first millennium BC.

The New Kingdom solar courts with associated chapel and the Edifice of Taharqa provide some insight into the background and development of the main concepts expressed on the walls of the *wabet* and court (i.e. the combination of solar and funerary motifs, and the role of the king, resulting in renewal) and the specific layout of the complex (i.e. open court and elevated chamber). A final important plausible prototype of the complex to be considered is the

[77] Parker, Leclant, and Goyon, *The Edifice of Taharqa*, p. 84, and Cooney, 'The Edifice of Taharqa by the Sacred Lake', pp. 25, n. 78, 27, and 45–46.

[78] Parker, Leclant, and Goyon, *The Edifice of Taharqa*, p. 84, and Cooney, 'The Edifice of Taharqa by the Sacred Lake', pp. 28–29, 33, and 39.

[79] For instance: Niwinski, 'The Solar–Osirian Unity', pp. 89–107, and Cooney, 'The Edifice of Taharqa by the Sacred Lake', pp. 41–43. See also Cruz-Uribe, 'Opening of the Mouth as Temple Ritual', pp. 69–73; Finnestad, 'Temples of the Ptolemaic and Roman Period', pp. 215–16; and Coppens, *The Wabet*, pp. 143, 158–59, and 206–08, for the presence of 'funerary' or 'mortuary' themes and rituals in the decorative programme of temples from Ptolemaic and Roman times.

Figure 5.9. The so-called dais room in the great temple of Amun-Nete (Temple M260) in Meroe. Photo: P. Onderka.

dais room found in a number of temples in Nubia dating to the Napatan period (Twenty-Fifth Dynasty, especially the reign of Taharqa) and the subsequent Meroitic era.[80] The chamber in question is usually found in a temple dedicated to Amun and appears to form a partly independent space. It is located in the immediate vicinity of the main sanctuary of the temple and is often accessible from the vestibule that precedes the sanctuary. A small staircase at its west end leads to a platform or altar. In the Napatan dais rooms, the platform abuts a

[80] Chapel B520 in the great Amun temple at Gebel Barkal/Napata (temple B500), rooms D and E in the temple of Amun in Sanam and in temple T at Kawa, and the unnumbered dais room in the Amun temple of Tabo on the island of Argo (all dated to the Napatan period, mainly to the reign of King Taharqa). The dais room in the temple of Amun in Dangeil (Kom H), chapel 266 in the Amun Temple M260 of Meroe, room 502 in the Eastern Temple (WBN 500) of Wad Ben Naga, and the dais room in the Amun temple N100 at Naga (all dated to Meroitic times, namely the reign of Queen Amanitore and King Natakamani). See Rocheleau, *Amun Temples in Nubia*, pp. 25, 28, 32, 33, 37, 41, and 54, and Onderka, 'The "Throne Rooms" in Amun Temples' with references.

wall, while in the Meroitic examples it is freestanding. The dais room is always orientated east–west, with the platform or altar in the west and facing the east, even if this implies that the layout and decoration of the space has to be reversed in comparison with the rest of the temple. The west part of the chapel was not roofed, allowing the morning sun rising in the east to throw its rays of light on the platform or dais in the west (Figure 5.9).

The exact function of this room is a matter of debate that has not yet been entirely resolved.[81] The Napatan temples containing the dais room are all known as 'coronation temples'. These temples were visited by each Nubian ruler when they came to power and played an important role in the legitimization of kingship in Nubia in Napatan times.[82] It is at present uncertain whether the Merotic temples incorporating the dais room should also be regarded as coronation temples or not.[83] The dais room was initially identified as the 'throne room' of the temple, and the steps leading to the platform at the west end of the chapel were seen as a part of the throne.[84] Laszlo Török has recently suggested that the ensembles are most likely chapels with an altar (rather than a throne) dedicated to the solar deity Ra-Harakhte. His identification is for a large part based on the decorative programme and finds from rooms D and E in Temple T in Kawa. He, and several other scholars, has also pointed out the similarities between these chambers in Nubian temples and the New Kingdom solar courts with an altar.[85] Although the final word on the identification and function of

[81] Török, *The Image of the Ordered World in Ancient Nubian Art*, p. 55, n. 56, and Rocheleau, *Amun Temples in Nubia*, pp. 77–78, provide a brief overview of the ongoing debate.

[82] On the coronation journey of the Nubian ruler, consult Hofmann, *Studien zum meroitischen Königstum*, pp. 18–25; Hakem, *Meroitic Architecture*, pp. 131–41; Kormysheva, 'Das Inthronisationsritual des Königs von Meroe', pp. 187–209; Lohwasser, 'Die Darstellung der kuschitischen Krönung', pp. 163–85; and Török, *The Image of the Ordered World in Ancient Nubian Art*, pp. 16–18.

[83] A suggestion made by Rocheleau, *Amun Temples in Nubia*, pp. 70–71 and 77–78.

[84] For instance Hofmann, *Studien zum meroitischen Königstum*, p. 22; Hakem, *Meroitic Architecture*, pp. 117–19; Kormysheva, 'Das Inthronisationsritual des Königs von Meroe', pp. 206–07 and 210; Lohwasser, 'Die Darstellung der kuschitischen Krönung', p. 170; Ernst, 'Altar oder Thron?', pp. 74–75; and Grzymski, *Meroe Reports*, p. 18.

[85] Török, *The Kingdom of Kush*, p. 310, and Török, *The Image of the Ordered World in Ancient Nubian Art*, pp. 55 and 110–13. See also Priesse, 'Die Statue des napatanisch Königs Aramatelqo', p. 222. Arnold, *Temples of the Last Pharaohs*, pp. 60 and 276; Traunecker, 'Les Ouabet des temples d'el-Qal'a et de Chenhour', pp. 272–75; Niederberger, *Elephantine XX*, pp. 114–16 and 120–21; and Coppens, *The Wabet*, pp. 209–18, link the New Kingdom solar courts with the Nubian dais room and the complex of *wabet* and court.

the dais room as either a solar chapel or throne room still needs to be said, one does not necessarily have to exclude the other. The themes of renewal through the rays of the sun and of the confirmation of the kingship feature extensively on the walls of the *wabet*, and in the New Kingdom solar courts both themes are also intertwined (cf. above). The texts describing the coronation journey of the Nubian ruler often relate it to the journey of Ra through the sky: the ruler was identified with the sun god.[86] In both Nubia and Egypt, the time of the New Year was considered one of if not the most suitable moment of the year to confirm the ruler's power. It was also the best suited moment for the renewal of the statues of the gods through their exposure to the rays of the sun.

The layout and the location of the dais room in the temples provide a few more indications that suggest a connection between the Nubian chapels and the younger ensembles. The existence of a partly uncovered chapel with an elevated platform in the very core of the temple already suggests a link between these spaces. The open court was in both sets of temples located in the immediate vicinity of the main sanctuary and often accessible through the vestibule that preceded the sanctuary. The strict adherence to an east–west orientation in the Nubian examples, even if it should have implied reversing the orientation of the decorative scheme, finds its counterpart in the temple of Philae. The ensemble in the temple of Philae, the oldest preserved complex, is also orientated along an east–west axis which is perpendicular to the axis of the temple (south–north).[87] These indirect indications suggest that the dais rooms of the Nubian temples and the ensembles in the Thirtieth Dynasty and Ptolemaic and Roman temples might not have been that different from each other. The ruinous state of most Nubian dais rooms unfortunately does not allow an unequivocal statement on the exact nature of this relation.

The previous analysis has made it clear that the complex of *wabet* and court is a stage in a development that started at least a millennium earlier. At the same time it is not possible to pinpoint its exact origin or follow in detail its development from the time of the New Kingdom solar courts (let alone before this period of time) to the initial appearance of the complex in temples at the end of the Thirtieth Dynasty and the beginning of Ptolemaic rule over Egypt. The poor state of preservation of many temples from between the end of the New Kingdom and the beginning of the Ptolemaic period simply does not allow

[86] Török, *The Image of the Ordered World in Ancient Nubian Art*, p. 17.

[87] Traunecker, 'Les Ouabet des temples d'el-Qal'a et de Chenhour', pp. 242–44; Coppens, 'The Open Court in the Temple of Philae', p. 27; and Coppens, *The Wabet*, pp. 22–26 and 73–74.

such an in-depth overview. The brief analysis of the solar courts of the New Kingdom temples, the dais rooms of the Nubian temples, and the Edifice of Taharqa near the sacred lake in Karnak indicates at least that the main themes in the architecture and the decorative scheme of the *wabet* and court and the complex's function in the temple draw upon age-old traditions that developed in the course of the preceding millennium. It bears witness to a continuous development and interpretation of age-old traditions and concepts in religion, architecture, and imagery. The idea of renewal and rejuvenation and the confirmation of kingship, the central themes running through the decorative scheme of the complex, is in one way or another already present in these older structures. The themes and the typical architectural layout that is found in many temples of the previous periods appear to have crystallized in the course of the fourth century BC in the ensemble of *wabet* and court which would reach its standard format in the temple of Edfu in the early Ptolemaic times.

Conclusion

The study of the complex of *wabet* and court and its prototypes in architecture, text, and imagery in this contribution can be seen as a specific case study providing some insight into how Egyptian priests designed sacred space in the Thirtieth Dynasty and the early Ptolemaic period. The priestly designers appear to have continuously searched for a balance between maintaining the traditional and developing contemporary forms in architecture and decoration as they analysed and interpreted the work of their predecessors. Although the complex of a light-well chamber and elevated chapel is a sacred space that is typical of temples dating to the twilight of the Pharaonic era and to the Ptolemaic and Roman periods, it is in the end the result of a development that started at least a millennium earlier. The reworked and edited elements from various architectural and ritual precursors, combined with new texts and imagery, resulted in the creation of a coherent architectural unit and decorative system that eloquently expressed the themes that played a central role in the function of the complex.

Works Cited

Secondary Studies

Alliot, M., *Le Culte d'Horus à Edfou au temps des Ptolémées*, Bibliothèque d'Etude, 20.1 (Cairo: Institut français d'archéologie orientale, 1949)

Arnold, D., *Building in Egypt: Pharaonic Stone Masonry* (Oxford: Oxford University Press, 1991)

——, *The Encyclopedia of Ancient Egyptian Architecture* (London: Tauris, 2003)

——, *Temples of the Last Pharaohs* (Oxford: Oxford University Press, 1999)

Assmann, J., *Ägypten, Theologie und Frömmigkeit einer frühen Hochkultur*, Urban Taschenbücher, 366 (Stuttgart: Kohlhammer, 1984)

——, *Tod und Jenseits im alten Ägypten* (München: Beck, 2001)

Badawy, A., 'The Approach to the Egyptian Temple in the Late and Graeco-Roman Period', *Zeitschrift für Ägyptische Sprache und Altertumskunde*, 102 (1975), 79–90

Barguet, A., *Le Temple d'Amon-Re à Karnak: essai d'exegese*, Recherches d'Archéologie, de Philologie et d'Histoire, 21 (Cairo: Institut français d'archéologie orientale, 1962)

Barta, W., 'Königskrönung', in *Lexikon der Ägyptologie*, ed. by W. Helck and E. Otto, 7 vols (Wiesbaden: Harrassowitz, 1980), pp. 531–33

Bell, L., 'Ancient Egyptian Personhood (Anthropology/Psychology): The Nature of Humankind, Individuality and Self-Identity', in *5. Ägyptologische Tempeltagung*, ed. by H. Beinlich and others, Ägypten und Altes Testament, 33/3 (Wiesbaden: Harrassowitz, 2002), pp. 38–42

Bialostocka, O., 'Hatshepsut's Regeneration in the Royal Cult Complex of her Temple at Deir el-Bahari', in *8th Egyptological Tempeltagung: Interconnections between Temples*, ed. by M. Dolinska and H. Beinlich, Königtum, Staat und Gesellschaft Früher Hochkulturen, 3.3 (Wiesbaden: Harrassowitz, 2010), pp. 13–24

Cauville, S., *Dendara V–VI: les cryptes du temple d'Hathor*, vol. I: *Traduction*, Orientalia Lovaniensia Analecta, 131 (Leuven: Peeters, 2004)

——, 'Les Inscriptions dédicatoires du temple d'Hathor à Dendara', *Bulletin de l'Institut français d'archéologie orientale*, 90 (1990), 83–114

——, 'Les Statues cultuelles de Dendera d'après les inscriptions pariétales', *Bulletin de l'Institut français d'archéologie orientale*, 87 (1987), 73–117

——, ed., *Le Temple de Dendara*, XIII (Cairo, 1998), available at <http://www.dendara.net/download>

Cauville, S., and D. Devauchelle, 'Les Mesures réelles du temple d'Edfou', *Bulletin de l'Institut français d'archéologie orientale*, 84 (1984), 23–34

Chassinat, E., 'Quelques parfums et onguents en usage dans les temples de l'Egypte ancienne', *Revue de l'Egypte Ancienne*, 3 (1931), 117–67

——, ed., *Le Temple de Dendara*, IV (Cairo: Institut français d'archéologie orientale, 1935)

——, ed., *Le Temple d'Edfou*, VI (Cairo: Institut français d'archéologie orientale, 1931)

——, ed., *Le Temple d'Edfou*, VII (Cairo: Institut français d'archéologie orientale, 1932)

Cooney, K. M., 'The Edifice of Taharqa by the Sacred Lake: Ritual Function and the Role of the King', *Journal of the American Research Center in Egypt*, 37 (2000), 15–47

Coppens, F., 'Creative Writing in Ptolemy II's Time: Texts from the Temple of Isis at Philae', in *Current Research in Egyptology 2004: Proceedings of the Fifth Annual Symposium*, ed. by R. J. Dann (Oxford: Oxbow, 2006), pp. 34–42

——, 'Funerary Practices in Ptolemaic and Roman Temples: A Case-Study of the Complex of *Wabet* and Court', in *Aegyptus et Pannonia IV: Acta Symposii anno 2006*, ed. by H. Győry (Budapest: MEBT-ÓEB, 2011), pp. 13–37

——, 'Linen, Unguents and Pectorals: Instruments of Regeneration in Ptolemaic and Roman Temples', in *8th Egyptological Tempeltagung: Interconnections between Temples*, ed. by M. Dolinska and H. Beinlich, Königtum, Staat und Gesellschaft Früher Hochkulturen, 3.3 (Wiesbaden: Harrassowitz, 2010), pp. 39–55

——, 'The Open Court in the Temple of Philae: A Complex of *Wabet* and Court in the Making', in *Aegyptus et Pannonia III: Acta Symposii anno 2004*, ed. by H. Győry (Budapest: MEBT-ÓEB, 2006), pp. 27–39

——, 'Temple Festivals of the Ptolemaic and Roman Periods', in *UCLA Encyclopedia of Egyptology*, ed. by J. Dieleman and W. Wendrich (Los Angeles: University of California, 2009), pp. 1–11, available at <http://escholarship.org/uc/item/4cd7q9mn> [accessed 15 June 2011]

——, 'A Variety of Designations: Some Terms for *Wabet* and Court in Graeco-Roman Temples', *Archiv Orientální*, 70/1 (2002), 13–26

——, 'The *Wabet*: An Old Kingdom Mortuary Workshop in a Graeco-Roman Temple?', in *Abusir and Saqqara in the Year 2001: Proceedings of the Symposium*, ed. by Filip Coppens, Archiv Orientální, 70.3 (Prague: Oriental Institute, 2002), pp. 309–18

——, *The Wabet: Tradition and Innovation in Temples of the Ptolemaic and Roman Period* (Prague: Charles University in Prague, 2007)

Coppens, F., and H. Vymazalová, 'Linen for the God: The Interpretation of Old Kingdom Clothing Rites in the Light of Ptolemaic and Roman Rituals', in *Aegyptus et Pannonia V: Acta Symposii anno 2008*, ed. by H. Győry (Budapest: MEBT-ÓEB, forthcoming)

——, 'Long Live the King! Notes on the Renewal of Divine Kingship in the Temple', in *Egypt in Transition: Social and Religious Development of Egypt in the First Millennium BCE*, ed. by L. Bareš, F. Coppens, and K. Smolárikoyá (Prague: Charles University in Prague, 2010), pp. 73–102

Coppens, F., and H. Willems, 'Chenhour et la region Coptite', in *Les Empereurs du Nil*, ed. by H. Willems and W. Clarysse (Leuven: Peeters, 1999), pp. 113–18

Cruz-Uribe, E., 'Opening of the Mouth as Temple Ritual', in *Gold of Praise: Studies of Ancient Egypt in Honor of Edward F. Wente*, ed. by E. Teeter and J. A. Larson, Studies in Ancient Oriental Civilization, 58 (Chicago: The Oriental Institute, 1999), pp. 69–73

Daumas, F., 'L'Interprétation des temples égyptiens anciens à la lumière des temples gréco-romains', *Karnak*, 6 (1980), 261–84

——, 'Sur trois représentations de Nout à Dendara', *Annales du Service des Antiquités de l'Egypte*, 51 (1951), 373–400

David, R., *A Guide to Religious Ritual at Abydos* (Warminster: Aris & Phillips, 1981)

Ernst, E., 'Altar oder Thron? Ein Monument Pianchis im Tempel des Amun von Napata', *Göttinger Miszellen*, 173 (1999), 73–78

Fassone, A., 'The Last Indigenous Dynasties and the Ptolemaic Period', in *Pharaonic Renaissance: Archaism and the Sense of History in Ancient Egypt*, ed. by F. Tiradritti (Budapest: Museum of Fine Arts, 2008), pp. 109–15

Finnestad, R. B., 'Temples of the Ptolemaic and Roman Period: Ancient Traditions in New Contexts', in *Temples of Ancient Egypt*, ed. by B. E. Shafer (New York: Tauris, 1997), pp. 185–237

Gaber, A., 'The Central Hall in the Egyptian Temples of the Ptolemaic Period' (unpublished doctoral thesis, Durham University, 2009), available at <http://etheses.dur.ac.uk/88/> [accessed 15 June 2011]

Goyon, J.-Cl., *Confirmation du pouvoir royal au Nouvel An*, Bibliothèque d'Etude, 52 (Cairo: Institut français d'archéologie orientale, 1972)

Grzymski, K. A., *Meroe Reports*, I (Mississauga: Benben Publications, 2003)

Hakem, A. M. A., *Meroitic Architecture: A Background of an African Civilization* (Khartoum: Khartoum University Press, 1988)

Hays, H. M., 'The Ritual Scenes in the Chapels of Amun', in *Medinet Habu IX. Plates 1–142. The Eighteenth Dynasty Temple I. The Inner Sanctuaries*, Oriental Institute Publications, 136 (Chicago: The Oriental Institute, 2009), pp. 1–14

Hofmann, I., *Studien zum meroitischen Königstum*, Monographies Reine Elisabeth, 2 (Bruxelles: Fondation Égyptologique Reine Élisabeth, 1971)

Hölbl, G., *Altägypten im Römischen Reich: der römische Pharao und seine Tempel III. Heiligtümer und religiöses Leben in den ägyptischen Wüsten und Oasen* (Mainz: Philipp von Zabern, 2005)

——, *A History of the Ptolemaic Empire* (London: Routledge, 2001)

Janák, J., 'A Question of Size: A Remark on Early Attestations of the Ba Hieroglyph', *Studien zur altägyptischen Kultur*, 40 (2011), 143–53

Janák, J., H. Vymazalová, and F. Coppens, 'The Fifth Dynasty "Sun Temples" in a Broader Context', in *Abusir and Saqqara in the Year 2010*, ed. by M. Bárta, F. Coppens, and J. Krejčí (Prague: Charles University in Prague, 2011), pp. 430–42

Karkowski, J., *Deir el-Bahari VI. The Temple of Hatshepsut. The Solar Complex* (Warsaw: Neriton, 2003)

Kockelmann, H., 'Birth House (Mammisi)', in *UCLA Encyclopedia of Egyptology*, ed. by W. Wendrich (Los Angeles: University of California, 2011), pp. 1–7, available at <http://escholarship.org/uc/item/8xj4k0ww> [accessed 15 June 2011]

Kormysheva, E., 'Das Inthronisationsritual des Königs von Meroe', in *Ägyptische Tempel: Struktur, Funktion und Programm*, ed. by R. Gundlach and M. Rochholz, Hildesheimer Ägyptologische Beiträge, 37 (Wiesbaden: Harrassowitz, 1994), pp. 187–209

Leitz, C., *Quellentexte zur ägyptischen Religion I. Die Tempelinschriften der griechisch–römischen Zeit*, ed. by L. Gestermann and C. Leitz, Einführungen und Quellentexte zur Ägyptologie, 2 (Münster: Lit, 2004)

Lohwasser, A., 'Die Darstellung der kuschitischen Krönung', in *3. Ägyptologische Tempeltagung: Systeme und Programme der ägyptischen Tempeldekoration*, ed. by D. Kurth, Ägypten und Altes Testament, 33.1 (Wiesbaden: Harrassowitz, 1995), pp. 163–85

Louant, E., 'Harsomtus the Child, Son of Horus of Edfu, and the Triple Confirmation of the Royal Power', in *Kindgötter im Ägypten der griechisch–römischen Zeit: Zeugnisse aus Stadt und Tempel als Spiegel des Interkulturellen Kontakts*, ed. by D. Budde, S. Sandri, and U. Verhoeven, Orientalia Lovaniensia Analecta, 128 (Leuven: Peeters, 2003), pp. 225–49

Möller, G., *Hieratische Papyrus aus den königlichen Museen zu Berlin 1: Rituale für den Kultus des Amon und für den Kultus der Mut* (Leipzig: Hinrichs, 1901)

Moret, A., *Le Rituel du culte divin journalier en Egypte d'après les papyrus de Berlin et les textes du temple de Séti Ier, à Abydos*, Annales du Musée Guimet. Bibliothèque d'études, 14 (Paris: Leroux, 1902)

Murnane, W. J., *United with Eternity: A Concise Guide to the Monuments of Medinet Habu* (Chicago: The Oriental Institute, 1980)

Niederberger, W., *Elephantine XX: Der Chnumtempel Nektanebos'II*, Archäologische Veröffentlichungen, 96 (Mainz: von Zabern, 1999)

Niwinski, A., 'The Solar–Osirian Unity as Principle of the Theology of the "State of Amun" in Thebes in the 21st Dynasty', *Jaarbericht van het Vooraziatisch Egyptisch Genootschap 'Ex Oriente Lux'*, 30 (1987–88), 89–107

Onderka, P., 'The "Throne Rooms" in Amun Temples', in *Wad Ben Naga 1821–2013*, ed. by P. Onderka and V. Vrtal (Prague: National Museum, 2013), pp. 83–88

Otto, E., *Das ägyptische Mundöffnungsritual*, Ägyptologische Abhandlungen, 3 (Wiesbaden: Harrassowitz, 1960)

Pantalacci, L., and C. Traunecker, eds, *Le Temple d'el-Qal'a*, II (Cairo: Institut français d'archéologie orientale, 1998)

Parker, R. A., J. Leclant, and J.-Cl. Goyon, *The Edifice of Taharqa by the Sacred Lake of Karnak*, Brown Egyptological Studies, 8 (Providence: Brown University Press, 1979)

Pevsner, N., *An Outline of European Architecture* (London: Thames and Hudson, 2009)

Preys, R., *Les Complexes de la Demeure du Sistre et du Trône de Rê: théologie et décoration dans le temple d'Hathor à Dendera*, Orientalia Lovaniensia Analecta, 106 (Leuven: Peeters, 2002)

Priesse, K.-H., 'Die Statue des napatanisch Königs Aramatelqo (Amtelqa) Berlin, Ägyptisches Museum Inv.–Nr. 2249', in *Festschrift zum 150 jährigen Bestehen des Berliner Ägyptischen Museums* (Berlin: Akademie, 1974), pp. 211–32

Raven, M. J., 'Charms for Protection during the Epagomenal Days', in *Essays on Ancient Egypt in Honour of Herman te Velde*, ed. by J. van Dijk, Egyptological Memoirs, 1 (Leiden: Brill, 1997), pp. 275–85

Reymond, E. A. E., *The Mythical Origin of the Egyptian Temple* (Manchester: Manchester University Press, 1969)

Rocheleau, C. M., *Amun Temples in Nubia: A Typological Study of New Kingdom, Napatan and Meroitic Temples*, British Archaeological Reports: International Series, 1850 (Oxford: Hadrian, 2008)

Rochemonteix, Marquis de, and E. Chassinat, eds, *Le Temple d'Edfou*, I, rev. and corr. by S. Cauville and D. Devauchelle (Cairo: Institut français d'archéologie orientale, 1984)

Sauneron, S., *Les Fêtes religieuses d'Esna aux derniers siècles du paganisme*, Esna, 5 (Cairo: Institut français d'archéologie orientale, 1962)

Smith, M., *The Liturgy of Opening the Mouth for Breathing* (Oxford: Griffith Institute, 1993)

Spencer, N., *A Naos of Nekhthorheb from Bubastis: Religious Iconography and Temple Building in the Thirtieth Dynasty*, British Museum Research Publications, 156 (London: The British Museum Press, 2006), pp. 47–52, available at <http://www.britishmuseum.org/research/research_publications/online_research_publications/a_naos_of_nekhthorheb.aspx> [accessed 15 June 2011]

Spencer, P., *The Egyptian Temple: A Lexicographical Study* (London: KPI, 1984)

Spiegelberg, W., *Demotische Papyrus aus den Königlichen Museen zu Berlin* (Leipzig: Giesecke und Devrient, 1902)

Stadelmann, R., '*šwt-Rcw* als Kultstätte des Sonnengottes im Neuen Reich', *Mitteilungen des Deutschen Archäologischen Instituts, Abteilung Kairo*, 25 (1969), 159–78

Stadler, M., 'Procession', in *UCLA Encyclopedia of Egyptology*, ed. by J. Dieleman and W. Wendrich (Los Angeles: University of California, 2008), pp. 1–12, avaialble at <http://escholarship.org/uc/item/679146w5> [accessed 15 June 2011]

Tiradritti, F., ed., *Pharaonic Renaissance: Archaism and the Sense of History in Ancient Egypt* (Budapest: Museum of Fine Arts, 2008)

Török, L., *The Image of the Ordered World in Ancient Nubian Art: The Construction of the Kushite Mind, 800 BC–300 AD*, Probleme der Ägyptologie, 18 (Leiden: Brill, 2002)

——, *The Kingdom of Kush: Handbook of the Napatan-Meroitic Civilization*, Handbuch der Orientalistik, 31 (Leiden: Brill, 1997)

Traunecker, C., 'Cryptes connues et inconnues des temples tardifs', *Bulletin de la société française d'égyptologie*, 129 (1994), 21–46

——, 'Dimensions réelles et dimensions imaginaires des dieux de l'Egypte: les statues secrètes du temple d'Opet à Karnak', *Ktèma*, 29 (2004), 51–65

——, 'Krypta', in *Lexikon der Ägyptologie*, ed. by W. Helck and E. Otto, 7 vols (Wiesbaden: Harrassowitz, 1980), III, 823–30

——, 'Les Ouabet des temples d'el-Qal'a et de Chenhour', in *3. Ägyptologische Tempeltagung: Systeme und Programme der ägyptischen Tempeldekoration*, ed. by D. Kurth, Ägypten und Altes Testament, 33.1 (Wiesbaden: Harrassowitz, 1995), pp. 241–82

Traunecker, C., and H. Willems, 'Chenhour: Rapport des travaux de 1996 et 1997', *Cahier de récherches de l'Institut de papyrologie et égyptologie de Lille*, 19 (1998), 167–209

Vymazalová, H., and F. Coppens, 'Statues and Rituals for Khentkaus II: A Reconsideration of Some Papyrus Fragments from the Queen's Funerary Complex', in *Abusir and Saqqara in the Year 2010*, ed. by M. Bárta, F. Coppens, and J. Krejčí (Prague: Charles University in Prague, 2011), pp. 785–99

Waitkus, Wolfgang, *Die Texte in den unteren Krypten des Hathortempels von Dendara*, Münchner Ägyptologische Studien, 47 (Mainz: von Zabern, 1997)

——, 'Zum funktionalen Zusammenhang von Krypta, Wabet und Goldhaus', in *3. Ägyptologische Tempeltagung: Systeme und Programme der ägyptischen Tempeldekoration*, ed. by D. Kurth, Ägypten und Altes Testament, 33/1 (Wiesbaden: Harrassowitz, 1995), pp. 283–303

Werbrouck, M., *Le Temple d'Hatshepsout à Deir el Bahari* (Brussels: Fondation Égyptologique Reine Élisabeth, 1949)

Willeitner, J., *Die ägyptischen Oasen: Städte, Tempel und Gräber in der Libyschen Wüste* (Mainz: Philipp von Zabern, 2003)

Žabkar, L. V., *A Study of the Ba Concept in Ancient Egyptian Texts*, Studies in Ancient Oriental Civilization, 34 (Chicago: The Oriental Institute, 1968)

Zauzich, K.-T., *Aegyptische Handschriften II*, Verzeichnis der orientalischen Handschriften in Deutschland, 19.2 (Wiesbaden: Franz Steiner, 1971)

Zivie-Coche, C., 'Late Period Temples', in *UCLA Encyclopedia of Egyptology*, ed. by W. Wendrich (Los Angeles: University of California, 2008), pp. 1–17, available at <http://escholarship.org/uc/item/30k472wh> [accessed 15 June 2011]

Places, Communities, and Individuals

THE KTMW STELE FROM ZINCIRLI: SYRO-HITTITE MORTUARY CULT AND URBAN SOCIAL NETWORKS

Virginia Rimmer Herrmann

Local religion — defined here as religious activities and loci that lie in scale and institutionalization between domestic and state cults — has usually been quite an elusive phenomenon for scholars of the ancient Near East. Compared with the officially archived texts and monumental architecture of state religion, evidence for local religion has been both less visible and less often sought after. However, a recent discovery at the site of Zincirli, Turkey, the ancient city of Sam'al, offers new insight into local mortuary and deity cult in one of the Syro-Hittite kingdoms of the early first millennium BC. In 2008, the Neubauer Expedition to Zincirli of the University of Chicago's Oriental Institute recovered in its original archaeological context an intact stone mortuary stele bearing a relief image and an Aramaic inscription. Subsequent enlargement of the excavations in the vicinity of the stele from 2008 to 2010 has revealed a large part of its building and neighbourhood. Alone, this unique document discloses a number of new details about the beliefs, practices, and setting of non-royal Syro-Hittite mortuary cult. The addition of the stele's architectural and urban context at Sam'al opens further possibilities for the interpretation of the social setting of this cult. The interplay of the stele's text, image, and context suggests that this sacred space was a central nexus in an urban social network of which the deceased was a prominent member.

* This contribution has been substantially revised from the paper presented at the conference 'Redefining the Sacred: Religious Identity, Ritual Practice and Sacred Architecture in the Near East and Egypt, 1000 BC – AD 300' in March 2009, as continued excavation of the KTMW stele's context since that time has revealed new information and inspired new interpretations.

Virginia Rimmer Herrmann (vrherrmann@gmail.com) Oriental Institute, University of Chicago.

Figure 6.1.
The KTMW Stele. Photo: Eudora Struble, used with the permission of the Neubauer Expedition to Zincirli.

The KTMW Stele and Syro-Hittite Mortuary Cult

The KTMW stele (see Figure 6.1) is approximately a metre tall and made of fine-grained basalt. Its top is rounded into an arch, and its back is convex, while the bottom is squared-off with a tenon 16 cm long protruding from it.[1] On the flat, front side, a scene and inscription are carved in low relief inside a plain border or frame. At the top, a winged sun-disk once arched over the scene below, but this motif has been nearly obliterated by ploughs scraping the top of the stele, and it can only be recognized by traces of the bottoms of the wings and

[1] For a full description and discussion of the stele's relief image and carving technique, see Struble and Herrmann, 'An Eternal Feast at Sam'al', pp. 16–29.

the curling volutes that hang down from the central disk. The rest of the scene shows a man seated in a high-backed chair with his feet on a low footstool, facing to the right. The man has a full beard, but does not appear to have hair on his head, beneath his peaked cap, from the tip of which dangles a small tassel. He wears an ankle-length, short-sleeved tunic and a fringed shawl over his shoulders. Indications of footwear are very faint, but he appears to be wearing low boots. In his right hand, the man holds up level with his mouth a wide cup with a flaring rim and apparently gadrooned sides, a type that is conventionally called a *phiale* and associated with elite drinking practices throughout the Near East and eastern Mediterranean in this period.[2] In his left hand, he holds out a stick that bears a slightly drooping oval shape, criss-crossed with incised lines. This is most likely intended to depict a conifer cone on a branch.[3] A low table with columnar legs and central brace sits before the man. On it are a small cylindrical box with a lid, a duck or goose in a footed bowl, and a stack of three curved pieces of bread (or two pieces of bread in a flat-bottomed bowl) topped by an ovoid object, probably another foodstuff. The thirteen-line inscription fills the space to the right of the man's upper half, below the winged sun-disk and above the table.

The inscription, carved in Aramaic-Phoenician script and written in a dialect of Aramaic or Sam'alian has been translated thusly by Dennis Pardee:

> (1) I am KTMW, servant of Panamuwa, who commissioned for myself (this) stele while (2) still living. I placed it in my eternal chamber(?) (*bsyr/d 'lmy*) and established a feast (at) (3) this chamber(?) (*syr/d*): a bull for Hadad QR/DPD/RL, a ram for NGD/R (4) ṢWD/RN, a ram for Šamš, a ram for Hadad of the Vineyards, (5) a ram for Kubaba, and a ram for my 'soul' (*lnbšy*) that (will be) in this stele. (6) Henceforth, whoever of my sons or (7) of the sons of anybody (else) should come into possession of (8) this chamber(!?) (*nsyr/d*), let him take from (9) the best (produce) of this vine(yard) (as) a (presentation?)-offering (10) year by year. He is also to perform the (11) slaughter (prescribed above) in (proximity to) my 'soul' (12) and is to apportion (13) for me a leg-cut.[4]

The inscription's first line appears to reveal the identity of the seated figure depicted in the relief scene, a man with the Luwian name of KTMW.[5] Two

[2] Struble and Herrmann, 'An Eternal Feast at Sam'al', pp. 23, 31.

[3] See discussion in Struble and Herrmann, 'An Eternal Feast at Sam'al', pp. 24–25, 32–33.

[4] Pardee, 'A New Aramaic Inscription from Zincirli', pp. 53–54.

[5] Proposals for the vocalization of this name include Kuttamuwa, Katimuwa (Pardee, 'A New Aramaic Inscription from Zincirli', p. 58), and now Katumuwa and Katamuwa (Younger,

kings of Sam'al named Panamuwa are known from royal inscriptions discovered near Zincirli over a century ago by the German Orient-Comité expedition.[6] Both inscription and relief of the new stele point to Panamuwa II as the king identified as KTMW's lord. This king reigned from *c.* 743/40 to 733/32 BC and is noted as a loyal client of King Tiglath-Pileser III of Assyria. The style of the stele's relief is very similar to that of a number of orthostats discovered in the palaces on the citadel of Zincirli that were commissioned by Barrākib, the son of Panamuwa II.[7] Furthermore, the sign forms of the KTMW inscription more closely resemble those used in the mortuary inscription written for Panamuwa II by Barrākib than those found in the earlier mortuary inscription of Panamuwa I.[8]

Due to the high quality of the stele and its clear affinities to royal Sam'alian sculpture of this period, KTMW's self-description as an *'bd*, 'servant', should be understood to mean that he was a retainer or high official of the king of Sam'al.[9] He gives no more specific title, but two idiosyncratic features of his depiction, his apparent baldness and the conifer cone that he holds up, might hint at his status or occupation.[10] It is difficult to say exactly what this might be, but baldness was often associated with the priesthood and states of ritual purity in the ancient Near East and Egypt.[11] Two Syro-Hittite mortuary steles from Neirab depicting bald men are accompanied by inscriptions identifying those depicted as priests of the moon-god Śahr.[12] On the other hand, unlike the men from Neirab, KTMW sports a full beard and moustache, and the marking of religious purity usually seems to have involved shaving all of the hair of the body, including the beard. The conifer cone, meanwhile, suggests an association with the

'Two Epigraphic Notes on the New Katumuwa Inscription from Zincirli').

[6] Von Luschan, Schrader, and Sachau, *Ausgrabungen in Sendschirli*; Tropper, *Die Inschriften von Zincirli*.

[7] Struble and Herrmann, 'An Eternal Feast at Sam'al', p. 16.

[8] Pardee, 'A New Aramaic Inscription from Zincirli', p. 54. For Panamuwa I, see Donner and Röllig, *Kanaanäische und aramäische Inschriften*, text 214. For Panamuwa II, see Donner and Röllig, *Kanaanäische und aramäische Inschriften*, text 215.

[9] For this terminology, see Lipiński, *The Aramaeans*, p. 500.

[10] Struble and Herrmann, 'An Eternal Feast at Sam'al', p. 42.

[11] See Collon, 'Clothing and Grooming in Ancient Western Asia', pp. 503–15; Olyan, 'What Do Shaving Rites Accomplish', pp. 611–22; Robins, 'Hair and the Construction of Identity in Ancient Egypt', p. 61; Galpaz-Feller, 'Hair in the Bible and in Ancient Egyptian Culture', pp. 75–94.

[12] Donner and Röllig, *Kanaanäische und aramäische Inschriften*, texts 225 and 276.

nearby Amanus Mountains, a perennial source of valuable pine and cedar products, though it could well have been a religious symbol instead in this context, representing a hope of regeneration or a reference to a particular deity.[13]

The KTMW stele clearly belongs to the corpus of over fifty Iron Age banquet steles from the northern Levant and southern Anatolia that has been studied extensively in the past few decades, from both stylistic and chronological as well as iconographical and iconological perspectives.[14] These are almost universally understood as personal mortuary monuments, based on their form, occasional inscriptions, and the connection of a small number of them with grave sites.[15] Three other, less common types of Syro-Hittite mortuary monuments are contemporary with and related to these banquet steles in form and seemingly also in function: colossal statues of standing male figures, usually thought to represent deceased kings, statues in the round of seated figures who often hold a cup in their right hand (a form which carries over from the second-millennium Levant), and aniconic steles with funerary inscriptions in Hieroglyphic Luwian, some carved to resemble rectangular towers with crenellations at the top.[16]

The banquet steles typically depict a seated person or a seated pair (occasionally same-sex, but most often a man and a woman, thought to represent a husband and wife) before a table laden with food, almost always including a stack of flatbreads, but sometimes augmented by meat.[17] The seated persons, thought to represent the deceased, nearly always hold an upraised cup in their

[13] Struble and Herrmann, 'An Eternal Feast at Sam'al', pp. 32–33.

[14] See Orthmann, *Untersuchungen zur späthethitischen Kunst*; Winter, 'North Syria in the Early First Millennium B.C.'; Genge, *Nordsyrisch-südanatolische Reliefs*; Voos, 'Studien zum syrohethitischen Totenkult'; Voos, 'Studien zur Rolle von Statuen', pp. 347–62; Voos, 'Bemerkungen zum Syrohethitischen Totenkult der Frühen Eisenzeit', pp. 349–60; Bonatz, *Das syro-hethitische Grabdenkmal*; Bonatz, 'Syro-Hittite Funerary Monuments', pp. 189–210.

[15] Orthmann, *Untersuchungen zur späthethitischen Kunst*; Voos, 'Bemerkungen zum Syrohethitischen Totenkult der Frühen Eisenzeit', p. 348; Bonatz, *Das syro-hethitische Grabdenkmal*, p. 151; see Struble and Herrmann, 'An Eternal Feast at Sam'al', pp. 29–31.

[16] For the standing statues, see Bonatz, *Das syro-hethitische Grabdenkmal*, pp. 24–27. For the seated statues, see Bonatz, *Das syro-hethitische Grabdenkmal*, pp. 27–31; Bonatz, 'Syro-Hittite Funerary Monuments'; Schachner, Schachner, and Karabulut, 'Vier Sitzbilder aus Bit-Bahiani', pp. 106–23; Röllig, 'Das Sitzbild des Kammaki vom Tell Halaf', pp. 421–32; Matthiae, 'High Old Syrian Royal Statuary from Ebla', pp. 111–28; Spycket, *La Statuaire du Proche-Orient Ancien*. For the tower-shaped steles, see Hawkins, 'Late Hittite Funerary Monuments', pp. 213–25; Hawkins, 'More Late Hittite Funerary Monuments', pp. 189–97.

[17] Bonatz, *Das syro-hethitische Grabdenkmal*, pp. 92–96.

right hand and often hold a botanical object, thought to symbolize the regeneration of life, or a symbol of identity or status, such as a distaff, spindle, or mirror for women, or a staff or folded cloth for men, in their left hand.[18] The seated figures are often accompanied by a smaller, standing figure (not found on the KTMW stele), who is sometimes embraced by the woman of the seated pair and obviously represents a child, and in other cases waves a fan or fly whisk or holds up a drinking cup or status- or regeneration-symbol of his or her own. While the latter have sometimes been interpreted as generic servants or worshipers, Bonatz argues that all of these smaller, standing figures represent the surviving heir of the deceased, who would have been responsible for offerings to and communication with the deceased at the memorial site and was probably often the commissioner of the monuments.[19] If we accept this plausible interpretation, the iconography of these steles appears all the more to emphasize the importance of the continuity of the immediate family, which is so clearly expressed in the intimate scenes of mother and child.

The depiction of apparently human (rather than divine) figures seated at a meal has been related plausibly to the funerary or mortuary meal described in texts from several areas and periods of the ancient Near East that formed the fundamental component of ancestor cult in this region.[20] Royal funerary and mortuary rituals from Ebla, Hattuša, and Ugarit, as well as the *kispum* ritual for deceased ancestors in Mesopotamia, stipulate regular food and drink offerings to nourish the deceased in the afterlife, and documentation of a belief in such a need for sustenance after death, including scenes of the deceased seated before food- and drink-laden tables, is abundant in all periods in Egypt.[21] The mortuary inscriptions of two of the eighth-century BC kings of Sam'al, Panamuwa I and Panamuwa II, on colossal stone statues found near Zincirli also describe the invocation of the deceased and the offering of food and drink. Through comparison with these texts, the iconography of the banquet scene shown on

[18] Bonatz, *Das syro-hethitische Grabdenkmal*, pp. 76–102.

[19] Bonatz, *Das syro-hethitische Grabdenkmal*, pp. 103–05, 116–17. For other interpretations, see e.g. Moortgat, *Die bildende Kunst des Alten Orients und die Bergvölker*; Orthmann, *Untersuchungen zur späthethitischen Kunst*, p. 375; Voos, 'Studien zur Rolle von Statuen und Reliefs', p. 358.

[20] Orthmann, *Untersuchungen zur späthethitischen Kunst*, p. 378; Voos, 'Bemerkungen zum Syrohethitischen Totenkult der Frühen Eisenzeit', p. 362; Bonatz, *Das syro-hethitische Grabdenkmal*, pp. 92–94.

[21] For a review of evidence for mortuary food- and drink-offerings in the ancient Near East and Egypt with relevant citations, see Bonatz, *Das syro-hethitische Grabdenkmal*, pp. 92–96.

the Syro-Hittite steles has sometimes been understood not only as symbolic of the blessed afterlife of the deceased, but as a prescription for the proper ritual actions to be carried out in its presence, namely food- and drink-offerings.[22] According to Bonatz, these steles thus offered a 'prospektiver Sicht' ('prospective vision') of the deceased,[23] and, far from being lifeless memorials, acted as 'Grenzsteine' ('boundary stones') between realms, marking the spot where the living and dead met and interacted through ritual.[24]

The description of food-offerings in the KTMW inscription seems to confirm, for the first time, the assumed connection between the banquet scene of steles of this type and actual mortuary offerings.[25] It is in fact the first inscribed Syro-Hittite mortuary stele to give explicit information about the rituals expected to be performed in its presence, including the nature and quantity of the offerings, as well as their recipients, practitioners, frequency, and source (though we should be cautious in assuming that these arrangements were typical). The sacrifice of a bull and five rams is stipulated for a list of deities and KTMW's own 'soul' (*nbš*) (lines 3–5), but later in the inscription, KTMW's specific portion is prescribed (a leg-cut of mutton, lines 12–13), and an additional offering of grapes or wine is mentioned (line 9). The offerings were intended to be annual in perpetuity (line 10), rather than limited to the time of death and burial, and seem to have been supported by an endowment of some sort, given the description of the source of the grape or wine offering as 'this vine(yard)' (line 9).[26]

In addition to these practical aspects of the mortuary ritual, the KTMW inscription furnishes new insights into the religious ideas behind the care for the dead by the living. The offerings are intended in part for KTMW's 'soul' (*nbš*) (lines 5 and 11), which is explicitly stated to reside 'in this stele' (line 5). The stone stele thus seems to be the means of transmission of the sacrifices to that part of the person that remained after death. In later periods, the term *nbš*

[22] Bonatz, *Das syro-hethitische Grabdenkmal*, pp. 115–17. Conversely, Orthmann, *Untersuchungen zur späthethitischen Kunst*, p. 378, Voos, 'Bemerkungen zum Syrohethitischen Totenkult der Frühen Eisenzeit', p. 361, and Kestemont, 'Survie et destin chez les Néo-Hittites', p. 59, have suggested that the meal depicted on the steles could have been merely symbolic or a substitute for actual offerings.

[23] Bonatz, *Das syro-hethitische Grabdenkmal*, p. 115. See also Jonker, *The Topography of Remembrance*, p. 189.

[24] Bonatz, *Das syro-hethitische Grabdenkmal*, p. 157.

[25] Struble and Herrmann, 'An Eternal Feast at Sam'al', p. 30.

[26] Pardee, 'A New Aramaic Inscription from Zincirli', p. 65.

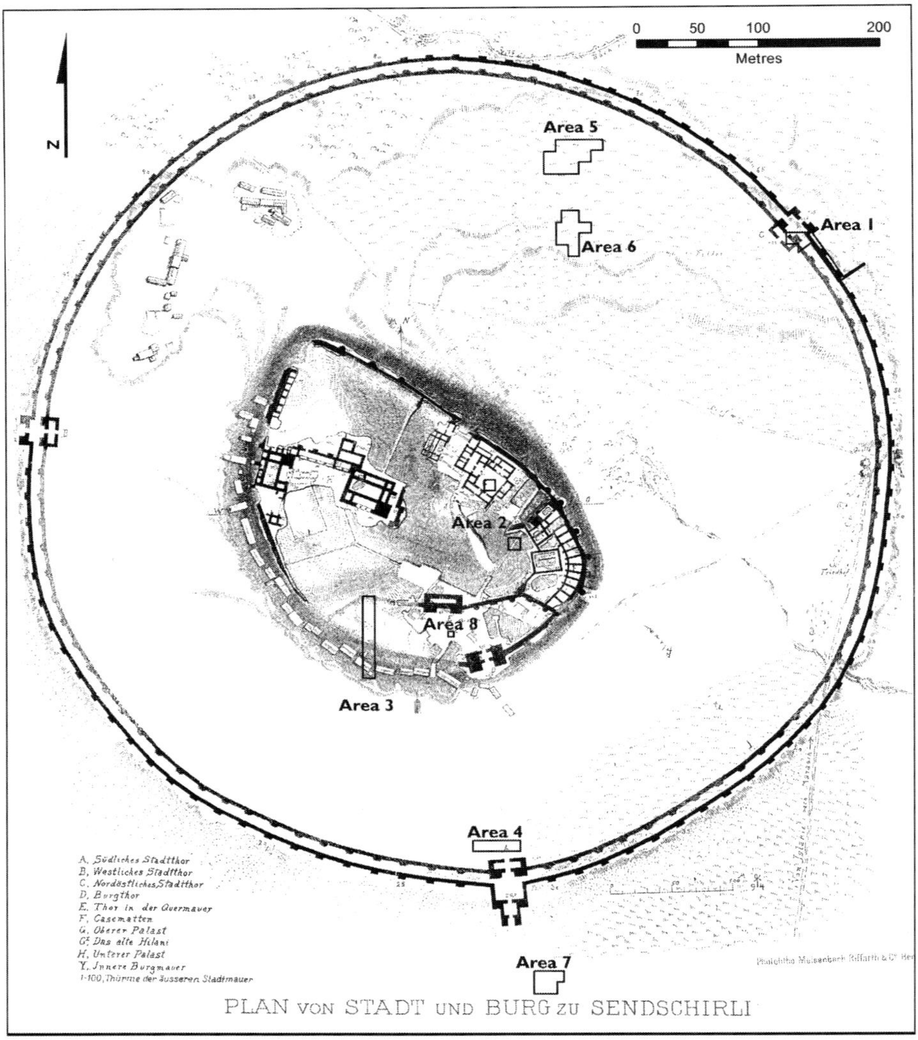

Figure 6.2. 2006–2010 excavation areas of the Neubauer expedition to Zincirli. The KTMW stele was found in Area 5, in the northern lower town. The plan shows the features excavated at Zincirli by the German Orient-Comité expedition as of 1898. After von Luschan and Jacoby, *Ausgrabungen in Sendschirli IV*, pl. XXIX.

or *npš* would come to be synonymous with the mortuary monument or tombstone itself in its function as representing the dead, but here in the eighth century BC, we still see a clear distinction between the stele (*nṣb*) and the *nbš* that is present within it.[27] It is an intriguing detail for the history of Aramaean and/or Luwian religion that KTMW's mortal remains have not been discovered in the vicinity of the stele, as this may indicate that the *nbš* was believed to be able to reside and be nourished in the afterlife in a cenotaph removed from the body.

Furthermore, a clear parallel can be seen between the KTMW inscription's list of gods for whom sacrificial animals are prescribed alongside the *nbš* of the deceased (lines 3–5) and part of the mortuary inscription of Panamuwa I of Sam'al on a statue of the Storm-God Hadad, in which the King's heir is urged to say, upon sacrificing to Hadad, 'May the "soul" (*nbš*) of Pana[muwa] eat with Hadad and may the "soul" of Panamuwa drink with H[adad]'.[28] This post-mortem meal with a god has sometimes been thought to have been a royal privilege, representing the deification of the king after death.[29] Just such a common meal with the gods certainly seems to be implied in the KTMW inscription, however, even for a man of less than royal, if still elite, status.

The Architectural Setting of Syro-Hittite Mortuary Cult: Chapel and Temple

The new stele from Zincirli is the first Syro-Hittite banquet stele to have been discovered in its original context in a controlled archaeological excavation, all previous examples having been found in secondary or tertiary contexts or in unscientific or poorly documented excavations. This fortunate circumstance gives us the opportunity to compare the setting of this stele with what is known of the surroundings of other types of memorial from the same period with the

[27] See Pardee, 'A New Aramaic Inscription from Zincirli', pp. 62–63. For the later meaning of *npš*, see Hoftijzer and Jongeling, *Dictionary of the North-West Semitic Inscriptions*, pp. 748–49; Triebel, *Jenseitshoffnung in Wort und Stein*.

[28] Donner and Röllig, *Kanaanäische und aramäische Inschriften*, text 214, lines 21–22. Translation after Younger, 'The Hadad Inscription (2.36)', pp. 156–58.

[29] Orthmann, *Untersuchungen zur späthethitischen Kunst*, p. 378; Voos, 'Bemerkungen zum Syrohethitischen Totenkult der Frühen Eisenzeit', p. 349; van der Toorn, *Family Religion in Babylonia, Syria and Israel*, p. 168. See also Niehr, 'Zum Totenkult der Könige von Sam'al', p. 62; Niehr, 'Ein weiterer Aspekt zum Totenkult der Könige von Sam'al', pp. 83–97; Niehr, 'Bestattung und Ahnenkult in den Königshäusern von Sam'al', pp. 111–39.

aim of identifying a regional tradition and its relationship with widely held beliefs about the situation of the dead.

Zincirli was first investigated in the late nineteenth century by an expedition of the German Orient-Comité headed by Felix von Luschan. These early excavations concentrated on the fortifications and palatial buildings of the 5-ha central citadel mound and the double wall and three gates of the perfectly circular, 40-ha lower town that surrounds it.[30] By contrast, a priority of the new Neubauer Expedition to Zincirli of the University of Chicago, led by David Schloen and Amir Fink, has been the investigation of the lower town itself, via both large-scale excavations and remote sensing.[31] Area 5 is located in the northern lower town, *c.* 40 m south of the outer fortification wall (see Figure 6.2), and has been expanded over the course of three seasons of excavation (2008–10) supervised by the author to 1100 m^2.[32] The KTMW stele was discovered on only the fifth day of the first season in this area, but over time the majority of both the building in which it was found and the larger architectural 'insula' to which it belonged have been exposed. This agglomeration of smaller buildings, called Complex A, is surrounded on all sides by streets or open 'plazas' (see Figure 6.3).

The stele was found standing upright, but fallen backward slightly against the wall behind it, in the north-western corner of the innermost room of a modest-sized building (*c.* 9 by 12–13 m, or *c.* 113m^2) on the north-eastern edge of Complex A, designated Building A/II (see Figure 6.3). This room had previously been somewhat larger and had housed two clay-and-sherd ovens, but when the stele was erected, the earth floor was raised several centimetres, putting the ovens out of use, and new walls were constructed in the east and south, making the room smaller with a narrower entrance, possibly so that it could be closed off by a door. The stele was framed in its corner of the room by a small flagstone pavement in front, a low stone bench to its right, and a stone 'pedestal' to its left. These modest features, proportional to the stele in size, would likely have served as the immediate setting for cultic activities related to

[30] Von Luschan, Schrader, and Sachau, *Ausgrabungen in Sendschirli I*; von Luschan, Humann, and Koldewey, *Ausgrabungen in Sendschirli II*; Luschan, *Ausgrabungen in Sendschirli III*; von Luschan and Jacoby, *Ausgrabungen in Sendschirli IV*; von Luschan and Andrae, *Die Kleinfunde von Sendschirli*.

[31] See Schloen and Fink, 'New Excavations at Zincirli Höyük in Turkey', pp. 1–13; Schloen and Fink, 'Searching for Ancient Sam'al', pp. 203–19.

[32] See Herrmann, 'Society and Economy under Empire at Iron Age Sam'al' for a detailed description of the results of the excavations in this area.

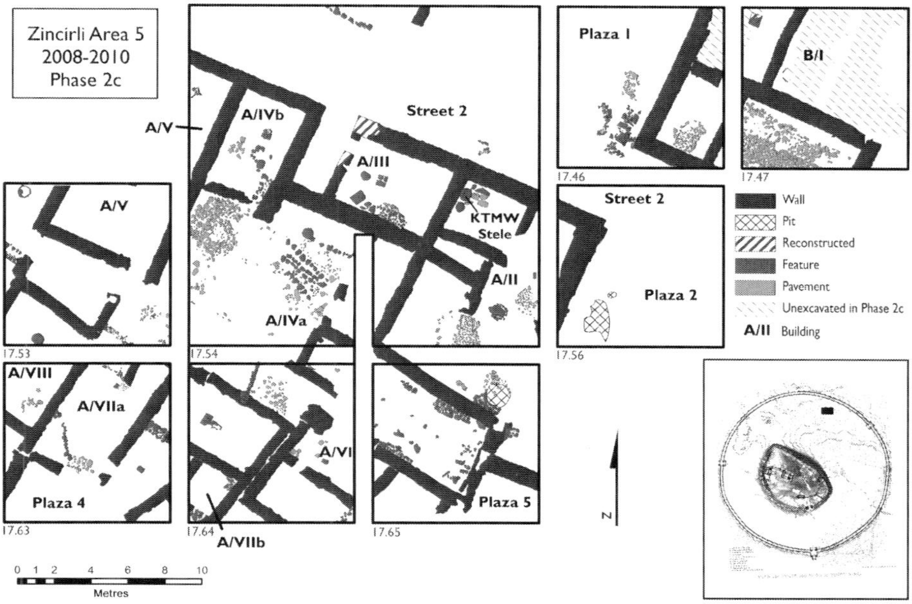

Figure 6.3. Plan of Zincirli Area 5, Phase 2c. The exposed architecture can be divided into two complexes: Complex A (in the south-west), composed of several smaller buildings including the stele building (A/II), and Complex B (in the north-east), consisting of a single large courtyard-building. Drawing provided by author.

it and possibly even as the places where food and drink offerings were deposited. Despite the implication of the stele's inscription that it was intended to represent its owner after his death, no trace of human remains has yet been found beneath the stele installation or elsewhere in the room.

Building A/II possessed three other rooms of roughly similar size, of which the stele room was the most secluded and the only one whose entrance could have been closed off with a door.[33] It may have been fronted by a walled forecourt to the east that has been only partially excavated. The building was fairly well cleaned out when it was later rebuilt, probably sometime in the seventh century BC, leaving few features and artefacts to inform us about the function of these outer rooms. Wide entrances gave access between them, marked by fragmentary stone pavements, one of which acted as a sloping ramp leading

[33] See Herrmann, 'Society and Economy under Empire at Iron Age Sam'al', pp. 268–71, 480–83, for full details of this building and its contents.

down into the vestibule before the stele room, as the floors of the northern two rooms were slightly lower than the southern two. A linear stone feature against the wall just inside the outermost entrance may have supported a low bench, and a massive, flat, but irregularly shaped stone next to the aforementioned 'ramp' may have formed the base of a wooden ceiling post.

The artefacts found abandoned on the floors of the rooms were quite various. Five stone bowl fragments found in the stele room and the vestibule before it, as well as two blue frit beads, a ceramic zoomorphic figurine fragment, a small bronze nail, two further fragments of bronze, and a thin silver ring or earring found elsewhere may have derived from cult furniture or votive offerings related to the mortuary cult. Other items relate to food preparation and storage, perhaps for the mortuary feast itself, and include a partial cooking pot, three handstones, a stone mortar, two ceramic jar or jug stoppers, three olive pits, and a number of large fragments of storage jars. An iron bar attached to two linked rings was found in the doorway to the stele room and may have been used to secure a wooden door. Still other artefacts found in the building attest to a range of activities that seem unrelated to the mortuary cult, including textile production (a spindle whorl, a ceramic loom weight fragment, and part of the base of a large ceramic vat or basin), metallurgy (three pieces of slag), and possibly agriculture (eight chert fragments).

Was Building A/II the house of KTMW? At first glance, this would seem to be a logical location for a mortuary cult that is believed from the evidence of the iconography and inscriptions of other steles to have been intimately linked to the deceased's family. While the building did contain some domestic implements, I think this is unlikely to have been the case. A geomagnetic survey carried out in 2007 shows that the north-eastern quadrant of Zincirli's lower town was dominated by very large buildings centred on one or two large courtyards, which were presumably the homes of the city's elite, including the top officials.[34] These buildings, parts of two of which have been excavated by the Neubauer Expedition, dwarf Building A/II, at five to ten or more times its size. KTMW's stele is of an impressive, if not quite royal, size and quality of carving, and he had himself portrayed as a servant of the king in the court dress of Sam'al. It seems more likely that such a person would have resided in one of the large courtyard residences immediately to the east and south, rather than in Building A/II itself.

[34] Casana and Herrmann, 'Settlement History and Urban Planning at Zincirli Höyük', pp. 55–80.

In the inscription itself, this building or part of it is referred to three times with the enigmatic terms *syr/d* (lines 2 and 3) or *nsyr/d* (line 8). The signs for *r* and *d* in this inscription are almost indistinguishable, creating still more uncertainty about the etymology and meaning of this word.[35] From its context, the *syr/d* appears to be the place where the stele was installed (line 2), modified by *'lmy* to make 'the SYR/D of my eternity' or 'my eternal SYR/D', and where the great mortuary or funerary feast is to be carried out (line 3). In its third occurrence (line 8), the *syr/d* or *nsyr/d* seems to be property that can be inherited or otherwise transferred and carries with it both the responsibility for the annual mortuary offerings and apparently the ownership or use of a vineyard nearby, which provides at least part of the offerings. Based on these contextual clues from the inscription together with the stele's archaeological context, Pardee provisionally translated this word as 'chamber'. He tentatively suggested, however, that it should be read *syr* and might be related to the Hebrew SR, 'turn aside', in which case it could mean something like 'the place to which one "turns aside", or to which one "travels", for the purpose of honouring the departed ancestor'.[36] Mazzini, on the other hand, has proposed a connection between *syr/d* and the West Semitic root *swd*, from which an ancient South Arabian word meaning 'hall, audience chamber, reception hall' was derived.[37] This meaning would fit nicely the architectural context of the stele and the term's usage in the inscription. In addition, more abstract derivations from this root meaning 'company, council, assembly' (i.e. the group of people who might gather in such a hall) are found in South Arabian, Hebrew, and Ugaritic.[38] This sense further supports the interpretation of Building A/II as a place of gathering for the practice of mortuary cult.

Whatever understanding of the word *syr/d* is favoured, the use of this special terminology for the place where the stele was installed strengthens the impression that this structure was a special-purpose building dedicated to the mortuary cult of one of the city's elite rather than the deceased's home (though it was converted from what was once perhaps a private residence). Such an interpretation for the building also finds support in the fragmentary evidence for the architectural context of other types of Syro-Hittite memorials and elite

35 Pardee, 'A New Aramaic Inscription from Zincirli', pp. 54–56.

36 Pardee, 'A New Aramaic Inscription from Zincirli', p. 60.

37 Mazzini, 'On the Problematic Term *syr/d*', pp. 505–07.

38 Mazzini, 'On the Problematic Term *syr/d*', p. 506.

burials.[39] The best-preserved example is the so-called 'Kultraum' building in the lower town of Tell Halaf (ancient Guzana) in eastern Syria, in which a statue of two figures seated side by side, one male and one female, was found. The building consisted of a small entrance room, a long, narrow 'cella', and three smaller side rooms. The double statue sat on a podium at the end of the cella, facing east, along with a statue of a standing male figure (usually understood to represent the Storm-God). The cella contained a great deal of evidence for cultic activity, including a long bench, a mudbrick altar with evidence of burning, several basalt vessels, and numerous basalt and bronze statuettes of male and female figures.[40] Other, more fragmentary freestanding structures containing stone memorials and/or cremation or inhumation burials were found elsewhere at Tell Halaf and at Carchemish, in some cases associated with temples, but often in an unclear urban context.[41]

Comparison with these structures in other Syro-Hittite capitals suggests that the stele building in the lower town of Zincirli forms part of a widespread regional tradition of the erection of a memorial (facing east, towards the rising sun) in a private sanctuary or chapel that was above ground and accessible, purpose-built for the mortuary cult of the deceased, but intimately connected with the worship of one or more deities.[42] This tradition of propinquity between Syro-Anatolian mortuary and deity cult seems to have been established already in the Bronze Age. The discovery of stone representations of deceased nobility in or around the temples of deities at Bronze Age Ebla, Alalakh, and Hazor, as well as in Hatti, recalls the juxtaposition of the statues of deity and deceased pair in the Iron Age Kultraum at Tell Halaf.[43] The duty of the pious son to erect a stele of his ancestor in the sanctuary, described in the Late Bronze Age Ugaritic Aqhat Epic,[44] evokes the partaking of both Panamuwa I and KTMW

[39] Struble and Herrmann, 'An Eternal Feast at Sam'al', pp. 36–39.

[40] Müller, 'Teil II: Das Stadtgebiet', pp. 357–60; Pucci, *Functional Analysis of Space in Syro-Hittite Architecture*, pp. 115–16, pls 13, 21.

[41] See Struble and Herrmann, 'An Eternal Feast at Sam'al', pp. 36–39; Langenegger, 'Teil I: Die Bauten und Schichten des Burghügels', pp. 100–03, 159–67, 169–78; Woolley, *Carchemish, Part II*, pp. 67–68, pl. 8; Woolley and Barnett, *Carchemish, Part III*, pp. 167, 180–81, 213, pls 29, 36a, 38, 49, 50a.

[42] Struble and Herrmann, 'An Eternal Feast at Sam'al', p. 38. For the identification of this tradition, see Bonatz, *Das syro-hethitische Grabdenkmal*, p. 152; Niehr, 'Bestattung und Ahnenkult in den Königshäusern von Sam'al'.

[43] See Bonatz, *Das syro-hethitische Grabdenkmal*, pp. 152–53.

[44] Dietrich, Loretz, and Sanmartín, *Die Keilalphabetischen Texte aus Ugarit*, 1.17 i, lines

in offerings to the gods in the Iron Age inscriptions of Sam'al. Drawing on these scattered indications in the northern Levantine inscriptions, along with certain passages in the Hebrew Bible, van der Toorn has surmised:

> In the Syro-Phoenician conception, the dead are presumed to dwell with the family god; in the hereafter, they eat and drink with their god. That is why the post-funerary offerings are to be accepted by the family god before they can reach the family ancestors. Unlike the Old Babylonian customs, the temple of the family god could serve as the place where the dead were addressed.[45]

The KTMW stele and its setting can be even more closely linked to this regional tradition of the indivisibility of deity and mortuary cult, if, as I propose, the building immediately adjacent to Building A/II on the north-west is understood as a small neighbourhood temple. Building A/III is a two-room building of approximately 6 by 9 m (*c.* 51 m^2) that was constructed at roughly the same time that A/II next door was repurposed for the cult of KTMW (see Figure 6.3). While the building contained no artefacts that are definitively cultic in nature, its architectural characteristics distinguish it from the other excavated buildings in this neighbourhood, and its plan and features can be compared to a certain group of Levantine temples.[46]

Though it is a small building, Building A/III has particularly wide wall foundations, suggesting that it could have had a tall, tower-like superstructure. The ragged ends of these walls hint that large, shaped stones were robbed from the doorways of the building in antiquity. A/III is the only building in this architectural complex that has an entrance directly onto the major street passing through the area, suggesting a semi-public character, and in its later reconstruction, this entrance was marked by a stone-paved porch and projecting stone buttress. The main, inner room possessed a stone foundation for a wide bench against the south wall, next to a large fragment of a well-hewn basalt block or 'table' with a shallow rectangular depression covering its upper surface.[47] In the centre of the room were two adjacent stone bases, one circular and one square, the latter with two shallow divots on opposite corners.

25–27; see Pardee, 'The 'Aqhatu Legend', pp. 343–56.

[45] Van der Toorn, *Family Religion in Babylonia, Syria and Israel*, p. 153.

[46] For a more detailed argument for the identification of Building A/III as a neighbourhood temple, see Herrmann, 'Society and Economy under Empire at Iron Age Sam'al', pp. 468–76.

[47] Compare the basalt 'offering tables' from Carchemish (Woolley and Barnett, *Carchemish, Part III*, p. 182, fig. 169) and the Tell Halaf Kultraum (Müller, 'Teil II: Das Stadtgebiet', p. 360).

Building A/III bears no resemblance to what is considered the typical temple plan of this region: a monumental, freestanding structure with a symmetric plan, whose cultic focus is approached directly on the central axis of the building.[48] It does, however, share a number of features with a smaller group of temples from the Late Bronze and Iron Age Levant called by A. Mazar temples with 'irregular plans and indirect access'.[49] These are usually smaller in size than the monumental symmetrical temples and often not freestanding. They have a corner entrance often through a smaller antechamber that sometimes requires a ninety-degree turn in order to view the cult image. Within, there are often benches along the walls, one or more pillars supporting the roof, a raised platform acting as the 'holy of holies', and often a back room that served as a storeroom or temple treasury. Building A/III at Zincirli fits this description in all details except its lack of a storeroom in the rear.

The KTMW stele installation was built against the wall shared between Building A/II and the main room of A/III. If the latter room can be considered a 'cella' that would have contained a cult image or symbol, the stele was located as close as possible to the divine presence without being in the room itself. The identification of Building A/III as a small neighbourhood temple belonging to this secondary tradition of Levantine cultic architecture thus provides a rationale for the location of the KTMW stele and its chapel on this site that is consonant with the other evidence reviewed above for the spatial and ritual link between the cult of the gods and the cult of the dead in this region.

Like the post-mortem communal meal with a god or gods, the construction of a private mortuary chapel in the Syro-Hittite city has sometimes been assumed to have been an exclusively royal privilege.[50] While it cannot be excluded that KTMW belonged to the royal family, he was certainly not a king. The discovery of his mortuary establishment at Sam'al thus supports the idea that, in this society, there was no categorical difference between royal and non-royal mortuary beliefs and practices, merely gradations in grandeur and scale.[51]

[48] See Mazar, 'Temples of the Middle and Late Bronze Ages and the Iron Age', pp. 161–90; Naumann, *Architektur Kleinasiens*, pp. 463–72; Werner, *Die entwicklung der Sakralarchitektur in Nordsyrien und Südostkleinasien vom Neolithikum*.

[49] Mazar, 'Temples of the Middle and Late Bronze Ages and the Iron Age', pp. 177–82; Mazar, *Excavations at Tell Qasile*, pp. 61–71; Mazar, 'The Temples and Cults of the Philistines', pp. 213–31. This type of temple has also been called the 'bench temple' by Dever, 'Palaces and Temples in Canaan and Ancient Israel', p. 610.

[50] E.g. Niehr, 'Bestattung und Ahnenkult in den Königshäusern von Sam'al'.

[51] See further in Struble and Herrmann, 'An Eternal Feast at Sam'al', p. 40.

As Pardee has suggested regarding the Syro-Hittite afterlife, 'the envisaged state was perhaps one where the hierarchies of human existence were retained but in immediate contact with the divine sphere'.[52]

Local Religion and Social Groups in a Syro-Hittite City

Beyond the light cast by the new stele from Zincirli on non-royal Syro-Hittite mortuary cult, the choice of this specific location within the urban fabric of Sam'al for the erection of his stele suggests that KTMW had a particular social audience in mind, whose identity can perhaps be conjectured from the archaeological evidence for the setting of this cult. Van de Mieroop has written of Mesopotamian cities that 'the major problem in the reconstruction of the social organization lies in the identification of groupings larger than the nuclear family, yet smaller than the entire city'.[53] Similarly, some historians of ancient Near Eastern religion have proposed an obscure and neglected level of 'local religion' intermediate between the domestic cult and state or official religion whose participants consist of the neighbourhood, village, or clan.[54] Most would agree that such more or less formal 'intermediate' social groups of various types, including religious groups, must have existed in ancient Near Eastern cities, but concrete evidence for them is usually difficult to wring out of our extant textual and archaeological sources, though micro-histories based on archives and architectural analysis of residential neighbourhoods are two fruitful approaches where the evidence allows.[55] In the case at hand, it is only the combination of a text with its archaeological context that hints at the existence of such a group. Below, a review of some clues from the Zincirli stele's text, iconography, and architectural and urban context will suggest that a social group of intermediate size and scope partook of the rites surrounding it. Then, two specific types of urban socio-religious groups attested in the ancient Near East and Mediterranean that we might tentatively identify with the participants in KTMW's cult are proposed.

[52] Pardee, 'A New Aramaic Inscription from Zincirli', p. 63.

[53] Van de Mieroop, *The Ancient Mesopotamian City*, p. 102.

[54] Albertz, *A History of Israelite Religion in the Old Testament Period*, pp. 91–92; van der Toorn, 'Religious Practices of the Individual and Family', pp. 423–24; Olyan, 'Family Religion in Israel and the Wider Levant', p. 113.

[55] See, e.g., Stone, *Nippur Neighborhoods*, and Schloen, *The House of the Father as Fact and Symbol.*

Comparison of the text and iconography of the KTMW stele with its urban context reveals something of a contradiction. The manner in which KTMW had himself depicted on his stele advertises his status at the court of Sam'al (by means of his clothing and the style of carving), and the inscription provides his relationship to the King of Sam'al as the deceased's sole identifying characteristic. The audience of this lofty self-depiction was neither the royal court on the citadel nor the public at large, however, as KTMW had his stele installed in a private, indoor setting in the residential lower town, in a complex of relatively modest buildings. We can reasonably infer from this that the stele's intended audience was a more restricted and localized social group. The fact that it was set up in a multi-room, special-purpose building adjacent to a local temple, rather than in the deceased's home, suggests, however, that some more extensive group than KTMW's immediate kin was envisaged. The feast prescribed by the inscription, including a bull and five rams, would have fed quite a substantial group. The neighbourhood temple and the adjacent private mortuary chapel thus make good candidates for the nucleus of a particular social network at Sam'al — one that had a religious basis, but almost assuredly overlapped with social groups founded on other (kinship, neighbourhood, economic, political, or personal) bases, too.

I proposed above that proximity to the small temple A/III next door to the stele building was the intended purpose behind the location of KTMW's mortuary cult. Furthermore, the list of gods found in the stele's inscription is quite idiosyncratic, departing dramatically from the standard pantheon found in the royal inscriptions of Sam'al (consisting of Hadad, El, Rakib-el, Šamaš, and sometimes Rašap), and may have been influenced by Luwian religion in its inclusion of Kubaba and Hadad of the Vineyards.[56] This suggests that KTMW selected these gods for specific reasons of personal devotion, family tradition, or cultic proximity.

The modest-sized Zincirli A/III temple, nestled among primarily domestic buildings, can be classified as a neighbourhood temple, defined here as a cultic building that was not segregated into a special religious quarter or royal precinct but rather closely integrated into a residential area. Other examples of this type of temple include several buildings in neighbourhood AH in Old Babylonian Ur, the Temple aux Rhytons at Late Bronze Age Ugarit, and the

[56] See Masson, 'La Stèle mortuaire de Kuttamuwa (Zincirli)', pp. 52–53, who also proposes to see the mysterious god NGD/R ṢWD/RN in the KTMW inscription as the Luwian god Nikarawas/Nikaruhas.

above-mentioned Kultraum at Iron Age Tell Halaf.[57] It is logical to suppose, due to their location and smaller size, that such neighbourhood temples were frequented primarily by local residents, who, as individuals or communal groups, may have in many cases also sponsored their construction and maintenance. Charpin, followed by van der Toorn, has argued from a variety of textual evidence that in early second-millennium Babylonia, an individual's personal god, who was usually passed from father to son and from husband to wife, was quite often not a major god or the god of his city, but one whose temple was located in the neighbourhood of his home.[58] Personal or family gods are also attested in the Bronze and Iron Age Levant, though less extensively, and van der Toorn proposes that certain stories in the Hebrew Bible demonstrate the organization of family religion in the Iron Age southern Levant around local sanctuaries at which clans would gather for monthly and annual festivals that included communion with their ancestors.[59]

Given this background, KTMW's decision to establish his mortuary cult next to the small temple A/III suggests that he had a strong personal or familial connection to the temple and its god(s), and thus probably also to its neighbourhood. His residence, possibly one of the large courtyard-buildings to the east and south of Complex A, is likely to have been nearby. The connection between the adherents of smaller temples like Building A/III and local residence raises the possibility that the devotees both of KTMW's mortuary cult in Building A/II and of temple A/III next door were, like KTMW himself, inhabitants of this area of the lower town of Sam'al. Many in this 'religious community' of sorts would likely have had some kind of relationship of kinship, dependency, or reciprocity with KTMW or his household, forming the kind of 'urban clan' or 'patronymic association' typically identified in Islamic Middle Eastern and North African cities that had its nucleus in a particular neighbourhood and was held together by the combination of residential proximity with both real and fictive kinship.[60] Though the stele building was located

[57] Woolley and Mallowan, *Ur Excavations VII*; Yon, 'The Temple of the Rhytons at Ugarit', pp. 405–22; Müller, 'Teil II: Das Stadtgebiet'.

[58] Charpin, 'Les Divinités famliales des Babyloniens', pp. 59–78; van der Toorn, *Family Religion in Babylonia, Syria and Israel*, pp. 66–78, 79–87.

[59] Van der Toorn, *Family Religion in Babylonia, Syria and Israel*, pp. 168–77, 211–18.

[60] Cohen, *Arab Border Villages in Israel*; Cohen, 'The Politics of Marriage in Changing Middle Eastern Stratification Systems', pp. 195–209. Eickelman, *The Middle East and Central Asia*, pp. 144–51. On the existence of 'patronymic associations' occupying particular neighbourhoods in Mesopotamia (the *bābtum*) and Israel (the *mišpāḥâ*), see Stone, 'Texts, Architecture and

on the edge of the elite quarter of the lower town, Complex A in which it was found contained only modest dwellings, so this group was probably of mixed social and economic status. The numerous small stone and bronze statuettes of men and women discovered on the floor surrounding the statues of the god and deceased couple in the Kultraum, the combined temple and mortuary chapel at Tell Halaf, suggest that a similar extended (real or fictive) kinship group of mixed socio-economic position used this building as well.[61]

The foundation of a mortuary institution that hosted an annual feast by a nobleman such as KTMW in this neighbourhood could be interpreted as an expression of his family's local solidarity, while the stele's relief and inscription vaunted his relationship to the king as legitimation for his or his family's leading role in the neighbourhood. In the historical context of the mid-eighth century BC at Sam'al, however, KTMW's religious patronage in this part of the lower town could be understood to have had an even more overt political motive. KTMW's lord Panamuwa II was placed on the throne of Sam'al by the Assyrian king Tiglath-Pileser III following a period of internal strife in which the rightful heir (Panamuwa's father Bar-Ṣūr) and many of his relatives were killed and the kingdom taken over by a usurper, at least according to the version of events found in Panamuwa II's mortuary inscription.[62] Though we know little about the circumstances of this civil war and restoration and even less about KTMW's background, it is possible that when KTMW was raised to his evidently high position at Sam'al, he was in some way a *novus homo* or upstart, a new occupant of one of the palatial residences of the northern lower town. His foundation of a relatively grand mortuary establishment (and possibly also the construction or renovation of temple A/III) was perhaps an attempt to legitimate his position in the eyes of the local audience of both gods and humans in a period of political factionalism and external interference. Through benefactions including the sponsorship of feasts at an institution such as this, he might have hoped

Ethnographic Analogy', 19–34; Stone, *Nippur Neighborhoods*; van de Mieroop, *The Ancient Mesopotamian City*, pp. 109–12; Schloen, *The House of the Father as Fact and Symbol*, pp. 112, 151–65, 287–89.

[61] Müller, 'Teil II: Das Stadtgebiet', pp. 357–60; Hrouda, *Tell Halaf IV*, pp. 5–7, 9–21, pls 2–4. Though it is often assumed that the statue of the man and woman represents a deceased royal couple (e.g. Niehr, 'Bestattung und Ahnenkult in den Königshäusern von Sam'al'), there is no direct evidence for their royal status.

[62] See Dion, *Les Araméens à l'âge du fer*, pp. 109–11; Herrmann, 'Society and Economy under Empire at Iron Age Sam'al', pp. 44–49.

to foster in his new neighbourhood the kind of local social links from which the above-mentioned urban clans were formed.

An alternative possibility is that the group who participated in the annual feast in Building A/II had quite a different basis with a more exclusive, upper-class character. Later in the first millennium BC, urban 'voluntary associations' of various types that were dedicated to different deities (e.g. Greek *thiasoi*, including Dionysiac cults, Roman *collegia*, mystery cults, professional groups, and even Jewish synagogues and early Christian churches) proliferated throughout the Hellenistic world. These associations frequently had their own meeting places, engaged in communal feasting and drinking, and provided for the funerals of their members through contributions.[63] While it has often been proposed that the greater social dislocation from civic and kinship groups in this later period was responsible for the widespread popularity of these compensatory associations, especially among the urban lower classes,[64] it is quite probable that similar organizations existed to a lesser degree in the pre-Hellenistic Near East to meet various social or religious needs.[65] Indeed, one type of such a religious voluntary association, the *marzeaḥ*, is known to have existed in the West Semitic world from the third millennium BC through the Late Roman period.

The *marzeaḥ* is attested sporadically in texts from Ebla, Ugarit, and Emar, in the prophetic books of the Hebrew Bible (Amos 6. 4–7, Jeramiah 16. 5), in Phoenician and Aramaic texts of the later first millennium BC, and in Nabataean and especially Palmyrene inscriptions of the early centuries of the Common Era. The most recent comprehensive review of the textual evidence for this association concluded that in all periods the *marzeaḥ* was an upper-

[63] The designation 'voluntary' is given to distinguish such associations from civic and familial groups to which membership was 'automatic'. See Wilson, 'Voluntary Associations', p. 1. See also Kloppenborg and Wilson, *Voluntary Associations in the Graeco-Roman World*; Chaniotis, 'Religious Organizations and Bodies: Greece', pp. 319–21; North, 'Religious Organizations and Bodies: Rome', pp. 321–23.

[64] E.g. Kloppenborg, 'Collegia and *Thiasoi*', pp. 17–18.

[65] Occasional references are made to defined religious groups in Ugaritic and Phoenician texts (del Olmo Lete, 'Religious Organizations and Bodies: Syria-Canaan', pp. 315–16) and various specific 'assemblies' (*puhrum*) are attested in addition to the city assembly in Old Babylonian texts, including 'the assembly of the *awīlû*, the assembly of the *pašīšu*-priests, the assembly of the innkeepers, the assembly of the troops, the assembly of the land, the assembly of kings; finally the assembly of the "nomads", and the assembly of the Amorites' (Seri, *Local Power in Old Babylonian Mesopotamia*, p. 166).

class, male religious drinking society.[66] The most abundant pre-Hellenistic evidence for these societies is found in several legal texts from late second-millennium BC Ugarit, from which it is apparent that each *marzeaḥ* was dedicated to a particular deity (Šatrana, the Hurrian Ištar, and Anat are attested), that more than one *marzeaḥ* could exist in close proximity, and that each had a defined membership, referred to as the 'men' or 'sons' of the *marzeaḥ*, and probably a 'head' (*rb*). This group could collectively own property, their right to which was recognized by the King of Ugarit and which could include a special 'house' for their meetings, as well as vineyards, fields, and substantial amounts of silver. The frequent mention of vineyards in connection with the *marzeaḥ*, in combination with a mythological text in which the supreme god El holds a *marzeaḥ* and gets extremely drunk, suggests that one of the main activities of these societies was drinking wine, often to excess.[67]

The activities and setting related to the KTMW stele, as indicated by its text, relief, and context, shared several features in common with those of the *marzeaḥ*. The inscription mentions an annual feast which includes the product of the vine and is dedicated to several deities, as well as the 'soul' of KTMW. The deceased is shown sitting at such a feast, holding aloft a vessel associated with elite wine consumption that is of the same type as a fourth-century BC example inscribed in Phoenician to indicate that it was intended for the *marzeaḥ* of Šamaš.[68] The stele was found in a building described by a particular term (*syr/d*) that may mean something like 'assembly' or 'reception hall'. This building, next to but distinct from a neighbourhood temple, could have accommodated a medium-sized group, and the inscription indicates that there was a vineyard associated with it. The description of the party responsible for the perpetuation of the feast which KTMW had established, 'whoever of my sons or of the sons of anybody (else) should come into possession of this *nsyr/d*' (lines 6–8), is so vague that one could potentially even take it as a reference to communal ownership of the building, rather than ownership by a particular family. While most scholars now reject the older idea that the *marzeaḥ* was a specifically funerary cult association,[69] the relevant passage in Jeremiah (16. 5) from the seventh or

[66] McLaughlin, *The Marzeah in the Prophetic Literature*, pp. 65–70.

[67] See McLaughlin, *The Marzeah in the Prophetic Literature*, pp. 11–33, for the *marzeaḥ* texts from Ugarit and their interpretation.

[68] Avigad and Greenfield, 'A Bronze *phiale* with a Phoenician Dedicatory Inscription', pp. 118–28; McLaughlin, *The Marzeah in the Prophetic Literature*, pp. 37–38.

[69] E.g. Lewis, *Cults of the Dead in Ancient Israel and Ugarit*, pp. 80–94; Schmidt, *Israel's*

sixth century BC indicates that it could in some cases have hosted a funereal wake such as KTMW's feast.

It must be noted that despite ample opportunity the KTMW inscription does not mention a *marzeaḥ*, instead repeatedly using the term *syr/d*, so it would be incautious to conclude that the stele building was a *marzeaḥ*-house. Nevertheless, given the similarities of the KTMW institution with what is known of the *marzeaḥ*, it is possible that this *syr/d* belonged to a similar type of religious voluntary association at Sam'al that was devoted to one or more of the deities listed in the inscription and included among its activities mortuary feasts for its most prominent or wealthiest member(s). Similarly to the *marzeaḥ*, the basis for inclusion in this group may have been wealth and political status rather than kinship or local origin, as is perhaps suggested by the inscription's reference to the King of Sam'al and the absence of a son and heir as either commissioner of the monument or attendant in the relief. Rather than the consolidation of local influence and solidarity, the purpose of the institution in which the stele was installed may instead have been to reinforce the social bonds among the kingdom's leading nobles and officials.

Summary and Conclusions

The KTMW stele from Zincirli is a rich new source that breathes life into one corner of an Iron Age Near Eastern city. The testimony of its inscription, relief, and archaeological context support several previous theories regarding the practice of mortuary cult in the Aramaean and Luwian kingdoms, such as the provision of regular food- and drink-offerings for the deceased, the belief that mourners could interact with the 'soul' through its stone representation, and the close connection of mortuary cult with deity cult, suggested by both the provision of offerings to several gods simultaneously with those for the deceased's 'soul' and the stele's proximity to what is argued to have been a small temple. The stele has also offered some surprises, however. The evidently non-royal status of its owner contradicts suggestions that the envisioned post-mortem meal with the gods and veneration in a private mortuary chapel were restricted to deceased (and 'deified') royalty, and its inscription presents us with a new term (*syr/d*) for the setting of such a cult.

In combination with its architectural and urban context, the KTMW stele also seems to provide a window onto urban social groups at the often elusive

Beneficent Dead; Pardee, '*Marzihu*, *Kispu* and the Ugaritic Funerary Cult', pp. 273–87; McLaughlin, *The Marzeah in the Prophetic Literature*, pp. 70–79.

level between the immediate family and the city or state as a whole and suggests that such groups may have been defined in part through shared religious practice. On the basis of comparative material ranging broadly in time and space, two alternative possibilities were suggested for the social background of the devotees of KTMW's mortuary cult. On the one hand, the stele building may have been intended to provide a space for the meeting of an urban 'clan' for annual or even more regular feasts in honour of patron gods and ancestors, under the leadership of KTMW's immediate family. On the other hand, the building could have served as the 'clubhouse' of a group of upper-class men who socialized at periodic religious feasts at which its deceased associates were also remembered. It may not be possible, given the current state of the evidence, to decide between these two, admittedly speculative, proposals. How we interpret the social context of KTMW's mortuary cult and which aspect of his social identity he sought to emphasize through his mortuary monument may depend ultimately on whether we consider urban social organization in the late Iron Age Near East to have been based fundamentally on local solidarity and kinship structures or increasingly on class and social status. Despite these unanswered questions, this case demonstrates that by putting such an inscribed monument into its broadest possible context we can gain new insight into little-known dimensions of ancient Near Eastern urban and religious life.

Works Cited

Secondary Studies

Albertz, R., *A History of Israelite Religion in the Old Testament Period*, vol. I: *From the Beginnings to the End of the Monarchy* (Louisville: Westminster John Knox, 1994)

Avigad, N,. and J. C. Greenfield, 'A Bronze *phiale* with a Phoenician Dedicatory Inscription', *Israel Exploration Journal*, 32 (1982), 118–28

Bonatz, D., *Das syro-hethitische Grabdenkmal: Untersuchungen zur Entstehung einer neuen Bildgattung in der Eisenzeit im nordsyrisch-südostanatolischen Raum* (Mainz: Philipp von Zabern, 2000)

——, 'Syro-Hittite Funerary Monuments: A Phenomenon of Tradition or Innovation?', in *Essays on Syria in the Iron Age*, ed. by G. Bunnens, Ancient Near Eastern Studies Suppl., 7 (Louvain: Peeters, 2000), pp. 189–210

Casana, J., and J. Herrmann, 'Settlement History and Urban Planning at Zincirli Höyük, Southern Turkey', *Journal of Mediterranean Archaeology*, 23 (2010), 55–80

Chaniotis, A., 'Religious Organizations and Bodies: Greece', in *Religions of the Ancient World: A Guide*, ed. by Sarah I. Johnston (Cambridge, MA: Harvard University Press, 2004), pp. 319–21

Charpin, D., 'Les Divinités famliales des Babyloniens d'après les légendes de leurs sceaux-cylindres', in *De la Babylonie à la Syrie en passant par Mari: mélanges offerts à Monsieur J.-R. Kupper à l'occasion de son 70e anniversaire*, ed. by Ö. Tunca (Liège: Université de Liège, 1990), pp. 59–78

Cohen, A., *Arab Border Villages in Israel* (Manchester: Manchester University Press, 1965)

——, 'The Politics of Marriage in Changing Middle Eastern Stratification Systems', in *Essays in Comparative Social Stratification*, ed. by L. Plotnicov and A. Tuden (Pittsburgh: University of Pittsburgh Press, 1970), pp. 195–209

Collon, D., 'Clothing and Grooming in Ancient Western Asia', in *Civilizations of the Ancient Near East*, vol. I, ed. by J. M. Sasson (New York: Scribners, 1995), pp. 503–15

Dever, W., 'Palaces and Temples in Canaan and Ancient Israel', in *Civilizations of the Ancient Near East*, vol. I, ed. by J. M. Sasson (New York: Scribner's, 1995), pp. 605–14

Dietrich, M., O. Loretz, and J. Sanmartín, *Die Keilalphabetischen Texte aus Ugarit*, Alter Orient und Altes Testament, 24.1 (Neukirschen-Vluyn: Neukirchener Verlag, 1976)

Dion, P., *Les Araméens à l'âge du fer: histoire politique et structures sociales* (Paris: Librairie Lecoffre, 1997)

Donner, H., and W. Röllig, *Kanaanäische und aramäische Inschriften*, 3rd edn (Wiesbaden: Harrassowitz, 1971)

Eickelman, D. F., *The Middle East and Central Asia: An Anthropological Approach*, 4th edn (Upper Saddle River: Prentice-Hall, 2002)

Galpaz-Feller, P., 'Hair in the Bible and in Ancient Egyptian Culture: Cultural and Private Connotations', *Biblische Notizien*, 125 (2005), 75–94

Genge, H., *Nordsyrisch-südanatolische Reliefs: eine archäologisch-historische Untersuchung, Datierung und Bestimmung* (København: Munksgaard, 1979)

Hawkins, J. D., 'Late Hittite Funerary Monuments', in *Death in Mesopotamia: Papers Read at the XXVIe Rencontre Assyriologique Internationale*, ed. by B. Alster (København: Akademisk, 1980), pp. 213–25

——, 'More Late Hittite Funerary Monuments', in *Anatolia and the Ancient Near East: Studies in Honor of T. Özgüç*, ed. by K. Emre and others (Ankara: Türk Tarih Kurum Basimevi, 1989), pp. 189–97

Herrmann, V. R., 'Society and Economy under Empire at Iron Age Sam'al (Zincirli Höyük, Turkey)' (unpublished doctoral dissertation, University of Chicago, 2011)

Hoftijzer, J., and K. Jongeling, *Dictionary of the North-West Semitic Inscriptions*, Handbuch der Orientalistik, Erste Abteilung, Der Nähe und Mittlere Osten, 21 (Leiden: Brill, 1995)

Hrouda, B., *Tell Halaf IV: Die Kleinfunde aus historischer Zeit* (Berlin: De Gruyter, 1962)

Jonker, G., *The Topography of Remembrance: The Dead, Tradition and Collective Memory in Mesopotamia* (Leiden: Brill, 1995)

Kestemont, G., 'Survie et destin chez les Néo-Hittites (IXe–VIIIe s. av. J.C.)', in *Vie et survie dans les civilisations orientales*, ed. by A. Théodoridès, P. Naster, and J. Ries, Acta Orientalia Belgica, 3 (Leuven: Éditions Peeters, 1983), pp. 55–64

Kloppenborg, J. S., 'Collegia and *Thiasoi*: Issues in Function, Taxonomy and Membership', in *Voluntary Associations in the Graeco-Roman World*, ed. by J. S. Kloppenborg and S. G. Wilson (London: Routledge, 1996), pp. 16–30

Kloppenborg, J. S., and S. G. Wilson, eds, *Voluntary Associations in the Graeco-Roman World* (London: Routledge, 1996)

Langenegger, F., 'Teil I: Die Bauten und Schichten des Burghügels', in *Tell Halaf II: Die Bauwerke*, ed. by R. Naumann (Berlin: De Gruyter 1950), pp. 3–324

Lewis, T. J., *Cults of the Dead in Ancient Israel and Ugarit*, Harvard Semitic Monographs, 39 (Atlanta: Scholar, 1989)

Lipiński, E., *The Aramaeans: Their Ancient History, Culture, Religion*, Orientalia Lovaniensia Analecta, 100 (Leuven: Peeters, 2000)

Luschan, F. von, *Ausgrabungen in Sendschirli III: Thorsculpturen*, Mittheilungen aus den Orientalischen Sammlungen, Königliche Museen zu Berlin, 13 (Berlin: Georg Reimer, 1902)

Luschan, F. von, and W. Andrae, *Die Kleinfunde von Sendschirli*, Mittheilungen aus den Orientalischen Sammlungen, Königliche Museen zu Berlin, 15 (Berlin: De Gruyter, 1943)

Luschan, F. von, C. Humann, and R. Koldewey, *Ausgrabungen in Sendschirli II: Ausgrabungsbericht und Architektur*, Mittheilungen aus den Orientalischen Sammlungen, Königliche Museen zu Berlin, 12 (Berlin: Spemann, 1898)

Luschan, F. von, and G. Jacoby, *Ausgrabungen in Sendschirli IV*, Mittheilungen aus den Orientalischen Sammlungen, Königliche Museen zu Berlin, 14 (Berlin: Georg Reimer, 1911)

Luschan, F. von, E. Schrader, and E. Sachau, *Ausgrabungen in Sendschirli I. Einleitung und Inschriften*, Mittheilungen aus den Orientalischen Sammlungen, Königliche Museen zu Berlin, 11 (Berlin: Spemann, 1893)

Masson, E., 'La Stèle mortuaire de Kuttamuwa (Zincirli): comment l'appréhender', *Semitica et Classica: International Journal of Oriental and Mediterranean Studies*, 3 (2010), 47–58

Matthiae, P., 'High Old Syrian Royal Statuary from Ebla', in *Von Uruk nach Tuttul: eine Festschrift für Eva Strommenger, Studien und Aufsätze von Kollegen und Freunden*, ed. by B. Hrouda, S. Kroll, and P. Z. Spanos (München: Profil, 1992), pp. 111–28

Mazar, A., *Excavations at Tell Qasile, Part One: The Philistine Sanctuary: Architecture and Cult Objects*, Qedem, 12 (Jerusalem: The Institute of Archaeology, Hebrew University of Jerusalem, 1980)

——, 'The Temples and Cults of the Philistines', in *The Sea Peoples and their World: A Reassessment*, ed. by E. D. Oren (Philadelphia: The University Museum, University of Pennsylvania, 2000), pp. 213–31

——, 'Temples of the Middle and Late Bronze Ages and the Iron Age', in *The Architecture of Ancient Israel from the Prehistoric to the Persian Periods*, ed. by A. Kempinski and R. Reich (Jerusalem: Israel Exploration Society, 1992), pp. 161–90

Mazzini, G., 'On the Problematic Term *syr/d* in the New Old Aramaic Inscription from Zincirli', *Ugarit Forschungen*, 41 (2009), 505–07

McLaughlin, J. L., *The Marzēaḥ in the Prophetic Literature*, Supplements to Vetus Testamentum, 86 (Leiden: Brill, 2001)

Mieroop, M. van de, *The Ancient Mesopotamian City* (Oxford: Clarendon Press, 1997)

Moortgat, A., *Die bildende Kunst des Alten Orients und die Bergvölker* (Berlin: Schoetz, 1932)

Müller, K., 'Teil II: Das Stadtgebiet', in *Tell Halaf II: Die Bauwerke*, ed. by R. Naumann (Berlin: De Gruyter, 1950), pp. 327–66

Naumann, R., *Architektur Kleinasiens von ihren Anfängen bis zum Ende der hethitischen Zeit* (Tübingen: Wasmuth, 1971)

Niehr, H., 'Bestattung und Ahnenkult in den Königshäusern von Sam'al (Zincirli) und Guzana (Tell Halaf) in Nordsyrien', *Zeitschrift des Deutschen Palästina-Vereins*, 122 (2006), 111–39

——, 'Ein weiterer Aspekt zum Totenkult der Könige von Sam'al', *Studi Epigrafici e Linguistici sul Vicino Oriente Antico*, 18 (2001), 83–97

——, 'Zum Totenkult der Könige von Sam'al im 9. und 8. Jh. v. Chr.', *Studi Epigrafici e Linguistici sul Vicino Oriente Antico*, 11 (1994), 57–73

North, J., 'Religious Organizations and Bodies: Rome', in *Religions of the Ancient World: A Guide*, ed. by S. I. Johnston (Cambridge, MA: Harvard University Press, 2004), pp. 321–23

Olmo Lete, G. del, 'Religious Organizations and Bodies: Syria-Canaan', in *Religions of the Ancient World: A Guide*, ed. by S. I. Johnston (Cambridge, MA: Harvard University Press, 2004), pp. 315–16

Olyan, S. M., 'Family Religion in Israel and the Wider Levant of the First Millennium BCE', in *Household and Family Religion in Antiquity*, ed. by J. Bodel and S. M. Olyan (Malden: Blackwell, 2008), pp. 113–26

——, 'What Do Shaving Rites Accomplish and What Do They Signal in Biblical Ritual Contexts?', *Journal of Biblical Literature*, 117 (1998), 611–22

Orthmann, W., *Untersuchungen zur späthethitischen Kunst*, Saarbrücker Beiträge zur Altertumskunde, 8 (Bonn: Rudolf Habelt, 1971)

Pardee, D., 'The 'Aqhatu Legend', in *The Context of Scripture*, ed. by W. W. Hallo, 3 vols (Leiden: Brill, 2000), I, 343–56

——, '*Marziḥu*, *Kispu* and the Ugaritic Funerary Cult: A Minimalist View', in *Ugarit, Religion and Culture: Proceedings of the International Colloquium on Ugarit, Religion and Culture, Edinburgh, July 1994*, ed. by N. Wyatt, W. G. E. Watson, and J. B. Lloyd, Ugaritisch-biblische Literatur, 12 (Münster: Ugarit, 1996), pp. 273–87

——, 'A New Aramaic Inscription from Zincirli', *Bulletin of the American Schools of Oriental Research*, 356 (2009), 51–71

Pucci, M., *Functional Analysis of Space in Syro-Hittite Architecture*, British Archaeological Reports. International Series, 1738 (Oxford: Archaeopress, 2008)
Robins, G., 'Hair and the Construction of Identity in Ancient Egypt', *Journal of the American Research Center in Egypt*, 36 (1999), 55–69
Röllig, W., 'Das Sitzbild des Kammaki vom Tell Halaf', in *Altertumswissenschaften im Dialog: Festschrift für Wolfram Nadel zur Vollendung seines 80. Lebensjahres*, ed. by R. Dittmann, C. Eder, and B. Jacobs, Alter Orient und Altes Testament, 306 (Münster: Ugarit, 2003), pp. 421–32
Schachner, A., S. Schachner, and H. Karabulut, 'Vier Sitzbilder aus Bit-Bahiani', *Zeitschrift für Assyriologie und Vorderasiatische Archäologie*, 92 (2002), 106–23
Schloen, J. D., *The House of the Father as Fact and Symbol: Patrimonialism in Ugarit and the Ancient Near East*, Studies in the Archaeology and History of the Levant, 2 (Winona Lake: Eisenbrauns, 2001)
Schloen, J. D., and A. S. Fink, 'New Excavations at Zincirli Höyük in Turkey (Ancient Sam'al) and the Discovery of an Inscribed Mortuary Stele', *Bulletin of the American Schools of Oriental Research*, 356 (2009), 1–13
——, 'Searching for Ancient Sam'al: New Excavations at Zincirli in Turkey', *Near Eastern Archaeology*, 72 (2009), 203–19
Schmidt, B. B., *Israel's Beneficent Dead: Ancestor Cult and Necromancy in Ancient Israelite Religion and Tradition* (Winona Lake: Eisenbrauns, 1994)
Seri, A., *Local Power in Old Babylonian Mesopotamia* (London: Equinox Publishing, 2005)
Spycket, A., *La Statuaire du Proche-Orient Ancien*, Handbuch der Orientalistik Studien, 1, B1a, L.2 (Leiden: Brill, 1981)
Stone, E., *Nippur Neighborhoods*, Studies in Ancient Oriental Civilization, 44 (Chicago: Oriental Institute, University of Chicago, 1987)
——, 'Texts, Architecture and Ethnographic Analogy: Patterns of Residence in Old Babylonian Nippur', *Iraq*, 43 (1981), 19–34
Struble, E., and V. R. Herrmann, 'An Eternal Feast at Sam'al: The New Iron Age Mortuary Stele from Zincirli in Context', *Bulletin of the American Schools of Oriental Research*, 356 (2009), 15–49
Toorn, K. van der, *Family Religion in Babylonia, Syria and Israel: Continuity and Change in the Forms of Religious Life*, Studies in the History and Culture of the Ancient Near East, 7 (Leiden: Brill, 1996)
——, 'Religious Practices of the Individual and Family: Introduction', in *Religions of the Ancient World: A Guide*, ed. by S. I. Johnston (Cambridge, MA: Harvard University Press, 2004), pp. 423–24
Triebel, L., *Jenseitshoffnung in Wort und Stein: Nefesch und Pyramidales Grabmal als Phänomene antiken jüdischen Bestattungswesens im Kontext der Nachbarkulturen*, Arbeiten zur Geschichte des Antiken Judentums und des Urchristentums, 56 (Leiden: Brill, 2004)
Tropper, J., *Die Inschriften von Zincirli: neue Edition und vergleichende Grammatik des phönizischen, samalischen und aramäischen Textkorpus*, Abhandlungen zur Literatur Alt-Syrien-Palästinas und Mesopotamiens, 6 (Münster: Ugarit, 1993)

Voos, J., 'Bemerkungen zum Syrohethitischen Totenkult der Frühen Eisenzeit', in *Šulmu: Papers on the Ancient Near East Presented at the International Conference of Socialist Countries*, ed. by P. Vavrousek and V. Soucek (Prague: Charles University in Prague, 1988), pp. 349–60

——, 'Studien zum syrohethitischen Totenkult: zur Rolle von Statuen und Reliefs im Totenkult der Fürstentümer Nordsyriens und Südostanatoliens während der frühen Eisenzeit' (unpublished doctoral dissertation, Zentralinstitut der Akademie der Wissenschaften der DDR, 1986)

——, 'Studien zur Rolle von Statuen und Reliefs im syrohethitischen Totenkult während der frühen Eisenzeit (etwa 10.–7. Jh. v. u. Z.)', *Ethnographisch-Archäologische Zeitschrift*, 29 (1988), 347–62

Werner, P., *Die entwicklung der Sakralarchitektur in Nordsyrien und Südostkleinasien vom Neolithikum bis in das 1. Jt. v. Chr.*, Münchener Vorderasiatische Studien, 15 (München: Profil, 1994)

Wilson, S. G., 'Voluntary Associations: An Overview', in *Voluntary Associations in the Graeco-Roman World*, ed. by J. S. Kloppenborg and S. G. Wilson (London: Routledge, 1996), pp. 1–15

Winter, I. J., 'North Syria in the Early First Millennium B.C. with Special Reference to Ivory Carving' (unpublished doctoral dissertation, Columbia University, 1973)

Woolley, L., *Carchemish, Part II: The Town Defences* (London: British Museum Press, 1921)

Woolley, L., and R. D. Barnett, *Carchemish, Part III: The Excavations in the Inner Town; The Hittite Inscriptions* (London: British Museum Press, 1952)

Woolley, L., and M. E. L. Mallowan, *Ur Excavations VII: The Old Babylonian Period* (London: British Museum, 1976)

Yon, M., 'The Temple of the Rhytons at Ugarit', in *Ugarit, Religion and Culture: Proceedings of the International Colloquium on Ugarit, Religion and Culture, Edinburgh, July 1994*, ed. by N. Wyatt, W. G. E. Watson, and J. B. Lloyd, Ugaritisch-biblische Literatur, 12 (Münster: Ugarit, 1996), pp. 405–22

Younger, K. L., 'The Hadad Inscription (2.36)', in *The Context of Scripture*, vol. II: *Monumental Inscriptions from the Biblical World*, ed. by W. W. Hallo and K. L. Younger, Jr (Leiden: Brill, 2000), pp. 156–58

——, 'Two Epigraphic Notes on the New Katumuwa Inscription from Zincirli', *Maarav*, 16 (2009), 159–79

TEMPLE AND CITY IN HELLENISTIC URUK: SACRED SPACE AND THE TRANSFORMATION OF LATE BABYLONIAN SOCIETY

Heather D. Baker

Introduction

This chapter examines an episode of wide-ranging cultic reform which took place in the Babylonian city of Uruk in the late Achaemenid period and explores its impact on urban spatial organization and on the relationship between temple and community. This was a critical period: as one scholar has recently observed,

> The second part of Achaemenid rule in Babylonia opened up a new chapter in the history of Babylonian temple religion, as many cultic, administrative and social transformations affected the operation of the temples and their priesthoods, but this period of change too remains to be fully investigated.[1]

As well as attempting to delineate some of the key ramifications of this cultic reform, the chapter also aims to trace further developments in the urban landscape of Uruk during the Seleucid era and to relate them to their socio-political context.

* This study arose originally out of work conducted under the auspices of the START Project 'The Economic History of Babylonia in the First Millennium BC' led by Michael Jursa at the University of Vienna and funded by the Austrian Science Fund (FWF). The present article was prepared within the framework of the project 'Royal Institutional Households in First Millennium BC Mesopotamia' led by the author since March 2009 as part of a National Research Network '"Imperium" and "Officium"– Comparative Studies in Ancient Bureaucracy and Officialdom'; this project is also funded by the Austrian Science Fund (grant S 10802-G18).

[1] Waerzeggers, 'The Babylonian Priesthood', p. 70.

Heather Baker (heather.baker@univie.ac.at) Institut für Orientalistik, Universität Wien.

It is perhaps only natural to think of the Babylonian temples as the principal sites within the city where cultic activity took place. However, we should not underestimate the extent to which cultic topography permeated, indeed was intertwined with, the urban fabric.[2] The cosmic dimension of the ancient Near Eastern capitals, especially Babylon itself, has been underlined by various scholars,[3] and it is clear that the values attached to urban living in general were bound up with the concept of civilization as something bestowed by the gods. Not only the temples bore religious ceremonial names, but also daises, shrines, and altars around the city, as well as processional streets, city walls, and gates.[4] Watercourses and quays were also important, especially for divine excursions within and between cities, such as the annual journey of the god Nabû from Borsippa to Babylon by ceremonial barge in order to participate in the New Year festival.[5] The city thus took on a 'divine personality', and the home of a god was not merely his temple but also his city.[6] It would be a mistake therefore to differentiate too sharply between the spatial context of 'everyday' activities and that of cultic practice: on one level the whole city was, effectively, sacred space. This is reflected, for example, in the prevalence in contemporary everyday documents of Babylonian toponyms and terms associated with cultic topography, for instance the popular characterization of major public streets as 'way of the gods and the king' and the references to city districts named after local temples.[7]

In the Mesopotamian context Pongratz-Leisten has distinguished between mythologized and ritualized sacred space.[8] The former comprises sacred space imbued with mythical or cosmological significance; this may be reflected in the ceremonial or programmatic names given to structures such as temples, city walls, and the like (see above). A ritualized place, by contrast, required sanctification through ritual acts. These acts may create sacred space intentionally (as in the case of building rituals) or the sanctification may be achieved de facto (for example, through the movement of a procession which brings before the

[2] For a succinct overview of the nature of sacred space in Mesopotamia, see Pongratz-Leisten, 'Sacred Places', pp. 253–55.

[3] See especially Maul, 'Die altorientalische Hauptstadt', pp. 109–24, and George, '"Bond of the Lands"', pp. 125–45.

[4] George, *Babylonian Topographical Texts*, passim.

[5] Waerzeggers, *The Ezida Temple of Borsippa*, pp. 119–30.

[6] George, '"Bond of the Lands"', p. 127.

[7] Baker, 'From Street Altar to Palace', pp. 536–37.

[8] Pongratz-Leisten, 'Sacred Places', p. 254.

public the gods, normally hidden from sight). Thus sacred space is created not by architectural features alone but rather by actions performed.

As in all periods of Mesopotamian history, members of the temple personnel formed a significant sector of the urban community, both in numerical terms and with respect to their crucial role in caring for the deities housed in the city's various temples and shrines. Their daily lives were regulated by the cultic calendar, revolving around the regular, daily provisions for the gods as well as the monthly, annual, and periodical festivals.[9] These events determined in large measure the rhythm of their days and their movements in and around the city. The duties of the temple prebendaries — those who held offices involving the performance of specialized tasks in the service of a deity (or deities) in return for a fixed share in temple income — required their physical attendance (although this might be circumvented to some degree by leasing the performance of prebendary duties to another suitably qualified individual).[10] These same personnel typically had other interests which served to supplement and diversify their sources of income: members of the Nappāḫu family of sixth- to early fifth-century Babylon, for example, owned some date orchards outside the city as well as small urban properties, both of which generated rental income.[11] However, out of the 291 tablets from their archive, only a handful (18) of those where the place of writing is both present and preserved and where the transaction directly involves a member of the archive-holding family were drawn up in a place other than Babylon. Moreover, in those instances the places in question are restricted to the three settlements in which the family's date orchards were situated, thus highlighting their relatively circumscribed geographical sphere of activity.[12] This picture is in stark contrast with contemporary entrepreneurial

[9] Waerzeggers, *The Ezida Temple of Borsippa*, pp. 111–52, for a treatment of temple worship and cult in Neo-Babylonian/early Achaemenid Borsippa; she distinguishes (p. 111) between the named festivals common to all deities and those which were associated with the particular mythology or attribute of a certain deity and thus lent a unique aspect to the local cultic calendar. For a similarly detailed account of the cultic occasions attested for Hellenistic Babylonia, see Linssen, *The Cults of Uruk and Babylon*.

[10] For a detailed discussion of Neo-Babylonian temple prebends as well as a general treatment of the priesthood and cult, see now the comprehensive study of the Nabû temple of Borsippa by Waerzeggers, *The Ezida Temple of Borsippa*.

[11] Baker, *The Archive of the Nappāḫu Family*, pp. 47–69.

[12] Higher ranking members of the temple personnel, including the temple scribes, are known to have travelled to Susa in connection with the fulfilment of tax obligations during the reign of Darius, but not the ordinary prebendaries (Waerzeggers, 'Babylonians in Susa', p. 806).

families such as the Egibis, whose interests were played out over a much greater geographical area, with a spatial network of connections covering the key cities of northern Babylonia as well as numerous small settlements and extending as far as Susa and Ecbatana in the east.[13]

The prebendaries were not only tied to the temple through their regular attendance for the performance of duties; they often also owned a physical stake in the temple itself. Some members of the temple personnel lived in residential areas located within the temple precincts of Eanna at Uruk and Esagila at Babylon.[14] Moreover, some of them also owned facilities located within the temple precinct which served as space for storage and/or workrooms: in the Neo-Babylonian and Achaemenid period, properties known as *šutummu*s are attested in private ownership,[15] while in the Hellenistic period at Uruk we are dealing with the rooms known as *bīt qāti*s located within the precincts of the Rēš and Ešgal temples.[16] The conditions attached to the allocation and ownership of these properties, which formed part of the temple's physical fabric, are not so very well documented, but it seems clear that ownership of a temple prebend was a precondition because these were spaces used in the performance of prebendary duties. Like the prebends themselves, they were alienable within the restricted group of consecrated temple personnel and could be passed on through inheritance, sale, and the like.

The introductory remarks made so far are intended to remind the reader of the extent to which cultic topography permeated the daily lives not only of the temple personnel but of all Babylonian city-dwellers. But what happened when the sacred landscape changed? We are relatively well informed as to temporary disturbances set against a general background of continuity in cultic prac-

[13] For example, the 144 tablets pertaining to the activities of Marduk-nāṣir-apli, key member of the fourth generation of the well-known Egibi family, were written in fifteen places apart from Babylon; see the catalogue of Abraham, *Business and Politics under the Persian Empire*, pp. 196–202. This picture would be greatly expanded if all five generations of the archive-holding family were taken into account, but that is beyond the scope of the present study.

[14] Baker, 'Beyond Planning'. There is some evidence that those who lived outside of a precinct tended nevertheless to live in proximity to the temple they served; see Baker, 'From Street Altar to Palace', p. 546.

[15] Waerzeggers, *The Ezida Temple of Borsippa*, pp. 11–13.

[16] The *bīt qāti*s within the Rēš are the subject of a detailed study by the present author which re-evaluates the cultic topography of the temple complex in its entirety and demonstrates the differential access to parts of the temple by different sectors of its personnel: Baker, 'Beneath the Stairs in the Rēš Temple of Hellenistic Uruk'.

tice, thanks to the wealth of royal inscriptions which commemorate specific instances of temple (re)building.[17] The act of rebuilding a temple inevitably led to some short-term disruption in cultic practice. The necessity of rebuilding was justified by recourse to the idea that the deity was dissatisfied with the quality of the previous construction, which had lacked the necessary divine approval, and in his/her anger that deity had caused it to collapse.[18] The deity abandoned the temple since it was no longer suitable for divine occupation and took up temporary residence in the temple of another deity while the rebuilding took place. Presumably temporary arrangements had also to be made for accommodating the tasks performed by the prebendary personnel serving that deity, such as the provision of cultic meals. The completed rebuilding of the sanctuary was marked by the ceremonial return of the deity to his/her abode and the ritual bringing in of the 'keybrick'.[19] Judging by the numerous temple rebuildings attested both in the texts and in the archaeological record, and given that each Babylonian city would have not only one but many temples,[20] such episodes were rather commonplace. But what happened in the case of major cultic reforms? In the remainder of this chapter I shall discuss the case of Uruk in the later first millennium BC, exploring the effects of wide-ranging cultic reform on the spatial organization of the city, on the composition of the urban elite, and on the lives of its inhabitants.

Uruk in the Later First Millennium BC

Uruk, a key site for the development of southern Mesopotamian urbanism already in the late fourth millennium BC, was still one of the major urban centres of Babylonia during the first millennium BC. The city witnessed a resurgence during the eighth century BC after which it flourished especially during the Neo-Babylonian and early Achaemenid period, and then again during the Hellenistic period. After the imposition of Greek rule following Alexander's

[17] Schaudig, 'The Restoration of Temples in the Neo- and Late Babylonian Periods', pp. 141–64; for the Assyrian evidence, cf. Novotny, 'Temple Building in Assyria', pp. 109–39.

[18] Ambos, 'Building Rituals from the First Millennium BC', pp. 224–29.

[19] Ambos, 'Building Rituals from the First Millennium BC', pp. 235–36.

[20] For example, forty-three temples in Babylon are listed in Tablet IV of the topographical series Tintir (George, *Babylonian Topographical Texts*, pp. 57–62). This excludes the numerous cultic daises, stations, and shrines scattered around the city, a couple of which may be identified with structures excavated in the streets of the Merkes quarter of the city (Baker, 'A Waste of Space?', pp. 96–97).

conquest in 331 BC, Uruk and Babylon were the two principal cities where the Babylonian cultural tradition continued to flourish, especially among the scholarly communities associated with their temples. Other Babylonian settlements were certainly still occupied at this time, but they have produced nothing like the abundance of written material that we have from these two sites. Aside from its importance for the study of Babylonia during the Hellenistic period, Uruk is vital for examining long-term developments in urbanism during the later phases of what has been termed 'cuneiform culture'.[21] Not only has it been relatively well served by excavation and subsequent publication of the results, but also it has produced a great many cuneiform tablets, many of which contain information about urban properties and city topography. Since these cover the period from the seventh century to the second century BC (given some inevitable unevenness of coverage over time), Uruk presents a remarkable case study for long-term continuity and change in Babylonian urbanism during this late period of Mesopotamian civilization. Moreover, the abundant evidence for developments in urbanism per se is complemented by our knowledge of the city's society and economy based on the contemporary documents.

Cultic Reform in Uruk

Various strands of evidence converge to indicate that a major episode of cultic reform took place in Uruk during the fifth century BC. This religious reform is reflected in our sources by two major changes. First, the Urukean onomasticon was transformed in such a way that personal names formed with the divine name Anu came completely to predominate (whereas before they had scarcely featured in the local onomastic repertoire). This change used to be dated in the fourth century BC, but it is now clear that it began after the reign of Darius I (521–486 BC) and was already well under way by the second half of the fifth century BC.[22] Second, the ancient Eanna temple dedicted to Ištar lost its role as the city's main temple, and Ištar herself was replaced by Anu as head of the local pantheon (hence the aforementioned change in the onomasticon). The Eanna temple as a functioning institution is last attested in everyday documents around the end of the reign of Darius I. It was effectively 'decommissioned', probably not long afterwards. At around the same time, the extensive residential

[21] Radner and Robson, *The Oxford Handbook of Cuneiform Culture*.

[22] Beaulieu, *The Pantheon of Uruk During the Neo-Babylonian Period*, p. 3.

quarters associated with the precinct were abandoned.[23] It is clear from archival documents found in situ that these residential quarters had housed the very people who made up the core of the temple personnel, that is, the middle-ranking staff such as prebendary bakers, brewers, and so on.[24] It comes as no great surprise therefore that their fates were intimately bound up with that of the temple which they had served (see below). Among the private archival tablets associated with this housing, the latest dated tablet was written in the thirty-third regnal year of Darius I, that is, 489/88 BC.[25] There are a few later references to Eanna in the written sources,[26] but these relate simply to the continuation of the cult, albeit on a vastly reduced scale. They do not speak against the stark fact that Eanna had lost its significance as the dominant institution in Uruk, both in cultic and economic terms.[27] This picture is supported also by the archaeological evidence which indicates that later work within Eanna was restricted to the renovation and extension of the ziggurat in the Seleucid era.[28] The rest of the precinct seems to have been abandoned to ruin or used for poor-status dwellings, with the exception of the Kassite-period Karaindaš temple, dedicated to the goddess Ištar, which was apparently restored in the Seleucid period.[29]

The Rēš temple

Following the decline of Eanna, the Rēš temple served as the main city temple of Uruk, housing the god Anu as new head of the local pantheon. Nearby, also in the centre of Uruk, was the Ešgal (or Irigal), the temple dedicated to the goddesses Ištar and Nanaya. Since the excavated plan of the Rēš is best known

[23] See Miglus, *Städtische Wohnarchitektur in Babylonien und Assyrien*, p. 180 with plan Taf. 93 Abb. 413, for a summary of the remains of this housing which was occupied over a period of two centuries from the reign of Sargon II (721–705 BC) to that of Darius I; as Miglus notes, the excavator Lenzen was of the opinion that the housing was destroyed along with Eanna during the reign of Darius.

[24] Some of the archival material is published by Kessler, *Urkunden aus Privathäusern*.

[25] Kessler, 'Urukäische Familien versus babylonische Familien', p. 239.

[26] As noted by Falkenstein, *Topographie von Uruk I*, pp. 40–41. See e.g. the colophon of the Seleucid-period tablet describing daily offerings in Uruk, AO 6451 r. 45 (Linssen, *The Cults of Uruk and Babylon*, pp. 173 and 179).

[27] Kleber, *Tempel und Palast*, p. 4.

[28] Kose, *Uruk: Architektur IV*, p. 257; *contra* Petrie, 'Seleucid Uruk', p. 88, who states: 'During the Seleucid period, the ancient E-anna temple and ziggurat appear to have been substantially rebuilt and continued to be utilised'.

[29] Kose, *Uruk: Architektur IV*, pp. 268 and 276.

to us by its Seleucid-period remains and by the inscriptions of Nikarchos and Kephalon (see below), it is often discussed as though it were a foundation of that period.[30] However, given the evidence for the cultic reform which took place in the fifth century BC, it is likely that it was at that time already that the Anu temple was (re)built on a scale fitting its new role as home to the city's patron deity: it would have been extraordinary if Anu, as newly elevated head of the pantheon, did not occupy the city's major temple. Unfortunately the Seleucid-era rebuilding of the temple obliterated any traces of its forebears: only sparse remains dating to the Achaemenid period (as well as some equally sparse remains of the Neo-Assyrian era) were found beneath the Seleucid level and above the archaic levels of Bauschicht 4 which comprised the earliest remains on the spot.[31] Given that Esarhaddon restored the Anu-ziggurat, it seems reasonable to suppose that the temple of Anu which is attested in Neo-Babylonian texts[32] was associated with the ziggurat and lay in close proximity, quite possibly under the later Rēš complex. However, since at that time the principal temple of Uruk was the Eanna, the Neo-Assyrian/Neo-Babylonian temple of Anu is likely to have been of a simpler plan, without an extensive precinct of its own.[33] In fact, Beaulieu has characterized the Neo-Babylonian Anu temple as 'one of the small independent sanctuaries of Uruk', and Anu himself is treated among the 'Minor Gods'.[34] In that case its seems legitimate to consider the Anu temple as represented by the (late Achaemenid/)Hellenistic Rēš to be a major new (re)foundation, clearly associated with the cultic reform that saw Anu elevated to the head of the Urukean pantheon in the fifth century BC.

In the Seleucid era, key work was carried out on the Rēš by two high officials of Uruk, Anu-uballiṭ, also known by the Greek name Nikarchos, and Anu-uballiṭ, also known as Kephalon.[35] According to his own cylinder inscription,

[30] E.g. Röllig, 'Hellenistic Babylonia', p. 126; Frahm, 'Zwischen Tradition und Neuerung', p. 96. In fact for the sake of brevity and simplicity the title of this paper refers only to the excavated Rēš of the Hellenistic era and not to its presumed precursor(s), but it should be clear from the contents that our main interest lies in the longer-term processes which shaped the temple and its surroundings.

[31] Kose, *Uruk: Architektur IV*, pp. 107–09.

[32] Falkenstein, *Topographie von Uruk I*, p. 8.

[33] Bearing in mind the customary distinction between a main city temple, surrounded by its own extensive precinct, and a minor temple which was typically 'free-standing'.

[34] Beaulieu, *The Pantheon of Uruk During the Neo-Babylonian Period*, p. 330.

[35] For further details of these individuals, see Doty, 'Nikarchos and Kephalon', pp. 95–118. On Nikarchos, see also Monerie, 'Notabilité urbaine et administration locale', pp. 333–43.

dated in 244 BC, Nikarchos laid out seven courtyards around the courtyard containing the 'dais of destinies', and he also completed the enclosure wall, the workrooms, and the cellas of the gods.[36] No trace of the main temple of Anu and Antu from this period has been excavated, but it must have been built on the same location as its baked brick successor, the 'Kernbau' built by Kephalon in 201 BC whose construction presumably removed all traces of its precursor.

Written as well as archaeological evidence demonstrates that the Rēš already existed prior to the phase which is associated with Nikarchos's work of 244 BC. There is a ritual text dated in 251 which describes the procession of the god Anu from the Rēš to the *akītu*-house outside of the city.[37] The excavators have identified three phases of level 2 which predate Nikarchos's work, namely 2θ (late Achaemenid-early Hellenistic), 2ε (early Seleucid, before 281 BC), and 2ζ (shortly before 244 BC). An earlier level (3) comprises the Assyrian king Esarhaddon's work on the Anu-ziggurat as well as Neo-Assyrian–Achaemenid-period remains (of housing?) under the later eastern corner of the Rēš.[38] So, although the layout of the Rēš complex as we know it reflects that established in the mid- to late third century BC, the presence of the temple on that spot can be traced back to the early Hellenistic era if not (as seems likely) the late Achaemenid period.

The Background to the Cultic Reforms

Through a close reading of the onomastic data from Achaemenid-period Uruk, Kessler has shown that the people most affected by the closure of Eanna were those members of the temple elite whose families originated in northern Babylonia.[39] As a result of the cultic reform the great temples of southern Babylonia gained greater independence vis-à-vis the north, and especially with regard to Esagila, the temple of Marduk in Babylon. According to Kessler, these reforms, which can only have been instigated by a ruler, can be dated early in the reign of Xerxes, at the very time when a great many archives of cuneiform tablets, both private and temple-related, came to an end.[40] In fact, Waerzeggers

[36] Falkenstein, *Topographie von Uruk I*, pp. 4–5.

[37] Clay, *Babylonian Records in the Library of J. Pierpont Morgan*, no. 7; Linssen, *The Cults of Uruk and Babylon*, pp. 209–14.

[38] Kose, *Uruk: Architektur IV*, p. 133.

[39] Kessler, 'Urukäische Familien versus babylonische Familien'.

[40] Kessler, 'Urukäische Familien versus babylonische Familien', pp. 252–53.

has demonstrated that this phenomenon of widespread archive deposition can be specifically related to the suppression of the Babylonian revolts that took place in Xerxes' second regnal year, in 484 BC.[41] The effects of Xerxes' reforms on the temple personnel of Uruk (as elsewhere) were momentous.[42] Kleber attributed the 'Zerstörung' of the temple to Xerxes,[43] although it seems that we are not dealing with actual physical destruction, but rather destruction by means of conscious demotion and deliberate neglect.[44]

The Reconfiguration of the Urban Elite

Accepting Kessler's argument that it was Xerxes who implemented the wide-ranging cultic reform at Uruk, it is worth considering in greater detail the implications of these events for the inhabitants of the city. There has been much recent discussion concerning the impact of the measures taken by Xerxes to suppress the Babylonian revolts which broke out in the summer of 484 BC, especially in relation to the temples and their personnel. Jursa states that 'the uprisings against Xerxes must be considered a watershed in the history of the country'.[45] Others have rather stressed aspects of continuity and have sought to diminish the negative impact of Xerxes' actions. For example, Henkelman et al. concede (with reference to Babylon) that 'Xerxes certainly did intervene in temple administration and deprived long established prebend holders from traditional families of their privileges', although they go on to claim that 'Xerxes did not diminish the cult itself by his actions'. They also characterize Xerxes' actions as 'yet another transformation of the temple administration' rather than a 'total disruption by a hostile outsider'.[46] As noted above, these comments

[41] Waerzeggers, 'The Babylonian Revolts against Xerxes', pp. 150–73.

[42] Kessler, 'Urukäische Familien versus babylonische Familien', pp. 250–51, followed by Beaulieu, 'Official and Vernacular Languages', p. 210 n. 54.

[43] Kleber, *Tempel und Palast*, p. 4.

[44] The Ningizzida temple, constructed in the Neo-Assyrian period within the casemate enclosure wall of Eanna, did actually suffer a burnt destruction some time after the early reign of Darius I, according to the testimony of dated tablets found in the debris (Kose, *Uruk: Architektur IV*, p. 273). However, it is not possible to date this event precisely, nor to determine whether the fire was accidental or deliberate.

[45] Jursa, 'The Transition of Babylonia', p. 90.

[46] Henkelman and others, 'Herodotus and Babylon Reconsidered', p. 452.

were made primarily with respect to Babylon and the north of the country. The case of Uruk deserves further, detailed consideration.

The local urban elites of Babylonia depended on royal sponsorship, but the ruler in turn relied on these same elites to maintain stability; thus, when Cyrus brought about a change in regime in 539 BC, many key Babylonian officials maintained their positions and the new king actively sought to promote himself as a supporter of the local temples.[47] However, in the case of Uruk, Xerxes effectively put the great Eanna temple out of use. Given that the building, endowment, and maintenance of temples and their cult was a cornerstone of Babylonian ruler ideology at this period,[48] such an action was the very antithesis of the conduct expected of a king. How he sought to justify this act remains uncertain (see below), but it is clear that the new cultic order required a newly configured elite class — one which would, presumably, be more loyal to the ruler. The implications of such a change of personnel have been evaluated in brief by Waerzeggers and Kessler.[49] They were indeed radical, since by its very nature the priesthood was a closed group: admission was carefully controlled, and one of the key qualifying criteria for consecration was family background, especially paternal descent,[50] with prebendary offices being passed down from father to son, generation after generation. This system also naturally served to regulate access to cultic space by determining who could participate in ritual activity, both within the temple and outside (for example on the occasion of the divine processions). Thus the cultic reform which promoted Anu at the expense of Ištar of Eanna necessitated the replacement of one substantial corps of temple personnel by another. What the former lost in terms of substantial economic benefits and social standing, the latter gained. This replacement was no small task since suitable candidates had to be found, and the new (or newly expanded) priesthood of Anu had to be initiated according to the ancient traditions. Given the scale of the reform and the apparent expulsion from the local priesthood of members of northern Babylonian origin, it seems unlikely that there would have been sufficient candidates available to be initiated who conformed to the strict criteria for admission to the priesthood of what had formerly been a very minor cult at Uruk. One can imagine that a degree of crea-

[47] Jursa, 'The Transition of Babylonia', pp. 76 and 78.

[48] Waerzeggers, 'The Pious King', pp. 726–27.

[49] Waerzeggers, 'The Babylonian Revolts against Xerxes', p. 162; Kessler, 'Urukäische Familien versus babylonische Familien', pp. 250–53.

[50] Waerzeggers and Jursa, 'On the Initiation of Babylonian Priests', pp. 1–38.

tivity would have been needed in establishing the legitimacy of the measures necessary to accomplish the replacement of the city's cultic personnel on such a wide scale. Traditionally, the Babylonian priesthood served to mediate between god and king (compared with Assyria, where the king himself was the supreme priest and representative on earth of the god Aššur).[51] One key effect, if not an actual aim of the cultic reform at Uruk, was to enable the ruler (assumed here, following Kessler, to be Xerxes; see above) to manipulate the composition of the priesthood — a significant sector of the urban elite — for his own ends and to ensure that its members were aligned more closely with his own interests.

The Scholarly/Theological Background

I have raised the question of how the ruler might have sought to legitimize his actions in implementing wide-scale cultic reform. There exists no programmatic statement by Xerxes attempting to explain what he did, since there is no extant building inscription associated with his reforms.[52] The scholarly elite must somehow have been convinced of the theological legitimacy of the measures to downgrade Ištar and elevate Anu in her stead — or perhaps, if they were not convinced, they risked being replaced by scholars who were. In fact, it is clear that Urukean scholars played a central role in reshaping tradition in line with the new religious order. This process of theological legitimation has been examined by Beaulieu and Frahm on the basis of scholarly libraries excavated in a house in Uruk in square U18, some way to the east of the religious complex at the heart of the city.[53] These libraries belonged to two families of *āšipu*s (exorcists), descendants of Šangû-Ninurta and Ekur-zākir respectively, who were active in the late Achaemenid and early Hellenistic periods.[54] Beaulieu and Frahm detected among the tablets of these libraries an ongoing

[51] Waerzeggers, 'The Pious King', pp. 734 and 737.

[52] In fact, we lack any building inscriptions of the Achaemenid rulers of Babylonia, with the exception of Cyrus; see Frahm, 'Zwischen Tradition und Neuerung', p. 77; Beaulieu, 'Official and Vernacular Languages', pp. 205–06; Baker, 'From Street Altar to Palace', p. 546.

[53] Beaulieu, 'Antiquarian Theology in Seleucid Uruk', pp. 47–76; Frahm, 'Zwischen Tradition und Neuerung'.

[54] As far as the late Achaemenid period is concerned, documents relating to temple affairs are pretty much restricted to this particular findspot. The cuneiform documentation from late Achaemenid Uruk — relatively scarce, albeit less so than was previously thought — is discussed in detail in Stolper, 'Late Achaemenid Legal Texts', pp. 559–662; none of the texts published by him betrays an evident temple connection and they contain no mention of prebendary affairs.

theological discourse relating to the new position of Anu in the Urukean pantheon. The earliest evidence comprises the scribal activities of Anu-ikṣur of the Šangû-Ninurta family, who was active *c.* 400 BC, but there is nothing to rule out the discourse itself having started somewhat earlier in the fifth century BC. It certainly continued into the Hellenistic era, as witnessed by the scribal activities of Iqīšâ of the Ekur-zākir family. What is particularly interesting is that Frahm observes among the scholarly tablets a concern with associating the cultic attributes of Anu with those of Enlil of Nippur, the ancient head of the Babylonian pantheon prior to the elevation of Marduk in the late second millennium BC; by contrast, the library tablets reveal no corresponding interest in Marduk-theology.[55] This signifies a distancing from Babylon, whose city god was Marduk, serving to reinforce the cultural independence of Uruk in the later centuries of the first millennium BC.[56]

A further development emerges from the study of these particular scholarly families from Uruk, one which suggests a change in the nature of temple prebend-holding (and thus of the priesthood) at this time compared with the Neo-Babylonian/early Achaemenid period. The aforementioned exorcist Iqīšâ is known to have owned a brewer's prebend.[57] Moreover, contemporary archival evidence from the central Babylonian city of Nippur indicates that scholars attached to the Enlil temple there were also active as temple brewers.[58] This may represent a significant change in the composition of the priesthood since there is only scarce evidence from earlier centuries for learned members of the higher echelons of the priestly hierarchy owning prebendary shares in professions involving food preparation. In her study of the Borsippa priesthood, Waerzeggers suggests that 'multi-priests' were associated with the smaller Neo-Babylonian and Seleucid temples, taking upon themselves a range of different tasks, while the personnel attached to Ezida, the great Nabû temple of Borsippa, were strictly specialized.[59] In spite of this it seems that a distinction was maintained between what van Driel called the 'ritualists' (including the prebendary exorcists and lamentation priests) and those prebendaries involved

[55] Frahm, 'Zwischen Tradition und Neuerung', pp. 89 and 96–97.

[56] Though note the suggestion of George that aspects of the temple and cult of Anu in Uruk were modelled on Marduk and his temple (Esagila) at Babylon (George, 'The Bricks of E-sagil', p. 194).

[57] Frahm, 'Zwischen Tradition und Neuerung', p. 83 n. 39.

[58] Frahm, 'Zwischen Tradition und Neuerung', p. 92.

[59] Waerzeggers, *The Ezida Temple of Borsippa*, p. 78.

in food preparation and crafts.[60] Before the later Achaemenid period there seems to be little evidence for 'ritualists' owning these kinds of prebends.[61] This phenomenon, which appears to have become more common in the later Achaemenid period, reached its high point in the Seleucid era when, for example, Lâbâši, son of Anu-zēr-iddin, of the Ekur-zākir family accumulated shares in the exorcist's prebend (*āšipūtu*) as well as several others, including the butcher's, brewer's, and baker's prebends.[62]

This development whereby learned 'ritualist' prebendaries came to own prebends more typically associated with the middle-ranking temple personnel might reflect one or more of a number of circumstances, including the smaller size of the temple establishments involved, as suggested by Waerzeggers (see above), and an increasing separation between prebend ownership and the actual performance of prebendary duties which made it possible for individuals to amass prebends in professions outside of their own specialization.[63] The background to this development remains obscure, but one wonders whether in Uruk it might have had its origins in a shortage of suitably qualified personnel vis-à-vis the range and variety of cultic duties to be performed. At any rate, the cases highlighted by Frahm (as discussed above) suggest that the scholars among the temple communities of Uruk and Nippur now extended their influence beyond their traditional sphere of activity, gaining a foothold in areas typically reserved for lower-ranking staff.

[60] Van Driel, *Elusive Silver*, pp. 34–37.

[61] Given the wealth of prosopographical data now available for the personnel of Neo-Babylonian temples at Sippar, Uruk, Borsippa, and to a lesser extent, Babylon, it seems likely that this reflects the actual situation, and the fact that the food purveying and craft professions tended to be dominated by family 'dynasties' rather supports this. The evidence for actual prebendary exorcists and lamentation priests remains slight: see Bongenaar, *The Neo-Babylonian Ebabbar Temple at Sippar*, p. 288, for the Sippar evidence, and note Waerzeggers, *The Ezida Temple of Borsippa*, pp. 38–39, on Borsippa (where no prebendary exorcists or lamentation priests are yet attested). A rare counter-example to the phenomenon noted here comprises the family of Bēl-rēmanni from Sippar, who were exorcists as well as prebendary brewers and bakers; see Jursa, *Neo-Babylonian Legal and Administrative Documents*, pp. 126–27. I am grateful to M. Jursa for drawing this case to my attention.

[62] Corò, *Prebende Templari in Èta Seleucide*, pp. 87–94.

[63] For further discussion of the prebendary professions and the evidence for the ownership of multiple prebends by certain individuals/families, see Jursa, *Aspects of the Economic History of Babylonia in the First Millennium BC*, pp. 157–61.

The Reshaping of the Urban Settlement

The precise shape of the Late Achaemenid city of Uruk is difficult to grasp owing to the lack of direct evidence, but given that the cultic reform which took place in the fifth century must have been accompanied by large-scale reorganization of the city centre, it is likely that the basic layout as we know it from the Seleucid-era remains reflects the essential structure of the city as it was when Alexander conquered Babylonia. Since these remains consist primarily of the Rēš and Ešgal temples themselves and a small area of excavated housing on the east side of the city, they do not afford a detailed insight into the urban layout. However, significant additional information on urban topography is contained in the contemporary cuneiform documents, and although the features mentioned in the tablets often cannot be located with precision on the ground, nevertheless these tablets shed some further light on the character of the urban settlement. The city spatial organization certainly underwent further modification during the Seleucid era (see below), but these changes represent alterations to the layout already in place by the end of the Achaemenid period, rather than a replacement of it.

The demise of Eanna and the abandonment of the residential areas associated with it, followed by the establishment of two major new shrines in the city centre, are likely to have precipitated a reorganization of the residential sectors of the city. In fact, the results of the Uruk surface survey show a shift in occupation in the Seleucid/Parthian eras compared with the preceding period, with a particularly dense concentration towards the northern end of the site where Neo- and Late Babylonian material is said to have been rather scarce.[64] Moreover, the topographical evidence drawn from the cuneiform legal documents suggests that the names of city districts which were current in the Neo-Babylonian period had largely fallen out of use by the Hellenistic era, and that by this late period a range of city district names were in use which were, for the most part, new. As I have suggested elsewhere, it seems to me likely that this phenomenon reflects not merely the renaming of already existing districts but is rather to be related to the shift in occupation which is suggested by the survey evidence.[65] If this reconstruction is correct, then the cultic reform resulted in a widescale reorganization of the settlement, one which was reflected in the topographical terminology used in the everyday documents. This reorganiza-

[64] Cancik, '5.7 Neu- und spätbabylonische Zeit', p. 210.

[65] Baker, 'The Property Portfolio of a Family of Builders', p. 35.

tion must in turn have resulted in alterations to the street network; in particular, the remodelling of the cultic sector at the heart of the city must have led to changes in the processional routes taken by the gods on ceremonial occasions.[66]

During the Seleucid era two new city districts were named after the major temples: the Rēš district and the Ešgal district. Given their names, it seems likely that these districts were located in immediate proximity to the temples themselves, just as in the Neo-Babylonian period residential quarters had been situated within the greater precinct of Eanna. In order to assess the status of these two particular city districts, and to compare them with others, it is necessary first to make some observations about ownership and tenure of urban land in Uruk at this time. From the extant archives we have a substantial number of legal documents which involve the transfer of urban properties located in residential areas, usually through sale but also by other means, especially inheritance. These properties can be divided into three categories: houses transferred on their own, houses transferred together with unbuilt plots, and unbuilt plots on their own. Many of them were privately owned with no apparent restrictions as to alienability etc. Others, however, were subject to certain (as yet rather unclear) conditions of tenure. In these cases the property was typically designated 'tenured land, property of Anu' (*bīt ritti makkūr Anu*) or an abbreviated version of this expression (either *bīt ritti* or *makkūr Anu*). These properties were almost always associated with a named individual, with a few exceptions involving unbuilt plots which probably represented land yet to be assigned by the authorities. Some documents make it clear that originally institutional land was apportioned as *bīt ritti* and that the holder was then responsible for constructing his house on his *bīt ritti* plot. He was in return obliged to perform certain unspecified duties, should the temple call upon him to do so. Only occasionally can the original land allocation process be detected in the written record; usually, we are dealing with houses which had existed for some time already, and in many cases their *bīt ritti* status must have extended over one or more previous generations. The earliest attestation known to me dates from 281 BC, and it is impossible to determine whether or not this system of urban land tenure goes back to the late Achaemenid period. However, even if it were an innovation of the Seleucid era, it certainly had its roots in native Babylonian institutions: tenured agricultural (but never urban) land designated *bīt ritti* is known already in

[66] The reconstruction of the processional route of Anu to the Akītu temple on the occasion of the New Year festival by Falkenstein, *Topographie von Uruk I*, pp. 45–49 (which has been followed by other scholars, e.g. Kose, *Uruk: Architektur IV*, p. 14, Abb. 4) has to be modified in the light of information that has become available since his study was published.

the Neo-Babylonian period,[67] and urban land allocation schemes are attested in late Achaemenid times in the form of 'bow-lots' (*bīt qašti*),[68] a form of tenure more typically associated with agricultural land.

An interesting feature about the distribution of these urban *bīt ritti* properties in Hellenistic Uruk is that all of the documented properties located in the Rēš and Ešgal city districts belonged to this category. This supports the idea that these particular districts were closely associated with the temples, as their names suggest. Thus while the temples themselves were accessible only to consecrated personnel, much of the land surrounding them in these Rēš and Ešgal districts was reserved for residents associated with the temples (though they were not necessarily members of the priesthood, since it seems that non-prebendary workers could own/occupy *bīt ritti* properties).[69] Beyond this zone, the other city districts always contained a mixture of *bīt ritti*s and non-*bīt ritti* properties, although some districts had a much higher concentration of *bīt ritti*s than others. The fact that the Rēš and Ešgal districts were reserved for temple personnel has parallels in earlier times. During the Neo-Babylonian period there existed a city district named after Eanna, and it seems likely that this district encompassed the housing area immediately to the west and south-west of Eanna which was itself enclosed by an outer precinct wall. In this case we know that temple prebendaries lived in this housing associated with the Eanna. The precinct of the ziggurat of Babylon also contained a housing area, and again textual evidence indicates that temple prebendaries lived there.[70]

Given these parallels, we might expect these residential areas associated with the Urukean temples to have been surrounded by an enclosure wall. In fact, a fortification wall extending from the eastern corner of the Rēš was identified by Loftus already in the nineteenth century, and this came to be known in the literature as the 'Seleucid Wall' (*Seleukidenmauer*), although according to Kose it is now rather dated in the early Parthian period. However, Kose also notes that a tablet dated in the time of Antiochus III (209–192 BC) provides a terminus post quem for the wall's construction,[71] which suggests that a late Seleucid date cannot be entirely excluded. This wall lay directly above some of the Neo-Babylonian and early Achaemenid housing associated with the long-

[67] Van Driel, *Elusive Silver*, pp. 305–08.

[68] Van Driel, *Elusive Silver*, p. 238.

[69] Baker, *The Urban Landscape in First Millennium BC Babylonia*.

[70] Baker, 'Beyond Planning'.

[71] Kose, *Uruk: Architektur IV*, p. 255.

defunct Eanna temple.[72] There was a corresponding wall connecting the Rēš at its southern corner with the Ešgal, but otherwise it is impossible to trace any outer enclosure belonging with the two temples.

The fortification of certain Babylonian temples is traditionally associated with the Parthian era.[73] However, there is evidence from the legal documents which indicates that the city districts named after the Rēš and Ešgal were conceived as fortified already in the late Seleucid era. The Ešgal district is not infrequently referred to as 'the village of the temple of the gods of Uruk', but a handful of tablets refer to it also as 'the fortress of Anu' (*dūru ša Anu*). Two further tablets make it clear that the Rēš district was also known by this name; therefore the Rēš and Ešgal districts seem to have been considered as forming one greater unit.[74] The earliest attestation of the 'fortress of Anu' is dated in 157/156 BC, while the 'village of the temple of the gods' is first mentioned in 168 BC, so these two appellations appear to have come into use at around the same time. In Akkadian toponyms the element Dūr(u) indicates a walled settlement, so the use of the term *dūru ša Anu* suggests that the temples together with their associated residential areas were enclosed if not fortified in the later Seleucid period. This does not exclude the possibility that they were already enclosed before this time, but whether they were or not it does indicate that this aspect of the settlement came to be emphasized by members of the urban community in written representations of their local environment. This development in terms of the urban community's self-representation is prefigured in the late Achaemenid era by the innovative form of a gentilic for 'Urukean' based on the compound 'territory of Anu', namely, ^{lú}*qaq-qar-*^{d}*a-nu*^{ki}*-u* 'Man of the territory of Anu'.[75] Again, this hints at the prominence of the Anu temple

[72] See Kose, *Uruk: Architektur IV*, p. 123, Abb. 72, for a plan of the wall in relation to the so-called 'Egibi house' which it directly overlay. It was in this house that three archives of temple prebendaries were found in successive occupation levels; the earlier two archives were published by Kessler, *Urkunden aus Privathäusern*, who is also scheduled to publish the third and latest archive, that of the Egibi family.

[73] For example, the late Parthian fortress at Nippur, built around the ancient ziggurat. See Keall, 'Political, Economic, and Social Factors on the Parthian Landscape', pp. 85–86 with plan p. 82, who suggests that the fortress was not primarily defensive in function but rather represented 'a strong presence of the imperial administration', a viewpoint echoed by Bergamini, 'Parthian Fortifications in Mesopotamia', pp. 208–09 n. 28, who identifies this as a long-lived Parthian trend.

[74] The documentary evidence for these districts will be discussed in detail by the author in a forthcoming study: Baker, *The Urban Landscape in First Millennium BC Babylonia*.

[75] Frahm, 'Zwischen Tradition und Neuerung', p. 89 n. 68, citing the tablet SpTU, no. 33 r. 11′.

in Uruk at this time, even though no unequivocal archaeological traces have been recovered.

This documentary information ties in well with the archaeological evidence. Building phase 2γ, attributed to the late Seleucid/early Parthian era (after 201 BC), involved the renovation of the north-eastern outer precinct wall of the Rēš with the construction of rectangular defensive towers at the corners.[76] The corner towers were subsequently rebuilt as circular bastions in phase 2β,[77] probably during the early Parthian period. In the case of Ešgal, the fortification of the temple took place some time after the third phase of its construction ('Tempelanlage III'), attributed to the work of Anu-uballiṭ (Kephalon) in around 200 BC.[78] In his excavation report Kose equates these fortification works with those of building phase 2α on the Rēš,[79] which would place them during the reign of Mithridates II (c. 124/123–88/87 BC).[80] In any case, the fortification works were certainly accomplished before the temple was destroyed by the fire which happened some time after 108 BC. If there is any possibility that the earliest fortification works on Ešgal may be dated in the late Seleucid era, like those of building phase 2γ of the Rēš (late Seleucid/early Parthian), then these alterations too may be associated with the characterization of the Rēš and Ešgal districts as 'fortress of Anu'.

Although the conversion of the Rēš and Ešgal into a fortified place of refuge for the city has been dated in the reign of Mithridates II,[81] the documentary evidence discussed above indicates that for the Urukeans this whole area was considered to be a fortress already somewhat earlier in the second century, by 157/156 BC (first explicit mention of the fortress), if not by 168 BC (first mention of the associated 'village'). Even if the so-called 'Seleukidenmauer' is early Parthian rather than late Seleucid (and this seems rather uncertain), nevertheless there were fortification works on the corner bastions of the Rēš which predated its construction. At any rate, on analogy with the housing area associated with Eanna in the Neo-Babylonian/early Achaemenid period, it seems highly

[76] Kose, *Uruk: Architektur IV*, p. 122, p. 133, Beilage 45 Plan 52 and Beilage 61.

[77] The circular bastion at the eastern corner was preserved and recovered through excavation while the one at the northern corner is restored (Kose, *Uruk: Architektur IV*, p. 8 Beilage 45 Plan 52).

[78] Kose, *Uruk: Architektur IV*, p. 215.

[79] Kose, *Uruk: Architektur IV*, p. 230.

[80] Cf. Kose, *Uruk: Architektur IV*, p. 133.

[81] Kose, *Uruk: Architektur IV*, p. 133, phase 2α.

likely that the residential districts named after the Rēš and Ešgal were enclosed within a perimeter wall, as implied by the use of the term *dūru ša Anu*. It remains uncertain whether this enclosure was a precursor of the 'Seleukidenmauer', or was the 'Seleukidenmauer' itself, or followed an entirely different course.

It is clear from this evidence that the Parthian fortification of the Urukean temples represents a continuation of a phenomenon which had already begun in the late Seleucid era and which is reflected in contemporary written sources. Moreover, with some of the features discussed above it is difficult to demonstrate with any certainty a dating either shortly before or shortly after the Parthian conquest; if the former, then the case presented here is strengthened somewhat. There is another strand of evidence, however, which suggests that Babylonian temples could assume a defensive function already during the Seleucid era. This comprises a Babylonian Chronicle text concerning the invasion of Mesopotamia by Ptolemy III (246–222 BC), who besieged Babylon in 246/245 BC.[82] In the Chronicle the invaders are said to have done battle with 'the commander of the Bēlet-Ninua citadel' (*rab birti ša Bēlet-Ninua*), whereupon the people who were in the citadel became afraid and came out and went to the royal palace but were killed.[83] Although the editors of this Chronicle, in their preliminary online edition, treat the *birtu ša Bēlet-Ninua* as a citadel located on the west bank of the Euphrates, there is no other evidence for such a fortress and it seems to me more likely that the passage refers to the temple itself being used as one. Egišḫurankia, the temple of the goddess Bēlet-Ninua (= Ištar of Nineveh) in western Babylon, is listed already in the topographical series Tintir which most likely dates from the later second millennium BC,[84] and it is clear that the temple survived into the Hellenistic period since it is mentioned in an Astronomical Diary entry for the year 321 BC.[85] The architectural features of Babylonian temples rendered them defensible if need be: they had massive walls with few, easily barred means of access, they had large internal courtyards which could accommodate refugees and/or troops, and the enemy could be fired upon from the roof.

[82] See the preliminary online edition of 'Ptolemy III Chronicle', ed. by van der Spek and Finkel.

[83] 'Ptolemy III Chronicle', ed. by van der Spek and Finkel, lines 9′–10′.

[84] Tintir IV 32 (George, *Babylonian Topographical Texts*, pp. 60–61; see p. 7 for a suggested date of the series Tintir in the twelfth century BC).

[85] Sachs and Hunger, *Astronomical Diaries and Related Texts from Babylonia*, pp. 226–27, r. 13′.

Returning to Uruk, the motivation behind the late Seleucid fortification of its great temple precincts may well have been the threat posed to Babylonia by the Parthian expansion during the reign of Mithridates I (171–138 BC) which culminated in the conquest of Babylonia in 141 BC. As a means of defence, really the only option open to the inhabitants of the city was to create a fortified citadel, because the walls of Uruk had lain in a state of disrepair for several centuries; in fact, they are said to have been long ruined already in the Achaemenid period.[86] In a study of the Babylonian city walls of the first millennium BC I have suggested that, with the exception of Babylon, the capital, they ceased to be actively maintained for defensive purposes after the Persian conquest since they were not crucial to the defence of the empire.[87] Moreover, already during the Neo-Babylonian period the Babylonian rulers, especially the great builder-king Nebuchadnezzar II, concerned themselves primarily with the defence of northern Babylonia because that was the direction from which it was perceived a threat might come. The southern city walls, including those of Uruk, were rather left to crumble, although down into the Seleucid era their remains continued to mark the division between urban space and the steppe beyond. City districts were still named after individual gates, though it seems likely that by now these represented mere breaks in the wall circuit marking well-worn routes into and out of the city, rather than standing structures. Thus the assumption of a defensive function — or at least an appearance thereof — by the Urukean temples has to be viewed in the light of longer-term political developments and is one aspect of the changing relationship between the local community and the imperial centre. We may be witnessing a phenomenon similar to that observed by Keall for the later Parthian era (see above), that is, a 'strong presence of the imperial administration', although in the case of Hellenistic Uruk it is quite unclear to what extent these changes were directed from the centre rather than rooted in the local community. Even in the case of the temple (re)buildings by Nikarchos and Kephalon, there remains an ongoing debate as to how far these powerful local officials were acting on their own initiative.[88]

[86] Kose, *Uruk: Architektur IV*, p. 9.

[87] Baker, 'Babylonian City Walls'.

[88] These issues are addressed in greater detail in Baker, 'The Image of the City in Hellenistic Babylonia'.

Conclusions

In Mesopotamian history it is often — frustratingly — the case that the most interesting episodes are the least accessible to the scholar, because social disruption typically entailed a cessation of the written record; moreover, the events and processes leading up to it are often not explicitly documented. One should, of course, be cautious about extrapolating the course of events solely from their after-effects, in the absence of contemporary 'live' testimony. On the other hand, it does seem legitimate to evaluate disruptions to cultic practice by weighing them against the better documented 'normal' state. In these pages I have attempted to explore some of the wider-ranging effects of one episode of cultic reform, tracing them beyond the confines of the temple itself to encompass the spatial organization of the city as a whole and the lives of its inhabitants. It appears that in the second half of the first millennium BC we witness in Uruk an increased self-identification of the urban community with the temple itself (though we may question the extent to which this appearance is a product of our source material, deriving as it does primarily from the temple sphere itself or that of its personnel). This hint of an increasingly entrenched temple community may be reflected in the fortification of the great Urukean temples, both metaphorical (in the spatial terminology of the everyday documents) and actual (according to the archaeological evidence), in the later Seleucid era and afterwards. The developments discussed here suggest significant changes over the course of the later first millennium in the relationship between the temple and wider Babylonian society. This changing relationship has in turn to be seen in the context of the shift from native Babylonian rule to rule by external powers, first Persian and then Greek. Above all, it should be clear that any approach to sacred space and its transformation in this context requires us to take into account the complex intersection of multiple factors: political events; religious reform (whether politically motivated or incremental); the nature of the priesthood and its relationship with the ruler; the composition of the elite and of the wider urban community; and, not least, cultic topography and urban spatial organization.

Works Cited

Primary Sources

'Ptolemy III Chronicle', ed. by R. van der Spek and I. Finkel, *Babylonian Chronicles of the Hellenistic Period*, 11 <http://www.livius.org/cg-cm/chronicles/bchp-ptolemy_iii/bchp_ptolemy_iii_01.html> [accessed 21 April 2012]

Secondary Studies

Abraham, K., *Business and Politics under the Persian Empire: The Financial Dealings of Marduk-nāṣir-apli of the House of Egibi (521–487 B.C.E.)* (Bethesda: CDL Press, 2004)

Ambos, C., 'Building Rituals from the First Millennium BC: The Evidence from the Ritual Texts', in *From the Foundations to the Crenellations: Essays on Temple Building in the Ancient Near East and Hebrew Bible*, ed. by M. J. Boda and J. Novotny, Alter Orient und Altes Testament, 366 (Münster: Ugarit-Verlag, 2010), pp. 221–37

Baker, H. D., *The Archive of the Nappāḫu Family*, Archiv für Orientforschung Beiheft, 30 (Wien: Institut für Orientalistik der Universität Wien, 2004)

——, 'Babylonian City Walls in a Historical and Cross-Cultural Perspective', in *Krieg und Frieden im Alten Vorderasien: 52e Rencontre Assyriologique Internationale/ International Congress of Assyriology and Near Eastern Archaeology, Münster, 17.–21. Juli 2006*, ed. by H. Neumann and others, Alter Orient und Altes Testament, 401 (Münster: Ugarit-Verlag, forthcoming)

——, 'Beneath the Stairs in the Rēš Temple of Hellenistic Uruk: A Study in Cultic Topography and Spatial Organization', *Zeitschrift für Orient-Archäologie*, 6 (2013), 18–42

——, 'Beyond Planning: How the Babylonian City was Formed', in *The Neo-Babylonian Workshop of the 53rd RAI: City Administration in Neo-Babylonian Times*, ed. by C. Wunsch, Babel und Bibel (Winona Lake: Eisenbrauns, forthcoming)

——, 'From Street Altar to Palace: Reading the Built Environment of Urban Babylonia', in *The Oxford Handbook of Cuneiform Culture*, ed. by K. Radner and E. Robson (Oxford: Oxford University Press, 2011), pp. 533–52

——, 'The Image of the City in Hellenistic Babylonia', in *Shifting Social Imaginaries in the Hellenistic Period: Narrations, Practices, and Images*, ed. by E. Stavrianopoulou, Mnemosyne, Suppl. 363 (Leiden: Brill, 2013)

——, 'The Property Portfolio of a Family of Builders from Hellenistic Uruk', in *Approaching the Babylonian Economy: Proceedings of the START Project Symposium held in Vienna, 1–3 July 2004*, ed. by H. D. Baker and M. Jursa (Münster: Ugarit-Verlag, 2005), pp. 7–43

——, *The Urban Landscape in First Millennium BC Babylonia* (forthcoming)

——, 'A Waste of Space? Unbuilt Land in the Babylonian Cities of the First Millennium BC', *Iraq*, 71 (2009), 89–98

Beaulieu, P.-A., 'Antiquarian Theology in Seleucid Uruk', *Acta Sumerologica*, 14 (1992), 47–76
——, 'Official and Vernacular Languages: The Shifting Sands of Imperial and Cultural Identities in First-Millennium B.C. Mesopotamia', in *Margins of Writing, Origins of Cultures*, ed. by S. L. Sanders, 2nd edn (Chicago: The Oriental Institute of the University of Chicago, 2007), pp. 191–220
——, *The Pantheon of Uruk During the Neo-Babylonian Period*, Cuneiform Monographs, 23 (Leiden: Brill/STYX, 2003)
Bergamini, G., 'Parthian Fortifications in Mesopotamia', *Mesopotamia*, 22 (1987), 195–214
Bongenaar, A. C. V. M., *The Neo-Babylonian Ebabbar Temple at Sippar: Its Administration and its Prosopography*, Publications de l'Institut historique-archéologique néerlandais de Stamboul, 80 (Istanbul: Nederlands Historisch-Archaeologisch Instituut te Istanbul, 1997)
Cancik, E., '5.7 Neu- und spätbabylonische Zeit', in *Uruk: Kampagne 35–37, 1982–1984. Die archäologische Oberflächenuntersuchung (Survey)*, ed. by U. Finkbeiner, Ausgrabungen in Uruk-Warka, Endberichte, 4 (Mainz: Philipp von Zabern, 1991), pp. 209–10
Clay, A. T., *Babylonian Records in the Library of J. Pierpont Morgan* (New Haven: Yale University Press, 1923)
Corò, P., *Prebende Templari in Èta Seleucide*, History of the Ancient Near East/ Monographs, 8 (Padua: SARGON Editrice e Libreria, 2005)
Dandamayev, M. A., 'Was Eanna Destroyed by Darius I?', *Archaeologische Mitteilungen aus Iran und Turan*, 25 (1992), 169–72
Doty, L. T., 'Nikarchos and Kephalon', in *A Scientific Humanist: Studies in Memory of Abraham Sachs*, ed. by E. Leichty, M. de J. Ellis, and P. Gerardi (Philadelphia: University Museum, Philadelphia, 1988), pp. 95–118
Driel, G. van, *Elusive Silver: In Search of a Role for a Market in an Agrarian Environment. Aspects of Mesopotamia's Society*, Publications de l'Institut historique-archéologique néerlandais de Stamboul, 95 (Istanbul: Nederlands Instituut voor het Nabije Oosten, 2002)
Falkenstein, A., *Topographie von Uruk I: Uruk zur Seleukidenzeit*, Ausgrabungen der Deutschen Forschungsgemeinschaft in Uruk-Warka, 3 (Leipzig: Harrassowitz, 1941)
Frahm, E., 'Zwischen Tradition und Neuerung: Babylonische Priestergelehrte im achämenidenzeitlichen Uruk', in *Religion und Religionskontakte im Zeitalter der Achämeniden*, ed. by R. G. Kratz (Gütersloh: Kaiser/Gütersloher, 2002), pp. 74–108
George, A. R., *Babylonian Topographical Texts*, Orientalia Lovaniensia Analecta, 40 (Leuven: Peeters, 1992)
——, '"Bond of the Lands": Babylon, the Cosmic Capital', in *Die orientalische Stadt: Kontinuität, Wandel, Bruch. 1. Internationales Colloquium der Deutschen Orient-Gesellschaft, 9.–10. Mai 1996 in Halle/Saale*, ed. by G. Wilhelm, Colloquien der Deutschen Orient-Gesellschaft, 1 (Saarbrücken: Saarbrücker, 1997), pp. 125–45
——, 'The Bricks of E-sagil', *Iraq*, 57 (1995), 173–97
Henkelman, W., and others, 'Herodotus and Babylon Reconsidered', in *Herodot und das Persische Weltreich / Herodotus and the Persian Empire*, ed. by R. Rollinger, B. Truschnegg, and R. Bichler (Wiesbaden: Harrassowitz, 2011), pp. 449–70

Jursa, M., ed., *Aspects of the Economic History of Babylonia in the First Millennium BC: Economic Geography, Economic Mentalities, Agriculture, the Use of Money and the Problem of Economic Growth*, Alter Orient und Altes Testament, 377 (Münster: Ugarit-Verlag, 2010)

——, *Neo-Babylonian Legal and Administrative Documents: Typology, Contents and Archives*, Guides to the Mesopotamian Textual Record, 1 (Münster: Ugarit-Verlag, 2005)

——, 'The Transition of Babylonia from the Neo-Babylonian Empire to Achaemenid Rule', in *Regime Change in the Ancient Near East and Egypt: From Sargon of Agade to Saddam Hussein*, ed. by H. Crawford, Proceedings of the British Academy, 136 (London: The British Academy, 2007), pp. 73–94

Keall, E. J., 'Political, Economic, and Social Factors on the Parthian Landscape of Mesopotamia and Western Iran: Evidence from Two Case Studies', in *Mountains and Lowlands: Essays in the Archaeology of Greater Mesopotamia*, ed. by L. D. Levine and T. Cuyler Young, Bibliotheca Mesopotamica, 7 (Malibu: Undena Publications, 1977), pp. 81–89

Kessler, K., *Urkunden aus Privathäusern: Die Wohnhäuser Westlich des Eanna-Tempelbereichs I*, Ausgrabungen in Uruk-Warka, Endberichte, 8 (Mainz: von Zabern, 1991)

——, 'Urukäische Familien versus babylonische Familien: die Namengebung in Uruk, die Degradierung der Kulte von Eanna und der Aufstieg des Gottes Anu', *Altorientalische Forschungen*, 31 (2004), 237–62

Kleber, K., *Tempel und Palast: Die Beziehungen zwischen dem König und dem Eanna-Tempel im spätbabylonischen Uruk*, Alter Orient und Altes Testament, 358 (Münster: Ugarit-Verlag, 2008)

Kose, A., *Uruk: Architektur IV, von der Seleukiden- bis zur Sasanidenzeit*, Ausgrabungen in Uruk-Warka, Endberichte, 17, 2 vols (Mainz: von Zabern, 1998)

Linssen, M. J. H., *The Cults of Uruk and Babylon: The Temple Ritual Texts as Evidence for Hellenistic Cult Practice*, Cuneiform Monographs, 25 (Leiden: Brill/STYX, 2004)

Maul, S. M., 'Die altorientalische Hauptstadt: Nabel und Abbild der Welt', in *Die orientalische Stadt: Kontinuität, Wandel, Bruch. 1. Internationales Colloquium der Deutschen Orient-Gesellschaft, 9.–10. Mai 1996 in Halle/Saale*, ed. by G. Wilhelm, Colloquien der Deutschen Orient-Gesellschaft, 1 (Saarbrücken: Saarbrücker, 1997), pp. 109–24

Miglus, P. A., *Städtische Wohnarchitektur in Babylonien und Assyrien*, Baghdader Forschungen, 22 (Mainz: Philipp von Zabern, 1999)

Monerie, J., 'Notabilité urbaine et administration locale en Babylonie du sud aux époques séleucide et parthe', in *Communautés locales et pouvoir central dans l'Orient hellénistique et romain*, ed. by C. Feyel, Études anciennes (Nancy: A.D.R.A., 2012), pp. 327–52

Novotny, J., 'Temple Building in Assyria: Evidence from Royal Inscriptions', in *From the Foundations to the Crenellations: Essays on Temple Building in the Ancient Near East and Hebrew Bible*, ed. by M. J. Boda and J. Novotny, Alter Orient und Altes Testament, 366 (Münster: Ugarit-Verlag, 2010), pp. 109–39

Petrie, C. A., 'Seleucid Uruk: An Analysis of Ceramic Distribution', *Iraq*, 64 (2002), 85–123

Pongratz-Leisten, B., 'Sacred Places', in *Religions of the Ancient World: A Guide*, ed. by S. I. Johnston (Cambridge, MA: The Belknap Press of Harvard University Press, 2004), pp. 253–55

Radner, K., and E. Robson, *The Oxford Handbook of Cuneiform Culture* (Oxford: Oxford University Press, 2011)

Röllig, W., 'Hellenistic Babylonia: The Evidence from Uruk', in *Ho Hellēnismos stēn Anatolē, International Meeting of History and Archaeology 1986, Delphi, Greece* (Athens: Europaïko politistiko kentro Delphōn, 1991), pp. 121–29

Sachs, A., and H. Hunger, *Astronomical Diaries and Related Texts from Babylonia*, vol. I: *Diaries from 652 B.C. to 262 B.C.*, Denkschriften der philosophisch-historischen Klasse, 195 (Wien: Österreichische Akademie der Wissenschaften, 1988)

Schaudig, H., 'The Restoration of Temples in the Neo- and Late Babylonian Periods: A Royal Prerogative as the Setting for Political Argument', in *From the Foundations to the Crenellations: Essays on Temple Building in the Ancient Near East and Hebrew Bible*, ed. by M. J. Boda and J. Novotny, Alter Orient und Altes Testament, 366 (Münster: Ugarit-Verlag, 2010), pp. 141–64

Stolper, M. W., 'Late Achaemenid Legal Texts from Uruk and Larsa', *Baghdader Mitteilungen*, 21 (1990), 559–662

Waerzeggers, C., 'The Babylonian Priesthood in the Long Sixth Century BC', *Bulletin of the Institute of Classical Studies*, 54.2 (2011), 59–70

——, 'The Babylonian Revolts against Xerxes and the "Ends of Archives"', *Archiv für Orientforschung*, 50 (2003/04), 150–73

——, 'Babylonians in Susa: The Travels of Babylonian Businessmen to Susa Reconsidered', in *Der Achämenidenhof / The Achaemenid Court*, ed. by B. Jacobs and R. Rollinger (Wiesbaden: Harrassowitz, 2010), pp. 777–813

——, *The Ezida Temple of Borsippa: Priesthood, Cult, Archives*, Achaemenid History, 15 (Leiden: Nederlands Instituut voor het Nabije Oosten, 2010)

——, 'The Pious King: Royal Patronage of Temples', in *The Oxford Handbook of Cuneiform Culture*, ed. by K. Radner and E. Robson (Oxford: Oxford University Press, 2011), pp. 725–51

Waerzeggers, C., and M. Jursa, 'On the Initiation of Babylonian Priests', *Zeitschrift für Altorientalische und Biblische Rechtsgeschichte*, 14 (2008), 1–38

Continuity, Discontinuity, and Change in Religious Life in Southern Syria during the Roman Period

Achim Lichtenberger

Introduction

One of the major problems in the study of the Hellenistic and Roman Near East is the search for cultural and religious continuity, discontinuity, and change in the traditional Bronze and Iron Age civilizations and their after-life in later periods. While some scholars claim a historical 'amnesia' for the Hellenistic and Roman societies in most parts of the Near East (with the exception of the Jews and the Phoenicians),[1] others reconstruct profound continuity and only superficial Hellenization and Romanization.[2] Surely in the Near East in the Bronze and Iron Ages complex societies developed and later civilizations could draw on this heritage. But can we really speak of heritage? Does 'heritage' imply that something is transmitted more or less directly? Unfortunately for many regions of the Near East we hardly know anything about their structure and material culture at the time of the Macedonian conquest.[3] What we do

[1] E.g. Millar, *The Roman Near East*, passim.

[2] E.g. Ball, *Rome in the East*, passim.

[3] On the Levant in the centuries before the Macedonian conquest, see e.g. Sader, *Les États araméens de Syrie depuis leur fondation jusqu'à leur transformation en provinces assyriennes*; Sartre, *D'Alexandre à Zénobie*, pp. 37–65; Lemaire, 'La Transeuphratène en transition (c. 350–300)', pp. 405–41 (on the Persian province Transeuphratene); Stern, *The Material Culture of the Land of the Bible in the Persian Period* (on the material culture in the Persian period).

Achim Lichtenberger (achim.lichtenberger@rub.de) Ruhr-Universität Bochum Institut für Archäologische Wissenschaften.

know is that there is a general decline of settlements, and population numbers were probably going down.[4] Thus it seems that in most regions of the Near East, the centuries immediately before the Macedonian conquest and even the early Hellenistic period are a kind of 'Dark Ages', and this makes it difficult to decide what and how earlier traditions might have been handed down to the Hellenistic and Roman periods.

In the following I discuss three cities of the Syrian Decapolis, namely Dion, Gerasa, and Gadara, and investigate what we can say about continuity, discontinuity, and change in their religious life. However, before doing this, we have to define the term 'continuity' in relation to religious life.[5] Of course continuity does not mean that the entire structure of a religion or major elements were transmitted completely unchanged, since no culture developed in isolation and all historical processes are processes of acculturation. Thus continuity always implies change, and we have to instead question the extent of change. How much 'change' is tolerable to still postulate 'continuity'? Does similarity between single formal elements allow us to speak of 'continuity' when, at the same time, the whole cultural, social, or religious framework has changed?

In this context, what is the difference between 'continuity' and 'discontinuity' as we can detect it in the archaeological record? Continuity in religious life, in my opinion, primarily requires continuity of a place of worship and/or of the deity worshipped. Thus discontinuity in religious life results from a radical change, an interruption in, or the end of a cult of, for example, a certain deity at a particular site. At a later point, another deity that might have had nothing to do with the former could be introduced at that place. More generally, the usefulness of the terms can be doubted, as 'continuity' always implies change and 'discontinuity' simply means too much change.

Patterns of Continuity, Discontinuity, and Change

If we want to talk about continuity, discontinuity, and change, we need a very clear picture of what was before, what was in between, and what is the outcome. And exactly here begins the problem. As mentioned, little is known about the

[4] On Transjordan in that time, see Hübner, *Die Ammoniter*, pp. 210–28; Thiel, *Studien zum hellenistischen Siedlungswesen in Palästina und Transjordanien*, pp. 363–64; Kennedy, *Gerasa and the Decapolis*, pp. 84–85.

[5] On 'continuity' and 'discontinuity' in archaeological terminology, see Knopf, *Kontinuität und Diskontinuität in der Archäologie*, pp. 11–28.

Figure 8.1. Dendara, Temple of Hathor, relief with Domitian, Ihi, Hathor, and Horus. After Hölbl, *Altägypten im römischen Reich: Tempel I*, p. 73, Abb. 80.

material culture of the southern Levant in the time immediately before the Hellenistic period, and we hardly have any evidence of religious activity. Our source material is so limited that one could dismiss the investigation from the start. However, I discuss here some examples from the Decapolis, introduced by three arbitrary examples of better documented cases from other Mediterranean regions and times, in order to demonstrate the range of possibilities and patterns of continuity, discontinuity, and change.

Traditional Egyptian Architecture and Iconography in Roman Egypt

I briefly point to one monument (out of many) that attests to the persistence of Bronze Age iconography and thought into the Roman period. The temple of Hathor at Dendara dates back to the Sixth Dynasty (late third millennium BC).[6] In it, Hathor, Horus, and Ihi were venerated. In the late Ptolemaic and Roman periods the temple was extensively rebuilt, but the overall plan remained a traditional Egyptian style. Additionally the reliefs depict deities and rulers in a traditional manner: a relief from the north gate showing the Pharaoh Domitian standing in front of Ihi (the small figure), Hathor, and Horus serves as an example (Figure 8.1). Specialists of later periods of Egyptian history can probably point to several innovative elements in such an image that do not simply copy Bronze Age models. However, what is important is the persistence of traditional imagery, deities, and thought that can be seen in this relief as a whole. This persistence can be traced in a more or less continuous sequence of monuments. Within the range of potential 'change' in the concept of 'continuity' outlined above we surely can observe a profound continuity of religious life from the Bronze Age into the Roman period.

The Temple of Aphaia at Aigina

The next example takes us to the Aegean island of Aigina. Excavations in the sanctuary of Aphaia, with its late archaic Doric temple and famous pediment sculptures, have demonstrated that there was already a shrine at this location in the Bronze Age.[7] From the Mycenaean votive terracottas found there it has been concluded that the cult referred to a female deity of fertility. We only know obscure things about the deity Aphaia who was later worshipped in the archaic temple.[8] She is said to be of Cretan origin and was assimilated to Artemis and Athena. This emphasizes that she was not completely equivalent with any single Greek Olympic deity and that she might have been influenced by Bronze Age religion.

In the archaeological excavation of the sanctuary, the sequence of strata has been carefully recorded, and there are rich ceramic finds. The latest Bronze Age

[6] On the temple at Dendara in the Hellenistic and Roman periods, see Hölbl, *Altägypten im römischen Reich: Tempel I*, pp. 72–87 (with further literature p. 121 n. 231).

[7] On the Bronze Age sanctuary, see Pilafidis-Williams, *The Sanctuary of Aphaia on Aigina in the Bronze Age*.

[8] Pausanias II. 30. 3. See on Aphaia Auffahrt, 'Diktynna', p. 572 (with further literature).

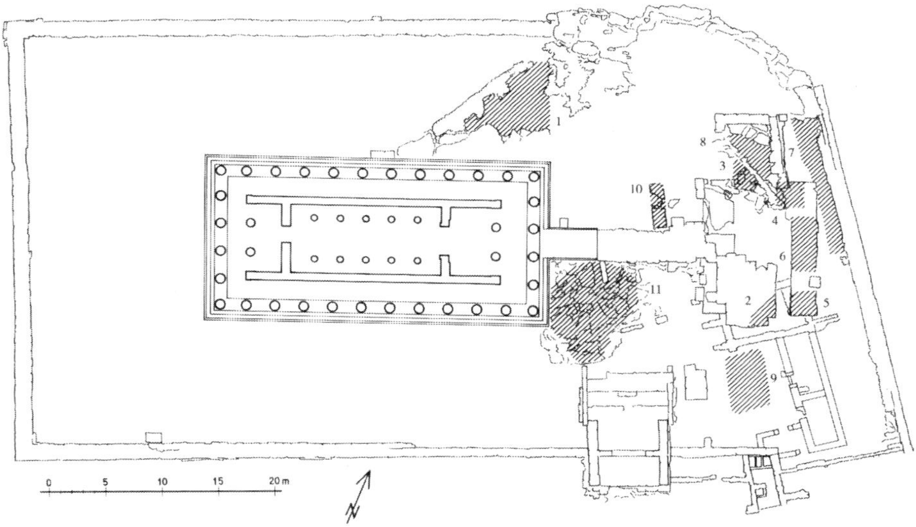

Figure 8.2. Aigina, Temple of Aphaia, Mycenaean find-contexts shaded. After Pilafidis-Williams, *The Sanctuary of Aphaia on Aigina in the Bronze Age*, fig. 2, plan by M. Ohly.

material is certainly middle LH III C (Figure 8.2). Sub-Mycenean and Early Protogeometric material is absent.[9] There is no evidence for cultic activity until Late Protogeometric, which means that there is a gap of settlement and cultic activity for about 150 to 200 years.[10]

What is the consequence? Can we assume any religious continuity, which may be suggested by the use of the same place and by the similar character of the deity worshipped there (a 'female deity of nature')? Or is the factual gap of 150 to 200 years (which is not an argument ex silentio because the strata were carefully observed) an obstacle to any assertion of continuity? The alleged similarity of the character of the deity would then be by chance.

The latter in fact could be the case as it fits with observations made by Snodgrass, Kyrieleis, and others for the transition from Late Bronze Age sanctuaries (e.g. Olympia) to the Early Greek period:[11] abandoned places with ancient ruined monuments seem to have been often deliberately chosen for

[9] Pilafidis-Williams, *The Sanctuary of Aphaia on Aigina in the Bronze Age*, pp. 159–60.

[10] Kraiker, *Aigina*, p. 11.

[11] Snodgrass, *The Dark Age of Greece*. pp. 394–416; Kyrieleis, *Anfänge und Frühzeit des Heiligtums von Olympia*, pp. 61–79. Cf. also in general Boardman, *The Archaeology of Nostalgia*.

Figure 8.3. Marash, stele, front.
Photo: M. Blömer.

Figure 8.4. Marash, stele, back.
Photo: M. Blömer.

cults as they were regarded as time-honoured, linking the present with a heroic past. Thus the time gap really attests to discontinuity, and what seems to be continuity is only a redefinition of the past.

The Stele from Marash

The third example stems from the Near East. In Marash in Commagene (north-western Syria) a stele in basalt was found that depicts a late Hittite weather god from the early seventh century BC on its front (Figure 8.3).[12] The god is shown in his typical attire with horned headgear, double axe, and thunderbolt. Above him is the winged sun-disc. The left side of the stele depicts the dedicant.

Especially relevant is the combination of this imagery with the inscription on the rear surface (Figure 8.4). This inscription is much later, the first century

[12] Şahin, 'Forschungen in Kommagene I: Epigraphik', pp. 99–111; Jacobs and Messerschmidt, 'Eine (provinzial-)assyrische Stele für Juppiter Dolichenus', pp. 105–14.

BC or AD. The dedicant is a certain Zarieris, son of Barnaios, who dedicated the stele to his *theos epekoos* after he had found it.

This stele with the inscription is one of the few attestations of centuries-old images which were later discovered and rededicated to current deities.[13] Although we have to assume that there must have been some aspect in the image of the seventh-century deity that reminded Zarieris of his *theos epekoos*, probably little continuity between the two deities can be postulated.

In this context one has to remember that in Commagene the image of Iuppiter Dolichenus had developed, and that the iconography of this mainly Roman deity can also be traced back to late Hittite antecedents.[14] We have to take into account that the iconography of Iuppiter Dolichenus also was shaped mainly by reference to centuries-old basalt reliefs that were redefined in the Hellenistic-Roman period.

These three examples attest to the range of possibilities for continuity, discontinuity, and change. We have seen that, as in Egypt, a spatial and iconographic religious continuity is possible. However in other cases, such as in Aigina, although a spatial and perhaps religious continuity at first glance seems conceivable, it nevertheless is unlikely; the interruption hints at discontinuity. The stele from Marash might also be evidence for such a discontinuity, which at a later date was redefined as continuity.

After these comparably well-documented examples we have to turn to the Decapolis where evidence is much more meagre.

Zeus at Dion

The Decapolis city of Dion belonged, in geographical terms, to southern Syria.[15] It was situated on Tell el-Ashari and, apart from some chance finds (mainly inscriptions), little archaeological investigation has taken place at the

[13] Another example might be the north Syrian rural sanctuary of Qadboun where we have Iron Age and Roman material. Although Bounni, 'La Permanence des lieux de culte en Syrie', pp. 777–89, proposes uninterrupted continuity at the site, a later rededication also seems possible.

[14] See now Bunnens, 'The Storm-God in Northern Syria and Southern Anatolia', pp. 57–82; Blömer, 'Statuen und Reliefs aus Zeugma und Umgebung', pp. 272–312; Blömer, 'Die Stele von Doliche', pp. 69–104.

[15] On Dion, see Augé, 'Sur le monnayage de Dion "de Coelé Syrie"', pp. 325–41; Sartre, 'Les Cites de Décapole septentrionale', pp. 149–51; Lichtenberger, *Kulte und Kultur der Dekapolis*, pp. 50–62; Riedl, 'Gottheiten und Kulte in der Dekapolis', pp. 90–93; Kropp, 'Dion of the Decapolis', pp. 125–44.

Figure 8.5.
Dion, civic bronze coin from the time of Geta, diameter: 23 mm. Münzen und Medaillen Deutschland, Auktion 32, 26.5.2010, lot 398.

site. Thus an important source for the cultural and religious history of the city is its bronze coinage which was minted by the city under Septimius Severus and Elagabalus. The reverse of coins of Geta and Elagabalus depict a standing deity flanked by two bulls (Figure 8.5).[16] The god is youthful with long hair, and he wears a kind of kalathos with horns in the shape of a lying crescent. His cloak is difficult to define. It may be a kind of cuirass or an ependytes like that of Artemis Ephesia.[17] His right arm rests on a sceptre surmounted by an eagle, and his left hand holds a Nike tendering a wreath to him.

There is no doubt that the iconography of this deity is quite similar to that of Jupiter Heliopolitanus of Baalbek who also owns a kalathos, is youthful, wears the ependytes, and is flanked by two bulls.[18] There are other similar deities in the region, and it is clear that they applied traditional iconographic schemata including the motif of the two flanking bulls and the hieratic statuary type.[19] The earliest attested deity that belongs to this group is the Zeus of Damascus who is attested for the first time on coins of the early first century BC.[20] Thus, although the deities seem to be quite old, we do not really know how genuine or 'traditional' the deities of this type are, and we must be very cautious in dating them too early.

[16] Spijkerman, *The Coins of the Decapolis and Provincia Arabia*, pp. 118–21, nos 6–8, 11–12.

[17] On Artemis Ephesia and her costume, see Fleischer, *Artemis von Ephesos und verwandte Kultstatuen*, esp. pp. 88–102.

[18] On Jupiter Heliopolitanus, see Fleischer, *Artemis von Ephesos und verwandte Kultstatuen*, pp. 326–69.

[19] Fleischer, *Artemis von Ephesos und verwandte Kultstatuen*.

[20] Houghton, Lorber, and Hoover, *Seleucid Coins*, pp. 609–10, nos 2471–72. On the iconography of the deity, see Fleischer, *Artemis von Ephesos und verwandte Kultstatuen*, pp. 379–80; Haider, Hutter, and Kreuzer, *Religionsgeschichte Syriens*, pp. 189–91.

After these general remarks on the type of deity, it is necessary to take a closer look at the Zeus of Dion who has two important features that differentiate him from Jupiter Heliopolitanus:

(1) Whereas Jupiter Heliopolitanus holds ears of corn and a whip in his hands, the Zeus of Dion has the eagle sceptre and the Nike. The attributes of Jupiter Heliopolitanus hint at his solar (whip) and fertility (ears of corn) character. Zeus of Dion has the typical attributes of the Greek Zeus Olympios (Nike and sceptre), who was widespread in the Decapolis.[21] We can assume that the attributes served to underscore that this local god was equivalent to the Greek Zeus. This is also supported by the toponym Dion which hints at Zeus being an important deity of that place.

(2) More difficult to understand are the horns of Zeus of Dion which are utterly exceptional. At first glance one could explain them as a traditional feature of the iconography of Near Eastern deities, since a wide array of such headgear with horns is attested.[22] But if we take a closer look at the different types, we realize that there is no horned headgear that fits into the late periods of this region. Thus one can consider whether the representation of Zeus of Dion shows a horizontal crescent rather than horns, or that an allusion to both was intended.

In the early Iron Age, Dion belonged to the Aramean kingdom of Damascus.[23] Late Hittite and Aramean images of deities often had horns[24] (as can be seen on the Marash stele, Figure 8.3), but we lack such evidence from the southern Levant. Thus it is difficult to postulate iconographic continuity, although there are some pre-Hellenistic remains at Tell el-Ashari that attest to earlier settlements, such as an Achaemenid seal[25] and a basalt stele.

[21] See for the attributes Lichtenberger, *Kulte und Kultur der Dekapolis*, p. 53. On Zeus Olympios in the Decapolis, see Lichtenberger, *Kulte und Kultur der Dekapolis*, pp. 341–43.

[22] On headgear with horns in the ancient Near East, see Boehmer, 'Hörnerkrone', pp. 431–34.

[23] Sader, *Les États araméens de Syrie depuis leur fondation jusqu'à leur transformation en provinces assyriennes*, pp. 231–70. See also the deity with horns (possibly from the Southern Levant) on a relief of Tiglatpilesar III from Nimrud (Unger, *Die Reliefs Tiglatpilesars III*, pl. IV no. 9; Unger, 'Diadem und Krone', p. 202).

[24] Boehmer, 'Hörnerkrone', p. 434.

[25] Kropp, 'Dion of the Decapolis', pp. 132–33.

Figure 8.6. Tell el-Ashari, basalt stele. After Bernett and Keel, *Mond, Stier und Kult am Stadttor*, p. 103.

In this context, I would like to draw attention to one basalt stele from Tell el-Ashari, datable to the ninth/eighth century BC (Figure 8.6).[26] Several such steles have been found in the region; for example, one in Awas (near Salchad) in the Hauran,[27] one at et-Turra (south of Tell el-Ashari),[28] and another at at-Tell near Lake Tiberias.[29] The one from Tell el-Ashari depicts a schematic tauromorphic figure with impressive horns and sword. This image, which also recurs on other monuments, is interpreted as a weather god like Hadad with aspects of a lunar god.[30] Such a deity might have been popular in the region in the early first millennium BC.[31]

An even older deity of the region was the local god on the 'Job-Stone' from Sheikh Sa'ad not far from Dion (Figure 8.7).[32] The basalt stele depicts the Egyptian Pharaoh Ramesses II (*c.* 1279–1213 BC) in front of a local deity

[26] Galling, 'Archäologisch-historische Erkenntnisse einer Reise in Syrien und Liban', pp. 186–87; Bernett and Keel, *Mond, Stier und Kult am Stadttor*, pp. 8–9.

[27] Bernett and Keel, *Mond, Stier und Kult am Stadttor*, pp. 9–10.

[28] Wimmer and Janaydeh, 'Eine Mondgottstele aus et-Turra/Jordanien', pp. 135–41.

[29] Bernett and Keel, *Mond, Stier und Kult am Stadttor*; Ornan, 'The Bull and its Two Masters', pp. 1–26.

[30] Galling, 'Archäologisch-historische Erkenntnisse einer Reise in Syrien und Liban', p. 187; Seyrig, 'Deux reliquaires', pp. 44–46; Bernett and Keel, *Mond, Stier und Kult am Stadttor*. See on the steles and on lunar deities of the Arameans Theuer, *Der Mondgott in den Religionen Syrien-Palästinas*, pp. 382–90.

[31] Further evidence for a lunar deity in the region in the first millennium BC might be a stamp seal from Abila with crescent and caprids (Lichtenberger, *Kulte und Kultur der Dekapolis*, pp. 75–76).

[32] Thanks are due to Andreas Kropp, Nottingham, who made me aware of the object. For the stele, see Schumacher, 'Der Hiobstein, Sachrat Eijub, im Hauran', pp. 142–47; Erman, 'Der

Figure 8.7.
Sheikh Sa'ad, 'Job-Stone'. After Erman, 'Der Hiobstein', p. 206.

with horns. Unfortunately the stele is badly weathered and the name of the deity is not fully legible. However the en face depiction (not typical for Egyptian deities) makes it plausible that it is a local south Syrian deity with horns.

We now have to ask whether or not there is any relationship between the Bronze and Iron Age precursors and the Zeus with horns and flanking bulls. At first glance this seems daring as we have no chronological continuity with comparable monuments for the later Iron Age and the Hellenistic period.[33] The only *tertium comparationis* is horns and — in the case of the Iron Age stele — bulls. But an influence from images like the Ramesside basalt stele could explain the unique motif of the horns of the Zeus of Dion, which has no contemporary comparison.[34] Thus images like the one from the stele could have

Hiobstein', pp. 205–11; Gressmann, *Altorientalische Texte zum Alten Testament*, p. 96, pl. XLV; Giveon, 'Two Egyptian Documents Concerning Bashan', pp. 197–200; Weber, *Sculptures from Roman Syria in the Syrian National Museum at Damascus*, pp. 42–43.

[33] However, in this region was situated the sanctuary of Atargatis at Karnain, which was destroyed 163 BC during the Maccabean revolt (I Maccabees 3. 26, 43–44; II Maccabees 12. 26; Flavius Josephus, Antiquitates Judaicae, 12. 344). The toponym Karnain ('horns') might relate to a local horned deity. On Karnain, see Möller and Schmitt, *Siedlungen Palästinas nach Flavius Josephus*, p. 121; Schmitt, 'Die Heimat Hiobs', pp. 56–63.

[34] Gawlikowski, 'Hadad', pp. 365–67, lists only our Zeus of Dion (p. 366, no. 11) as a 'Hadad' with horns. There is only one possible fourth century BC candidate for a Hadad with horns, on coins of (north Syrian) Hierapolis (Seyrig, 'Le Monnayage de Hiérapolis de Syrie a

inspired the image of the Zeus of Dion; Zeus might have drawn his horns from the tauromorphic creature. This hypothesis gains further weight when we consider that such monuments were also available in later periods; the stele from Tell el-Ashari was found in secondary use in a Roman tomb.[35] If this iconographic deduction is correct, the image of the Zeus of Dion can structurally be compared to the Marash stele: the traditional iconography does not hint at continuity but instead to discontinuity and a later redefinition of the past.

Zeus Olympios and Artemis at Gerasa

The next example stems from Gerasa in the Decapolis.[36] In this city two important sanctuaries are attested. A temple of Zeus Olympios stood in the southern part of the city, and in the north a temple of Artemis had been erected.[37]

The cult of Zeus Olympios is widely attested in inscriptions since the first century AD. The earliest evidence for cultic activity on the terrace of the temple of Zeus Olympios stems from the second century BC. Iron Age finds from the seventh/sixth century BC were also discovered at this site.[38] These finds lead to the widely accepted assumption that the cult of Zeus Olympios is the *interpretatio Graeca* of a former local deity, to which direct continuity is postulated.[39]

The time difference of a couple of hundred years, however, hints that at the site of the later temple of Zeus in Gerasa we are not dealing with continuity, but with discontinuity, and it is probable that there, as in Aigina, an old ritual place was consciously or coincidentally put back into use. We have to be

l'époque d'Alexandre', p. 16, no. 1). This, however, remains very controversial (cf. Seyrig, 'Le Monnayage de Hiérapolis de Syrie a l'époque d'Alexandre', p. 15). Kropp, 'Dion of the Decapolis', p. 135, is reminded by the horns of a 'lying crescent'. Such a large horizontal crescent on the head would also find no comparison with contemporary male deities. The crescent-like appearance of the horns would, however, fit with the tauromorphic deity from the Iron Age where the horns are shaped like a crescent.

[35] Seyrig, 'Deux reliquaires', p. 45.

[36] On Gerasa, see Kraeling, *Gerasa*. For more recent literature, see note 37, below.

[37] On Zeus Olympios and Artemis in Gerasa in the following, see Lichtenberger, 'Artemis and Zeus Olympios in Roman Gerasa and Seleucid Religious Policy', pp. 133–53. See also Lichtenberger, *Kulte und Kultur der Dekapolis*, pp. 191–243; Riedl, 'Gottheiten und Kulte in der Dekapolis', pp. 147–225 (with further literature).

[38] Seigne, 'De la grotte au périptère', p. 955; Seigne, 'Gerasa-Jerash – Stadt der 1000 Säulen', p. 13.

[39] See e.g. Thiel, 'Überlegungen zur Kultur- und Religionspolitik König Antiochos', p. 151.

extremely careful in postulating an internal or structural connection ('continuity') between the two cults. All the evidence we have regarding Zeus Olympios speaks for his introduction under the Seleucids as a genuine Greek cult for a new Greek settlement, which in Gerasa was named Antioch.

The case of Artemis in Gerasa is different. She is also attested in several inscriptions from the first century AD on. Most of the inscriptions mention epicleses which are not typical for Greek deities, but hint at a specific Near Eastern background.[40] This is also supported by iconographic evidence. Although we cannot entirely exclude that this character results from a contamination from the surrounding cultural setting,[41] I suggest that Artemis in Roman Gerasa is in fact an *interpretatio Graeca* of a traditional Near Eastern deity. However, although I postulate continuity, this deity underwent considerable changes when she experienced an *interpretatio Graeca*. This clearly sets her apart from the kind of continuity we encounter in Egypt. Also crucial is the fact that in Gerasa we cannot prove continuity on the spot. Thus we even have to consider that the Near Eastern deity was not local, but brought to this place from another region in the Near East. I suggest that this can be observed at the last place I discuss here, at Gadara.

Zeus and Heracles at Gadara

According to civic coinage of Gadara, the city had two important deities: Heracles (Figure 8.8) and Zeus (Figure 8.9).[42] With Zeus, the case is comparable to that at Gerasa. He seems to have been venerated as Zeus Olympios and brought to the city in the context of the implementation of a Seleucid settlement (Antioch and/or Seleucia). The temenos with temples of Zeus Olympios from the second century BC was found to the north of the city.[43] Again Iron Age remains (in fact one object)[44] were discovered in the vicinity, and continu-

[40] See for this phenomenon in the Decapolis, Lichtenberger, 'Probleme der interpretatio Graeca von Gottheiten in der syrischen Dekapolis', pp. 242–43.

[41] Lichtenberger, 'Probleme der interpretatio Graeca von Gottheiten in der syrischen Dekapolis', p. 243.

[42] On Gadara, Zeus, and Heracles, see in the following Lichtenberger, *Kulte und Kultur der Dekapolis*, pp. 83–114; Riedl, 'Gottheiten und Kulte in der Dekapolis', pp. 94–146. On Gadara in general, see Weber, *Gadara Decapolitana*.

[43] Hoffmann, 'Ein hellenistisches Heiligtum in Gadara', pp. 795–831. See for recent archaeological work Deutsches Archäologisches Institut, 'Gadara/Umm Qais (Jordanien)', pp. 247–49.

[44] C. Bührig, personal communication (2 March 2009), Berlin. The relevant object is mentioned in Hoffmann, 'Ein hellenistisches Heiligtum in Gadara', p. 805 with n. 27.

Figure 8.8.
Gadara, civic bronze coin from the time of Marcus Aurelius, diameter: 26 mm. Classical Numismatic Group, Electronic Auction 198, 5.11.2008, lot 202.

Figure 8.9.
Gadara, civic bronze coin from the time of Elagabalus, diameter: 24/26 mm. Spijkerman, *The Coins of the Decapolis and Provincia Arabia*, pp. 150–51, no. 80.

ity with an old 'High Place' to the cult of Zeus Olympios has been postulated.[45] The chronological gap between the Iron Age and the second century BC, however, is too wide. Thus we also have to assume that — just as in Gerasa — the Hellenistic cult place simply occupied a prominent location ('Aigina').

The cult of Heracles in Gadara is more complex. Already under Augustus the representation of a club on small bronze coins from the city hints at Heracles.[46] From the time of Antoninus Pius, the coins depict the bust of young beardless Heracles with laurel wreath (Figure 8.8).[47] Later coins show Heracles fighting with a thunderbolt against a snake-like creature (Figure 8.9).[48] The thunderbolt is also found as an attribute of Heracles on some coins minted in the time of Lucius Verus (Figure 8.10).[49] The thunderbolt as an attribute of Heracles

[45] Hoffmann, 'Ein hellenistisches Heiligtum in Gadara', pp. 804–05.

[46] Spijkerman, *The Coins of the Decapolis and Provincia Arabia*, pp. 130–31, no. 10.

[47] Spijkerman, *The Coins of the Decapolis and Provincia Arabia*, pp. 136–47, nos 32, 37–41, 53–56, 62, 68, 74.

[48] Lichtenberger, *Kulte und Kultur der Dekapolis*, MZ 40–41.

[49] Spijkerman, *The Coins of the Decapolis and Provincia Arabia*, pp. 142–43, nos 54–55; Lichtenberger, *Kulte und Kultur der Dekapolis*, MZ 36–37.

Figure 8.10. Gadara, civic bronze coin from the time of Lucius Verus, diameter: 25 mm. Classical Numismatic Group, Electronic Auction 207, 25.3.2009, lot 314.

requires explanation. Usually it belongs to Zeus as the highest deity of the pantheon. There is no place in Greece where Heracles held such a position.

But in Phoenicia, Melqart, who as Baal of Tyre could also be master of the thunderbolt,[50] was interpreted as Heracles, and the same is probably true for Gadara. Further evidence suggests that Heracles of Gadara was related to Heracles-Melqart of Tyre: the Gadarean coin type of the young laureate Heracles[51] corresponds to the main Heracles-Melqart type of Tyre (Figure 8.11) that was widespread in the southern Levant since the second century BC.[52] The same type is also attested in Philadelphia in the Decapolis[53] where a specific ritual of the cult of Heracles-Melqart, the *egersis*, is mentioned in an inscription.[54] Thus the appropriation of a specific coin type might hint at the character of the deity. In Gadara, as in Philadelphia, a Heracles was venerated that was probably related to Melqart of Tyre.

[50] On Melqart, see Bonnet, *Melqart*. On Melqart and the thunderbolt, see Lichtenberger, *Kulte und Kultur der Dekapolis*, p. 90. Thus, in the image of (Heracles-)Melqart, a fusion of the iconography of Greek Heracles and Greek Zeus took place. Because the Phoenician god was not equivalent to one Greek deity (since it had characteristics of a young Hero and of a supreme god), the deity in the *interpretatio Graeca* was translated into two Greek deities. I designate this phenomenon as 'double *interpretatio Graeca*'; Lichtenberger, 'Probleme der interpretatio Graeca von Gottheiten in der syrischen Dekapolis'.

[51] Cf. above, note 47.

[52] Hill, *Catalogue of the Greek Coins of Phoenicia*, pp. 233–53, nos 44–245; p. 254, no. 251; p. 257, nos 268–74; pp. 259–60, nos 288–98; pp. 264–65, nos 331–37; pp. 267–68, nos 356–66. On Heracles-Melqart in Tyre cf. Bonnet, *Melqart*, pp. 27–113.

[53] Spijkerman, *The Coins of the Decapolis and Provincia Arabia*, pp. 246–57, nos 9, 11–14, 17, 20, 27–28, 42.

[54] Gatier, *Inscriptions de la Jordanie*, pp. 51–54, no. 29. On Heracles(-Melqart) in Philadelphia, see Bonnet, *Melqart*, pp. 145–48; Lichtenberger, *Kulte und Kultur der Dekapolis*, pp. 248–55, 257–58, 260–61; Riedl, 'Gottheiten und Kulte in der Dekapolis', pp. 254–63.

Figure 8.11.
Tyre, civic bronze coin dated 84/85 AD, diameter: 25 mm. Münzen und Medaillen Deutschland, Auktion 17, 4.10.2005, lot 1061.

What is the consequence of this observation? Does this mean that we can trace continuity with an early first-millennium BC Phoenician cult in the Decapolis? This is unlikely as we have no evidence for Phoenician presence in the hinterland at that time. In the Persian and early Hellenistic periods, however, we can assume that Phoenician cities had interests in the hinterland.[55] Thus it is conceivable that Melqart was brought to the Decapolis under Phoenician influence in that period.[56] This means that the deity — although of Near Eastern origin — would not be a 'genuine', local one. His Near Eastern origin appears to be evidence of continuity, but closer analysis proves that he was a new deity, introduced comparably late.

Epilogue

In concluding these case studies of evidence for religion in the Decapolis we can summarize that continuity to the extent that can be observed in Egypt is nowhere to be found. We have no evidence for the persistence of Bronze Age and Iron Age religion at a single place or in relation to a single deity. This agrees with what we know about settlement patterns in the centuries immediately before the Macedonian conquest. There seems to be a general decline of population in the region which resulted in a broad cultural and religious discontinuity.

But this discontinuity does not mean that the religious life of the Decapolis in the Hellenistic and Roman periods was predominantly Western, Greek,

[55] Lichtenberger, 'The Decapolis and Phoenicia'.

[56] In Philadelphia it is conceivable that the Phoenician Melqart was related to the earlier Ammonite Milkom. This however remains difficult to verify; Bonnet, *Melqart*, p. 148; Lichtenberger, *Kulte und Kultur der Dekapolis*, pp. 251–52; Riedl, 'Gottheiten und Kulte in der Dekapolis', pp. 262–63.

or Roman (whatever that means), since redefinitions of the past, as with the Marash stele, Zeus of Dion, and the cults of Zeus Olympios at former ritual sites, happened. Of course internal Near Eastern developments also took place as with the probably Phoenician Heracles-Melqart in Gadara. And sometimes we do not know the origin of supposed Near Eastern deities, as is the case with Artemis in Gerasa.

Sometimes, however, and this must be stressed, continuity definitely existed. The best examples are toponyms which survived from the Bronze Age to the Byzantine period and beyond (e.g. Rabbatammon, Philadelphia, and Amman).[57] The mechanisms for their persistence apparently eludes the capacity of our archaeological and historical methods.

[57] See for the phenomenon of the reappearance of pre-Hellenistic toponyms Jones, *The Cities of the Eastern Roman Provinces*, pp. 228–30.

Works Cited

Secondary Studies

Auffahrt, C., 'Diktynna', *Der Neue Pauly*, 3 (1997), 572
Augé, C., 'Sur le monnayage de Dion "de Coelé Syrie"', in *Geographie historique au Proche-Orient*, ed. by P.-L. Gatier, B. Helly, and J.-P. Rey-Coquais (Paris: CNRS, 1988), pp. 325–41
Ball, W., *Rome in the East: The Transformation of an Empire* (London: Routledge, 2000)
Bernett, M., and O. Keel, *Mond, Stier und Kult am Stadttor: Die Stele von Betsaida (et-Tell)* (Freiburg: Universitätsverlag and Vandenhoeck and Ruprecht, 1998)
Blömer, M., 'Statuen und Reliefs aus Zeugma und Umgebung' (unpublished doctoral dissertation, University of Münster, 2008)
——, 'Die Stele von Doliche', in *Von Kummuḫ nach Telouch: Historische und archäologische Untersuchungen in Kommagene*, ed. by E. Winter (Bonn: Habelt, 2011), pp. 69–104
Boardman, J., *The Archaeology of Nostalgia: How the Greeks Re-created their Mythical Past* (London: Thames and Hudson, 2002)
Boehmer, R. M., 'Hörnerkrone', in *Reallexikon der Assyriologie und Vorderasiatischen Archäologie*, ed. by M. P. Streck (Berlin: De Gruyter, 1972–75), IV, 431–34
Bonnet, C., *Melqart: cultes et mythes de l'Héraclès tyrien en méditerranée* (Leuven: Peeters, 1988)
Bounni, A., 'La Permanence des lieux de culte en Syrie: l'exemple du site de Qadboun', *Topoi*, 7 (1997), 777–89
Bunnens, G., 'The Storm-God in Northern Syria and Southern Anatolia from Hadad of Aleppo to Iupiter Dolichenus', in *Offizielle Religion, lokale Kulte und individuelle Religiosität*, ed. by M. Hutter and S. Hutter-Braunsar (Münster: Ugarit, 2004), pp. 57–82
Deutsches Archäologisches Institut, 'Gadara/Umm Qais (Jordanien)', in *Jahresbericht 2007, Archäologischer Anzeiger*, 1 Beiheft (2008), 247–49
Erman, A., 'Der Hiobstein', *Zeitschrift des Deutschen Palästina-Vereins*, 15 (1892), 205–11
Fleischer, R., *Artemis von Ephesos und verwandte Kultstatuen aus Anatolien und Syrien* (Leiden: Brill, 1973)
Galling, K., 'Archäologisch-historische Erkenntnisse einer Reise in Syrien und Liban im Spätherbst 1952', *Zeitschrift des Deutschen Palästina-Vereins*, 69 (1953), 181–87
Gatier, P.-L., *Inscriptions de la Jordanie: II Région central (Amman – Hesban – Madaba – Main – Dhiban)* (Paris: Geuthner, 1986)
Gawlikowski, M., 'Hadad', in *Lexicon Iconographicum Mythologiae Classicae*, vol. IV (München: Artemis, 1984), pp. 365–67
Giveon, R., 'Two Egyptian Documents Concerning Bashan from the Time of Ramses II', *Rivista degli studi orientali*, 40 (1965), 197–202
Gressmann, H., *Altorientalische Texte zum Alten Testament*, 2nd edn (Berlin: De Gruyter, 1926)
Haider, P. W., M. Hutter, and S. Kreuzer, eds, *Religionsgeschichte Syriens* (Stuttgart: Kohlhammer, 1996)

Hill, G. F., *Catalogue of the Greek Coins of Phoenicia: A Catalogue of the Greek Coins in the British Museum* (London: Trustees of the British Museum, 1910)

Hoffmann, A., 'Ein hellenistisches Heiligtum in Gadara', *Topoi*, 9 (1999), 795–831

Hölbl, G., *Altägypten im römischen Reich. Die römische Pharao und seine Tempel I: Römische Politik und altägyptische Ideologie von Augustus bis Diocletian. Tempelbau in Oberägypten* (Mainz: von Zabern, 2000)

Houghton, A., C. Lorber, and O. Hoover, *Seleucid Coins: A Comprehensive Catalogue. Part II Seleucus IV through Antiochos XIII* (New York: American Numismatic Society, 2008)

Hübner, U., *Die Ammoniter: Untersuchungen zur Geschichte, Kultur und Religion eines transjordanischen Volkes im 1. Jahrtausend v. Chr.* (Wiesbaden: Harrassowitz, 1992)

Jacobs, B., and W. Messerschmidt, 'Eine (provinzial-)assyrische Stele für Juppiter Dolichenus', *Epigraphica Anatolica: Zeitschrift für Epigraphik und historische Geographie Anatoliens*, 19 (1992), 105–14

Jones, A. H. M., *The Cities of the Eastern Roman Provinces*, 2nd edn (Oxford: Clarendon Press, 1971)

Kennedy, D., *Gerasa and the Decapolis: A 'Virtual Island' in Northwest Jordan* (London: Duckworth, 2007)

Knopf, T., *Kontinuität und Diskontinuität in der Archäologie: Quellenkritisch-vergleichende Studien* (Münster: Waxmann, 2002)

Kraeling, C. H., ed., *Gerasa: City of the Decapolis* (New Haven: American Schools of Oriental Research, 1938)

Kraiker, W., *Aigina: Die Vasen des 10. bis 7. Jahrhunderts v. Chr.* (Berlin: Mann, 1951)

Kropp, A., 'Dion of the Decapolis: *Tell al-Ash'ari* in Southern Syria in the Light of Ancient Documents and Recent Discoveries', *Levant*, 38 (2006), 125–44

Kyrieleis, H., *Anfänge und Frühzeit des Heiligtums von Olympia: Die Ausgrabungen am Pelopion 1987–1996*, Olympische Forschungen, 31 (Berlin: De Gruyter, 2006)

Lemaire, A., 'La Transeuphratène en transition (c. 350–300)', in *La Transition entre l'empire achéménide et les royaumes hellénistiques*, ed. by P. Briant and F. Joannès (Paris: De Boccard, 2006), pp. 405–41

Lichtenberger, A., 'Artemis and Zeus Olympios in Roman Gerasa and Seleucid religious policy', in *The Variety of Local Religious Life in the Near East in the Hellenistic and Roman Periods*, ed. by T. Kaizer (Leiden: Brill, 2008), pp. 133–53

——, 'The Decapolis and Phoenicia', *ARAM Society for Syro-Mesopotamian Studies*, 23 (2011), 559–83

——, *Kulte und Kultur der Dekapolis: Untersuchungen zu numismatischen, archäologischen und epigraphischen Zeugnissen* (Wiesbaden: Harrassowitz, 2003)

——, 'Probleme der interpretatio Graeca von Gottheiten in der syrischen Dekapolis', in *Die Welt der Götterbilder*, ed. by B. Groneberg and H. Spieckermann (Berlin: De Gruyter, 2008), pp. 237–54

Millar, F., *The Roman Near East: 31 BC – AD 337* (Cambridge, MA: Harvard University Press, 1993)

Möller, C., and G. Schmitt, *Siedlungen Palästinas nach Flavius Josephus* (Wiesbaden: Harrassowitz, 1976)

Ornan, T., 'The Bull and its Two Masters: Moon and Storm Deities in Relation to the Bull in Ancient Near Eastern Art', *Israel Exploration Journal*, 51 (2001), 1–26

Pilafidis-Williams, K., *The Sanctuary of Aphaia on Aigina in the Bronze Age* (München: Hirmer, 1998)

Riedl, N., 'Gottheiten und Kulte in der Dekapolis' (unpublished doctoral dissertation, Freie Universität Berlin, 2003), available at <http://www.diss.fu-berlin.de/diss/receive/FUDISS_thesis_000000001712> [accessed 15 June 2011]

Sader, H. S., *Les États araméens de Syrie depuis leur fondation jusqu'à leur transformation en provinces assyriennes* (Wiesbaden: Steiner, 1987)

Şahin, S., 'Forschungen in Kommagene I: Epigraphik', *Epigraphica Anatolica: Zeitschrift für Epigraphik und historische Geographie Anatoliens*, 18 (1991), 99–111

Sartre, M., 'Les Cites de Décapole septentrionale: Canatha, Raphana, Dion et Ahadra', *ARAM Society for Syro-Mesopotamian Studies*, 4 (1992), 139–56

——, *D'Alexandre à Zénobie: Histoire du Levant antique. IVe siècle av. J.-C. – IIIe siècle ap. J.-C.* (Paris: Fayard, 2001)

Schmitt, G., 'Die Heimat Hiobs', *Zeitschrift des Deutschen Palästina-Vereins*, 40 (1985), 56–63

Schumacher, G., 'Der Hiobstein, Sachrat Eijub, im Hauran', *Zeitschrift des Deutschen Palästina-Vereins*, 14 (1891), 142–47

Seigne, J., 'De la grotte au périptère: le sanctuaire de Zeus Olympien à Jérash', *Topoi*, 7 (1997), 993–1004

——, 'Gerasa-Jerash – Stadt der 1000 Säulen', in *Gadara – Gerasa und die Dekapolis*, ed. by A. Hoffmann and S. Kerner (Mainz: Philipp von Zabern, 2002), pp. 6–22

Seyrig, H., 'Deux reliquaires', *Syria*, 36 (1959), 43–48

——, 'Le Monnayage de Hiérapolis de Syrie a l'époque d'Alexandre', *Revue numismatique*, 13 (1971), 11–21

Snodgrass, A. M., *The Dark Age of Greece: An Archaeological Survey of the Eleventh to the Eighth Centuries BC* (Edinburgh: Edinburgh University Press, 1971)

Spijkerman, A., *The Coins of the Decapolis and Provincia Arabia* (Jerusalem: Studium Biblicum Franciscanum, 1978)

Stern, E., *The Material Culture of the Land of the Bible in the Persian Period 538–332 B.C.* (Warminster: Aris and Philips, 1982)

Theuer, G., *Der Mondgott in den Religionen Syrien-Palästinas* (Freiburg: Universitätsverlag; Göttingen: Vandenhoeck and Ruprecht, 2000)

Thiel, W., *Studien zum hellenistischen Siedlungswesen in Palästina und Transjordanien: Historische und archäologische Untersuchungen zur städtebaulichen Entwicklung ausgewählter Siedlungen unter den Ptolemäern und Seleukiden* (München: Dr Hut, 2007)

——, 'Überlegungen zur Kultur- und Religionspolitik König Antiochos' IV: Epiphanes am Beispiel der Entwicklung des Heiligtums des Zeus Olympios/Akraios von Nysa-Skythopolis', in *Kult und Kommunikation: Medien in Heiligtümern der Antike*, ed. by C. Frevel and H. von Hesberg (Wiesbaden: Reichert, 2007), pp. 121–63

Unger, E., 'Diadem und Krone', *Reallexikon der Assyriologie und Vorderasiatischen Archäologie*, ed. by M. P. Streck, 13 vols (Berlin: De Gruyter), II (1938), 201–11

——, *Die Reliefs Tiglatpilesars III. aus Nimrud* (Konstantinopel: Ihsan, 1917)

Weber, T., *Gadara Decapolitana: Untersuchungen zur Topographie, Geschichte, Architektur und der Bildenden Kunst einer 'Polis Hellenis' im Ostjordanland* (Wiesbaden: Harrassowitz, 2002)

——, *Sculptures from Roman Syria in the Syrian National Museum at Damascus* (Worms: Werner, 2006)

Wimmer, S. J., and K. Janaydeh, 'Eine Mondgottstele aus et-Turra/Jordanien', *Zeitschrift des Deutschen Palästina-Vereins*, 127 (2011), 135–41

The Imperial Office and the Church in Ephrem the Syrian

Volker Menze

When the first Christian emperor, Constantine, came to power in Eburacum in Britain in 306, at the other end of the Roman Empire, in Nisibis, Ephrem, arguably the most important poet of the Syrian tongue, was born into a Christian family.[1] While the new Emperor slowly made his way from the province to the centres of power — having defeated Maxentius in the famous battle at the Milvian bridge outside Rome in 312, and having founded his new capital in Constantinople in 324 — Ephrem remained provincial. Ephrem may have been acquainted with Greek education and philosophy, and was not the purely Syrian-Semitic poet scholars once believed.[2] However, Ephrem never saw the Roman centres of powers with his own eyes:[3] he served

* A previous version of this article has been presented at a conference on 'Regionalisation and the Integration of the Mediterranean World in Late Antiquity' in Heidelberg and Frankfurt in June 2010. I am indebted to Andrew Palmer for comments and corrections.

[1] About Ephrem's life, see especially McVey's introduction in Ephrem the Syrian, *Hymns, trans. by McVey*, pp. 5–28, the introduction by Mathews in Ephrem the Syrian, *Selected Prose Works*, trans. by Mathews and Amar, pp. 12–37, and Lange's introduction in Lange, *Ephraem der Syrer*, pp. 9–34; see also Brock, *The Luminous Eye*, pp. 13–21; Ephrem the Syrian, *Hymns on Paradise, ed. and trans. by Brock*, pp. 8–25; for a general introduction to his life and work, see El-Khoury, *Die Interpretation der Welt bei Ephraem dem Syrer*.

[2] For Ephrem and Greek influence, see Koonammakkal, 'St. Ephrem and "Greek Wisdom"', pp. 169–76 and Possekel, *Evidence of Greek Philosophical Concepts in the Writings of Ephrem the Syrian*.

[3] However, note that Andrew Palmer argues that Ephrem might have been more widely travelled than most scholars suppose — including a visit to Nicomedia: Palmer, 'A Single Human Being Divided in Himself', § 8; against e.g. Bundy, 'Vision for the City', p. 189.

Volker Menze (theodora.volker@gmail.com) Department of Medieval Studies, Central European University.

his home church and the Nicene bishops of Nisibis until 363, when Emperor Jovian — after the fatal Persian campaign of Julian Apostata — had to hand over Nisibis to the Persians. Ephrem moved to Edessa where he lived and served the local bishop as deacon until he died in 373.

Here is no place for a full scholarly treatment of either Constantine or Ephrem, but in a series on contextualizing the sacred in the Near East, it seems appropriate to situate Ephrem and his self-understanding as a late antique Christian of Syrian origin in the context of the Later Roman Empire in the fourth century and investigate his provincial perception of imperial power and the imperial office in relation to the Church.

Ephrem's works do not form the average source material modern historians are used to working with. The rich, poetic imagery and language of his *madrāshê* — instructional teaching hymns — pose difficulties to use for historical contextualization.[4] For decades no scholarly consensus existed of the quality of Ephrem's oeuvre. Highly praised in antiquity since Theodoret's remark that Ephrem was 'the harp of the Holy Spirit, who waters daily the people of Syria with the streams of grace',[5] the perception of Ephrem's work in modern scholarship has gone a long way from despising his *madrāshê* as 'turgid, humourless and repetitive'[6] to regarding Ephrem 'the only theologian-poet to rank beside Dante'.[7] Also, placing the poet in his historical context has varied almost as much as the judgement of the quality of his works. Whereas fifty years ago Robert Murray could consider him as unattached from Greek thinking, Edmund Beck, Ephrem's tireless editor and translator, and others demonstrated that Ephrem had been involved with the Greek-speaking environment.[8] Samuel Lieu rightly summarizes Ephrem's fame early onwards by stating that Ephrem 'was the only Syriac theologian before the Monophysite controversy to be universally admired and the epithet of "the Syrian" testifies to his unique position'.[9]

[4] For a discussion of Ephrem's poetry, see especially Beck, 'Ephrem des Syrers Hymnik', pp. 345–79.

[5] Theodoret of Cyrrhus, *Epistulae*, 146, in Theodoret of Cyrrhus, *Correspondance, ed. and trans by Azéma*, pp. 190–91.

[6] Segal, *Edessa 'The Blessed City'*, p. 89.

[7] Murray, *Symbols of Church and Kingdom*, p. 31; the judgements on Ephrem's works are collected by Griffith, 'Ephraem, the Deacon of Edessa, and the Church of the Empire', pp. 22–23, and Shepardson, *Anti-Judaism and Christian Orthodoxy*, pp. 12–13.

[8] Murray, 'St Ephrem the Syrian on Church Unity', p. 164: 'St Ephrem [...] represents an entirely Semitic Christianity'. However, see now Koonammakkal, 'St. Ephrem and "Greek Wisdom"' and Possekel, *Evidence of Greek Philosophical Concepts in the Writings of Ephrem the Syrian*.

[9] Lieu, *The Emperor Julian*, p. 97.

Ephrem was a contemporary of the first two Christian emperors, Constantine I (306–37) and his son Constantius II (337–61), as well as the apostate Julian (361–63) and his two Christian successors Jovian (363–64) and Valens (364–78). As the poet served his local church at the fringes of the empire, neither profane historiography nor imperial politics were one of his major interests. However, considering the religious changes that these emperors brought about for the Roman Empire — Constantine made Christianity an official *religio* and held the council of Nicaea in 325 that condemned Arius, Constantius on the other hand was regarded an 'Arian', Julian an Apostate, and Valens an 'Arian' again[10] — it does not come as a complete surprise that Ephrem reflected on imperial politics in his *Hymns against Julian*. Constantine, Constantius, and Julian are featured here, and the texts vouchsafe the modern reader to get a rare glimpse of the poet's view of the empire as well as the impact of imperial power on the universal Church, Ephrem's home church, and also his home town, Nisibis.[11]

This article attempts to analyse Ephrem's perception and understanding of emperors and imperial power in relation to the Church as it can be perceived from his *Hymns against Julian*.[12] It argues that in contrast to Eusebius of Caesarea (*c.* 264/65–339/40) — the first Christian author who draws a model of how Christianity would fit into the existing Roman Empire — Ephrem attributes no spiritual role to the imperial office. The emperors' sponsorship for and protection of the Christian Church are acknowledged when they occurred. Furthermore, the jurisdiction of the imperial office is not questioned also in religious matters. However, the cases of the apostate Julian and the Arian emperors demonstrate that the (Nicene) Church had to exist without the patronage of the emperors. Therefore, unlike Eusebius, who constructed his Church of the Empire around Emperor Constantine the Great,[13] from Ephrem's provincial perception the imperial office did not play a role in his ecclesiology.

[10] The term 'Arian' is here used for convenience; for a discussion of the history of the controversy and also for terminology, see Hanson, *The Search for the Doctrine of God*; Brennecke, *Studien zur Geschichte der Homöer*; Ayres, *Nicaea and its Legacy*; Gwynn, *The Eusebians*.

[11] Russell, 'Nisibis as the Background to the Life of Ephrem the Syrian', § 5, rightly emphasizes the importance of Nisibis for Ephrem's cultural background: it was not Edessa — as references in scholarship to Ephrem of Edessa sometimes imply — that shaped Ephrem for most of his life.

[12] The Roman emperors and their relation to the Church comes up occasionally in other hymns as well, for example the *Carmina Nisibena*. See below.

[13] For Constantine and Eusebius's image of him, see Cameron, 'Eusebius's *Vita Constantini*

Since Edmund Beck's critical editions and translations of Ephrem the Syrian's work in 1955–79, scholarship dedicated to Ephrem has immensely increased.[14] Subsequent translations of a good number of his hymns into English by Sebastian Brock and Kathleen McVey have made Ephrem more accessible in the Anglo-Saxon world.[15] In 2002 Kees van Biesen published a *Bibliography of St. Ephrem the Syrian* that comprises almost four hundred pages.[16] The bibliography also shows in which directions research on Ephrem is undertaken: it contains chapters on editions, translations (ancient as well as modern), symbolic theology and theological hermeneutics, poetry, Ephrem's treatment of the *Diatessaron*, his exegesis of the Scriptures, his theology of Paradise, Mariology, Christian Life, Asceticism and Spirituality, etc. It is notable that historical studies form only a tiny minority among the many publications on Ephrem. Considering the already mentioned nature of Ephrem's poetic-theological work, this is not surprising but hardly satisfactory for a historian.

For placing Ephrem in his historical context and providing a historical analysis, Sidney Griffith's article on 'Ephraem, the Deacon of Edessa, and the Church of the Empire' from 1986 remains the seminal contribution to the field.[17] To this article one should add — at least partially — several of Griffith's further contributions on Ephrem in the following decades as well as Samuel Lieu's *The Emperor Julian: Panegyric and Polemic*, Andrew Palmer's articles on 'A Single Human Being Divided in Himself: Ephraim the Syrian, the Man in the Middle' and 'The Prophet and the King: Mår Afrem's Message to the Eastern Roman Emperor', and most recently Christine Shepardson's monograph on *Anti-Judaism and Christian Orthodoxy: Ephrem's Hymns in Fourth-Century Syria*.[18] Griffith rightly noted that Ephrem has often been neglected

and the Construction of Constantine', pp. 145–74. For a recent historical assessment, see Stephenson, *Constantine*.

[14] Griffith, 'A Spiritual Father for the Whole Church'.

[15] Furthermore Andrew Palmer has announced new editions and translations of Ephrem's *madrāshê* and homilies on faith; see Palmer, 'A Single Human Being Divided in Himself'.

[16] Van Biesen, *Bibliography of St. Ephrem the Syrian*. In an e-mail communication in 2010 Kees van Biesen announced that a second edition of his bibliography is forthcoming.

[17] Griffith, 'Ephraem, the Deacon of Edessa, and the Church of the Empire', pp. 22–52.

[18] Griffith, 'Ephraem the Syrian's Hymns "Against Julian"', pp. 238–66; Griffith, 'Setting Right the Church of Syria', pp. 97–114; Griffith, 'The Marks of the "True Church"', pp. 125–40; Lieu, *The Emperor Julian*; Palmer, 'A Single Human Being Divided in Himself'; Palmer, 'The Prophet and the King', pp. 213–36; Shepardson, *Anti-Judaism and Christian Orthodoxy*.

among 'the mainstream of modern patristic scholarship'.[19] This is even more so the case with historical studies which merely mention Ephrem in passing — not the least due to the fact that it is hardly possible to read Ephrem's works as a historical narrative.[20]

The *communis opinio* is that Ephrem was a staunch defender of the Council of Nicaea and strove to bring Syrian Christianity in line with the Nicene Church.[21] Ephrem started his work for the Church — probably already in Nisibis as deacon — under the Nicene Bishop Jacob of Nisibis (308/09–38) who had attended the Council of Nicaea, and whom Theodoret of Cyrrhus praised for his piety.[22] In this troublesome time for the Church, it is hard to imagine that Ephrem could have served Jacob as deacon for decades if he did not at least silently agreed with the doctrinal perception of his superior. In any case, there are no traces of any Arian leanings in Ephrem's works. However, Hanns Christof Brennecke's meticulous observation that Ephrem only started to promote Nicaea since 363 or 364 is notable, and even then Ephrem praised the 'Arian' Emperor Constantius II for his piety.[23] Brennecke regards this posi-

[19] Griffith, 'A Spiritual Father for the Whole Church', § 3, points as example to Hanson's seminal monograph on the 'Arian controversy' (already noted by Russell, *St. Ephraem the Syrian and St. Gregory the Theologian Confront the Arians*, p. 4): Hanson, *The Search for the Doctrine of God*.

[20] A recent example is Rosen, *Julian*. Bowersock, *Julian the Apostate*, pp. 104, 114, etc., had been fonder of Ephrem. Lightfoot, 'The Third Siege of Nisibis', p. 111, almost apologizes that he cannot make more of Ephrem's account of the siege of Nisibis as it does 'not constitute a precise historical record but contribute only brief, unconnected allusions' in a 'poetic and in content religious-didactic' form.

[21] As Ephrem complained that 'orthodox' Christians were called Palûtians in Edessa after a legendary Bishop Palût, Ephrem's community certainly competed with other Christians groups for (universal) recognition. See also Lange, *Ephraem der Syrer*, pp. 31–32 and 41–42.

[22] For Ephrem already made deacon in Nisibis, see Lange, *Ephraem der Syrer*, p. 12; for a legendary account of Jacob's life, see Theodoret of Cyrrhus, *Historia Religiosa*, 1.10 (Price, *A History of the Monks of Syria by Theodoret of Cyrrhus*); for a critical review of Jacob, see Bundy, 'Jacob of Nisibis as a Model for the Episcopacy', pp. 235–49; see also Fiey, *Nisibe*, pp. 21–26.

[23] Brennecke, *Studien zur Geschichte der Homöer*, pp. 84–85 and 199. Christian Lange in his introduction to Ephrem's *Commentary on the Diatessaron* misinterprets Brennecke when he believes that Brennecke actually stated that Ephrem was a Homoian; Lange, *Ephraem der Syrer*, p. 29 with n. 114. Brennecke clearly speaks of Ephrem as an author 'aus den Kreisen der neunizänischen Orthodoxie' (p. 84). Ephrem mentions the Council of Nicaea first in *Hymns against Heresies* 22.20, in Ephrem the Syrian, *Hymnen contra Haereses*, ed. and trans. by Beck; see also Lange, *Ephraem der Syrer*, p. 32; also pp. 33–34 and 41–42 where he dates the hymns against heresies to Ephrem's stay in Edessa after 363.

tive image of Constantius — which also other authors like Andrew Palmer and C. S. Lightfoot have noted[24] — as based in Ephrem's profound opposition to the apostate Julian, but it can be taken for granted that Ephrem never sided with the Homoian party.

In his 'Ephraem, the Deacon of Edessa', Griffith attempts to analyse 'an aspect of his ecclesiology [...], viz., Ephraem's ideas about the organizational constitution of the church, and its relationship to the newly Christian Roman empire'.[25] Griffith argues that 'Ephraem was [...] doing everything in his power to bring the Syriac-speaking community into line with the "Church of the Empire"'.[26] In order to define the 'Church of the Empire', Griffith refers especially to Karl Baus, who regarded the relationship of State and Church as very close, especially in the public sphere.[27] Griffith investigates Ephrem's understanding of the Christian Church, his image of the emperor, the relationships between emperor and bishops, and his view on the Arians. He concludes that Ephrem promoted 'an almost Eusebian doctrine of the church of the Empire'.[28]

Griffith reiterates his understanding of Ephrem's perception of the Church of his time as an almost Eusebian one in his further articles, and subsequent scholars refer the reader for Ephrem's understanding of Church and State back to Griffith's contributions.[29] Influenced by Griffith's contributions, Christine Shepardson regards Ephrem as struggling 'to fit his local Christian community into an imperial mold of Nicence Christianity'.[30] She compares Ephrem with Athanasius of Alexandria (328–73) and concludes that, like Athanasius, 'Ephrem emerges as a vocal Nicene Christian leader struggling to prevail in the topsy-turvy political and religious context of the fourth-century eastern Empire'.[31]

[24] Palmer, 'A Single Human Being Divided in Himself', § 6; Lightfoot, 'The Third Siege of Nisibis', p. 122.

[25] Griffith, 'Ephraem, the Deacon of Edessa, and the Church of the Empire', p. 24.

[26] Griffith, 'Ephraem, the Deacon of Edessa, and the Church of the Empire', p. 28.

[27] Baus, 'The Development of the Church of the Empire', pp. 89–90.

[28] Griffith, 'Ephraem, the Deacon of Edessa, and the Church of the Empire', p. 48.

[29] Griffith, 'Setting Right the Church of Syria', pp. 97–98: 'Ephraem was a staunch, even insistent, supporter of an ecclesiology reminiscent of that of Eusebius of Caesarea'; see also here p. 110 and below; Lieu, *The Emperor Julian*, p. 104; Shepardson, *Anti-Judaism and Christian Orthodoxy*, p. 21 n. 1, p. 23 n. 6, etc.

[30] Shepardson, *Anti-Judaism and Christian Orthodoxy*, p. 62.

[31] Shepardson, *Anti-Judaism and Christian Orthodoxy*, p. 160.

The Eusebian model of Church and State cannot be discussed here in full, but scholarship on Constantine and the depiction of the Emperor by Eusebius has greatly advanced in the last decades.[32] Against the background of the Trinitarian (and later the Christological) controversies, contemporary Christian authors became less certain than Eusebius how to understand Christian emperors. Although Athanasius of Alexandria, like Eusebius, constructed his interpretation of the imperial office within a biblical framework, in his *History of the Arians* he understood Constantius II as Pharaoh — or even as Anti-Christ.[33] The fact that Ephrem was a Nicene Christian who lived under either so-called Arian emperors or, with Julian, even under a pagan emperor should make scholars cautious of assuming an underlying Eusebian perception of Church and State in Ephrem's works.

One of Ephrem's objectives visible in most of his writings is his refusal of (non-Nicene) heresies and his despise of those who caused disputes by inquiring about God. In his *Sermons on Faith* written in Nisibis, Ephrem depicts a questionable state of the Christian Church in his time:[34]

> If you dispute like this there, the kingdom will not accept you,
> lest you should enter and spread discord in the place full of harmony.
> But that kingdom will exact retribution for holy Church.
> The troublers who have made trouble shall not enter that kingdom;
> those who have caused dissension shall not enter that garden of peace.
> This [present] Church of truth is the likeness of that kingdom.
> Just as there is harmony in the kingdom, so in holy Church there ought to be agreement.[35]

Ephrem wrote these as well as many further verses against the Arians whom he did not regard as Christians because they were named after their leader Arius,[36]

[32] Averil Cameron, Bernd Isele, Claudia Rapp, and others have worked on the Eusebian model of Constantine as bishop, Constantine as (new) Moses, etc. See e.g. Cameron, 'Eusebius's *Vita Constantini* and the Construction of Constantine'; Cameron, 'Form and Meaning', pp. 72–88; Rapp, 'Imperial Ideology in the Making', pp. 685–95; Isele, 'Moses oder Pharao?', pp. 103–18.

[33] Isele, 'Moses oder Pharao?', p. 111.

[34] For the date, see Lange, *Ephraem der Syrer*, p. 39 with n. 163.

[35] Ephrem the Syrian, *Sermons on Faith*, 6.315–330; Ephrem the Syrian, *Sermones de Fide*, ed. and trans. by Beck, p. 48 (p. 69); here translation quoted from Murray, *Symbols of Church and Kingdom*, p. 244.

[36] As already mentioned above, the term 'Christians' was disputed in Syria between the various Christian groups.

they inquired about God instead of believing in him (and Ephrem makes a clear distinction between the knowledge of the intellect and the knowledge of faith),[37] and they were like the Jews because they denied Christ to be uncreated and eternal.[38]

Ephrem places the responsibility for heresies exclusively within the Church. The emperor's sphere and the ecclesiastical spheres supplement each other but are clearly separated. This becomes obvious in his *Carmina Nisibena*, which is a collection of hymns written in celebration of the divine protection of the city of Nisibis.[39] In one of these hymns Ephrem points out,

> As the [first] priest and the first king, they were depicted in one another, and weighted [against each other] on a scale — also Vologeses and the son of the king were humble and gentle [...].
>
> From the king's office laws, and from the priesthood atonements; that both are soft would be odious, that both are forceful grievous. Let one be powerful, the other be pleasing [...]. Let our priests be mild and our kings be vigorous. [...]
>
> Let the priests pray for the kings that they may be the wall for mankind. From the kings be victory, from the priests be faith. May victory guard the bodies, and faith the souls. May kings end the fight, priests end the inquiry; may disputing and fighting cease![40]

This hymn is an extraordinary document as it can be dated to the short period of probably a few days between the very end of June 363 — when the news of Julian's death in Persia on 26 June 363 CE and the election of Jovian as his successor reached Nisibis — and the arrival of the defeated Roman army at Nisibis.[41]

[37] Palmer, 'The Prophet and the King', p. 225.

[38] For Ephrem's anti-Arianism, see Russell, *St. Ephraem the Syrian and St. Gregory the Theologian Confront the Arians*, and Bruns, 'Arius hellenizans?', pp. 21–57.

[39] Only the first twenty-one hymns (out of seventy-seven) deal with the city of Nisibis, 1–12 with the sieges and deliverances of the city in the Persian wars, 13–21 with the bishops of Nisibis. For the composition of the *Carmina Nisibena*, see Martikainen, 'Some Remarks about the Carmina Nisibena', pp. 345–51.

[40] Ephrem the Syrian, *Carmina Nisibena*, XXI.21–23; Ephrem the Syrian, *Carmina Nisibena*, ed. and trans. by Beck, pp. 58–59 (pp. 72–73). Here my translation; see also the nineteenth-century English translation in Schaff and Wace, *A Select Library of Nicene and Post-Nicene Fathers*, p. 193.

[41] Ephrem praises a new and 'righteous king' which can only refer to Jovian; *Carmina Nisibena*, XXI.14; Ephrem the Syrian, *Carmina Nisibena*, ed. and trans. by Beck, p. 57 (p. 70). See below.

After this point Jovian conveyed to the inhabitants of Nisibis that they had to leave their home city as Nisibis was to be handed over to the Persians.[42]

The 'first priest' refers to the first Bishop of Nisibis, Jacob, who is compared to the 'first [Christian] king', Constantine. And in the same way Vologeses, the (third) Bishop of Nisibis (346–61 CE), is matched with Emperor Constantius II — although the latter is not mentioned by name.[43] Ephrem also does not name Jovian in this hymn, but the praise for the 'new king' — a 'righteous king' as Ephrem points out — can only refer to the newly appointed Christian emperor, Jovian.[44] Jovian and the Bishop of Nisibis, Abraham (361–63), were supposed to run empire and local church as smoothly as had been the case in previous times under Christian rulership.[45] The positive attitude towards Constantine, Constantius, and Jovian is all the brighter against the background of Julian's reign. Nevertheless, considering the impact of Julian's short reign for Christianity in the Roman Empire, Ephrem's praise for Christian emperors remains nuanced.

Ephrem applied traditional attributes to the emperors: they should be strong and victorious and were supposed to take care of the physical well-being of their subjects.[46] In a discussion of Ephrem's perception of empire and church, it should be remembered that for an inhabitant of a border city this function of the emperor played an important role. Paul Russell rightly pointed out that the inhabitants of Nisibis had 'a natural tendency to pay greater attention to the peoples and powers around them and to be more careful to develop a good understanding of the practicalities of power'.[47] Under Constantius II Nisibis had been besieged by the Persians several times, and the Emperor proved to be unable to help out the inhabitants by sending troops.[48] Ephrem makes his

[42] See Ammianus, *Res Gestae*, XXV.7.11 and 8.13–9.6; *Ammianus Marcellinus*, ed. and trans. by Rolfe, pp. 534–35, pp. 542–51.

[43] Jacob's immediate successor as Bishop of Nisibis was Babu; see Fiey, *Nisibe*, pp. 26–29.

[44] For Vologeses, see Fiey, *Nisibe*, pp. 29–33. For Jovian as 'righteous king', see Ephraem, *Carmina Nisibena*, XXI.14; Ephrem the Syrian, *Carmina Nisibena*, ed. and trans. by Beck, p. 57 (p. 70).

[45] For Abraham, see Fiey, *Nisibe*, pp. 34–38.

[46] Similarly, also Ephrem's exhortation that the priests should pray for the emperor is a well-established role. For Griffith this strophe 'expresses a commitment to the "Church of the Empire" which is unmistakable': Griffith, 'Ephraem, the Deacon of Edessa, and the Church of the Empire', p. 32.

[47] Russell, 'Nisibis as the Background to the Life of Ephrem the Syrian', § 72.

[48] Constantius II was in Nisibis once in 345 CE; see *Codex Theodosianus* XI.7.5; Theodosiani, *Libri XVI cum constitutionibus Sirmondianis*, ed. by Mommsen and Meyer, p. 586. See

personified city dwell upon her deplorable military situation several times in the *Carmina Nisibena*:

> They flew, my Lord, and deserted [me], my children, and were like chickens which an eagle pursued. Lo! They hide in a refuge. May your peace bring them back! [...]
>
> The sound of terror I heard on my bulwarks; for my defenders scream while they guard my walls. Silence them through the voice of your peace![49]

Therefore Ephrem's prayer for the king's victory may have its origin not just in the fact that Ephrem applied a traditional image to the Emperor, but it also gives voice to the hope of the inhabitants of a border city which had suffered several times from the Persian army devastating its countryside.[50] Ephrem's description of the city's pitiful state of affairs did not flatter Constantius: 'How, my Master, may a deserted city, whose (son of) the king [=Constantius, as son of Constantine] is far off, and her enemy near, make stand without [your] mercy?'[51] However, Ephrem expressed his hopes that the Emperor would be able to end the war. For the poet the army and the well-being of the empire were the Emperor's primary domain and responsibility.

In contrast, Ephrem did not call upon the Emperor to take interest in ecclesiastical problems: it was the task of the priests to 'end the inquiry', a terminology in Ephrem's works that refers to the quarrels with the 'Arians' who inquired

also Ephram, *Carmina Nisibena*, XIII.4; Ephrem the Syrian, *Carmina Nisibena*, ed. and trans. by Beck, p. 35 (p. 40). Barnes, 'Imperial Chronology, A.D. 337–350', p. 163 n. 14, points out that the sources do not support the idea that Constantius was actually in Nisibis to relieve the city from a Persian siege but stayed in the city shortly before the siege.

[49] Ephram, *Carmina Nisibena*, IV.23 and 25; Ephrem the Syrian, *Carmina Nisibena*, ed. and trans. by Beck, p. 17 (p. 18); my translation.

[50] For the Roman-Persian wars and the sieges of Nisibis by the Persians during Constantius II's reign, see Dodgeon and Lieu, *The Roman Eastern Frontier and the Persian Wars*, pp. 164–230, who conveniently collected the sources in translation.

[51] Ephram, *Carmina Nisibena*, IV.18; Ephrem the Syrian, *Carmina Nisibena*, ed. and trans. by Beck, p. 16 (p. 17); my translation. However, to be fair, Ephrem also noted that the Emperor's piety saved Nisibis from the Persian armies; *Hymns against Julian*, II.19: 'The king by his sackcloth preserved it'; Ephrem the Syrian, *Hymnen de Paradiso und Contra Julianum*, ed. and trans. by Beck, p. 79 (p. 74); Ephrem the Syrian, *Hymns, trans. by McVey*, p. 240. Pedro Barceló does not regard Constantius's piety as the life-saver of the city, but he argues — against Ammianus — that Constantius's preventive defence-measures of Mesopotamia helped to save the city; Barceló, *Constantius II und seine Zeit*, p. 90.

about God.[52] Ephrem expects the bishops — not the imperial office — to eliminate heterodox opinions and establish an Orthodox Nicene doctrine within the Church.[53]

Considering that Ephrem held the imperial office responsible for setting down the law as quoted above, the omission of any biblical comparison for the emperor as law-giver is quite striking. If 'Ephraem's support of the Roman emperor is nothing short of Eusebian in its full dimension',[54] the Moses-typology used by Eusebius would have been in place here. However, while Constantine actually issued laws in favour of Eusebius's church, the apostate Julian but also the non-Nicene emperors Constantius and Valens opposed Ephrem's Nicene church openly. Andrew Palmer has argued forcefully that one of Ephrem's *Hymns on Faith* from after 363 can be regarded as a bold address to Valens requesting the heterodox Emperor to abstain from deciding questions of doctrine within the Church.[55] The poet did not blame Valens directly but the Christian clergy for advising the Emperor wrongly on matters of doctrine.[56] In other words, Ephrem did not question the imperial office's authority in laying down the law in general, even if it acted against the Church. However, in contrast to Eusebius who saw in Constantine a political as well as spiritual authority comparable to Moses, Ephrem understood the imperial office merely as an office for jurisdiction. Emperors could not be made responsible for decisions on any doctrinal matter because they had no authority in this. In other words, the imperial office remained without any spiritual component in Ephrem's perception.[57]

When Ephrem did use Old Testament typologies for rulers, he referred in his *Hymns against Julian* to the Persian king as the king of Babylon, and to Julian as the 'Hellenic king', a terminology that underlines Julian's paganism as well as referring to the book of Daniel.[58] Julian 'angered God and denied

[52] See the quote above; Ephrem the Syrian, *Carmina Nisibena*, ed. and trans. by Beck, p. 73 n. 40.

[53] This perception of the Church and her apparent inability to deal with the difficult doctrinal situation can also be seen in Ephrem's *Hymns on Nicomedia*; see Bundy, 'Jacob of Nisibis as a Model for the Episcopacy', pp. 242–43.

[54] Griffith, 'Setting Right the Church of Syria', p. 110.

[55] Palmer, 'The Prophet and the King', p. 235.

[56] Palmer, 'The Prophet and the King', pp. 213–16.

[57] For Eusebius's understanding, see Rapp, 'Imperial Ideology in the Making', here p. 692; Cameron, 'Eusebius's *Vita Constantini* and the Construction of Constantine', pp. 158–61.

[58] Ephrem the Syrian, *Hymns against Julian*, I.20; Ephrem the Syrian, *Hymnen de Paradiso und Contra Julianum*, ed. and trans. by Beck, p. 75 (p. 69); Ephrem the Syrian, *Hymns, trans. by McVey*, p. 232.

Daniel'[59] by attempting to rebuild the Jewish temple in Jerusalem:[60] Ephrem referred here to the Old Testament prophecy of Daniel[61] which Ephrem and other Patristic authors understood as a testimony of the permanent destruction of the Jewish temple. In another *Hymn against Julian* Ephrem compared Julian also to Ahab and other Old Testament kings who introduced Baal-worship in Israel.[62] According to the poet, Julian was judged and condemned near Babylon for denying the Old Testament prophecy and for offending God with his paganism.[63]

Ephrem's *Hymns against Julian* are a unique because almost contemporary source. All but the first were composed in the summer of 363, very likely still in Nisibis, just before Ephrem and all the other inhabitants of Nisibis had to leave the city or shortly afterwards.[64] The first hymn he probably already wrote when Julian came to the East in 362 CE, in order to prepare his military campaign against Persia.[65] The hymn is a meditation on the situation of the Christian Church in a time of fear and persecution:

> The kings who used to provide shade, cooled us in the droughts.
> We ate their fruits; we were ungrateful for their branches.
> Our soul luxuriated in the bounties and shadows.
> Our mouth raved and attacked our Creator.
> Battles in the shadows we waged with our investigations.
> He has stripped away our shade to make us mindful of our drought!
> Blessed is He Whose grace provides shade for us!
> Blessed is He Who worked in us grace without measure![66]

[59] Ephrem the Syrian, *Hymns against Julian*, I.20.

[60] See Ephrem the Syrian, *Hymns, trans. by McVey*, p. 232 n. 54. For Julian's attempt to rebuild the Jewish temple in Jerusalem, see Hahn, 'Kaiser Julian und ein dritter Tempel?', pp. 237–62.

[61] Daniel 9. 24–27.

[62] Ephrem the Syrian, *Hymns against Julian*, II.2; Ephrem the Syrian, *Hymnen de Paradiso und Contra Julianum*, ed. and trans. by Beck, p. 76 (p. 70); Ephrem the Syrian, *Hymns, trans. by McVey*, pp. 234–35.

[63] Ephrem the Syrian, *Hymns against Julian*, I.20; Ephrem the Syrian, *Hymnen de Paradiso und Contra Julianum*, ed. and trans. by Beck, p. 75 (p. 69); Ephrem the Syrian, *Hymns, trans. by McVey*, p. 232.

[64] Ammianus, *Res Gestae*, XXV.7.11 and 8.13–9.6; *Ammianus Marcellinus*, ed. and trans. by Rolfe, pp. 534–35, pp. 542–51.

[65] It was probably written when Julian was in Antioch or on his way to Persia.

[66] Ephrem the Syrian, *Hymns against Julian*, 'On the Church' 15; Ephrem the Syrian, *Hymnen de Paradiso und Contra Julianum*, ed. and trans. by Beck, p. 70 (p. 64); Ephrem the

By the time Ephrem wrote this, Roman emperors had favoured the Christian Church for almost half a century. The 'kings who used to provide shade' refer to Constantine and Constantius, and Ephrem depicted them as protectors who gave the Church shade and comfort. The first Christian emperors made laws in favour of the Christian Church which allowed the Church also to grow financially. It was certainly a time in which any Christian could 'luxuriate' with regard to the unexpected turn of events following the battle at the Milvian bridge in 312 CE.[67] Ephrem's 'fruits' are likely to mean donations by the emperors — in the form of church buildings, bibles, land, etc. Again Ephrem castigated the man-made quarrels within the Church and reminded his listeners that the real 'shade', the real hope of protection for the Church, lay with God, and that God would always provide it — no matter which religion was favoured by imperial policy.[68] In other words, Ephrem recognized Christian emperors as protectors and sponsors of the Church, but in his ecclesiological concept the imperial office as such did not enjoy a special status. In times of a non-Christian emperor, the Church was on its own again:

> Rely on the truth and fear not, my brothers,
> for our Lord is not weak that He should desert us in trials.
> He is the power on Whom depend the creation and its inhabitants.
> On Him depends the hope of His church.
> Who is able to cut off its heavenly roots?
> Blessed is He Whose power came down and was mingled with his churches![69]

After Constantius died and a pagan emperor returned to power, the Church only appears to be bereft of its protector. Ephrem ensured his listeners that there is no need to fear as they could always rely on God who would never desert them. However, Ephrem was very much aware of the earthly dangers the Church had to face from a pagan emperor:

> The sons of truth, then grow large on this Branch of Truth;
> They have been perfected and have become fruits fit for the kingdom.

Syrian, *Hymns, trans. by McVey*, pp. 224–25.

[67] For this change in religious policy and the consequences for the Church under Constantine, see Drake, *Constantine and the Bishops* and Girardet, *Die Konstantinische Wende*.

[68] The 'investigations' are again a reference to the Arians and their inquiries into the nature of God; see also above.

[69] Ephrem the Syrian, *Hymns against Julian*, 'On the Church' 1; Ephrem the Syrian, *Hymnen de Paradiso und Contra Julianum*, ed. and trans. by Beck, p. 67 (p. 61); Ephrem the Syrian, *Hymns, trans. by McVey*, pp. 221–22.

But, although the Branch is living, on it are also
Dead fruits that blossom [only] apparently.
The wind tested them and shook down the wild grapes.
Blessed is He Who crowned by it those who held fast in Him![70]

Ephrem complained about Julian's apparent success — about the many who denied the 'universal Life-giver', God, and converted to the 'diadem of mortality' as Ephrem phrased it.[71] Probably in the same way as some pagans started to adhere to the Christian God after Constantine, Christians now followed the example of Julian and apostatized from the Christian faith. The Church was on its own against the 'others' without any imperial support. The 'others' included pagans, heretics, as well as Jews whom Ephrem regarded as Julian's natural allies against the Church.[72] They were all the forces of 'evil', the left hand in a cosmic battle against God and the angels. This perception allowed Ephrem to understand Julian's death not only as the downfall of paganism but as that of Judaism as well.[73]

At this time of universal ecclesiastical crisis — an apostate ruling the empire and Christians following his example by defecting from the Church — Ephrem painted an image of how a Christian emperor should rule:

The sceptre of kingship shepherds humankind,
care for cities, drives away wild animals.
The opposite was the sceptre of the king who apostatized.
the wild animals saw it and exulted:
the wolves were his partisans; the leopard and the lion raged;
even the foxes raised their voices.[74]

Christian emperors were true shepherds for humankind and their subjects by providing care for the empire and its cities. If 'wild animals' is to be understood as pagans and heretics, this might be a hint that Ephrem hoped emperors would also take care of keeping heretics and non-Christians at bay so that the Church

[70] Ephrem the Syrian, *Hymns against Julian*, 'On the Church' 5; Ephrem the Syrian, *Hymnen de Paradiso und Contra Julianum*, ed. and trans. by Beck, p. 68 (p. 62); Ephrem the Syrian, *Hymns, trans. by McVey*, pp. 222–23.

[71] Ephrem the Syrian, *Hymns against Julian*, III.6.

[72] Griffith, 'Ephraem the Syrian's Hymns "Against Julian"', p. 254.

[73] Griffith, 'Ephraem the Syrian's Hymns "Against Julian"', pp. 256–60.

[74] Ephrem the Syrian, *Hymns against Julian*, I.1; Ephrem the Syrian, *Hymnen de Paradiso und Contra Julianum*, ed. and trans. by Beck, p. 71 (p. 65); Ephrem the Syrian, *Hymns, trans. by McVey*, p. 227.

could flourish.[75] It seems likely that the reign of Julian and the apostate's support for pagans as well as non-Nicene Christians revealed to Ephrem for the first time the importance of the imperial office for the ecclesiastical life of the Church.[76] Ephrem's image of the ideal emperor was caused by and developed against the image of the apostate Julian who sponsored 'wild animals' against the Nicene Church.

Sudden relief came for Ephrem and the Church with Julian's unexpected death in Persia at the end of June 363. The corpse was brought to Nisibis, and Ephrem could not resist the temptation but went to go outside the city and mock the dead Emperor in his coffin:

> Believe in 'yes' and 'no', the word of a trustworthy man,
> that I went right up, my brothers, to the coffin of the filthy one,
> and I stood over him and derided his paganism
> and said, 'Is this indeed he who exalted himself
> against the Living Name and forgot that he is dust?'
> [God] turned him back into his dust to let him know he was of dust.
> I stood and wondered at him whose downfall I had so fully seen.
> 'This is his majesty and this is his pomp!
> This is his kingship and this is his chariot!
> This is a clump of earth that has disintegrated!'
> I argued with myself, 'Why in [the time of] his power
> Did I not foresee this would be his end?'[77]

Griffith interprets the last verse as Ephrem nurturing 'an image of harmony between emperor and church, which virtually canonized the emperor'.[78] However, any canonization of Roman emperors can hardly been read into this. The poet blames himself that he did not foresee Julian's tragic end: Julian was a pagan, an apostate even, who had tried to rule against God and his Church on earth! Ephrem who in his previous *Hymns against Julian* had asked his com-

[75] For the interpretation of 'wild animals' as heretics (as well as apostates and Jews), see Griffith, 'Ephraem, the Deacon of Edessa, and the Church of the Empire', p. 33, and Griffith, 'Ephraem the Syrian's Hymns "Against Julian"', p. 252.

[76] Unfortunately, there is not enough evidence as to what the poet thought about the Roman emperor before Julian in order to investigate if there is a development in Ephrem's understanding of the emperor's role for the Church.

[77] Ephrem the Syrian, *Hymns against Julian*, III.4–5; Ephrem the Syrian, *Hymnen de Paradiso und Contra Julianum*, ed. and trans. by Beck, p. 82 (p. 77); Ephrem the Syrian, *Hymns, trans. by McVey*, pp. 244–45.

[78] Griffith, 'Ephraem the Syrian's Hymns "Against Julian"', p. 248.

munity to rely on God and believe that God, not the emperors, was responsible for the well-being of the Church — especially in times of persecution — was stunned that his own words had been fulfilled so soon.

Griffith conclusively argues that even the surrender of Nisibis to the Persians was in Ephrem's understanding a defeat of paganism. Ephrem inspected the corpse of the Emperor in his coffin outside the gates of Nisibis, and at the same time he could see the Persian flag being put up on the citadel of Nisibis. It was not the Christian Nisibis — which had withstood Persian armies three times during the last two decades — that was surrendered, but the Nisibis which had been ruled by a pagan emperor. Such an ideological interpretation obviously ignored the fact that it was actually the Christian Emperor Jovian who made the peace treaty that contained the unfortunate clause about Nisibis's surrender to the Persians. However, this detail could not prevent Ephrem's excitement about the apostate's death.

Following the fall of Nisibis, Griffith regards Ephrem's move to Edessa — after a probably short stay in Amida[79] — also as a sign of the poet's close ties to the 'Church of the Empire': Ephrem 'chose to live the latter part of his life under the Roman emperors, rather than under the great kings of Persia, as his move to Edessa after 363 testifies'.[80] However, this seems highly unlikely: although Ephrem did not record his motives, Ammianus Marcellinus leaves no doubt about the political state of affairs: 'Nisibis and Singara should pass into control of the Persians without their inhabitants'.[81] Han Drijvers thought maybe only 'the Christian elite left the town to find a refuge in the Roman West'.[82] However, Ammianus Marcellinus states that 'the emperor gave orders that all must leave the walls within three days', Ephrem did not seem to have the choice to stay: 'men were appointed to drive them out, and threatened with death all who hesitated to leave'.[83] Some inhabitants may have preferred to stay,

[79] The duration of the stay remains unknown, but Andrew Palmer points out that Ephrem most certainly stayed long enough to compose homilies in Amida; however, the refugee may not have felt welcome and subsequently moved to Edessa; see Palmer, 'A Single Human Being Divided in Himself', § 1 with n. 1.

[80] Griffith, 'Ephraem, the Deacon of Edessa, and the Church of the Empire', p. 47. In Griffith, 'Setting Right the Church of Syria', p. 112, Griffith acknowledges that Ephrem was forced to leave Nisibis.

[81] Ammianus, *Res Gestae*, XXV.7.11; *Ammianus Marcellinus*, ed. and trans. by Rolfe, pp. 534–35.

[82] Drijvers, 'Jews and Christians at Edessa', p. 97.

[83] Ammianus, *Res Gestae*, XXV.9.4–5; *Ammianus Marcellinus*, ed. and trans. by Rolfe,

including Ephrem if he had been given the chance. In this case he would never have been referred to as 'deacon of Edessa', a term that overemphasizes Ephrem's last decade of life in a city that must have felt foreign to him.

* * *

In conclusion, Ephrem was a firm supporter of the Nicene party who wished the Trinitarian creed to become the ruling doctrine in the Church. In this regard he resembled Athanasius but in a quite different social and ecclesiastical position than the Bishop of Alexandria.[84] Ephrem was a servant of his local church with a limited political horizon, not a 'Church leader' involved in making the 'orthodox' doctrine for centuries to come.

In order to understand Ephrem as a Nicene Christian who promoted his understanding of orthodoxy against various other Christian groups within Syrian Christianity, one should understand Ephrem's ecclesiology in its own right considering his identity and biography. Adherence to Nicene Christianity does not necessarily entail giving one's allegiance to the imperial office and the 'Church of the Empire' which for most of Ephrem's lifetime remained Arian. Leaving for Edessa and seeking refuge in the Christian Roman Empire might have been preferable to staying in Persia.[85] However, to interpret this as if Ephrem acted as the 'deciding voice [...] of Roman imperial authority'[86] downplays Ephrem's predominant concern with the Church — the universal as well as his local church and its bishops.[87] In Ephrem's mind the imperial-political context came in only when he was faced with attacks by the Persians or confronted with an apostate emperor. Julian's reign revealed to Ephrem the importance of the imperial office because the apostate directed its power against the Church. After and against him, Ephrem meditates on Roman emperors and their relations to the Church.

pp. 550–51. Considering this testimony, it seems highly unlikely that Ephrem stayed for several more years in Nisibis; but see Fiey, *Nisibe*, p. 36.

[84] Ephrem gives Syrian Nicene Christianity a voice which — as the later reference beyond the confines of Syrian Christianity proves — was quite influential, but he was hardly a 'leader' as Shepardson concludes; Shepardson, *Anti-Judaism and Christian Orthodoxy*, p. 160.

[85] Griffith, 'Setting Right the Church of Syria', pp. 112–13. Again, if this was indeed an option at all: more likely, Jovian ensured Nisibis's citizens remained 'his' subjects and were not allowed to live in the Persian Empire.

[86] Griffith, 'Setting Right the Church of Syria', p. 98.

[87] Griffith, 'Setting Right the Church of Syria', pp. 112–13.

Comparing Ephrem's ecclesiastical understanding with that of Eusebius one should note the different historical circumstances in which they wrote. Both authors met in their lifetime an emperor who inspired them to write about him and contemplate the role of the imperial office — both in their respective genres and both with their respective results. Eusebius composed his *Life of Constantine* in order to construct a model of the imperial office for a Christian Roman Empire, whereas Ephrem wrote his *Hymns against Julian* in order to comfort his Church and — after Julian's death — to analyse the fall of paganism within a biblical framework.[88] Ephrem's biography prevented him from sharing Eusebius's excitement about the imperial office which with Constantine for the first time recognized and even favoured Christianity. On the contrary, in Ephrem's hymns the knowledge is already present of how fickle late antique religious politics could be.

Eusebius and Ephrem took the Old Testament as their basis for explaining their respective emperors, but while in the *Life of Constantine* Constantine is depicted as a second Moses, Julian becomes the 'Hellenic king', the king of Greece of the book of Daniel who looks like a he-goat — an unflattering reference to Julian's beard.[89] The imperial office turned out to be quite different than Eusebius imagined, although the two authors were only divided by one generation. The fact that Ephrem resisted from applying Old Testament imagery to Christian emperors demonstrates that the imperial office had in the poet's perception no spiritual role to play in the Church.

Ephrem's ideal emperor would make the laws so that the Nicene Church could flourish. However, rooted in her firm faith in God she could also survive without a favourable religious and jurisdictional framework set by the imperial office. Neither did Ephrem's ecclesiology depend on this framework, nor did he consider the Roman emperor to be a sacred part of salvation history like Eusebius.[90] Ephrem's (provincial) ecclesiology is autonomous in this respect: it functions universally without the historical circumstances of a Christian imperial office in mind.[91] Later in the fifth century, the bishops of Rome, the papacy, would develop another ecclesiastical model — also based on the Nicene faith

88 And with that — as discussed above — also the fall of Judaism.

89 See Griffith, 'Ephraem the Syrian's Hymns "Against Julian"', pp. 254–55.

90 For Eusebius, see Cameron, 'Eusebius's *Vita Constantini* and the Construction of Constantine', pp. 160–61.

91 See also Wood, *'We have no king but Christ'*, especially chapters 1 and 3, who argued for regional identities within the Roman Empire and within (Christian) 'Roman Orthodoxy'.

— against the Eusebian model. Ephrem's rudimentary ecclesiastical model cannot compete with the evolving ideology of the papacy, but both presuppose an ecclesiastical independence from the imperial office.[92]

[92] Centuries later, in the Christological controversy of the sixth century, the Syrian Orthodox Bishop John of Tella developed an ecclesiological model explicitly against the Eusebian which had by then become the imperial model of ruling church and state; Menze and Akalın, *John of Tella's 'Profession of Faith'*, pp. 44–54.

Works Cited

Primary Sources

Ammianus Marcellinus, ed. and trans. by J. C. Rolfe, Loeb Classical Library, 315 (Cambridge, MA: Harvard University Press, 1940; repr. 1986)

Des heiligen Ephraem des Syrers Carmina Nisibena, ed. and trans. by E. Beck, Corpus Scriptorum Christianiorum Orientalium, 218–19, 2 vols (Leuven: Secrétariat du CSCO, 1961)

Des heiligen Ephraem des Syrers Hymnen contra Haereses, ed. and trans. by E. Beck, Corpus Scriptorum Christianiorum Orientalium, 169–70, 2 vols (Leuven: Peeters, 1957)

Des heiligen Ephraem des Syrers Hymnen de Paradiso und Contra Julianum, ed. and trans. by E. Beck, Corpus Scriptorum Christianiorum Orientalium, 174–75, 2 vols (Louvain: Peeters, 1957)

Ephrem the Syrian: Hymns, trans. by K. E. McVey (Mahwah: Paulist Press, 1989)

St. Ephrem the Syrian: Hymns on Paradise, ed. and trans. by S. Brock (Crestwood: St. Vladimir's Press, 1998)

St. Ephrem the Syrian: Selected Prose Works, trans. by E. G. Mathews and J. P. Amar, The Fathers of the Church, 91 (Washington, DC: Catholic University of America Press, 1994)

Des heiligen Ephraem des Syrers Sermones de Fide, ed. and trans. by E. Beck, Corpus Scriptorum Christianiorum Orientalium, 212–13 (Louvain: Secrétariat du CSCO, 1961)

Théodoret de Cyr Correspondance, ed. and trans. by Y. Azéma, Sources chrétiennes, 111 (Paris: Éditions du CERF, 1965)

A History of the Monks of Syria by Theodoret of Cyrrhus, trans. by R. M. Price, Cistercian Studies Series, 88 (Kalamazoo: Cistercian Publications, 1985)

Theodosiani libri XVI cum constitutionibus Sirmondianis et leges novellae ad Theodosianum pertinentes, ed. by T. Mommsen and P. Meyer (Berlin: Weidmann 1905)

Secondary Studies

Ayres, L., *Nicaea and its Legacy: An Approach to Fourth-Century Trinitarian Theology* (Oxford: Oxford University Press, 2004)

Barceló, P., *Constantius II und seine Zeit: Die Anfänge des Staatskirchentums* (Stuttgart: Klett-Cotta, 2004)

Barnes, T., 'Imperial Chronology, A.D. 337–350', *Phoenix*, 34 (1980), 160–66

Baus, K., 'The Development of the Church of the Empire within the Framework of the Imperial Religious Policy', in *History of the Church*, vol. II, ed. by H. Jedin and J. Dolan, 10 vols (New York: Seabury Press, 1980), pp. 3–90

Beck, E., 'Ephrem des Syrers Hymnik', in *Liturgie und Dichtung*, ed. by H. Becker and R. Kaczynski (St Ottilien: EOS Press, 1983), pp. 345–79

Biesen, K. van, *Bibliography of St. Ephrem the Syrian* (Giove in Umbria, 2002)

Bowersock, G. W., *Julian the Apostate* (Cambridge, MA: Harvard University Press, 1977)

Brennecke, H. C., *Studien zur Geschichte der Homöer* (Tübingen: Mohr Siebeck, 1988)

Brock, S., *The Luminous Eye: The Spiritual World Vision of Saint Ephrem the Syrian*, Cistercian Studies Series, 124 (Kalamazoo: Cistercian Publications, 1992)

Bruns, P., 'Arius hellenizans? Ephräm der Syrer und die neoarianischen Kontroversen seiner Zeit', *Zeitschrift für Kirchengeschichte*, 101 (1990/91), 21–57

Bundy, D., 'Jacob of Nisibis as a Model for the Episcopacy', *Le Muséon*, 104 (1991), 235–49

——, 'Vision for the City: Nisibis in Ephrem's *Hymns on Nicomedia*', in *Religions of Late Antiquity in Practice*, ed. by R. Valantasis (Princeton: Princeton University Press, 2000), pp. 189–206

Cameron, A., 'Eusebius's *Vita Constantini* and the Construction of Constantine', in *Portraits: Biographical Representations in the Greek and Latin Literature of the Roman Empire*, ed. by M. J. Edwards and S. C. R. Swain (Oxford: Clarendon Press, 1997), pp. 145–74

——, 'Form and Meaning: The Vita Contantini and the Vita Antonii', in *Greek Biography and Panegyric in Late Antiquity*, ed. by T. Hägg and P. Rousseau (Berkeley: University of California Press, 2000), pp. 72–88

Dodgeon, M. H., and S. N. C. Lieu, eds, *The Roman Eastern Frontier and the Persian Wars AD 226–363: A Documentary History* (London: Routledge, 1991)

Drake, H. A., *Constantine and the Bishops: The Politics of Intolerance* (Baltimore: Johns Hopkins University Press, 2000)

Drijvers, H. W., 'Jews and Christians at Edessa', *Journal of Jewish Studies*, 36 (1985), 88–102

El-Khoury, N., *Die Interpretation der Welt bei Ephraem dem Syrer (4. Jahrhundert): Beitrag zur Geistesgeschichte*, Tübinger Theologische Studien, 6 (Tübingen, 1976)

Fiey, J.-M., *Nisibe: métropole syriaque orientale et ses suffragants des origines à nos jours*, Corpus Scriptorum Christianiorum Orientalium, 388 (Louvain: Secrétariat du Corpus SCO, 1977)

Girardet, K. M., *Die Konstantinische Wende: Voraussetzungen und geistige Grundlagen der Religionspolitik Konstantins des Grossen* (Darmstadt: Wissenschaftliche Buchgesellschaft, 2006)

Griffith, S. H., 'Ephraem, the Deacon of Edessa, and the Church of the Empire', in *Diakonia: Studies in Honor of Robert T. Meyer*, ed. by T. Halton and J. P. Williman (Washington, DC: Catholic University of America Press, 1986), pp. 22–52

——, 'Ephraem the Syrian's Hymns "Against Julian": Meditations on History and Imperial Power', *Vigiliae Christianae*, 41 (1987), 238–66

——, 'The Marks of the "True Church" according to Ephraem's *Hymns against Heresies*', in *After Bardaisan: Studies on Continuity and Change in Syriac Christianity in Honour of Professor Han J. W. Drijvers*, ed. by G. J. Reinink and A. C. Klugkist (Leuven: Peeters, 1999), pp. 125–40

——, 'Setting Right the Church of Syria: Saint Ephraem's *Hymns against Heresies*', in *The Limits of Ancient Christianity: Essays on Late Antique Thought and Culture in Honor of R. A. Markus*, ed. by W. E. Klingshirn and M. Vessey (Ann Arbor: University of Michigan Press, 1999), pp. 97–114

——, 'A Spiritual Father for the Whole Church: The Universal Appeal of St. Ephraem the Syrian', *Hugoye: Journal of Syriac Studies*, 1.2 (1998), 197–220, available at <http://syrcom.cua.edu/Hugoye/vol1No2/HV1N2Griffith.html> [accessed 6 August 2013]

Gwynn, D. M., *The Eusebians: The Polemic of Athanasius of Alexandria and the Construction of the 'Arian Controversy'* (Oxford: Oxford University Press, 2007)

Hahn, J., 'Kaiser Julian und ein dritter Tempel? Idee, Wirklichkeit und Wirkung eines gescheiterten Projektes', in *Der Jerusalemer Tempel und seine Zerstörungen: Geschehen – Wahrnehmung – Bewältigung*, ed. by J. Hahn, Wissenschaftlische Untersuchungen zum Neuen Testament, 147 (Tübingen: Mohr Siebeck, 2002), pp. 237–62

Hanson, R. P. C., *The Search for the Doctrine of God: The Arian Controversy, 318–381* (London: T & T Clark, 1988)

Isele, B., 'Moses oder Pharao? Die ersten christlichen Kaiser und das Argument der Bibel', in *Die Bibel als politisches Argument: Voraussetzungen und Folgen biblizistischer Herrschaftslegitimation in der Vormoderne*, ed. by A. Pečar and K. Trampedach (München: R. Oldenbourg, 2007), pp. 103–18

Koonammakkal, T., 'St. Ephrem and "Greek Wisdom"', in *VI. Symposium Syriacum 1992*, ed. by R. Lavenant (Roma: Pontificio Istituto Orientale, 1994), pp. 169–76

Lange, C., ed., *Ephraem der Syrer: Kommentar zum Diatessaron*, vol. I, Fontes Christiani, 54/1 (Turnhout: Brepols, 2008)

Lieu, S. N. C., ed., *The Emperor Julian: Panegyric and Polemic*, Translated Texts for Historians, 2 (Liverpool: Liverpool University Press, 1989), pp. 89–104

Lightfoot, C. S., 'The Third Siege of Nisibis (A.D. 350)', *Historia*, 37.1 (1988), 105–25

Martikainen, J., 'Some Remarks about the Carmina Nisibena as a Literary and a Theological Source', *Orientalia Christiana Analecta*, 197 (1974), 345–51

Menze, V., and K. Akalın, *John of Tella's 'Profession of Faith': The Legacy of a Sixth-Century Syrian Orthodox Bishop*, Texts from Christian Late Antiquity, 25 (Piscataway: Gorgias, 2009)

Murray, R., 'St Ephrem the Syrian on Church Unity', *Eastern Churches Quarterly*, 15 (1963), 164–76

——, *Symbols of Church and Kingdom: A Study in Early Syriac Tradition* (Cambridge: Cambridge University Press, 1975)

Palmer, A., 'The Prophet and the King: Mar Afrem's Message to the Eastern Roman Emperor', in *After Bardaisan:. Studies on Continuity and Change in Syriac Christianity in Honour of Professor Han J. W. Drijvers*, ed. by G. J. Reinink and A. C. Klugkist (Leuven: Peeters, 1999), pp. 213–36

——, 'A Single Human Being Divided in Himself: Ephraim the Syrian, the Man in the Middle', *Hugoye: Journal of Syriac Studies*, 1.2 (1998), 119–63, available at <http://syrcom.cua.edu/Hugoye/vol1No2/HV1N2Palmer.html> [accessed 6 August 2013]

Possekel, U., *Evidence of Greek Philosophical Concepts in the Writings of Ephrem the Syrian* (Louvain: Peeters, 1999)

Rapp, C., 'Imperial Ideology in the Making: Eusebius of Caesarea on Constantine as "Bishop"', *Journal of Theological Studies*, 49 (1998), 685–95

Rosen, K., *Julian: Kaiser, Gott und Christenhasser* (Stuttgart: Klett-Cotta, 2006)

Russell, P. S., 'Nisibis as the Background to the Life of Ephrem the Syrian', *Hugoye*, 8 (2005), 179–235, available at <http://syrcom.cua.edu/hugoye/Vol8No2/HV8N2Russell.html> [accessed 6 August 2013]

——, *St. Ephraem the Syrian and St. Gregory the Theologian Confront the Arians*, Mōrān 'Ethō Series, 5 (Kerala: St. Ephrem Ecumenical Research Institute, 1994)

Schaff, P., and H. Wace, eds, *A Select Library of Nicene and Post-Nicene Fathers of the Christian Church*, vol. XIII (repr. Edinburgh: Clark, 1997)

Segal, J. B., *Edessa 'The Blessed City'* (Oxford: Clarendon Press, 1970)

Shepardson, C., *Anti-Judaism and Christian Orthodoxy: Ephrem's Hymns in Fourth-Century Syria* (Washington, DC: Catholic University of America Press, 2008)

Stephenson, P., *Constantine: Roman Emperor, Christian Victor* (New York: Overlook Press, 2010)

Wood, P., *'We have no king but Christ': Christian Political Thought in Greater Syria on the Eve of the Arab Conquest (c. 400–585)* (Oxford: Oxford University Press, 2010)

Index

CONTEXTUALIZING THE SACRED

All volumes in this series are evaluated by an Editorial Board, strictly on academic grounds, based on reports prepared by referees who have been commissioned by virtue of their specialism in the appropriate field. The Board ensures that the screening is done independently and without conflicts of interest. The definitive texts supplied by authors are also subject to review by the Board before being approved for publication. Further, the volumes are copyedited to conform to the publisher's stylebook and to the best international academic standards in the field.

Titles in Series

Anika Greve, *Sepulkrale Hofarchitekturen im Hellenismus: Alexandria—Nea Paphos—Kyrene* (2014)

Inge Nielsen, *Housing the Chosen: The Architectural Context of Mystery Groups and Religious Associations in the Ancient World* (2014)

In Preparation

Religious Identities in the Levant from Alexander to Muhammed: Continuity and Change, ed. by Michael Blömer, Achim Lichtenberger, and Rubina Raja

Phönizische, griechische und römische Gottheiten im historischen Wandel, ed. by Linda-Marie Günther and Bärbel Morstadt